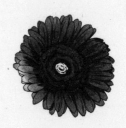

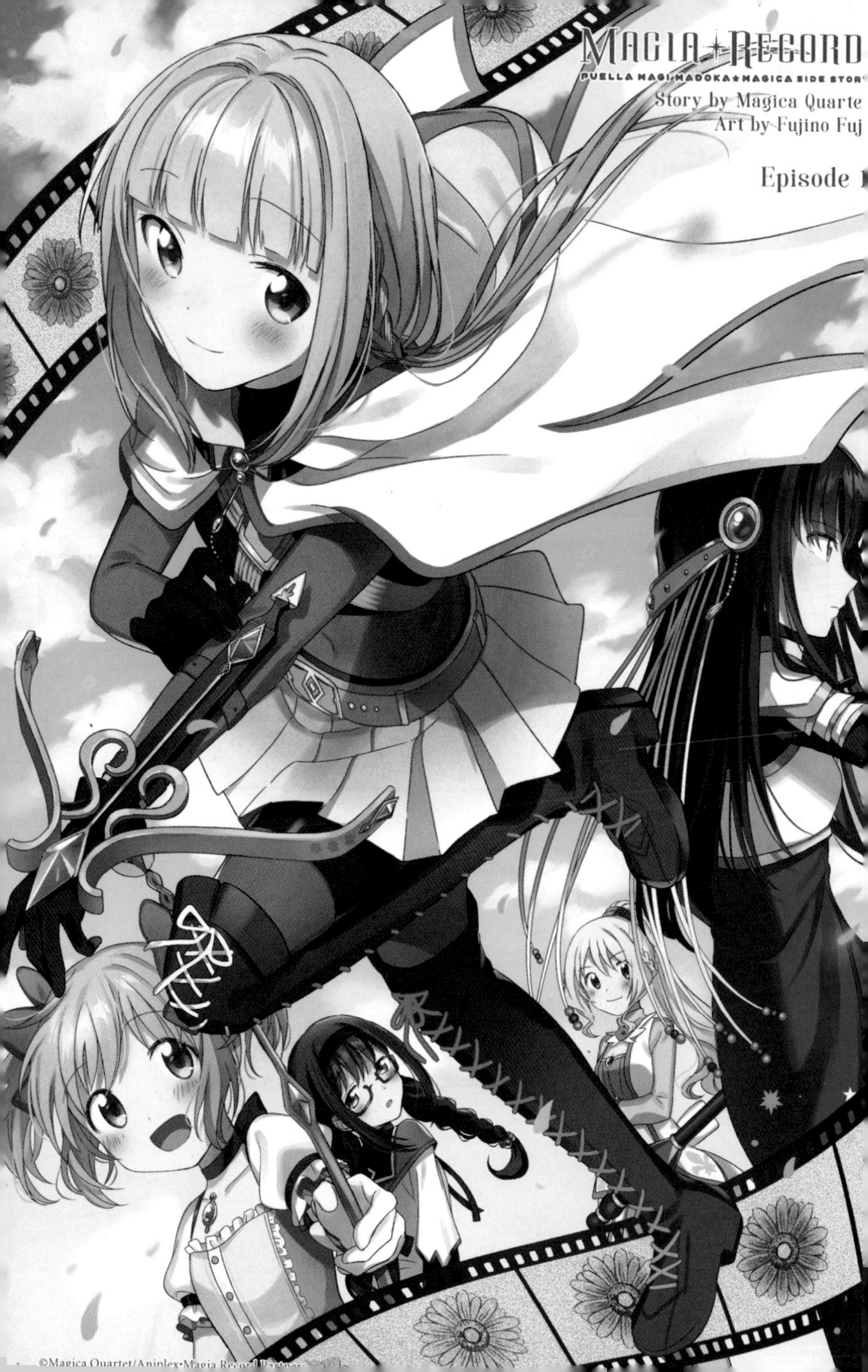
MAGIA RECORD
PUELLA MAGI MADOKA MAGICA SIDE STOR
Story by Magica Quarte
Art by Fujino Fuj
Episode 1
©Magica Quartet/Aniplex•Magia Record Partners

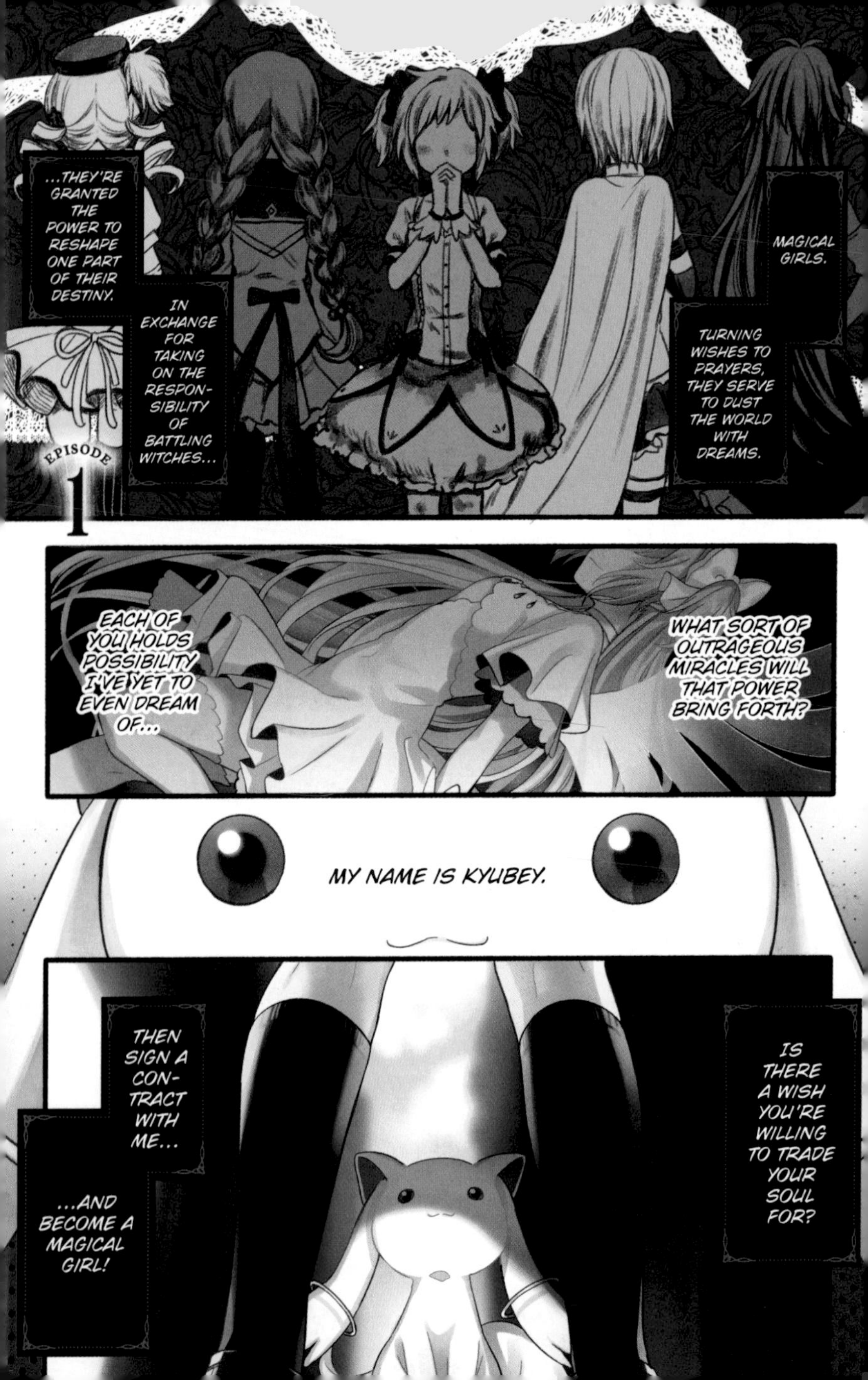
MAGICAL GIRLS.
TURNING WISHES TO PRAYERS, THEY SERVE TO DUST THE WORLD WITH DREAMS.
IN EXCHANGE FOR TAKING ON THE RESPON-SIBILITY OF BATTLING WITCHES...
...THEY'RE GRANTED THE POWER TO RESHAPE ONE PART OF THEIR DESTINY.
EPISODE 1
WHAT SORT OF OUTRAGEOUS MIRACLES WILL THAT POWER BRING FORTH?
EACH OF YOU HOLDS POSSIBILITY I'VE YET TO EVEN DREAM OF...
MY NAME IS KYUBEY.
IS THERE A WISH YOU'RE WILLING TO TRADE YOUR SOUL FOR?
THEN SIGN A CON-TRACT WITH ME...
...AND BECOME A MAGICAL GIRL!

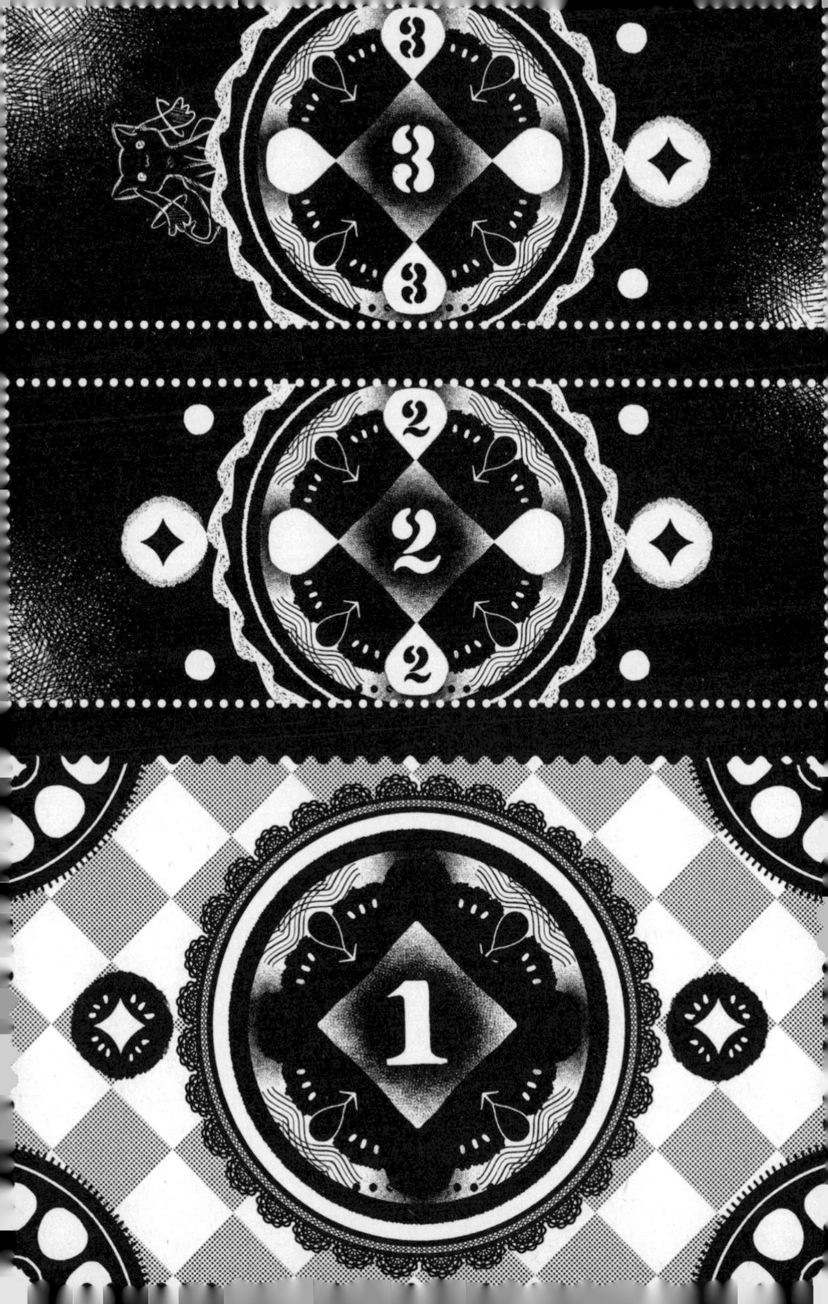
3
2
1

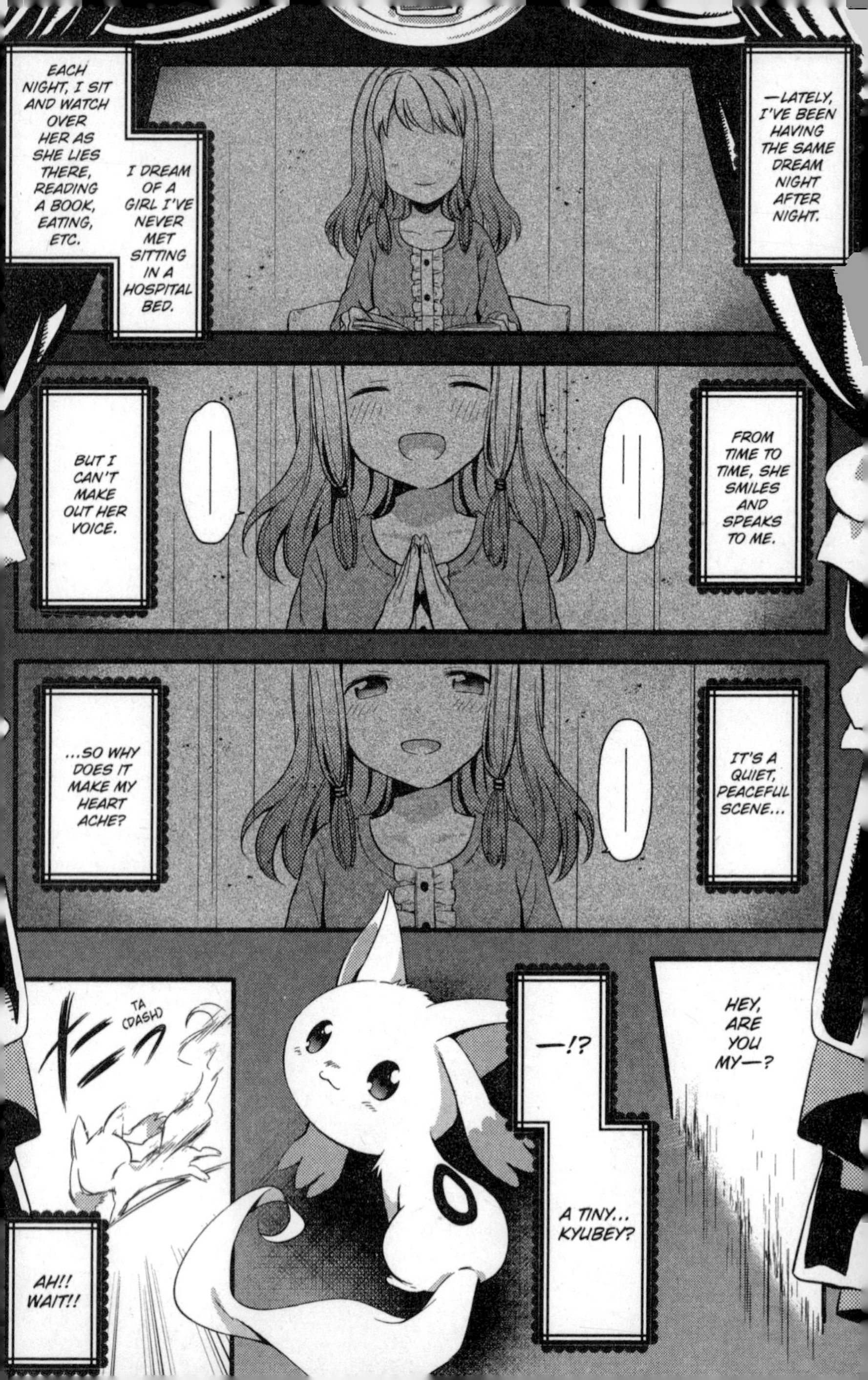
—LATELY, I'VE BEEN HAVING THE SAME DREAM NIGHT AFTER NIGHT.
I DREAM OF A GIRL I'VE NEVER MET SITTING IN A HOSPITAL BED.
EACH NIGHT, I SIT AND WATCH OVER HER AS SHE LIES THERE, READING A BOOK, EATING, ETC.
FROM TIME TO TIME, SHE SMILES AND SPEAKS TO ME.
—
—
BUT I CAN'T MAKE OUT HER VOICE.
IT'S A QUIET, PEACEFUL SCENE...
—
...SO WHY DOES IT MAKE MY HEART ACHE?
HEY, ARE YOU MY—?
—!?
A TINY... KYUBEY?
TA (DASH)
AH!! WAIT!!

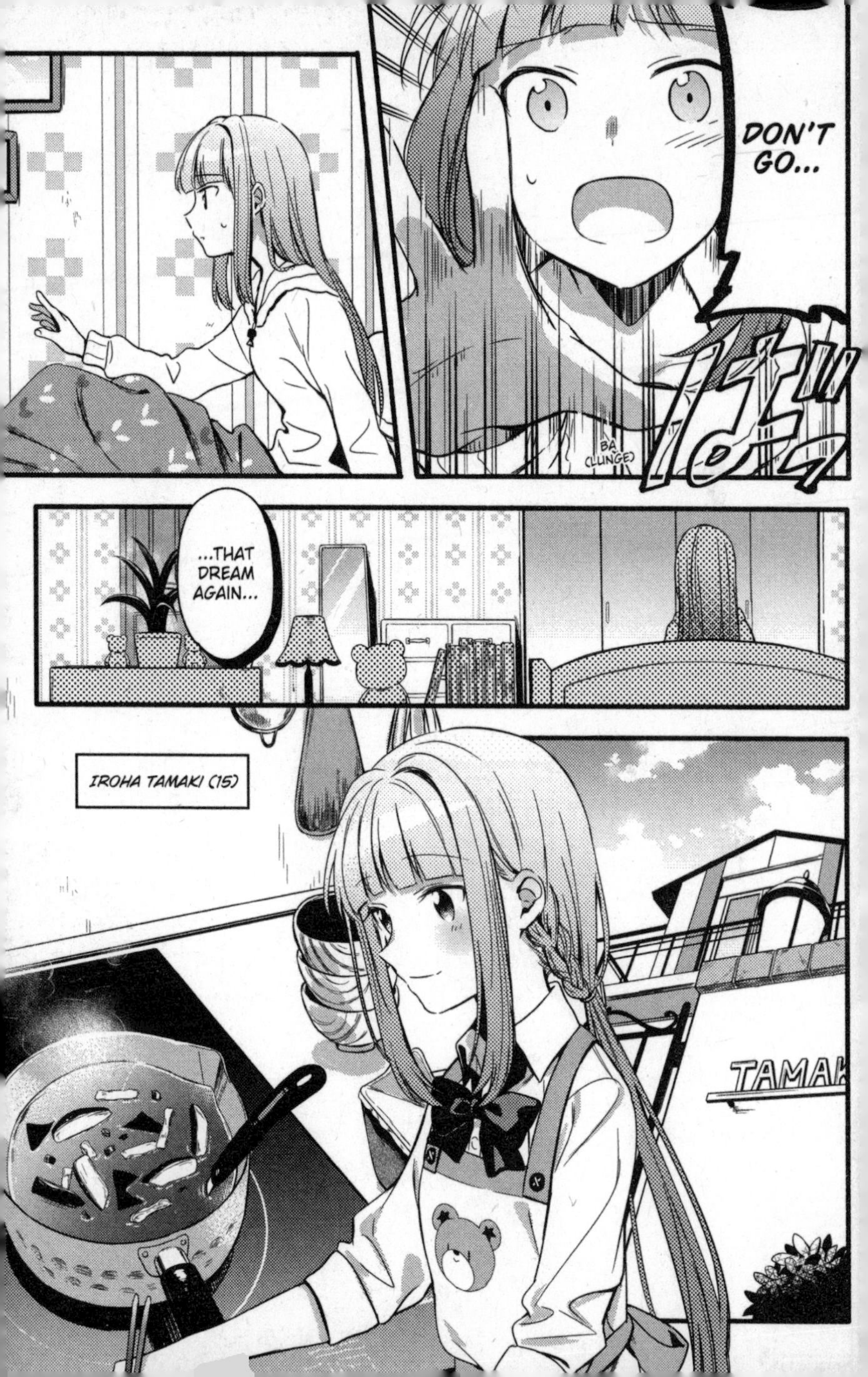
DON'T GO...
BA (LUNGE)
...THAT DREAM AGAIN...
IROHA TAMAKI (15)
TAMAK

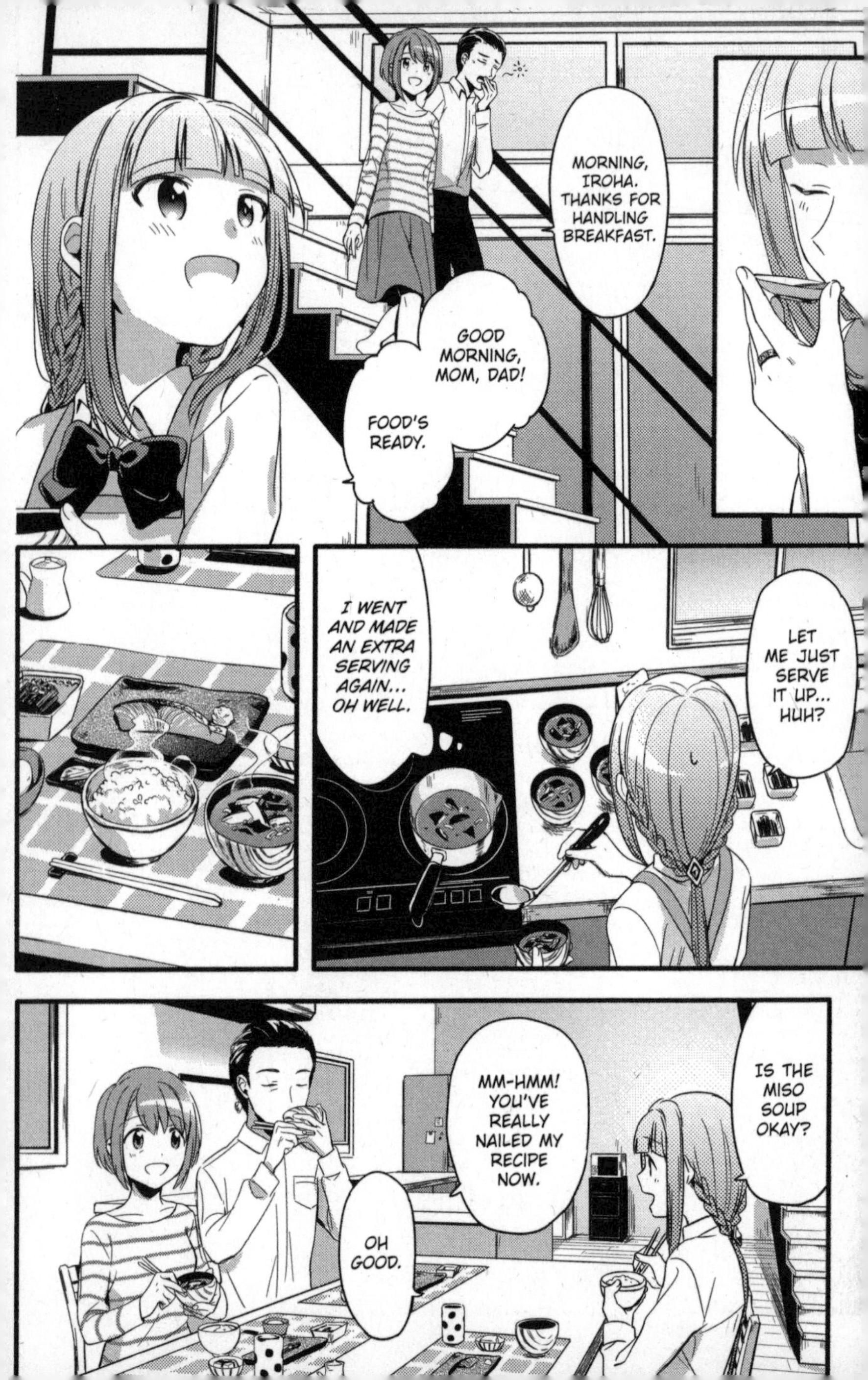
MORNING, IROHA. THANKS FOR HANDLING BREAKFAST.
GOOD MORNING, MOM, DAD!
FOOD'S READY.
LET ME JUST SERVE IT UP... HUH?
I WENT AND MADE AN EXTRA SERVING AGAIN... OH WELL.
IS THE MISO SOUP OKAY?
MM-HMM! YOU'VE REALLY NAILED MY RECIPE NOW.
OH GOOD.

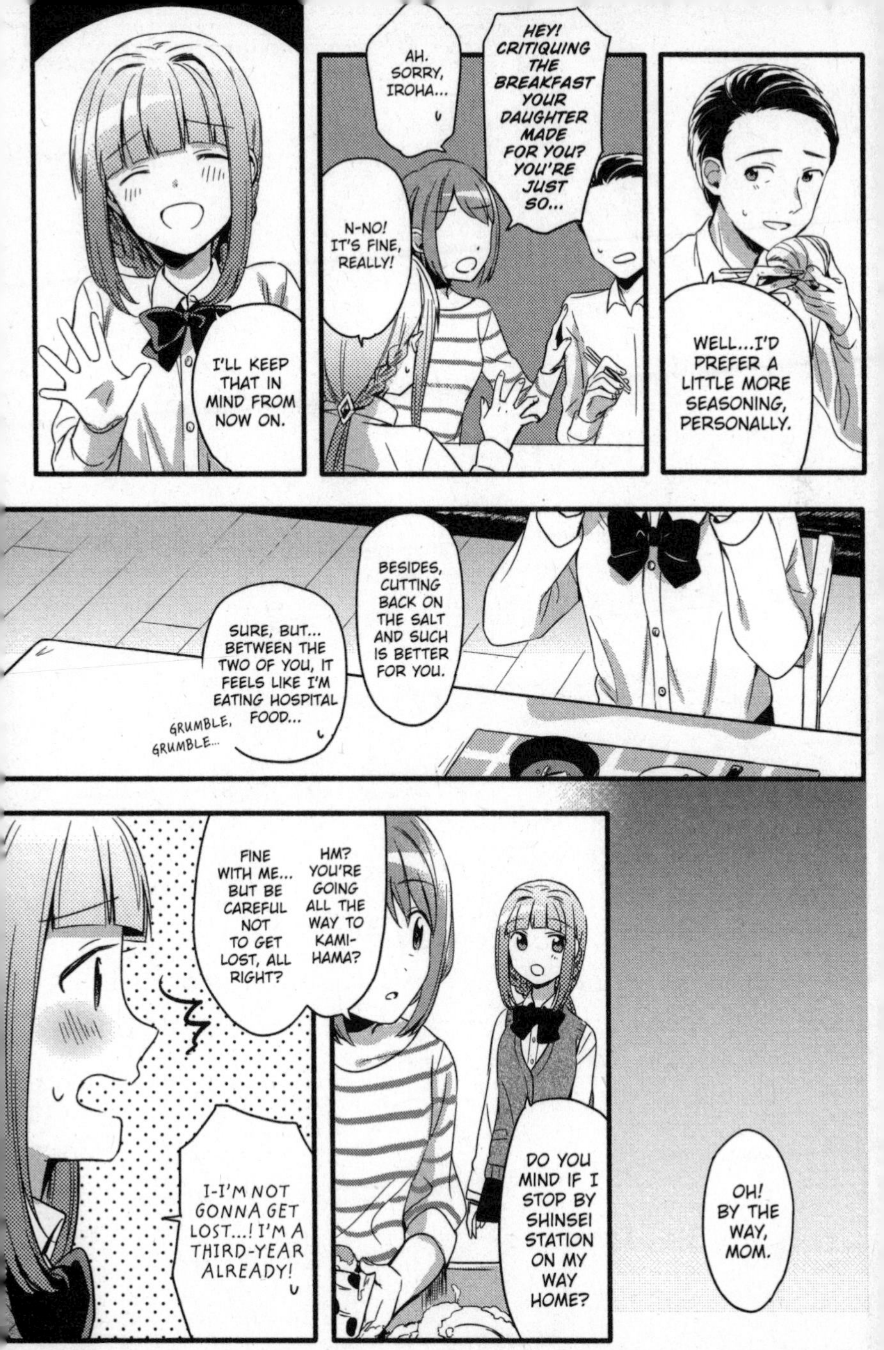
WELL...I'D PREFER A LITTLE MORE SEASONING, PERSONALLY.
HEY! CRITIQUING THE BREAKFAST YOUR DAUGHTER MADE FOR YOU? YOU'RE JUST SO...
AH. SORRY, IROHA...
N-NO! IT'S FINE, REALLY!
I'LL KEEP THAT IN MIND FROM NOW ON.
BESIDES, CUTTING BACK ON THE SALT AND SUCH IS BETTER FOR YOU.
SURE, BUT... BETWEEN THE TWO OF YOU, IT FEELS LIKE I'M EATING HOSPITAL FOOD...
GRUMBLE, GRUMBLE...
OH! BY THE WAY, MOM.
DO YOU MIND IF I STOP BY SHINSEI STATION ON MY WAY HOME?
HM? YOU'RE GOING ALL THE WAY TO KAMI-HAMA?
FINE WITH ME... BUT BE CAREFUL NOT TO GET LOST, ALL RIGHT?
I-I'M NOT GONNA GET LOST...! I'M A THIRD-YEAR ALREADY!

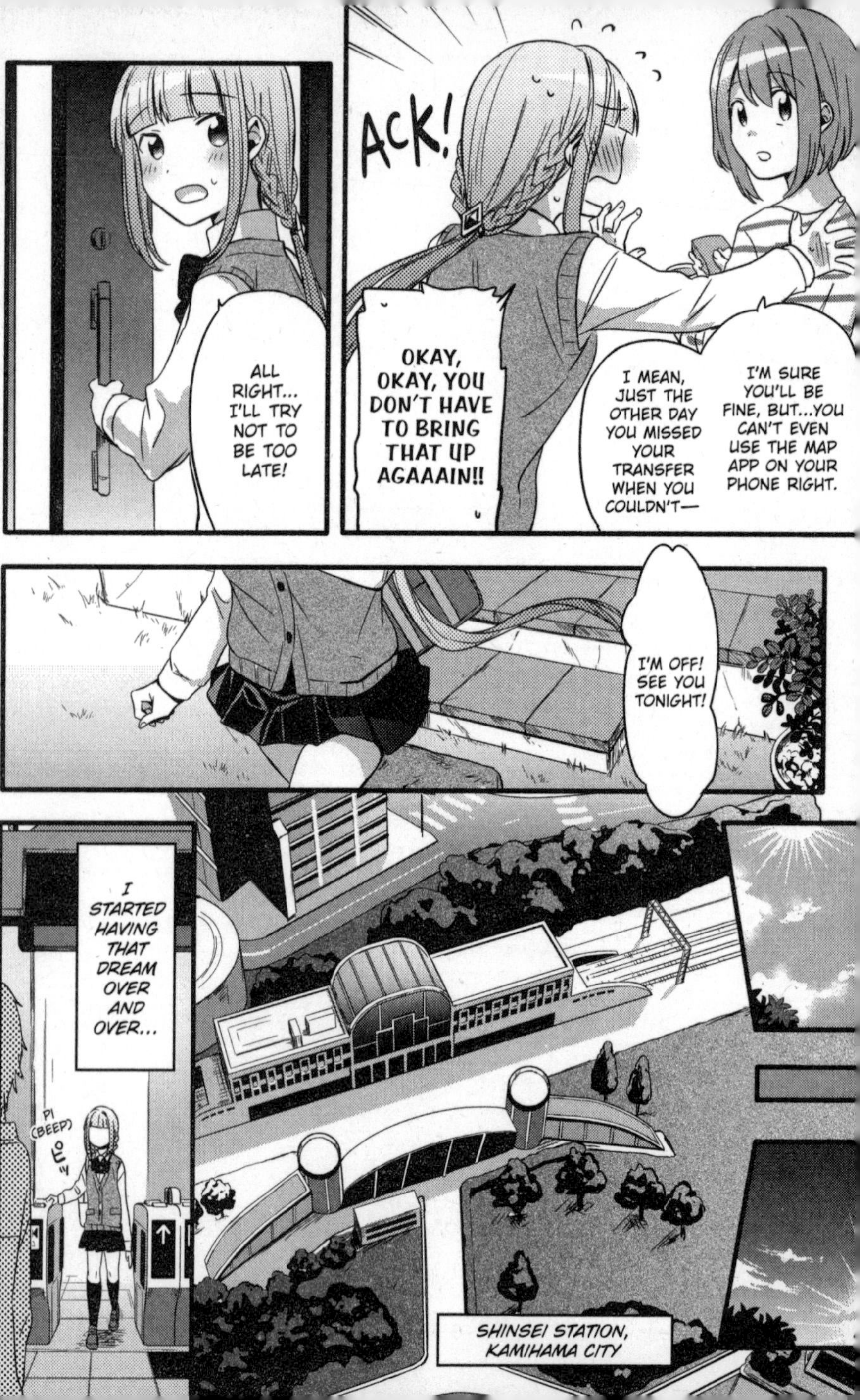
I'M SURE YOU'LL BE FINE, BUT...YOU CAN'T EVEN USE THE MAP APP ON YOUR PHONE RIGHT.
I MEAN, JUST THE OTHER DAY YOU MISSED YOUR TRANSFER WHEN YOU COULDN'T—
ACK!
OKAY, OKAY, YOU DON'T HAVE TO BRING THAT UP AGAAAIN!!
ALL RIGHT... I'LL TRY NOT TO BE TOO LATE!
I'M OFF! SEE YOU TONIGHT!
SHINSEI STATION, KAMIHAMA CITY
I STARTED HAVING THAT DREAM OVER AND OVER...
PI (BEEP)

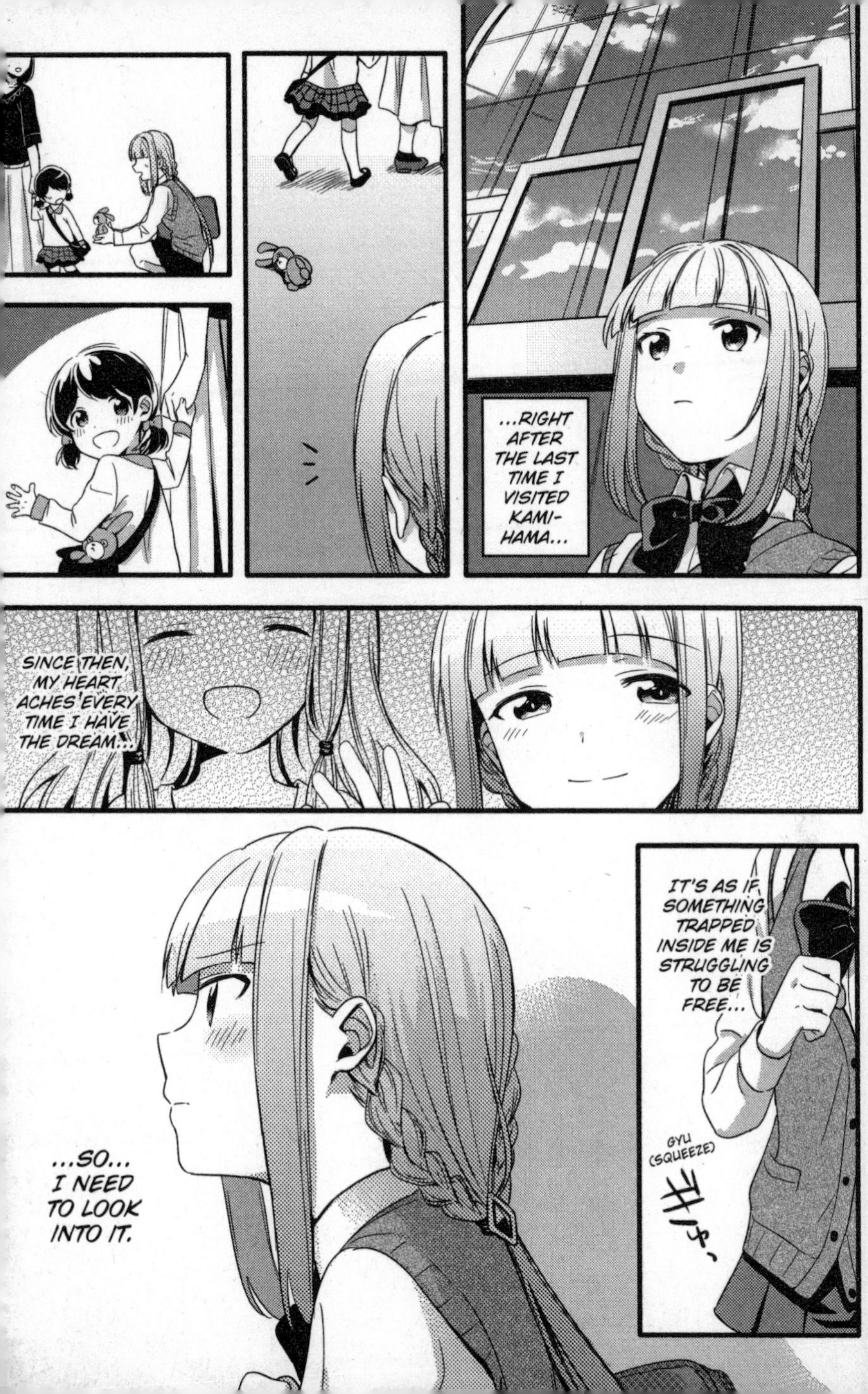
...RIGHT AFTER THE LAST TIME I VISITED KAMI-HAMA...
SINCE THEN, MY HEART ACHES EVERY TIME I HAVE THE DREAM...
IT'S AS IF SOMETHING TRAPPED INSIDE ME IS STRUGGLING TO BE FREE...
GYU (SQUEEZE)
...SO... I NEED TO LOOK INTO IT.

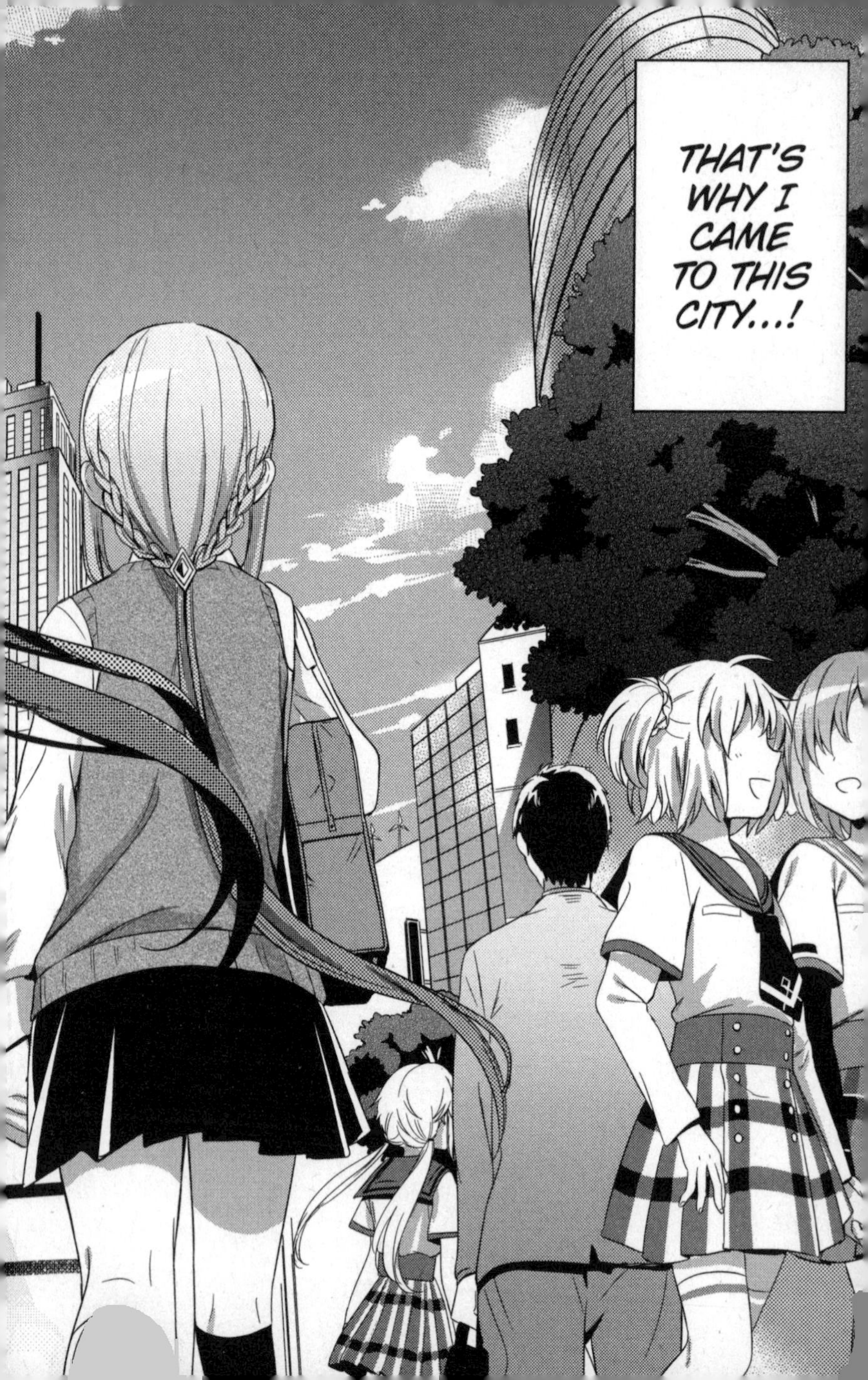
THAT'S WHY I CAME TO THIS CITY...!

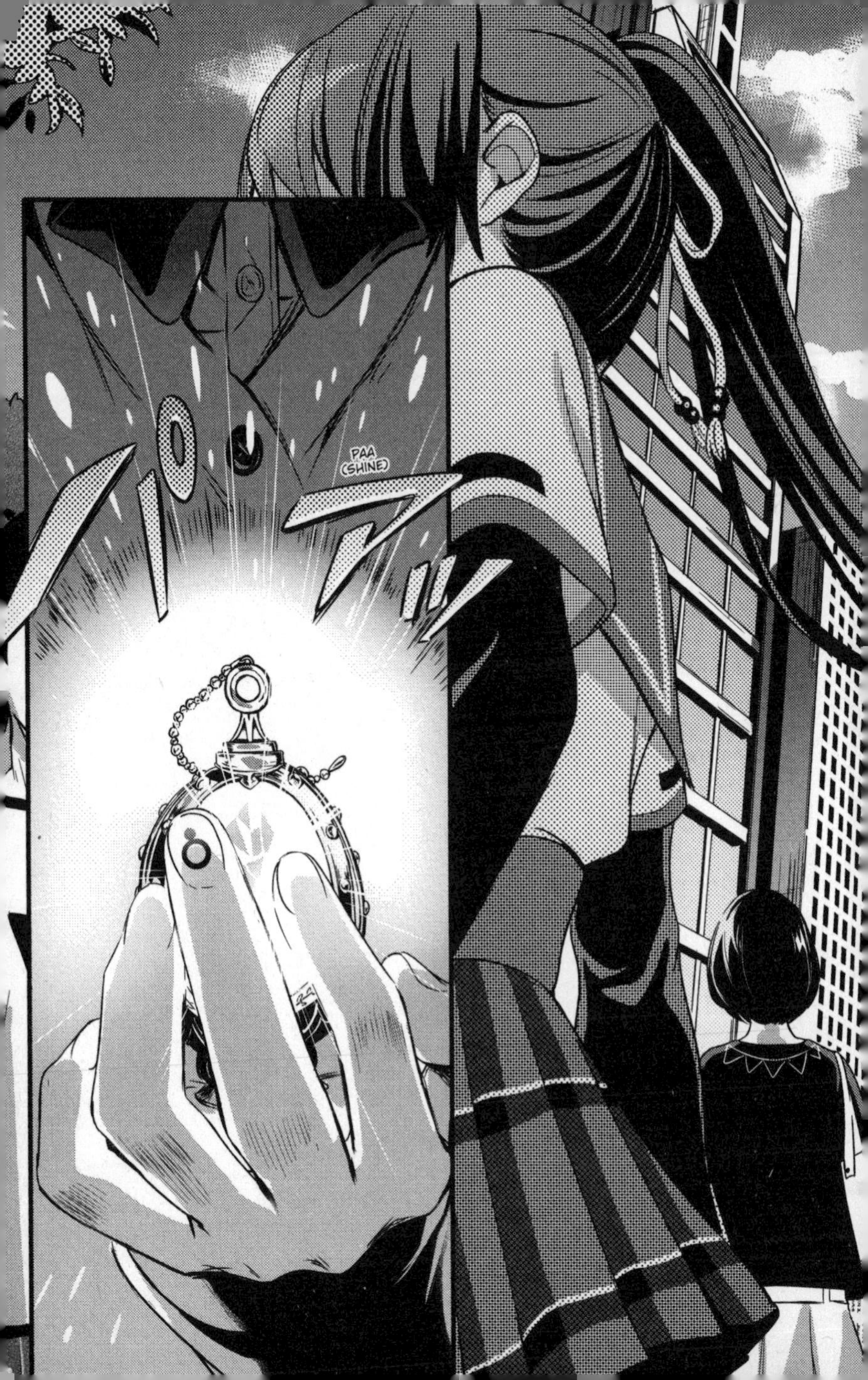
PAA
(SHINE)

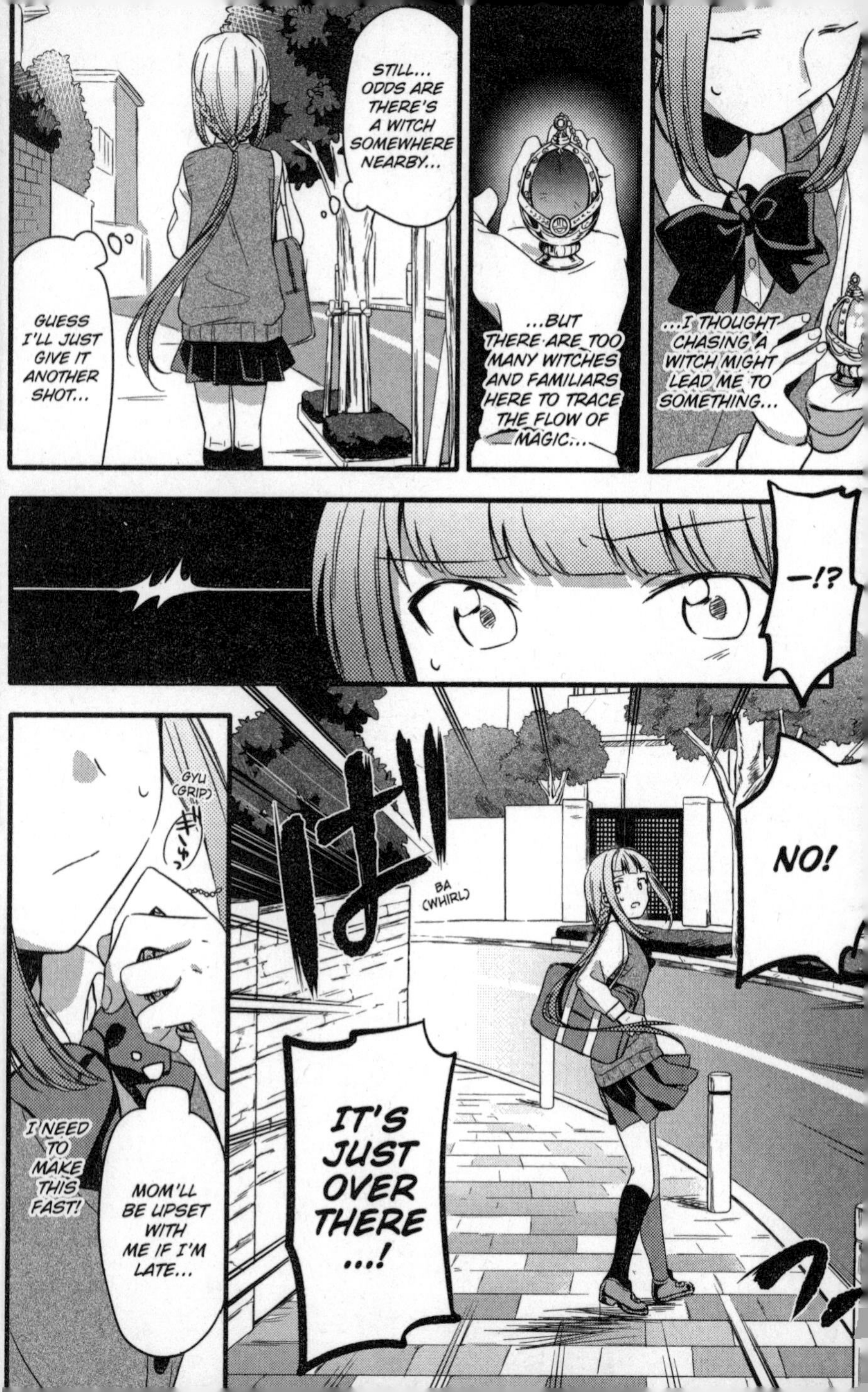
...I THOUGHT CHASING A WITCH MIGHT LEAD ME TO SOMETHING...
...BUT THERE ARE TOO MANY WITCHES AND FAMILIARS HERE TO TRACE THE FLOW OF MAGIC...
STILL... ODDS ARE THERE'S A WITCH SOMEWHERE NEARBY...
GUESS I'LL JUST GIVE IT ANOTHER SHOT...
—!?
NO!
BA (WHIRL)
IT'S JUST OVER THERE...!
GYU (GRIP)
MOM'LL BE UPSET WITH ME IF I'M LATE...
I NEED TO MAKE THIS FAST!

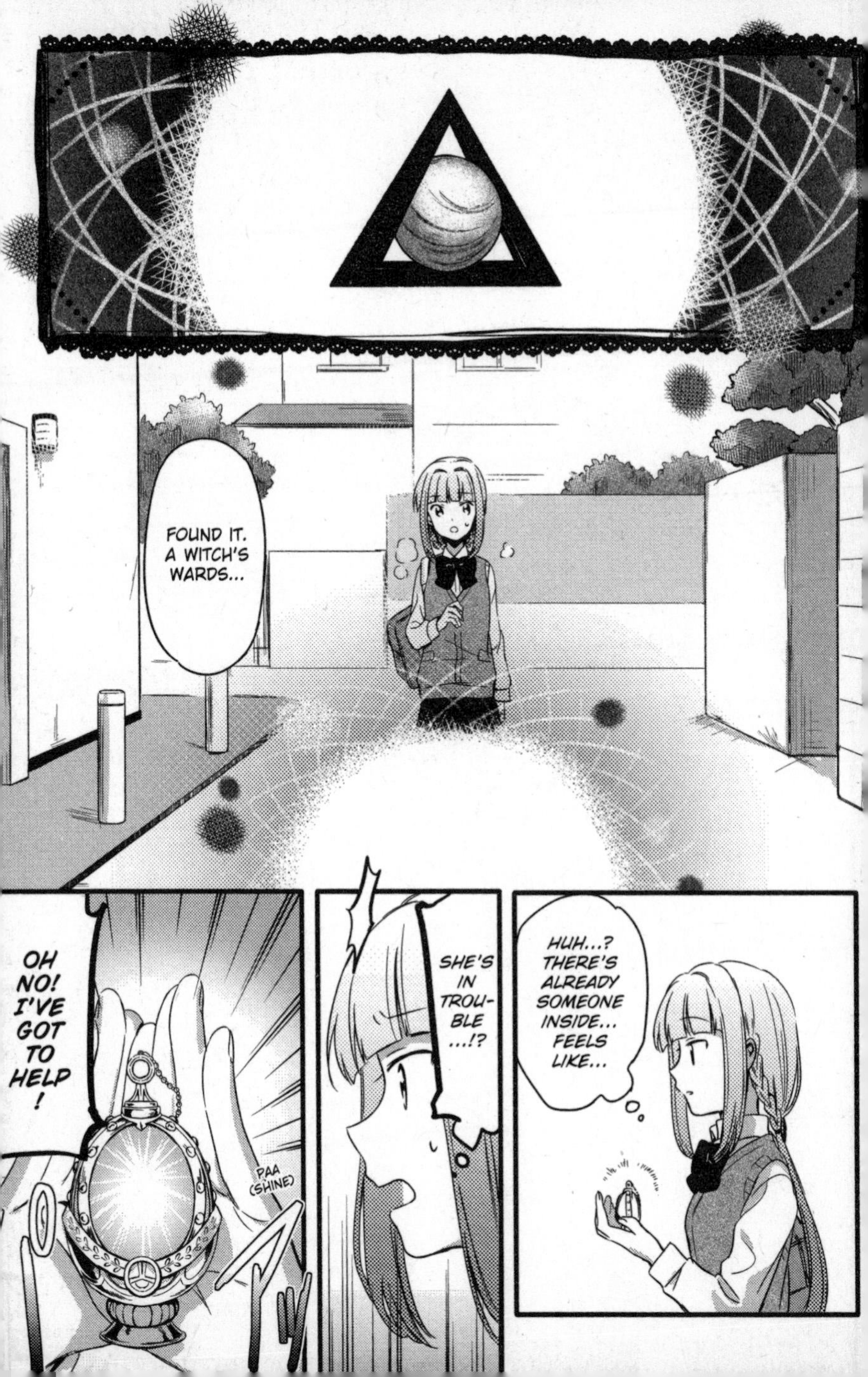
FOUND IT. A WITCH'S WARDS...
HUH...? THERE'S ALREADY SOMEONE INSIDE... FEELS LIKE...
SHE'S IN TROU-BLE...!?
OH NO! I'VE GOT TO HELP!
PAA (SHINE)

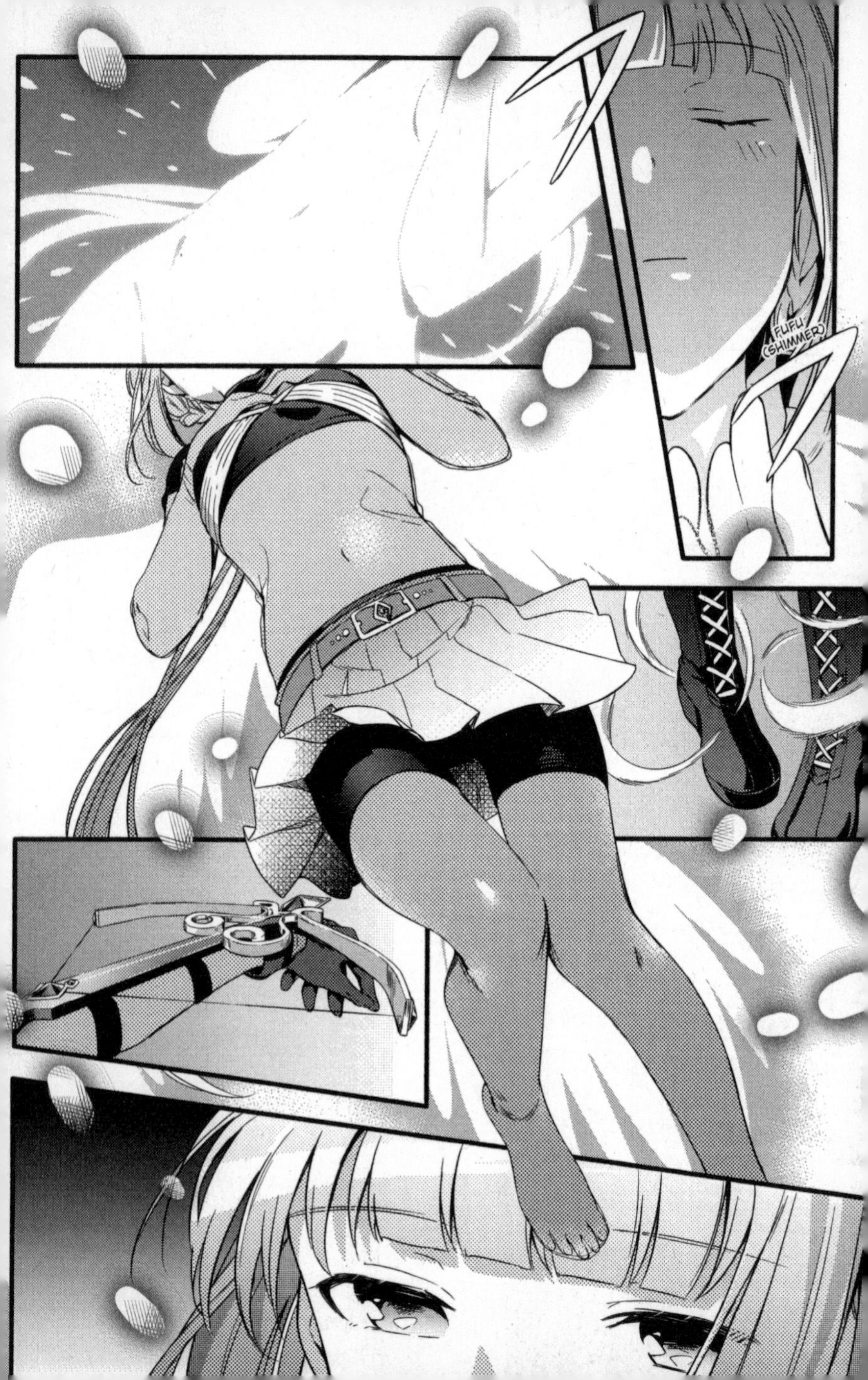
FUFU (SHIMMER)

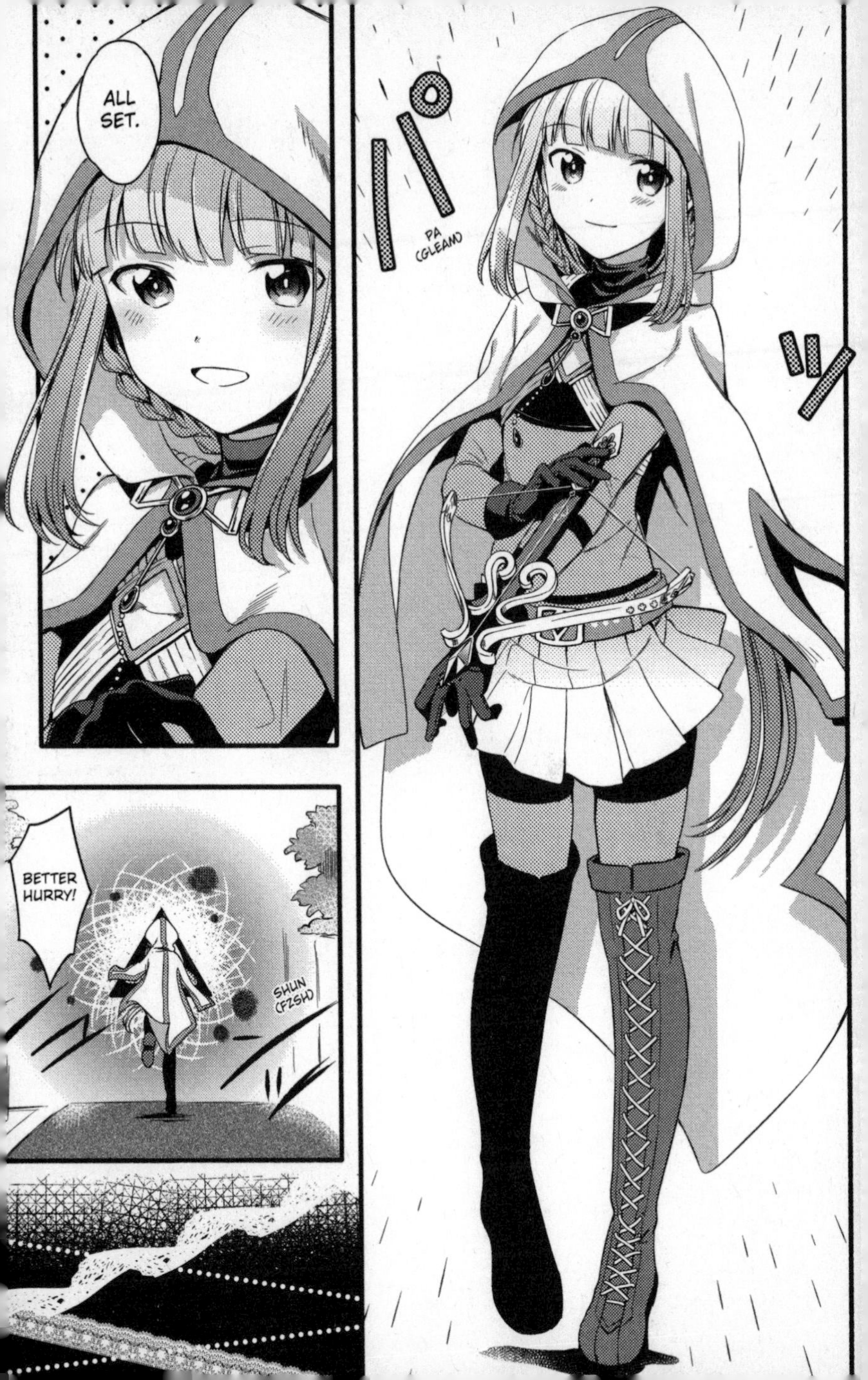
PA (GLEAM)
ALL SET.
BETTER HURRY!
SHUN (FZSH)

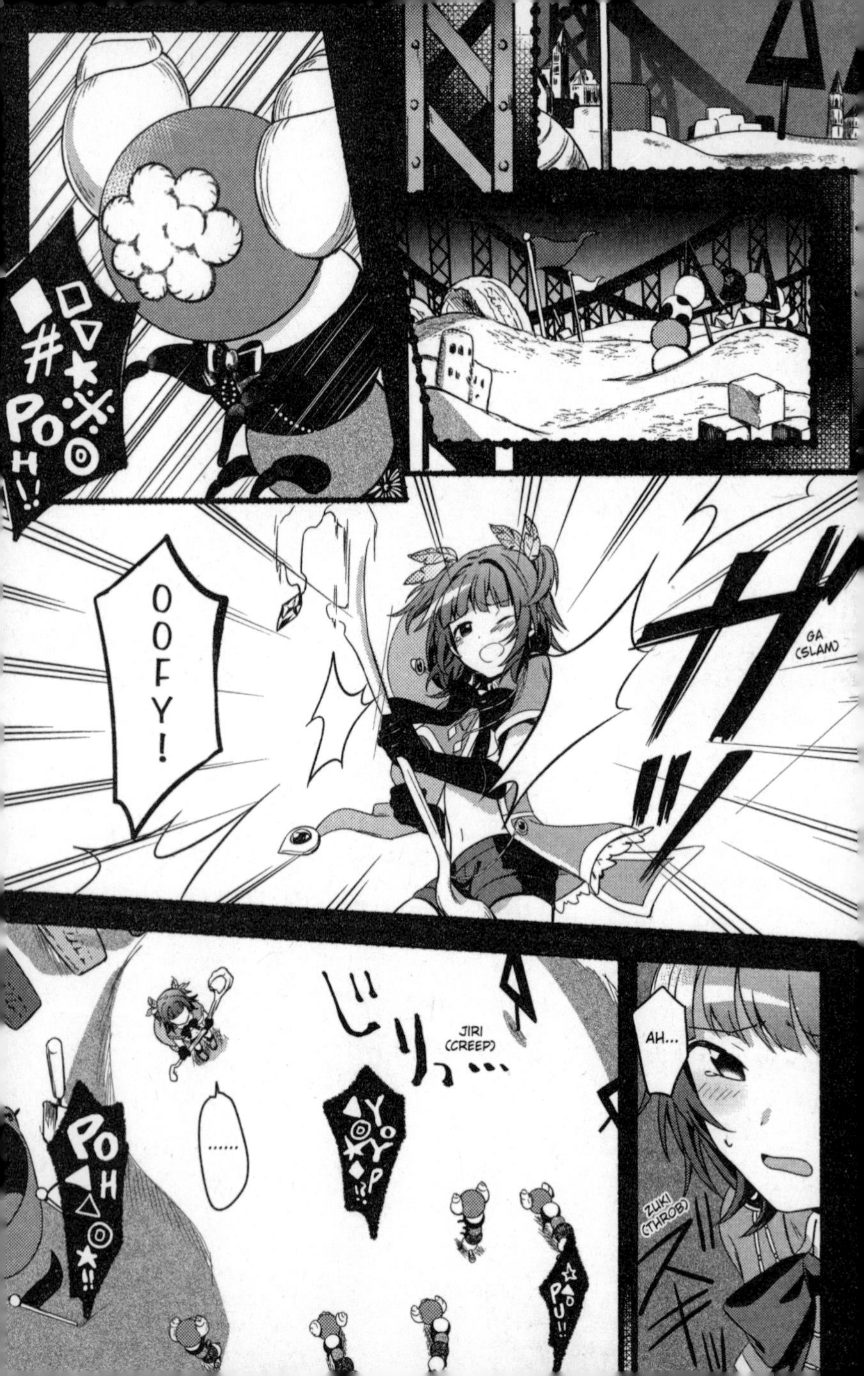

POH!!
ザッ
GA (SLAM)
OOFY!
AH...
ZUKI (THROB)
じりっ…
JIRI (CREEP)
YOYP!?!!
......
POH!!
PU!!

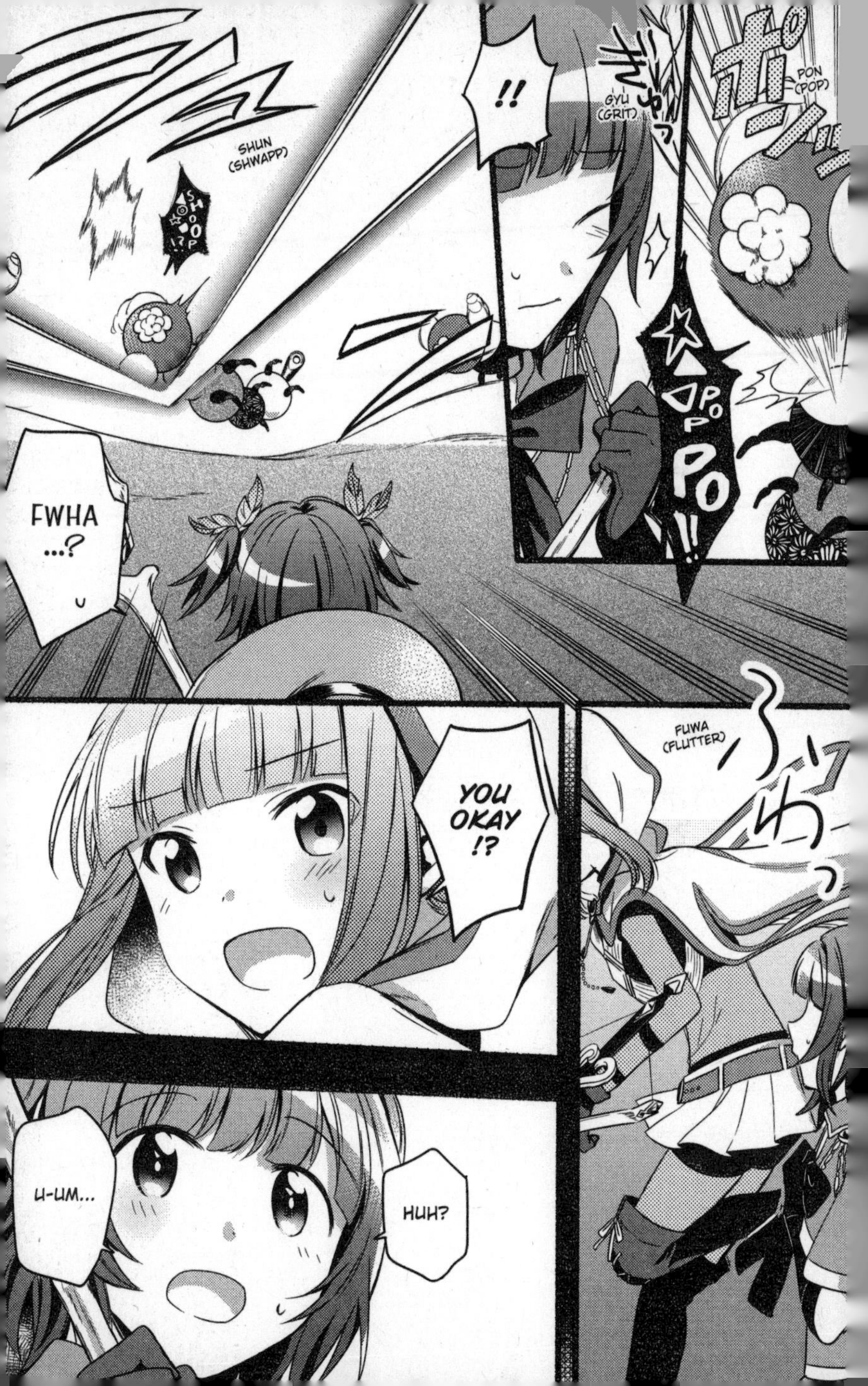
PON (POP)
GYU (GRIT)
!!
POPOPO!!
SHUN (SHWAPP)
SHOOP!?
FWHA...?
FUWA (FLUTTER)
YOU OKAY!?
HUH?
U-UM...

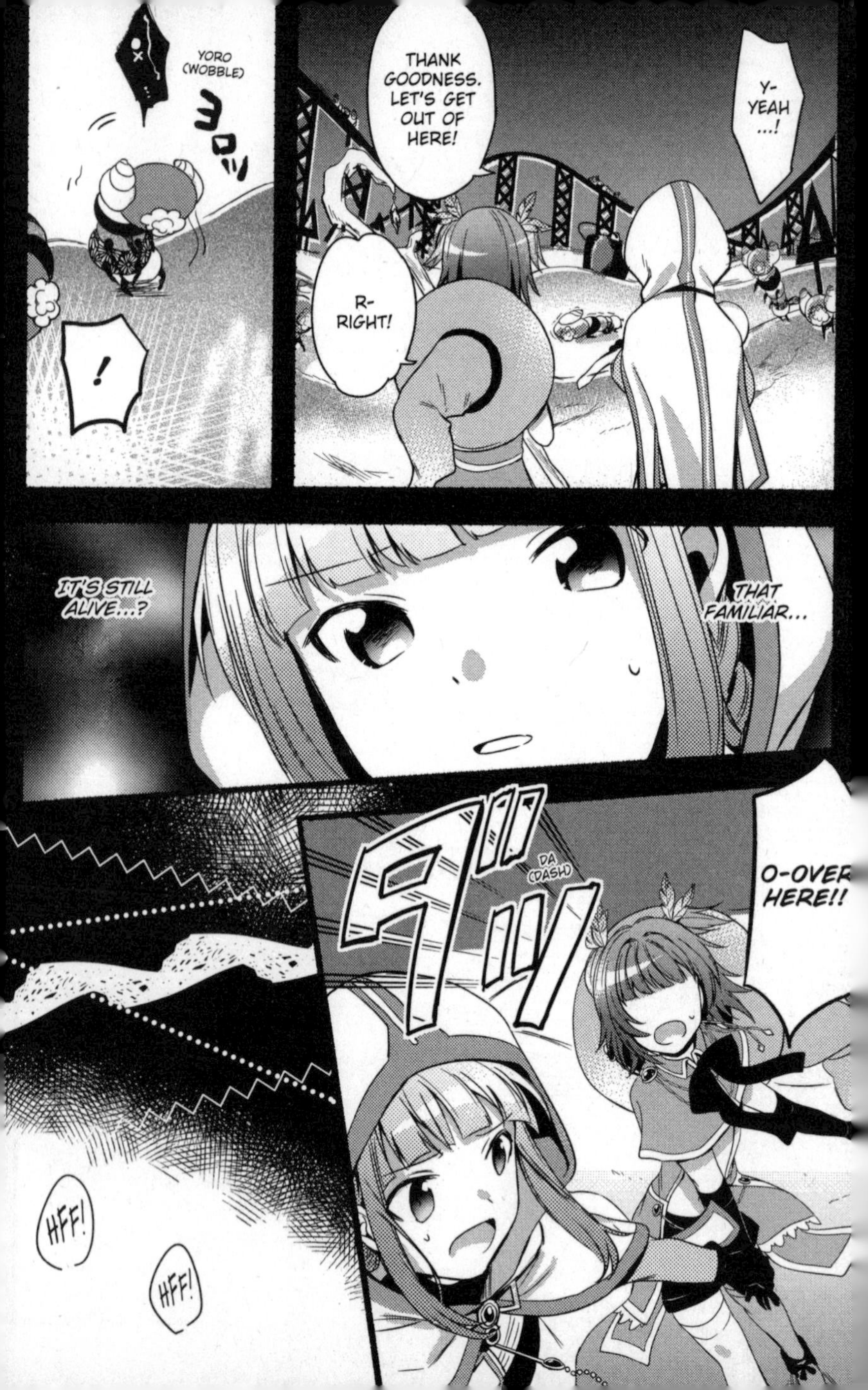
Y-YEAH ...!
THANK GOODNESS. LET'S GET OUT OF HERE!
R-RIGHT!
YORO (WOBBLE)
ヨロッ
!
THAT FAMILIAR...
IT'S STILL ALIVE...?
O-OVER HERE!!
ダッ
DA (DASH)
HFF!
HFF!

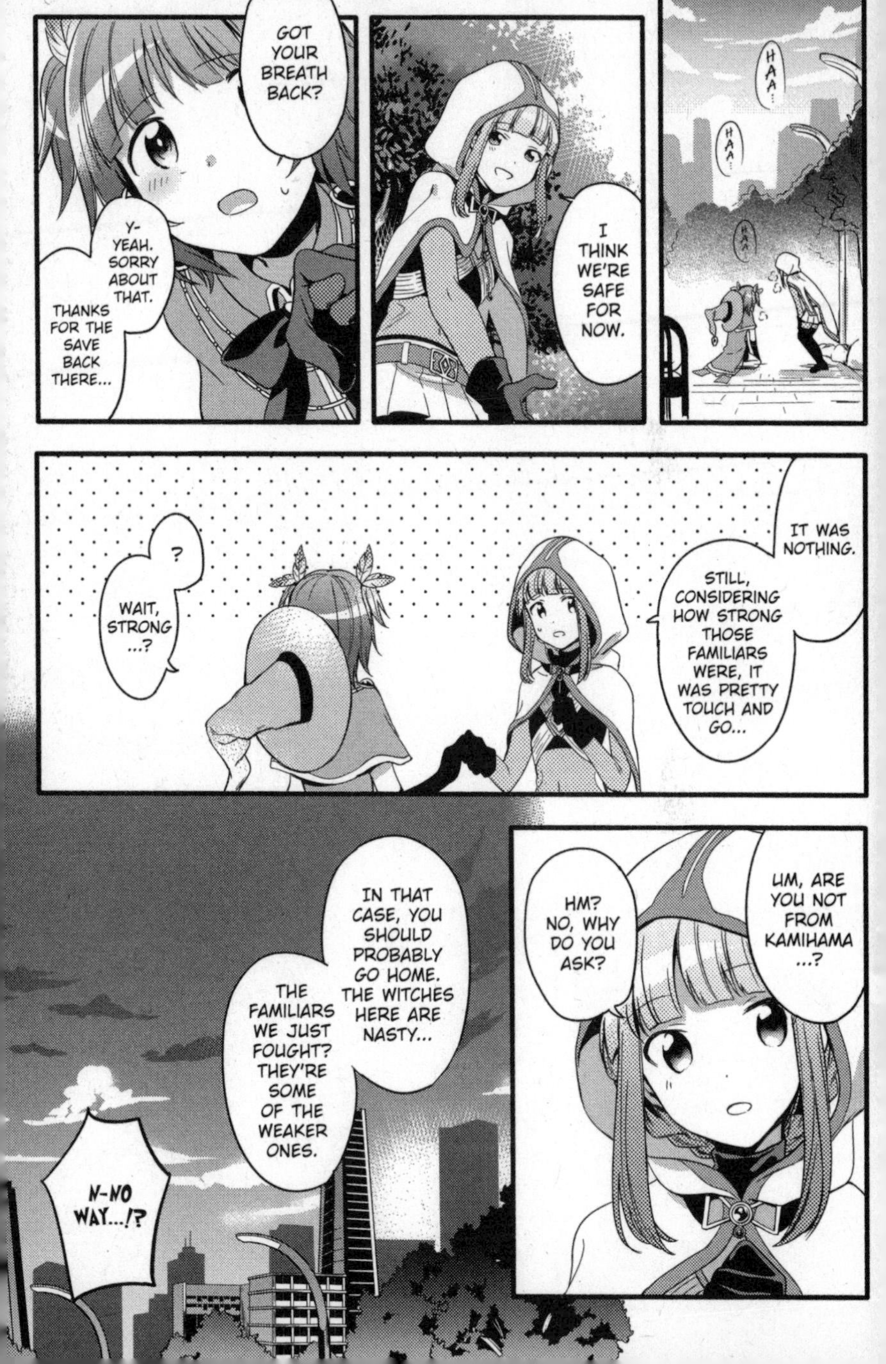
HAA...
HAA...
HAA...
I THINK WE'RE SAFE FOR NOW.
GOT YOUR BREATH BACK?
Y-YEAH. SORRY ABOUT THAT.
THANKS FOR THE SAVE BACK THERE...
IT WAS NOTHING.
STILL, CONSIDERING HOW STRONG THOSE FAMILIARS WERE, IT WAS PRETTY TOUCH AND GO...
?
WAIT, STRONG ...?
UM, ARE YOU NOT FROM KAMIHAMA ...?
HM? NO, WHY DO YOU ASK?
IN THAT CASE, YOU SHOULD PROBABLY GO HOME. THE WITCHES HERE ARE NASTY...
THE FAMILIARS WE JUST FOUGHT? THEY'RE SOME OF THE WEAKER ONES.
N-NO WAY...!?

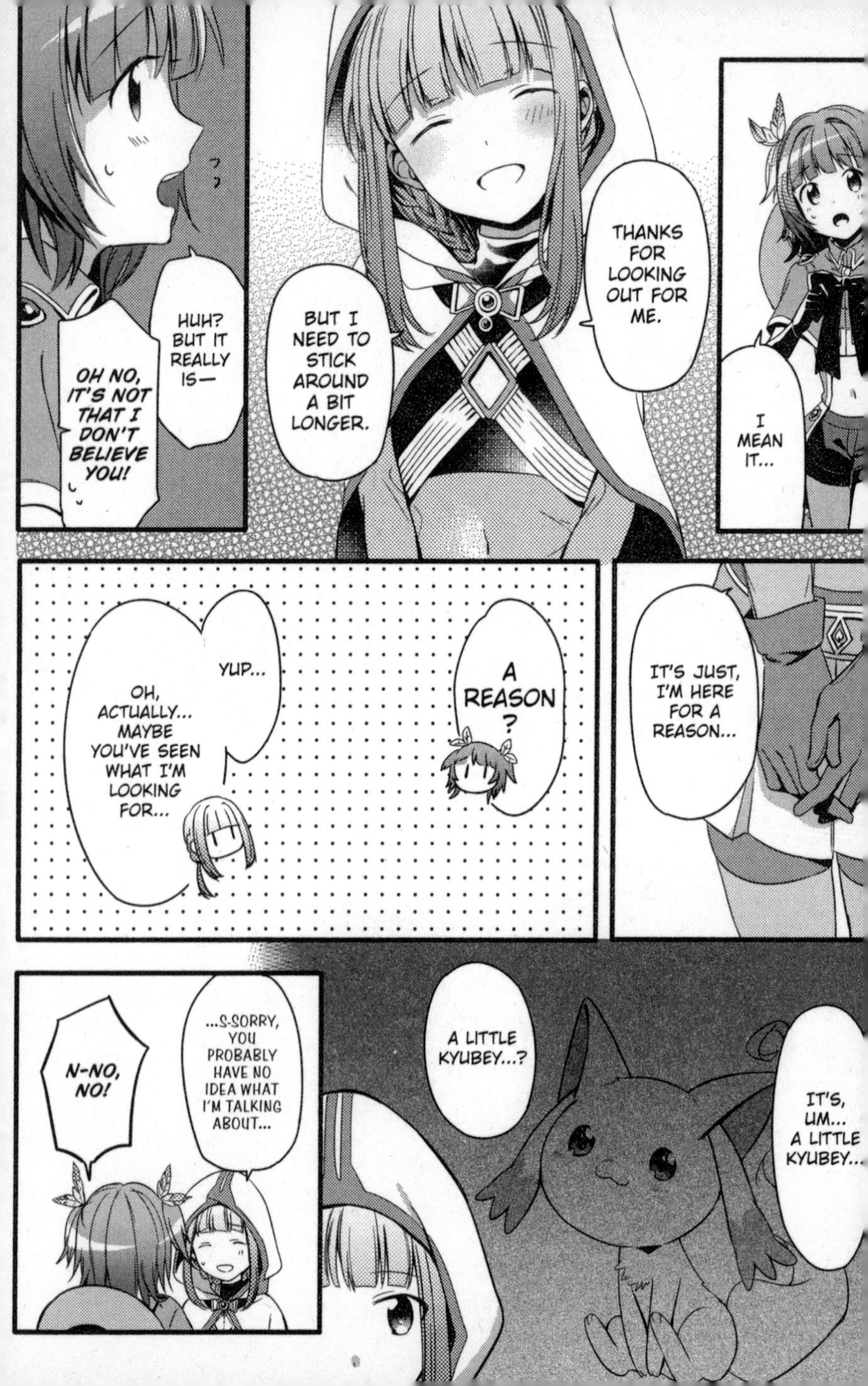
I MEAN IT...
THANKS FOR LOOKING OUT FOR ME.
BUT I NEED TO STICK AROUND A BIT LONGER.
HUH? BUT IT REALLY IS—
OH NO, IT'S NOT THAT I DON'T BELIEVE YOU!
IT'S JUST, I'M HERE FOR A REASON...
A REASON?
YUP...
OH, ACTUALLY... MAYBE YOU'VE SEEN WHAT I'M LOOKING FOR...
IT'S, UM... A LITTLE KYUBEY...
A LITTLE KYUBEY...?
...S-SORRY, YOU PROBABLY HAVE NO IDEA WHAT I'M TALKING ABOUT...
N-NO, NO!

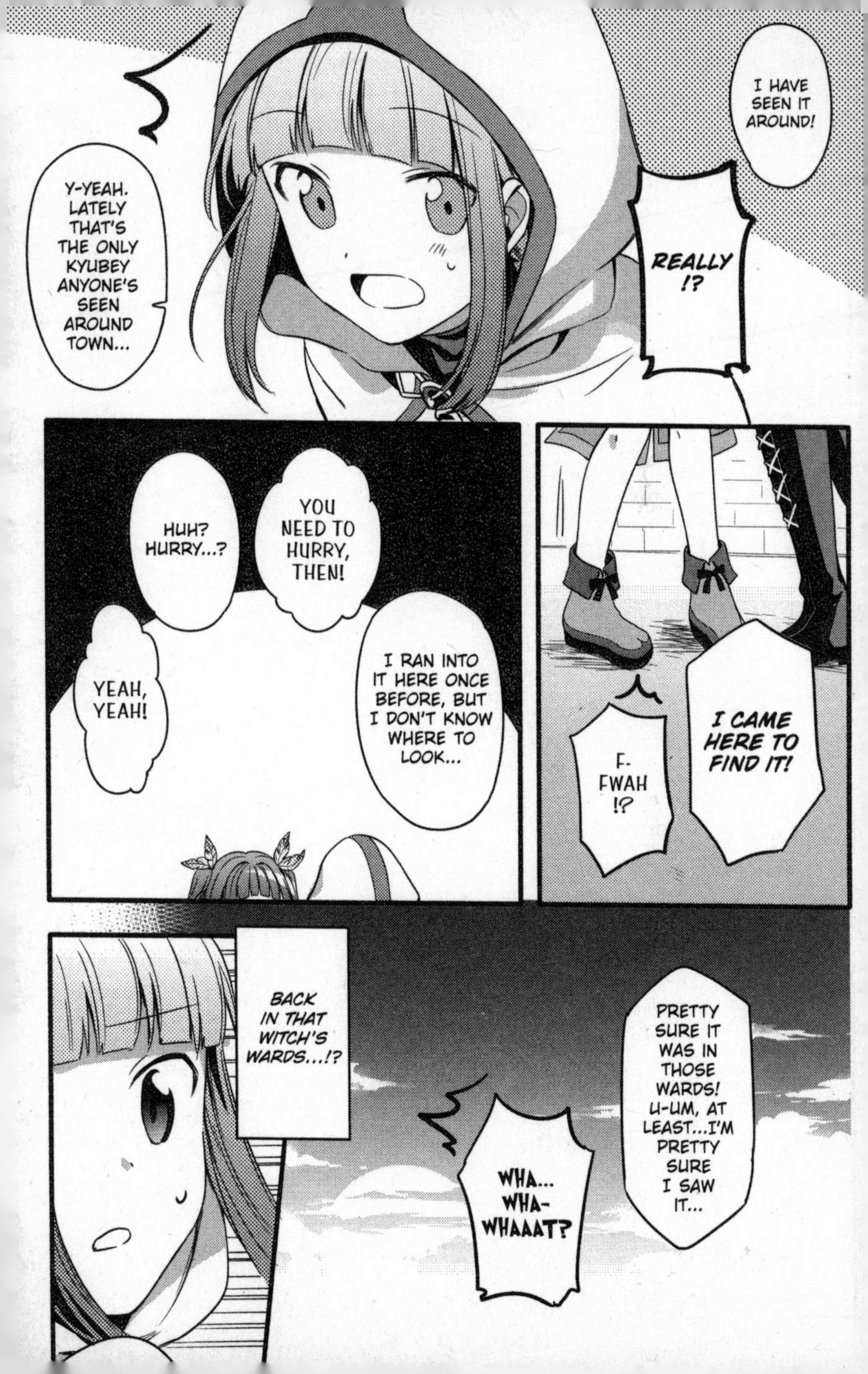
I HAVE SEEN IT AROUND!
REALLY!?
Y-YEAH. LATELY THAT'S THE ONLY KYUBEY ANYONE'S SEEN AROUND TOWN...
I CAME HERE TO FIND IT!
F-FWAH!?
YOU NEED TO HURRY, THEN!
HUH? HURRY...?
I RAN INTO IT HERE ONCE BEFORE, BUT I DON'T KNOW WHERE TO LOOK...
YEAH, YEAH!
PRETTY SURE IT WAS IN THOSE WARDS! U-UM, AT LEAST...I'M PRETTY SURE I SAW IT...
WHA... WHA-WHAAAT?
BACK IN THAT WITCH'S WARDS...!?

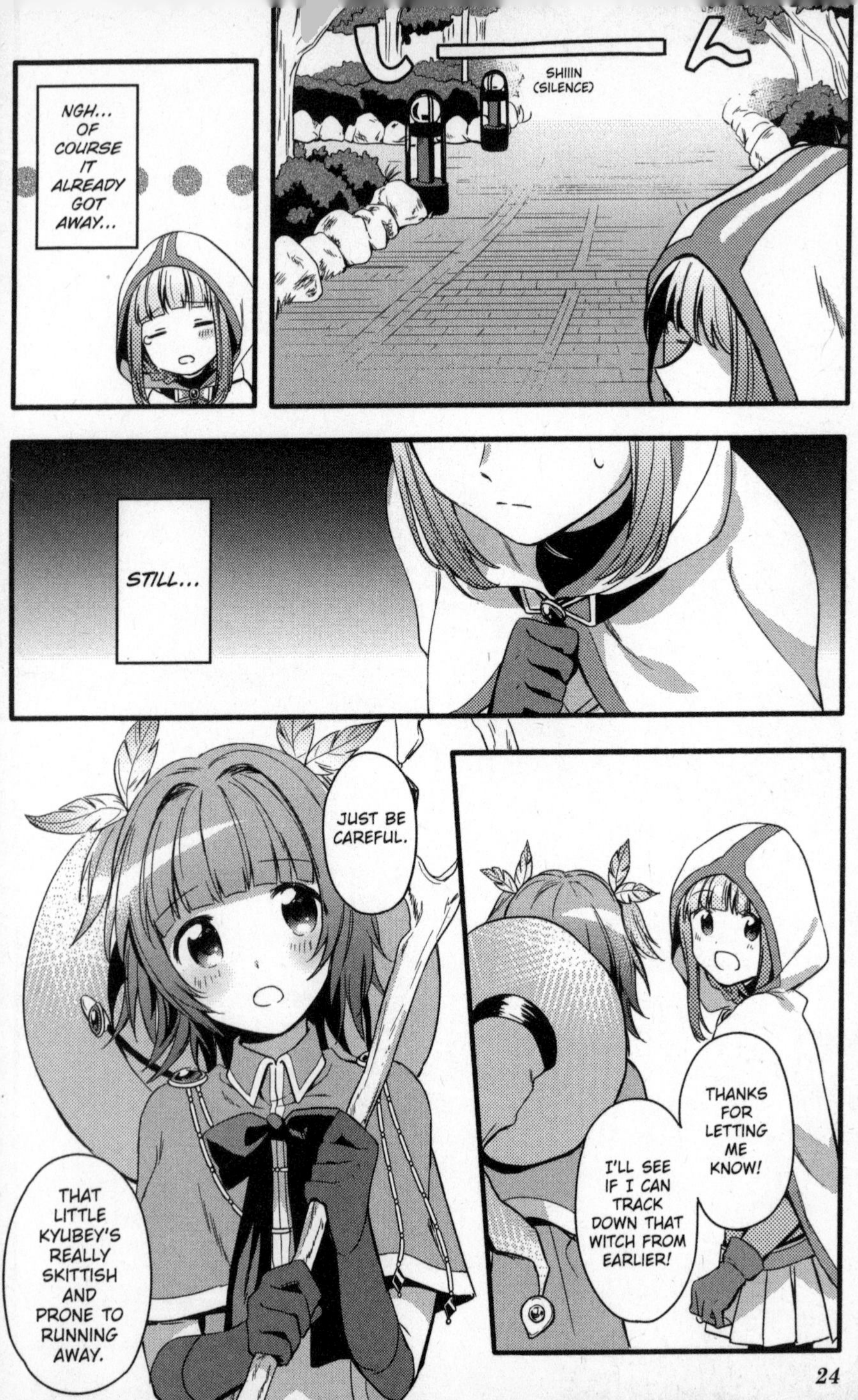
SHIIIN (SILENCE)
NGH... OF COURSE IT ALREADY GOT AWAY...
STILL...
THANKS FOR LETTING ME KNOW!
I'LL SEE IF I CAN TRACK DOWN THAT WITCH FROM EARLIER!
JUST BE CAREFUL.
THAT LITTLE KYUBEY'S REALLY SKITTISH AND PRONE TO RUNNING AWAY.

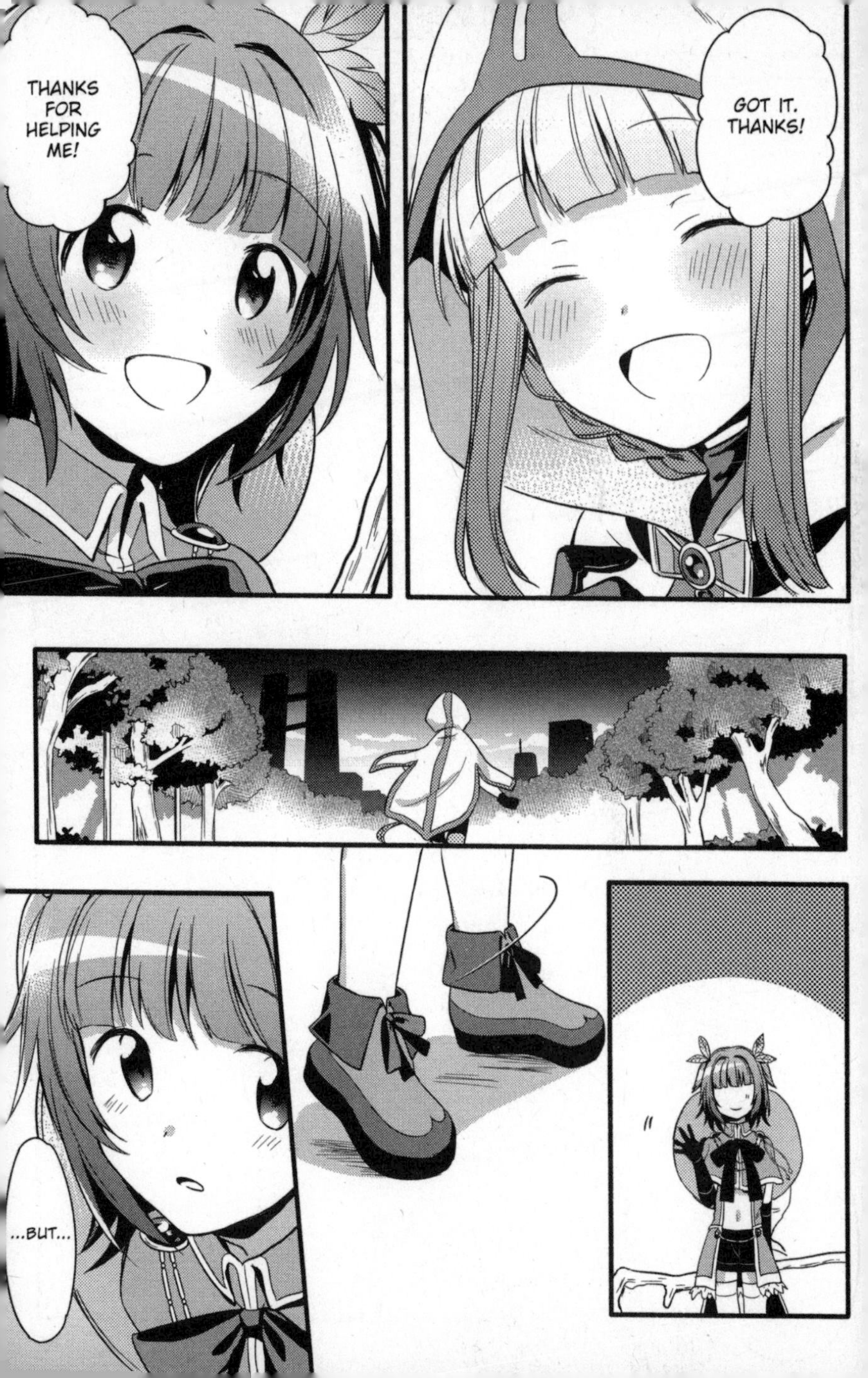
GOT IT. THANKS!
THANKS FOR HELPING ME!
...BUT...

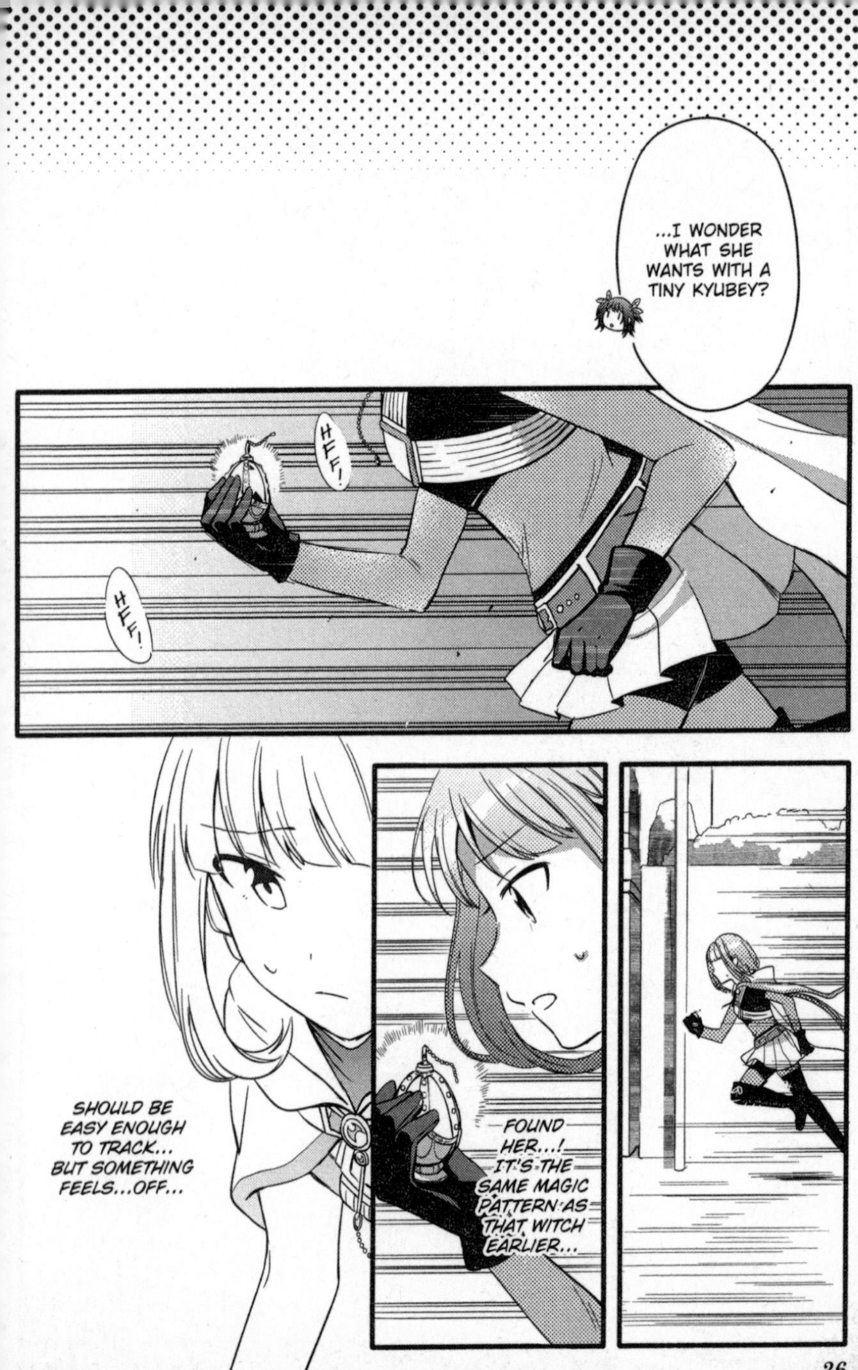
...I WONDER WHAT SHE WANTS WITH A TINY KYUBEY?
HFF!
HFF!
FOUND HER...! IT'S THE SAME MAGIC PATTERN AS THAT WITCH EARLIER...
SHOULD BE EASY ENOUGH TO TRACK... BUT SOMETHING FEELS...OFF...

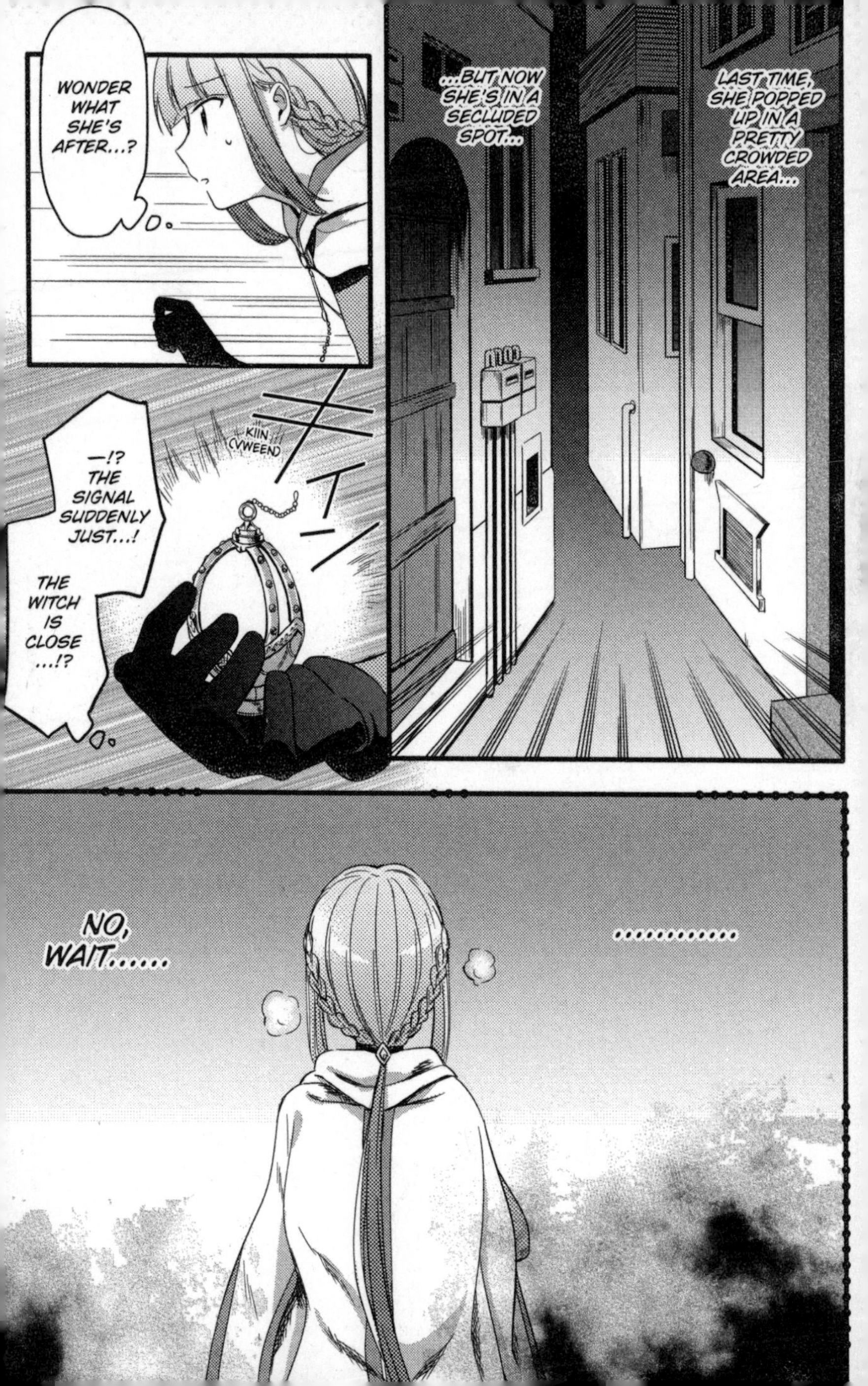
LAST TIME, SHE POPPED UP IN A PRETTY CROWDED AREA...
...BUT NOW SHE'S IN A SECLUDED SPOT...
WONDER WHAT SHE'S AFTER...?
KIIN (VWEEN)
—!? THE SIGNAL SUDDENLY JUST...!
THE WITCH IS CLOSE...!?
....
NO, WAIT......

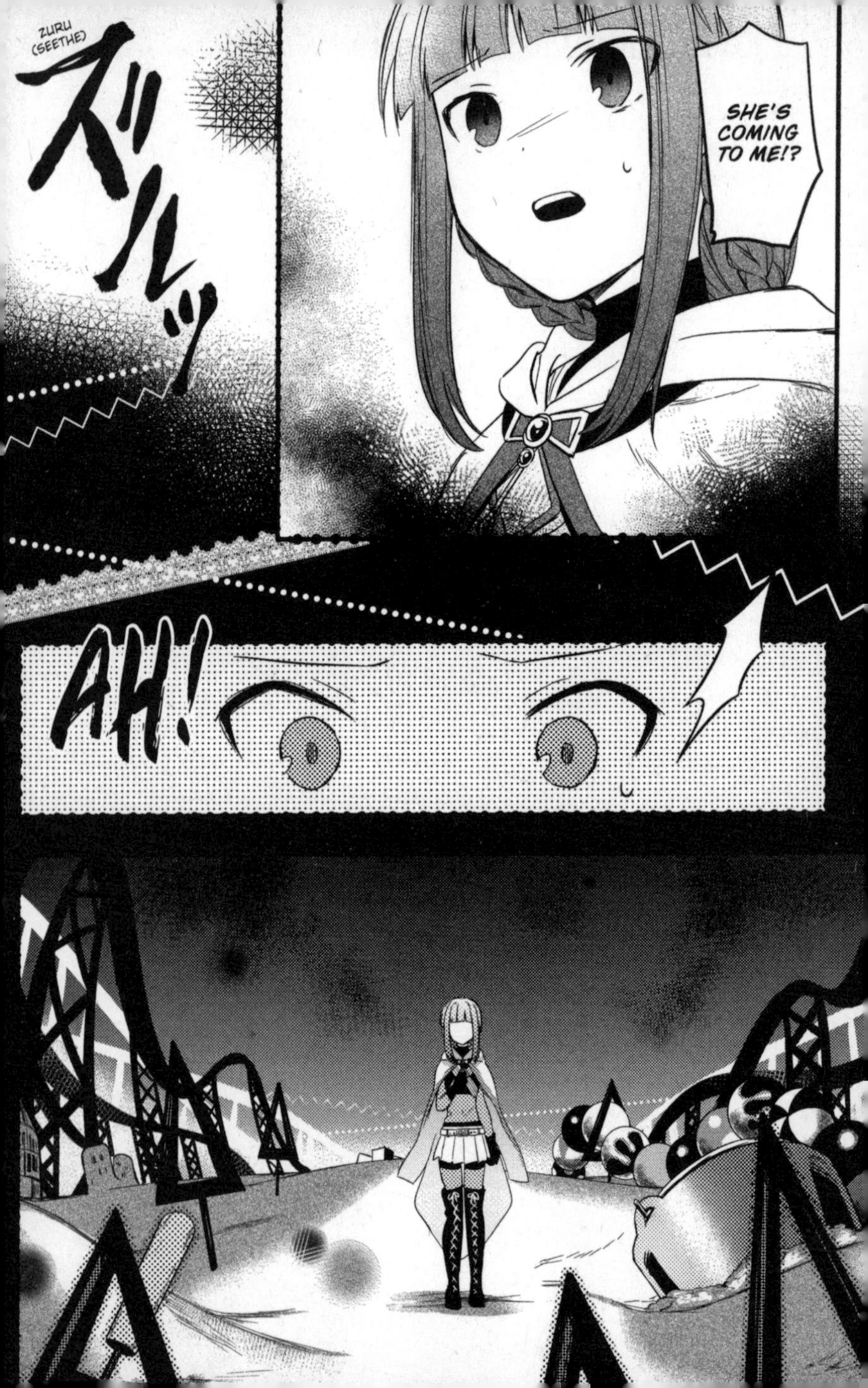
SHE'S COMING TO ME!?
ZURU (SEETHE)
ズルッ
AH!

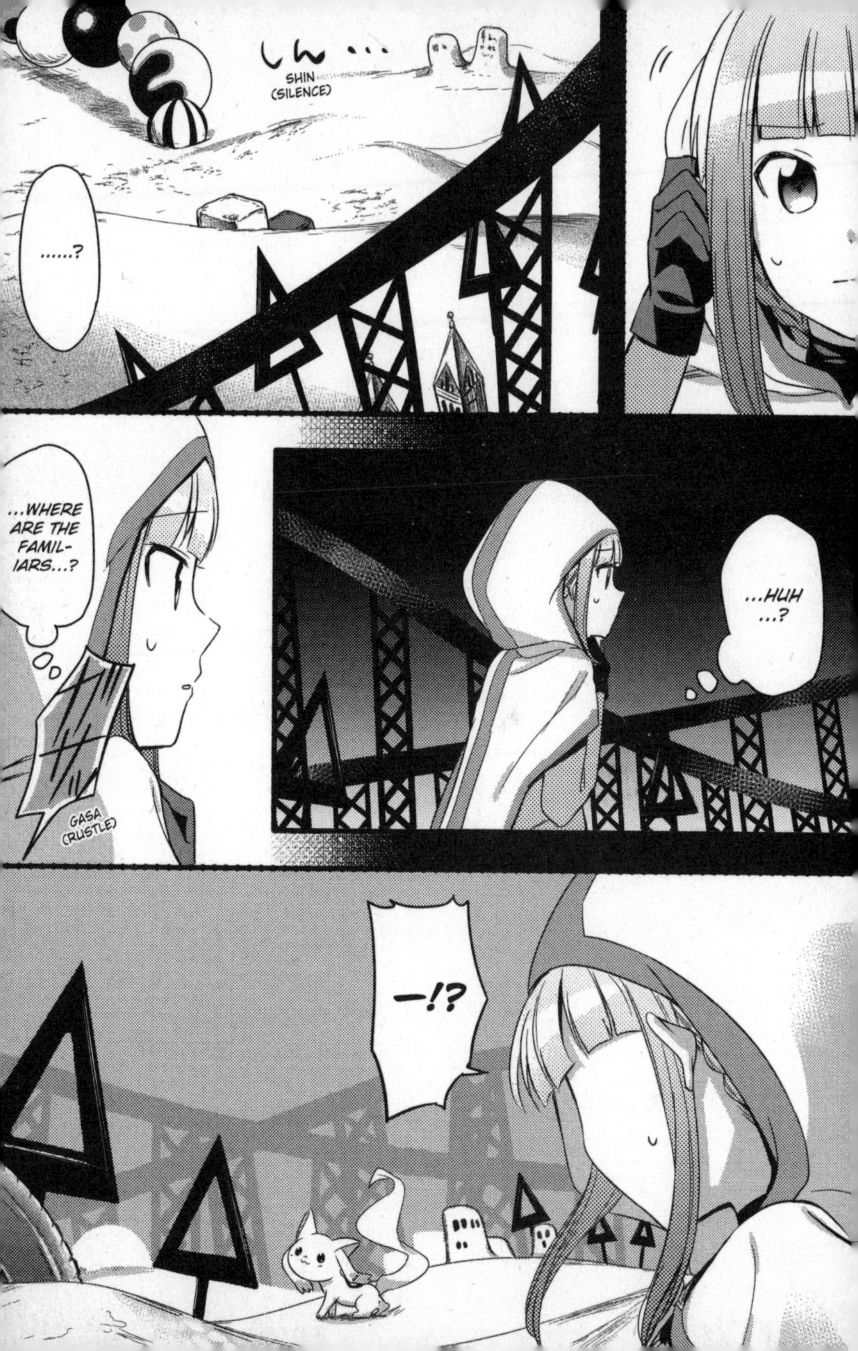
しん…
SHIN (SILENCE)
......?
...HUH ...?
...WHERE ARE THE FAMILIARS...?
GASA (RUSTLE)
—!?

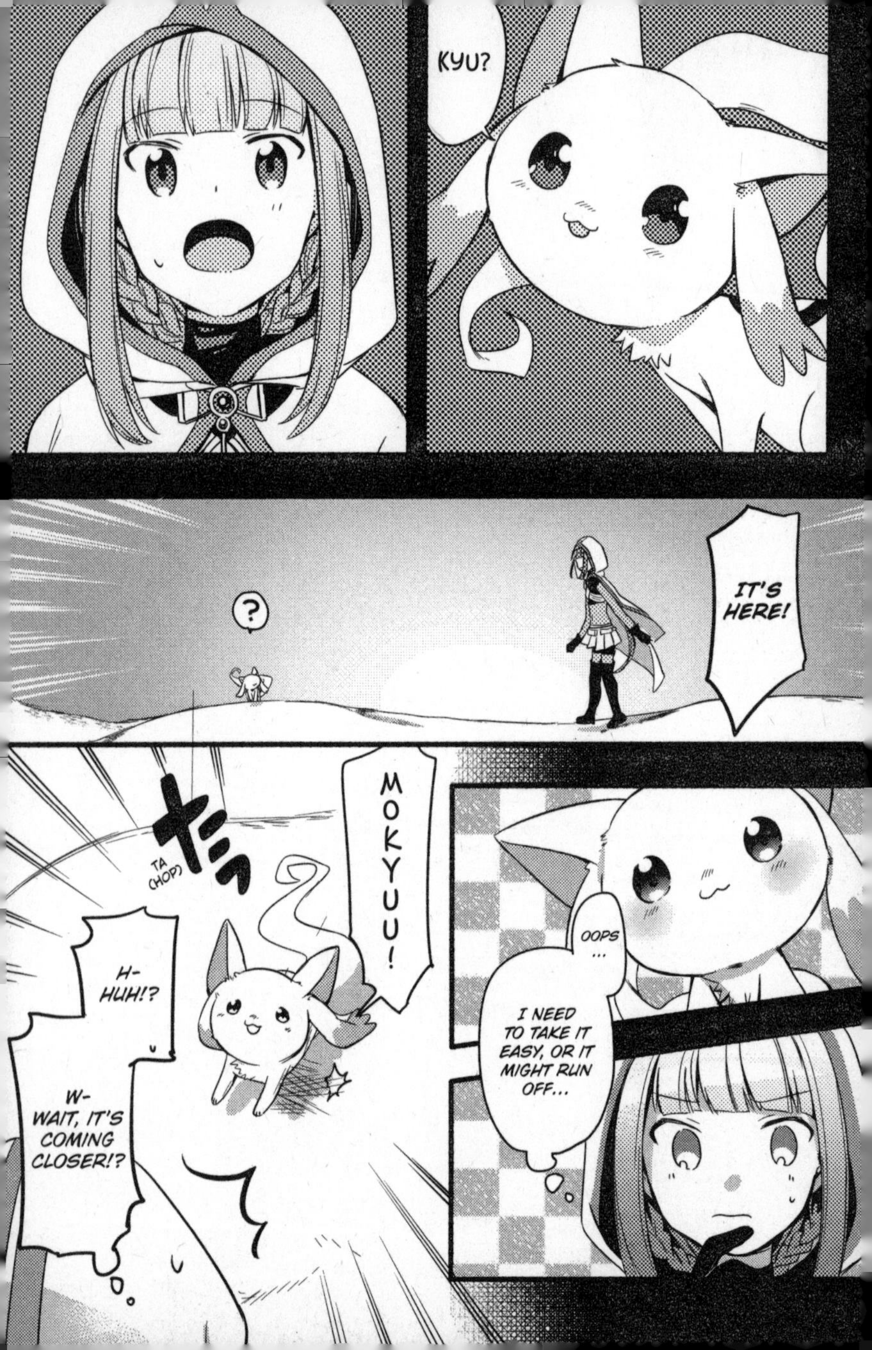
KYU?
IT'S HERE!
?
OOPS...
I NEED TO TAKE IT EASY, OR IT MIGHT RUN OFF...
MOKYUU!
TA (HOP)
H-HUH!?
W-WAIT, IT'S COMING CLOSER!?

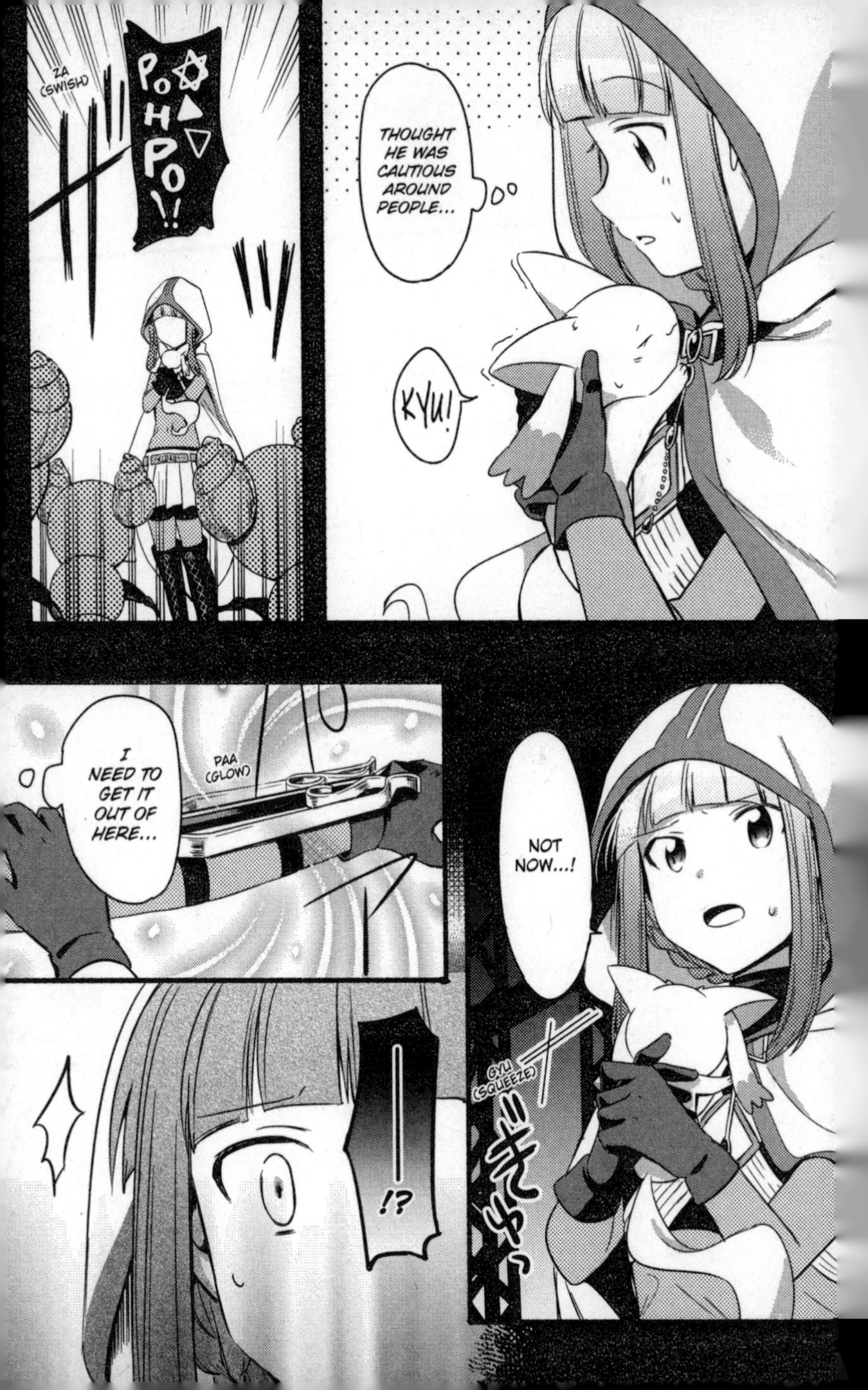
THOUGHT HE WAS CAUTIOUS AROUND PEOPLE...
KYU!
ZA (SWISH)
POHPO!!
NOT NOW...!
GYU (SQUEEZE)
I NEED TO GET IT OUT OF HERE...
PAA (GLOW)
—!?

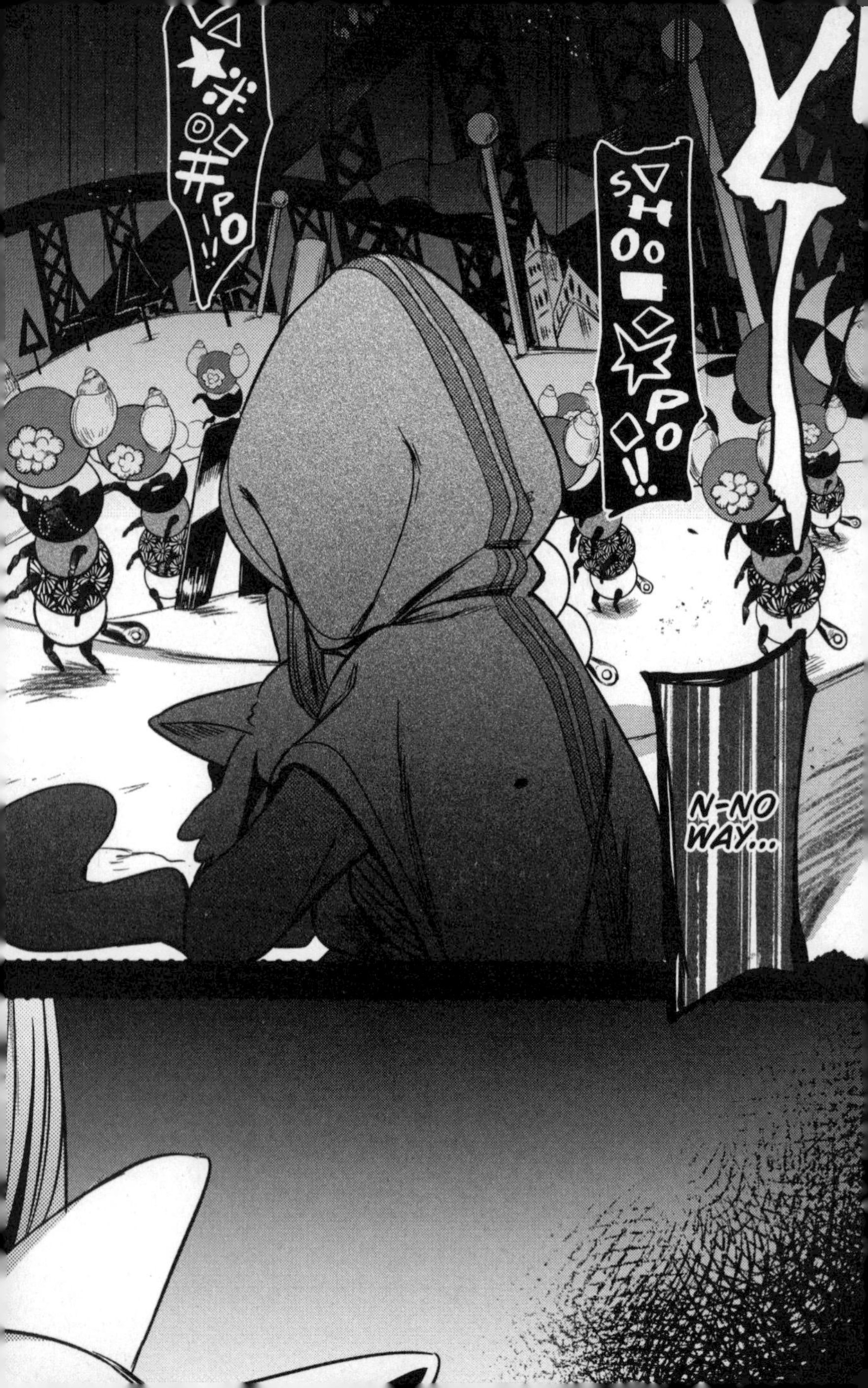
S△HOO■◇★PO◇!!
△★※◎◇#PO!!
N-NO WAY...

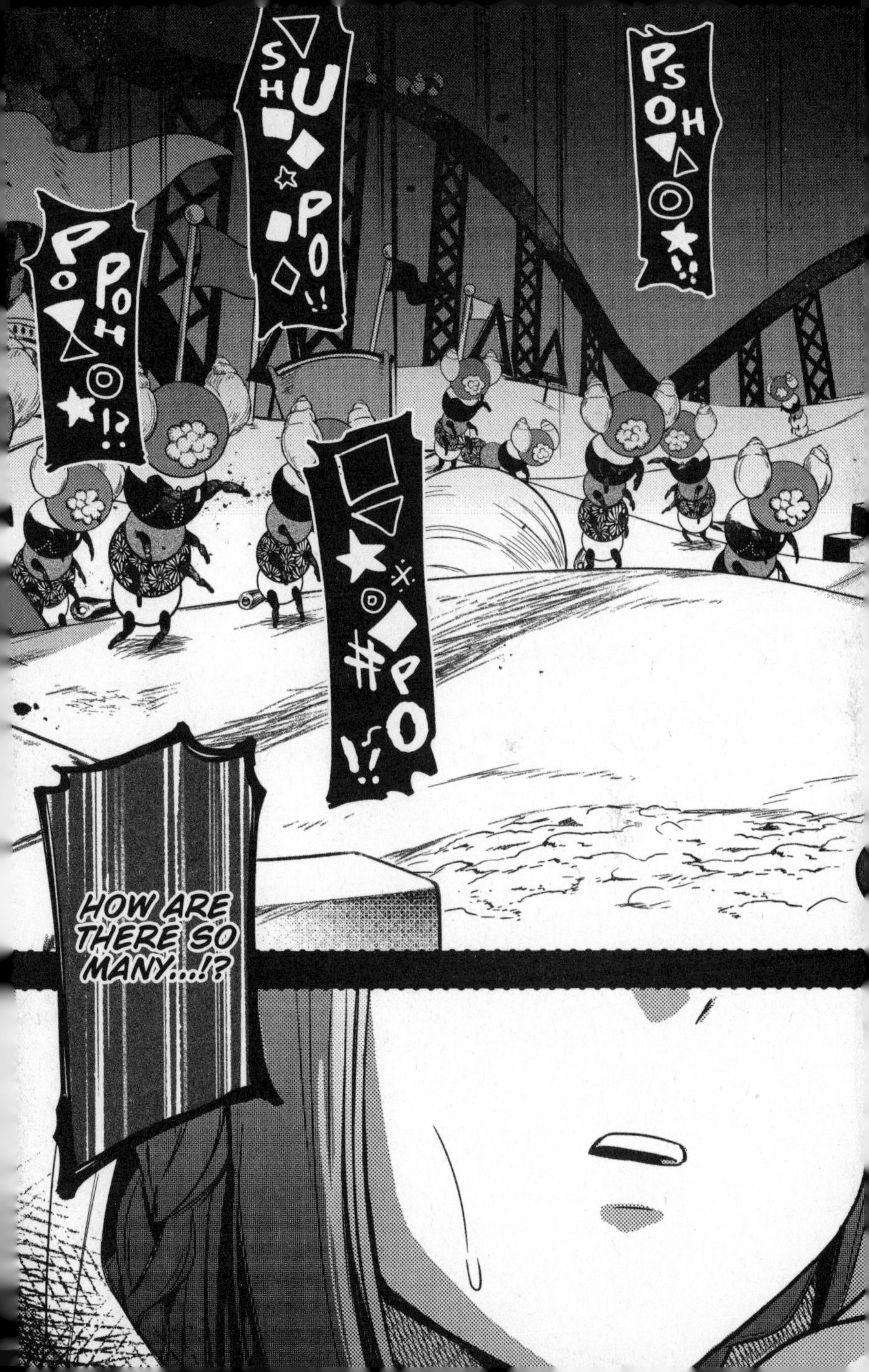
PSOH!!
SHUPO!!
POPOH!?
PO!!
HOW ARE THERE SO MANY...!?

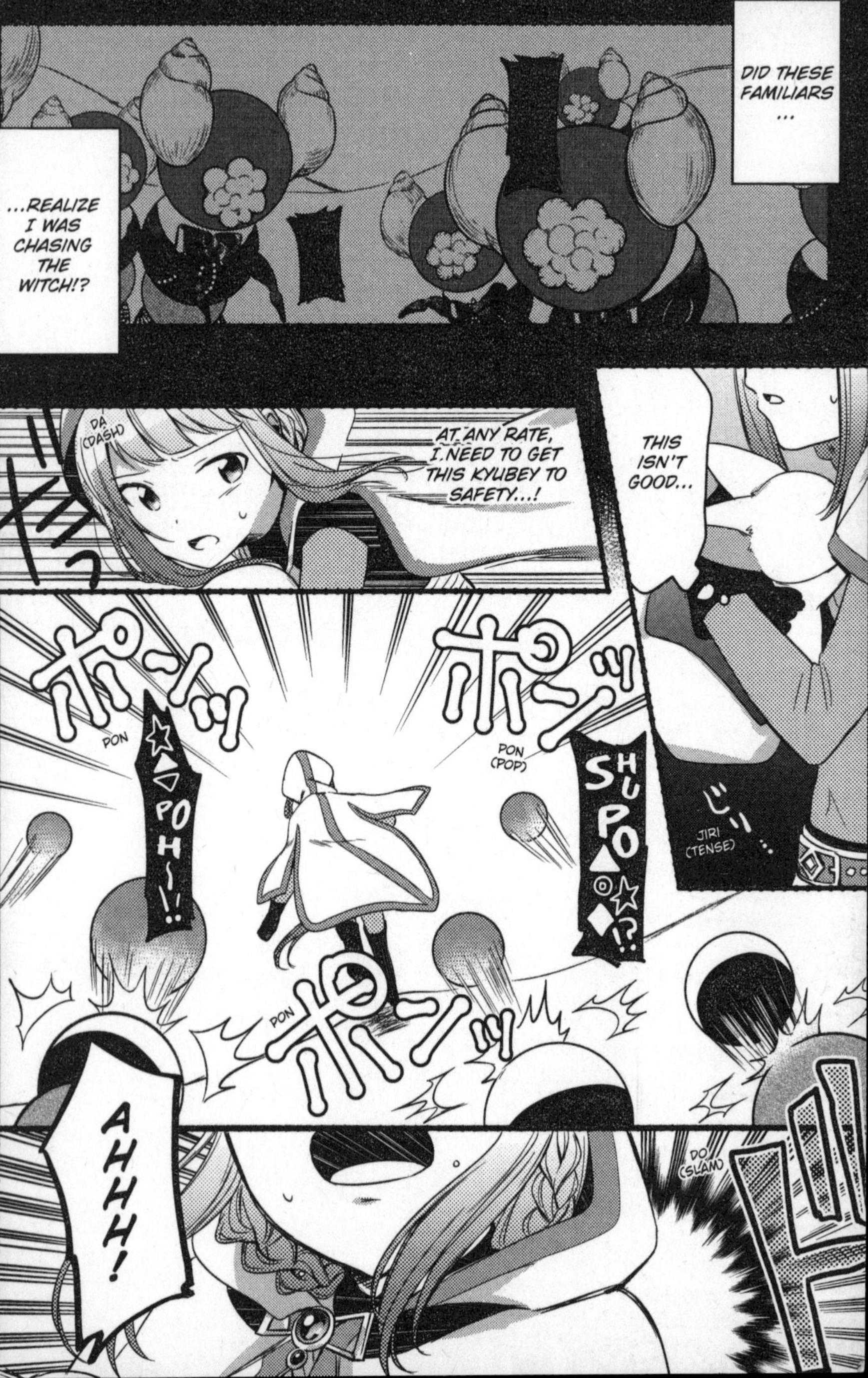
DID THESE FAMILIARS ...
...REALIZE I WAS CHASING THE WITCH!?
THIS ISN'T GOOD...
じりっ...
JIRI (TENSE)
DA (DASH)
AT ANY RATE, I NEED TO GET THIS KYUBEY TO SAFETY...!
ポーンッ
PON (POP)
SHUPO▲◎◆☆!?
ポーンッ
PON
☆▲◁POH~!!
ポーンッ
PON
DO (SLAM)
AHHH!

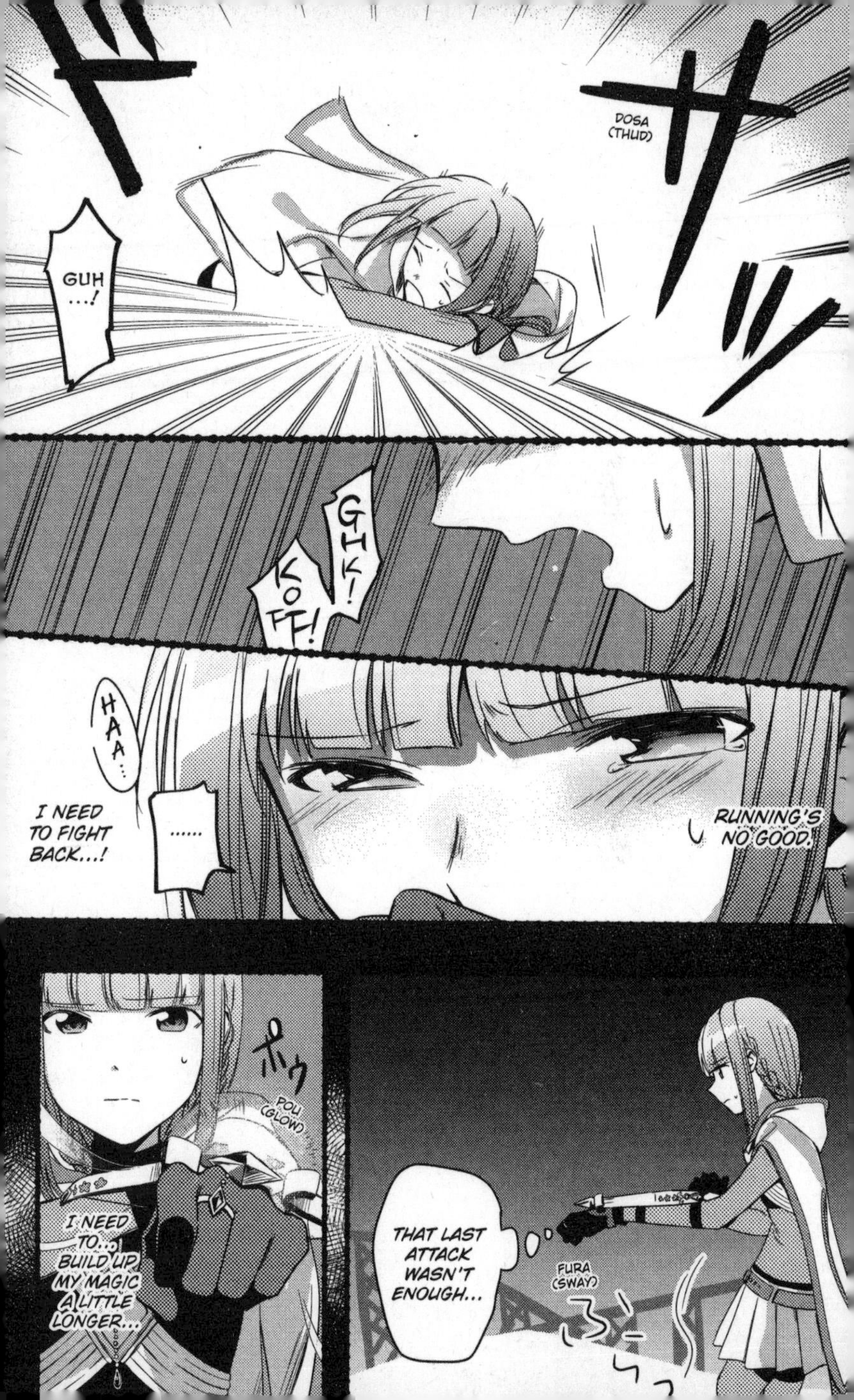
ドサッ
DOSA (THUD)
GUH ...!
GHK! KOFF!
RUNNING'S NO GOOD.
......
HAA...
I NEED TO FIGHT BACK...!
THAT LAST ATTACK WASN'T ENOUGH...
FURA (SWAY)
ポウ
POU (GLOW)
I NEED TO... BUILD UP MY MAGIC A LITTLE LONGER...

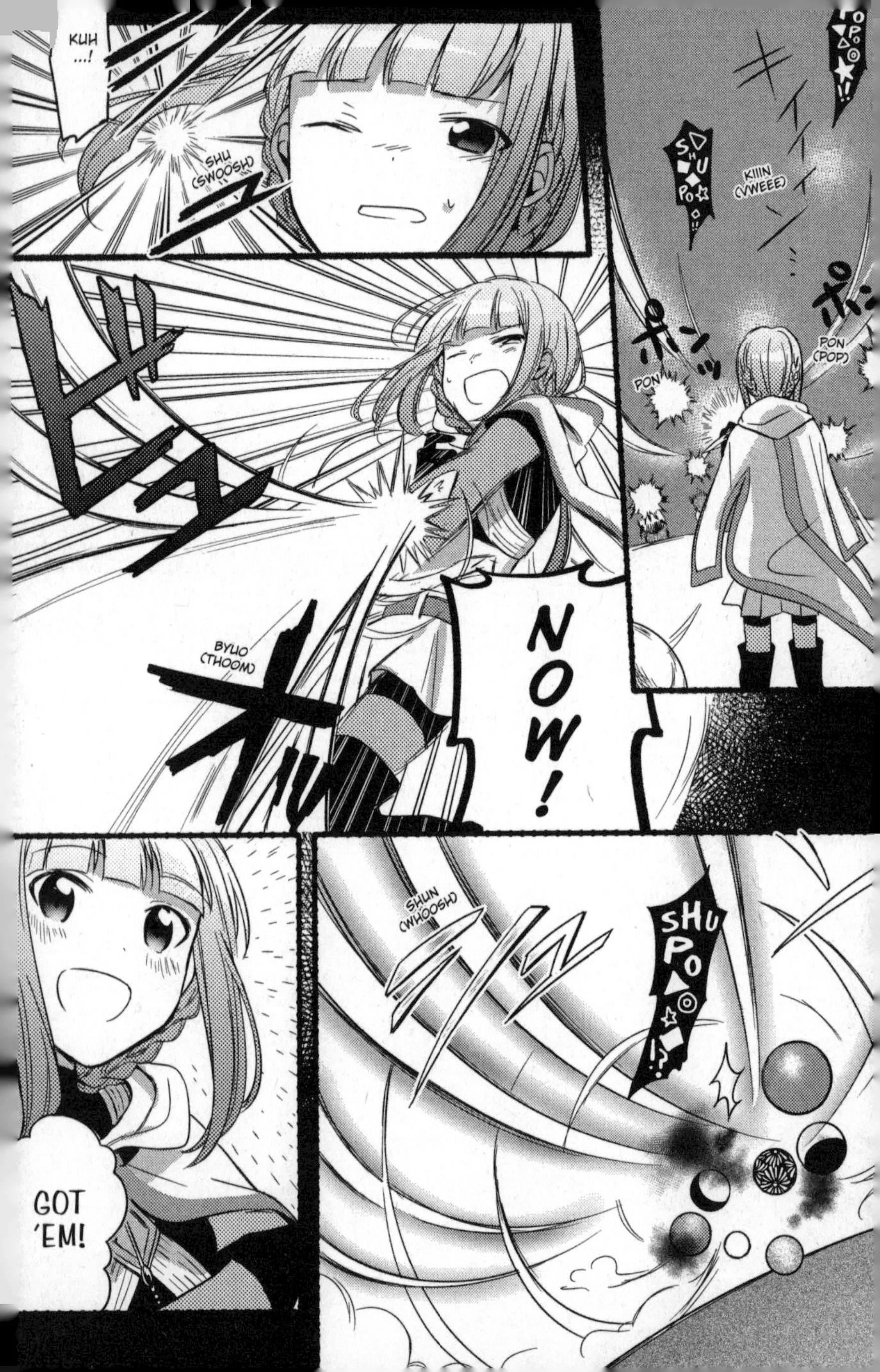

POPO!!
KIIN (VWEEE)
SHUPO!!
PON (POP)
PON
KUH ...!
SHU (SWOOSH)
NOW!
BYUO (THOOM)
SHUPO!?
SHUN (WHOOSH)
GOT 'EM!

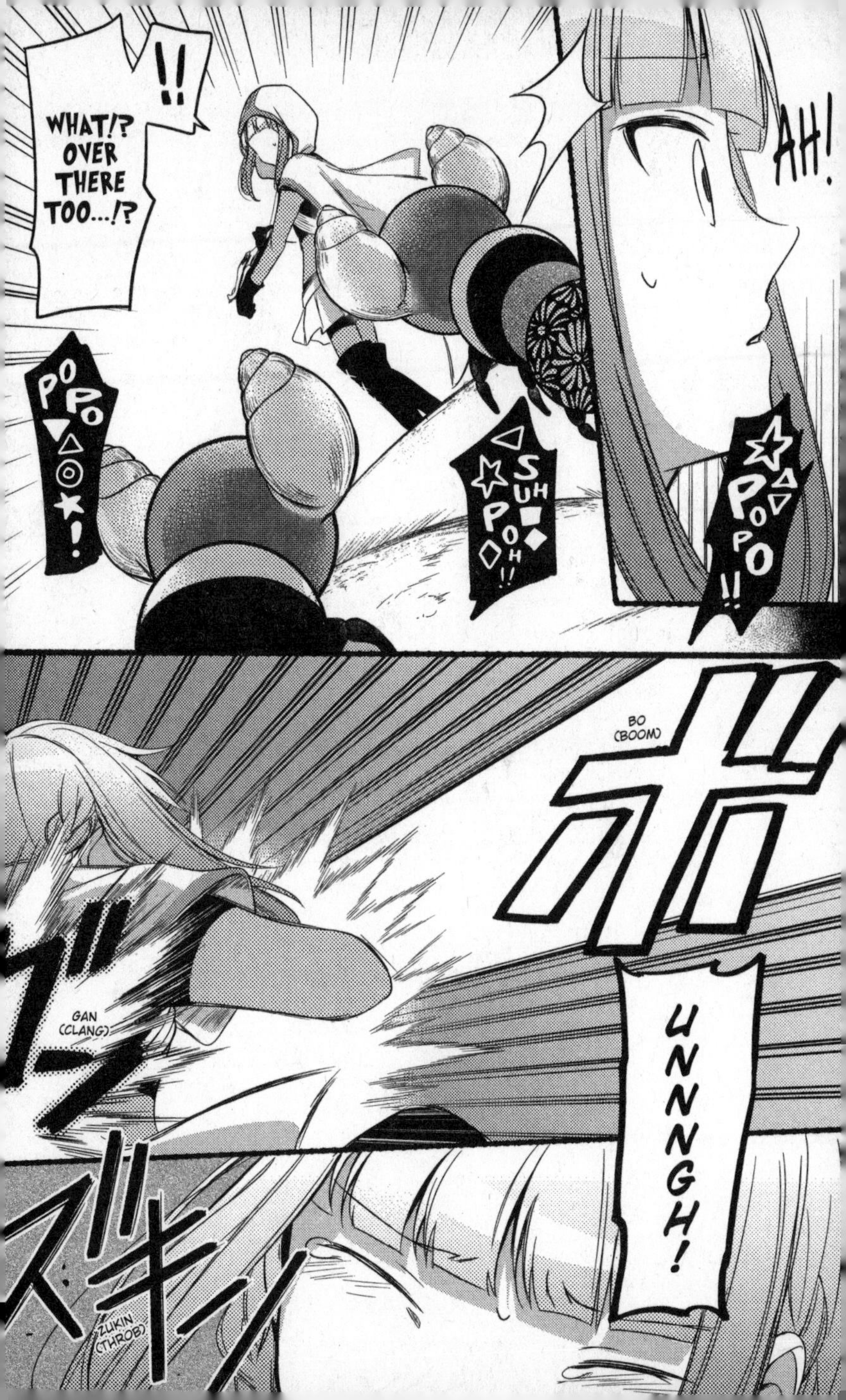
AH!
!!
WHAT!? OVER THERE TOO...!?
POPO!!
SUH POH!!
POPO!
BO (BOOM)
GAN (CLANG)
UNNNGH!
ZUKIN (THROB)

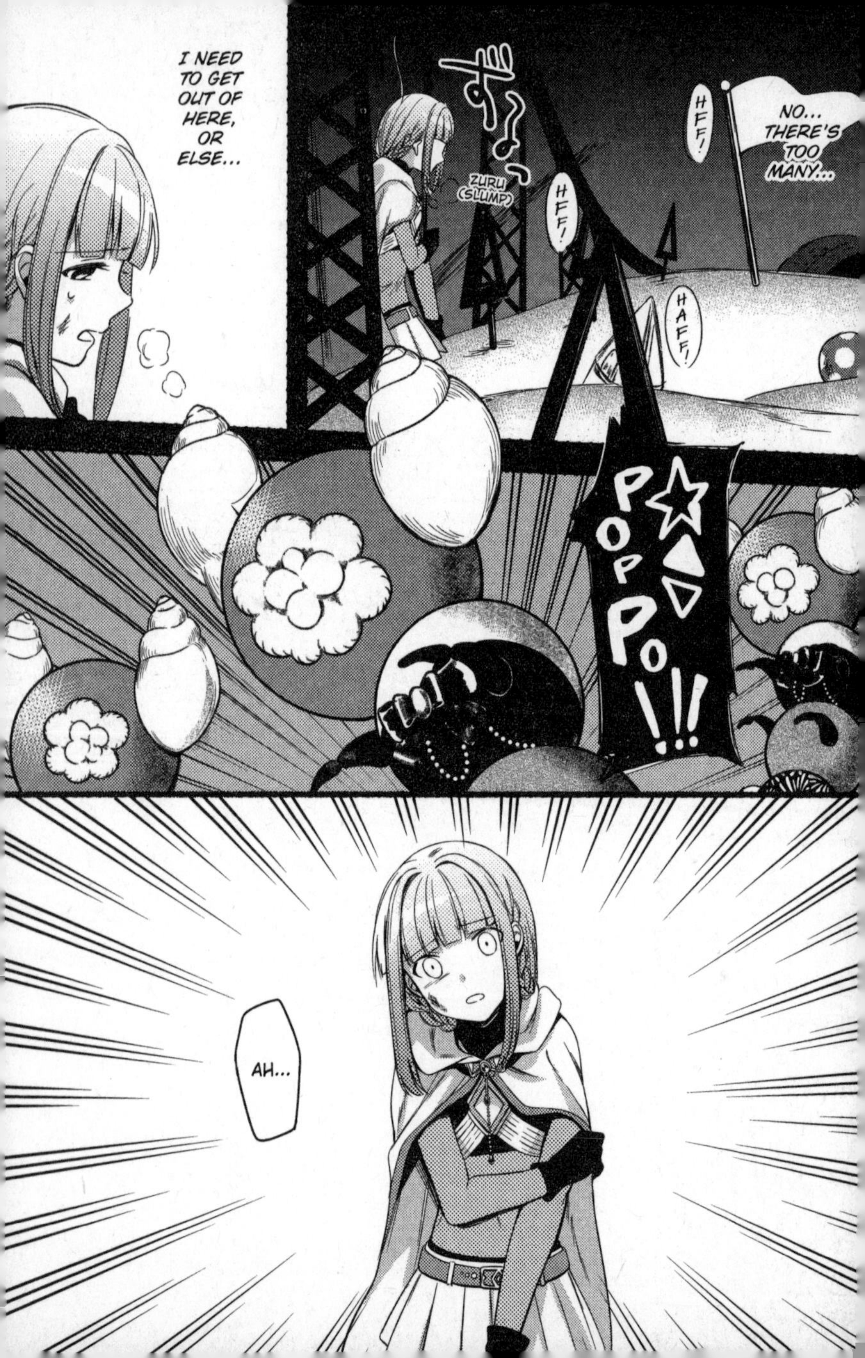
NO... THERE'S TOO MANY...
HFF!
HFF!
HAFF!
ずるっ
ZURU (SLUMP)
I NEED TO GET OUT OF HERE, OR ELSE...
POP POP!!!
AH...

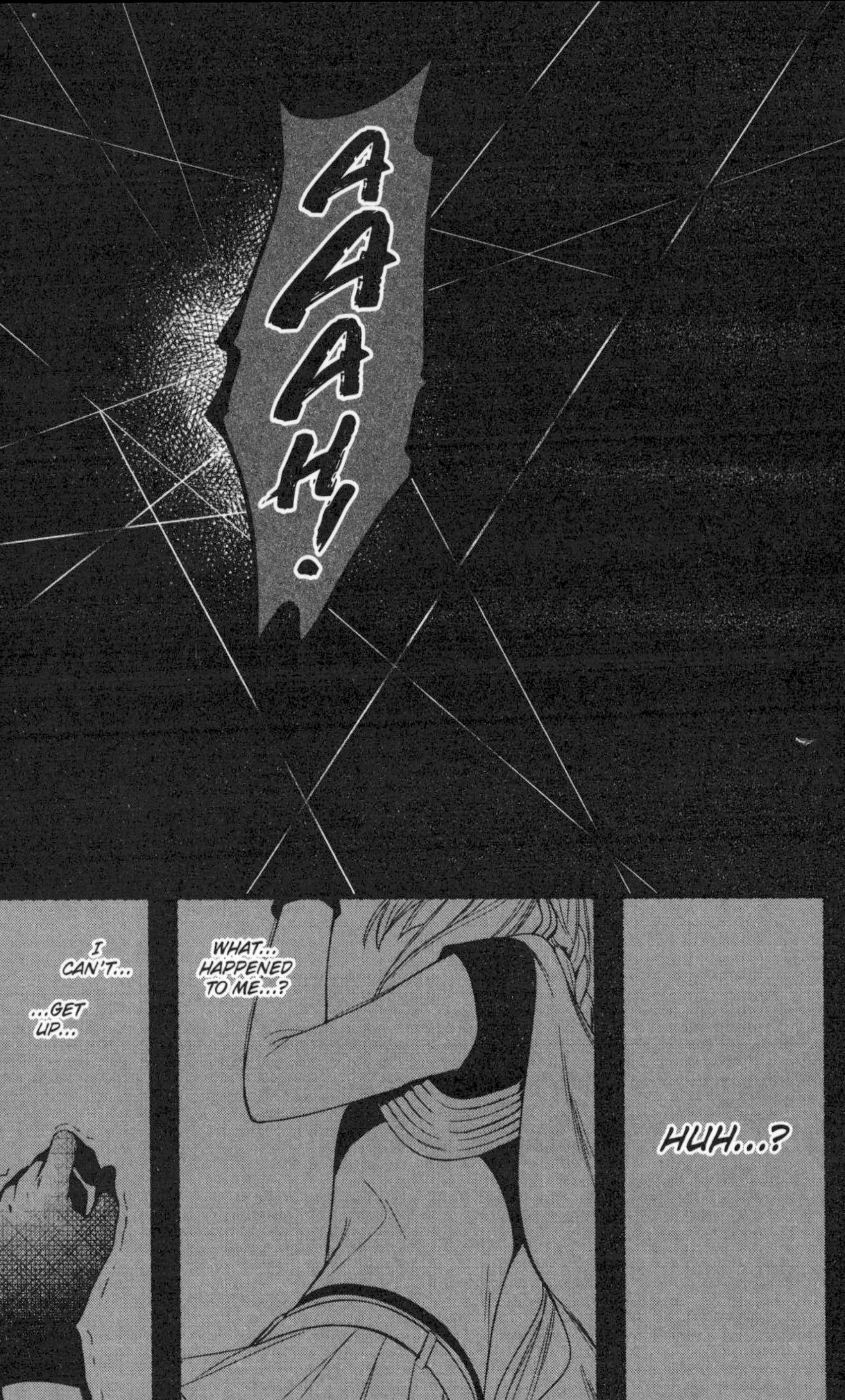
AAAH!
HUH...?
WHAT... HAPPENED TO ME...?
I CAN'T...
...GET UP...

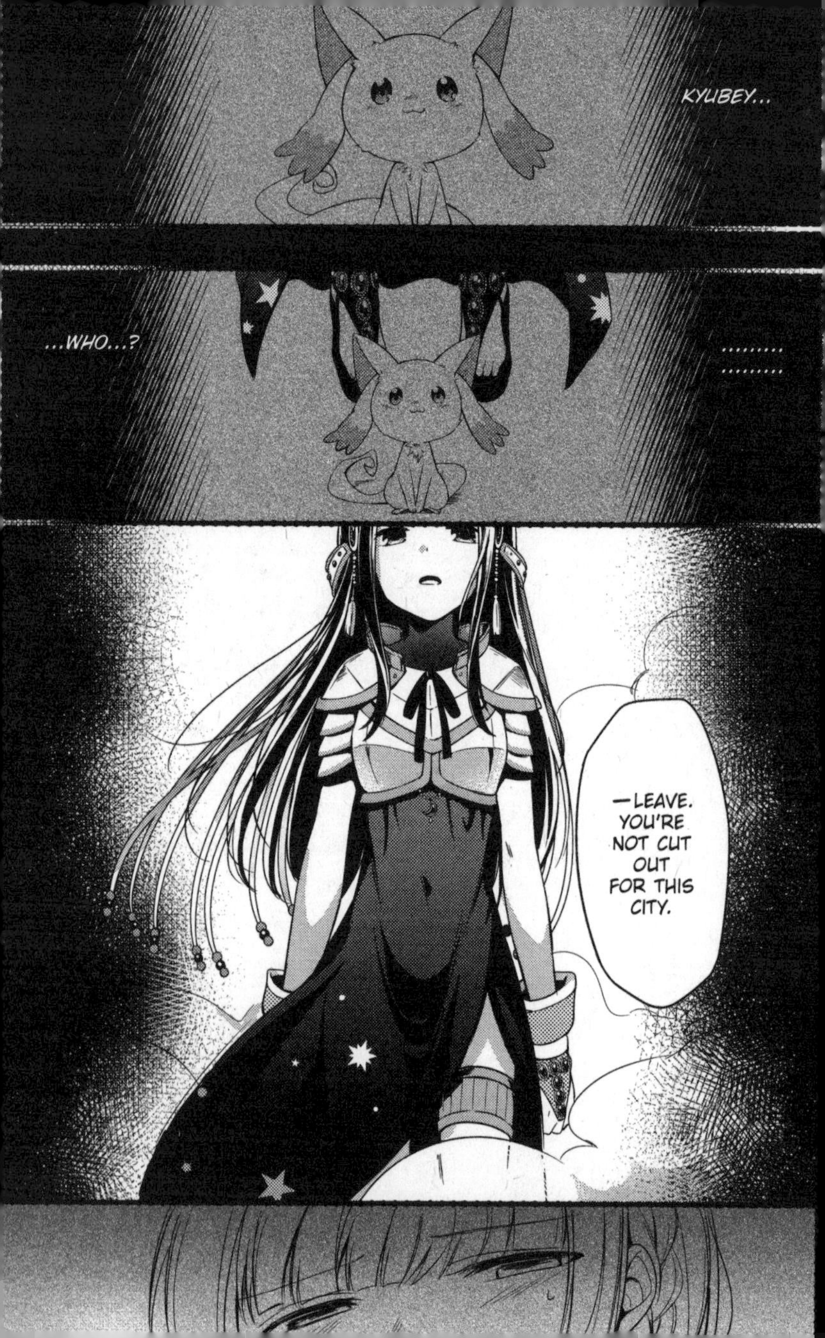
KYUBEY...
....
....
...WHO...?
—LEAVE. YOU'RE NOT CUT OUT FOR THIS CITY.

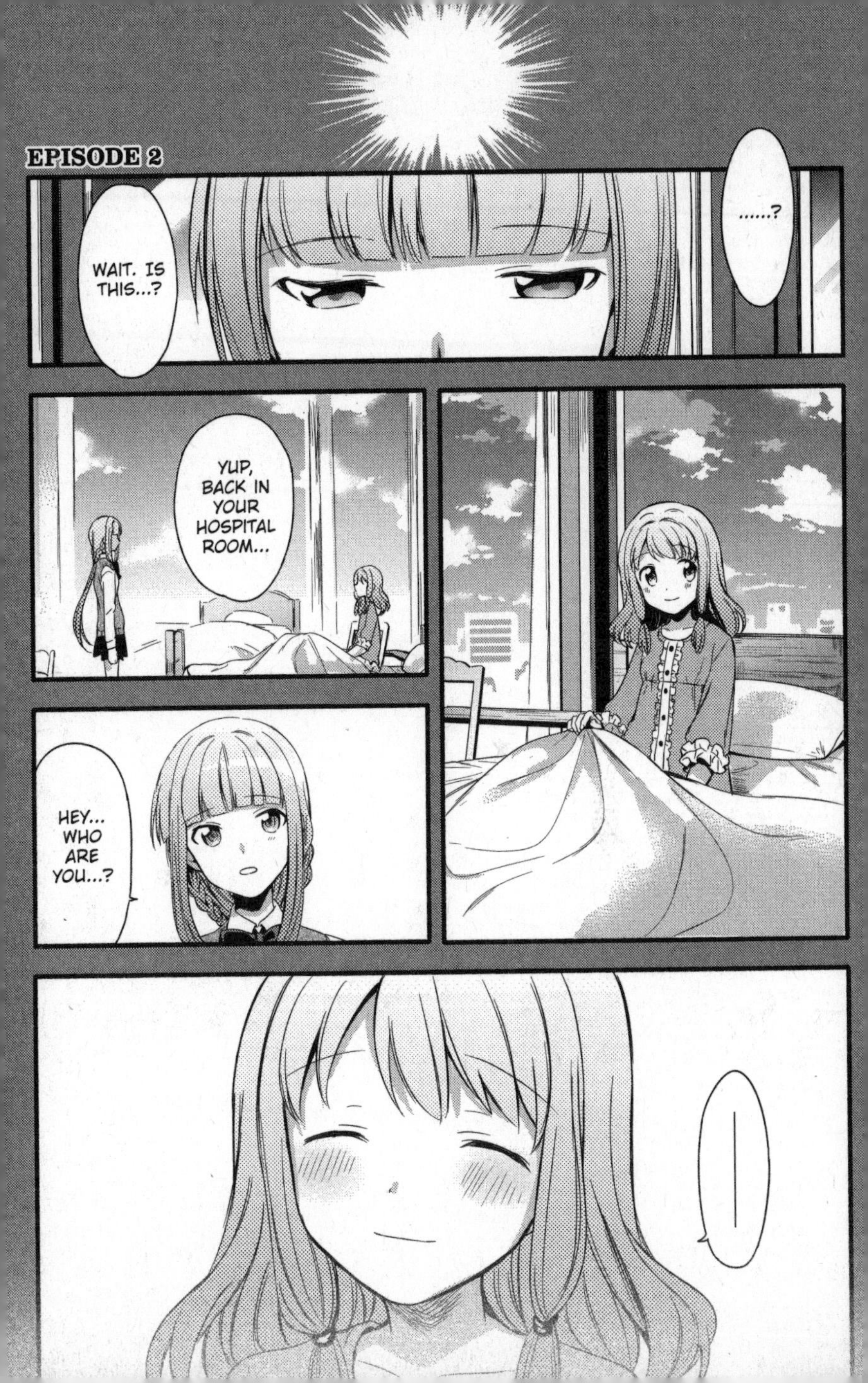
EPISODE 2
......?
WAIT. IS THIS...?
YUP, BACK IN YOUR HOSPITAL ROOM...
HEY... WHO ARE YOU...?
—

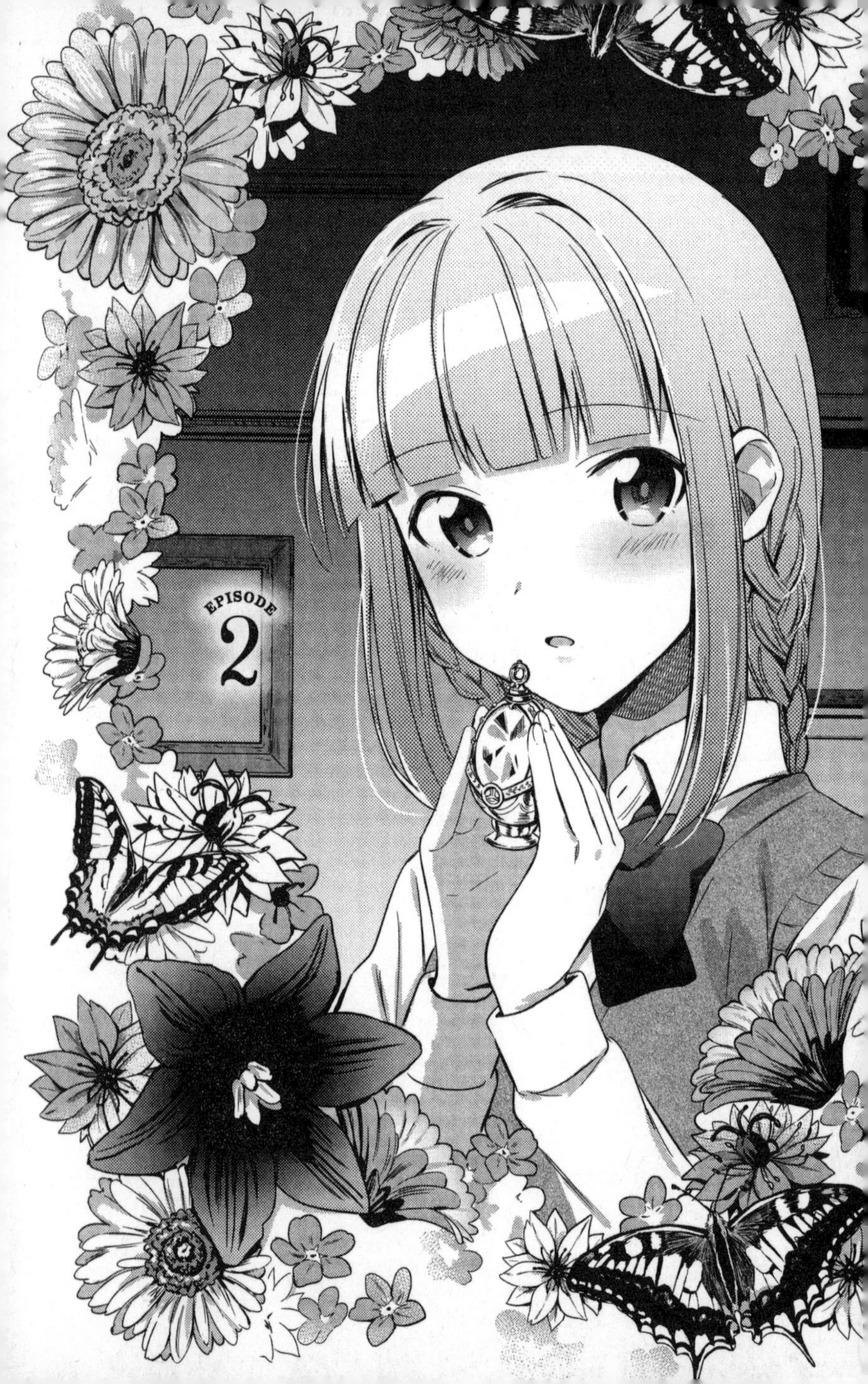
EPISODE
2

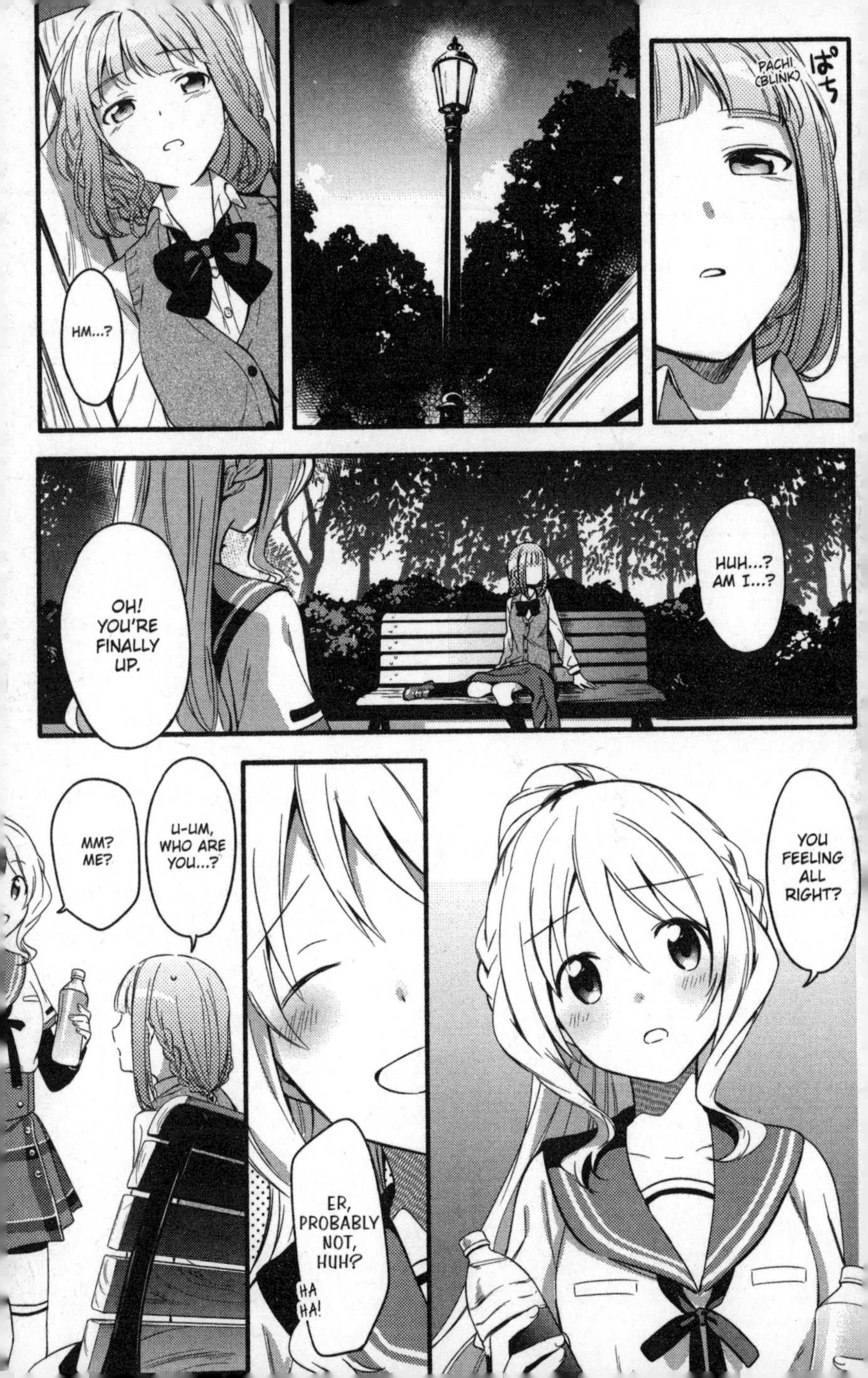
PACHI (BLINK)
ぱち
HM...?
HUH...? AM I...?
OH! YOU'RE FINALLY UP.
YOU FEELING ALL RIGHT?
ER, PROBABLY NOT, HUH?
HA HA!
U-UM, WHO ARE YOU...?
MM? ME?

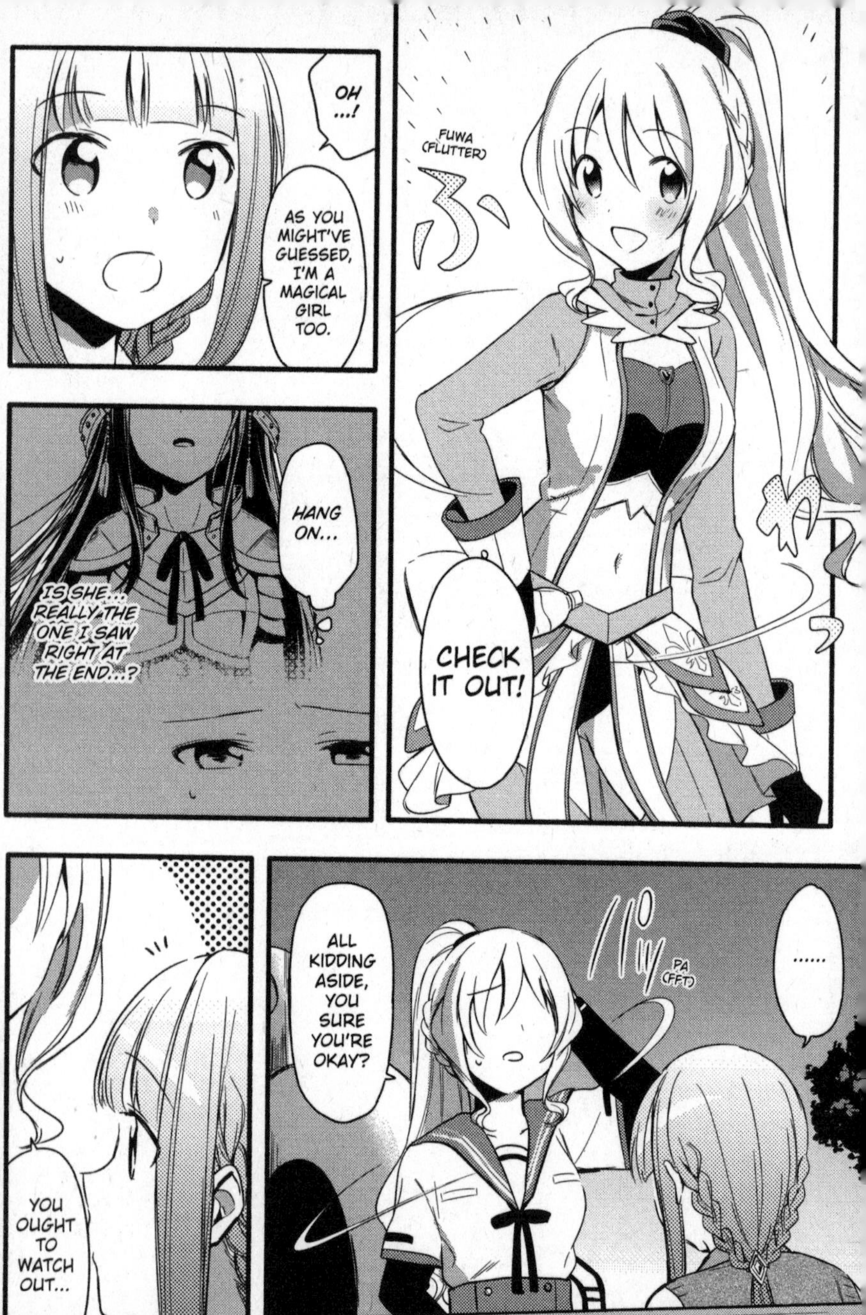
FUWA (FLUTTER)
CHECK IT OUT!
OH ...!
AS YOU MIGHT'VE GUESSED, I'M A MAGICAL GIRL TOO.
HANG ON...
IS SHE... REALLY THE ONE I SAW RIGHT AT THE END...?
......
PA (FFT)
ALL KIDDING ASIDE, YOU SURE YOU'RE OKAY?
YOU OUGHT TO WATCH OUT...

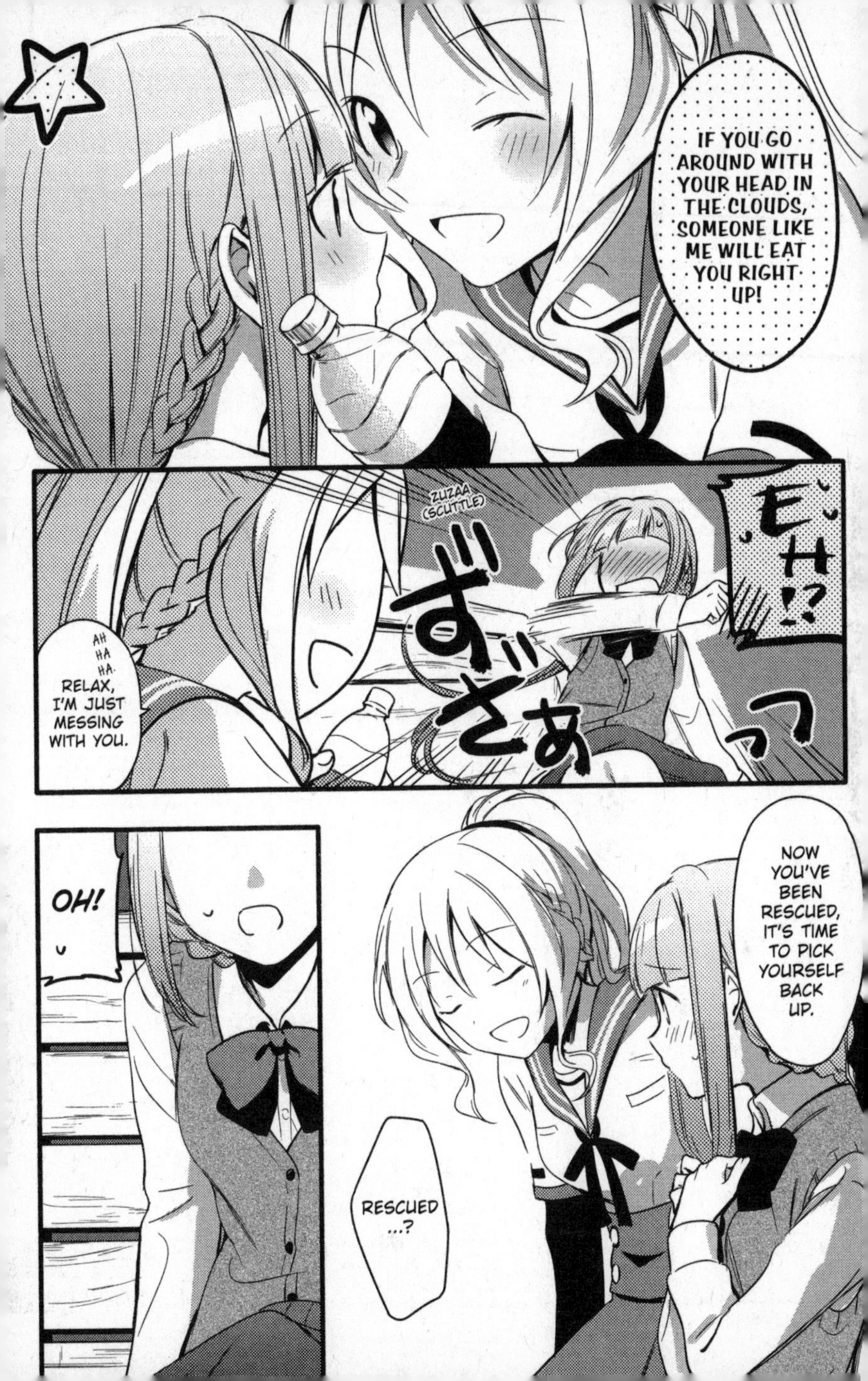
IF YOU GO AROUND WITH YOUR HEAD IN THE CLOUDS, SOMEONE LIKE ME WILL EAT YOU RIGHT UP!
EH!?
ZUZAA (SCUTTLE)
ずざぁっ
AH HA HA.
RELAX, I'M JUST MESSING WITH YOU.
NOW YOU'VE BEEN RESCUED, IT'S TIME TO PICK YOURSELF BACK UP.
RESCUED ...?
OH!

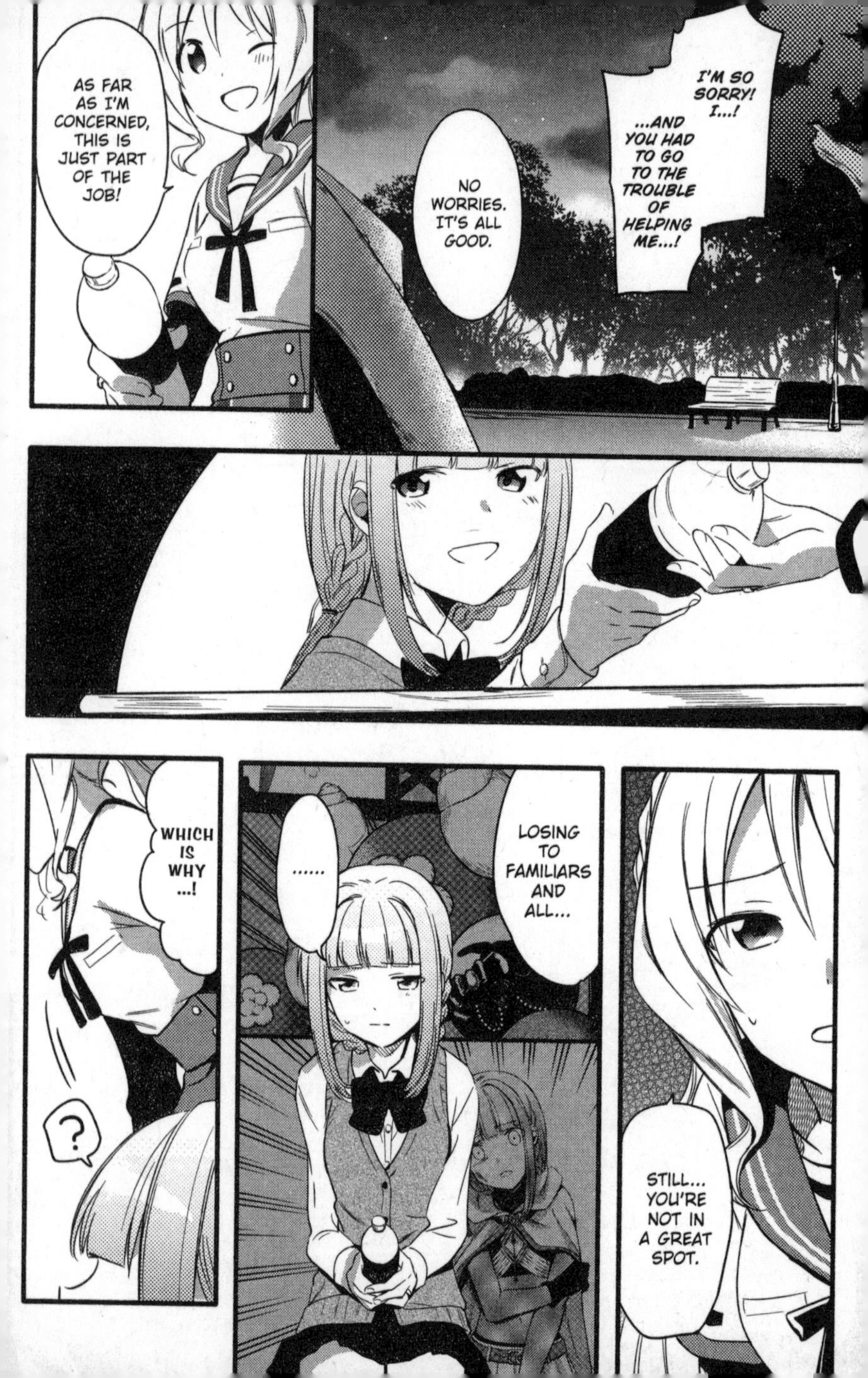
I'M SO SORRY! I...!
...AND YOU HAD TO GO TO THE TROUBLE OF HELPING ME...!
NO WORRIES. IT'S ALL GOOD.
AS FAR AS I'M CONCERNED, THIS IS JUST PART OF THE JOB!
STILL... YOU'RE NOT IN A GREAT SPOT.
LOSING TO FAMILIARS AND ALL...
......
WHICH IS WHY ...!
?

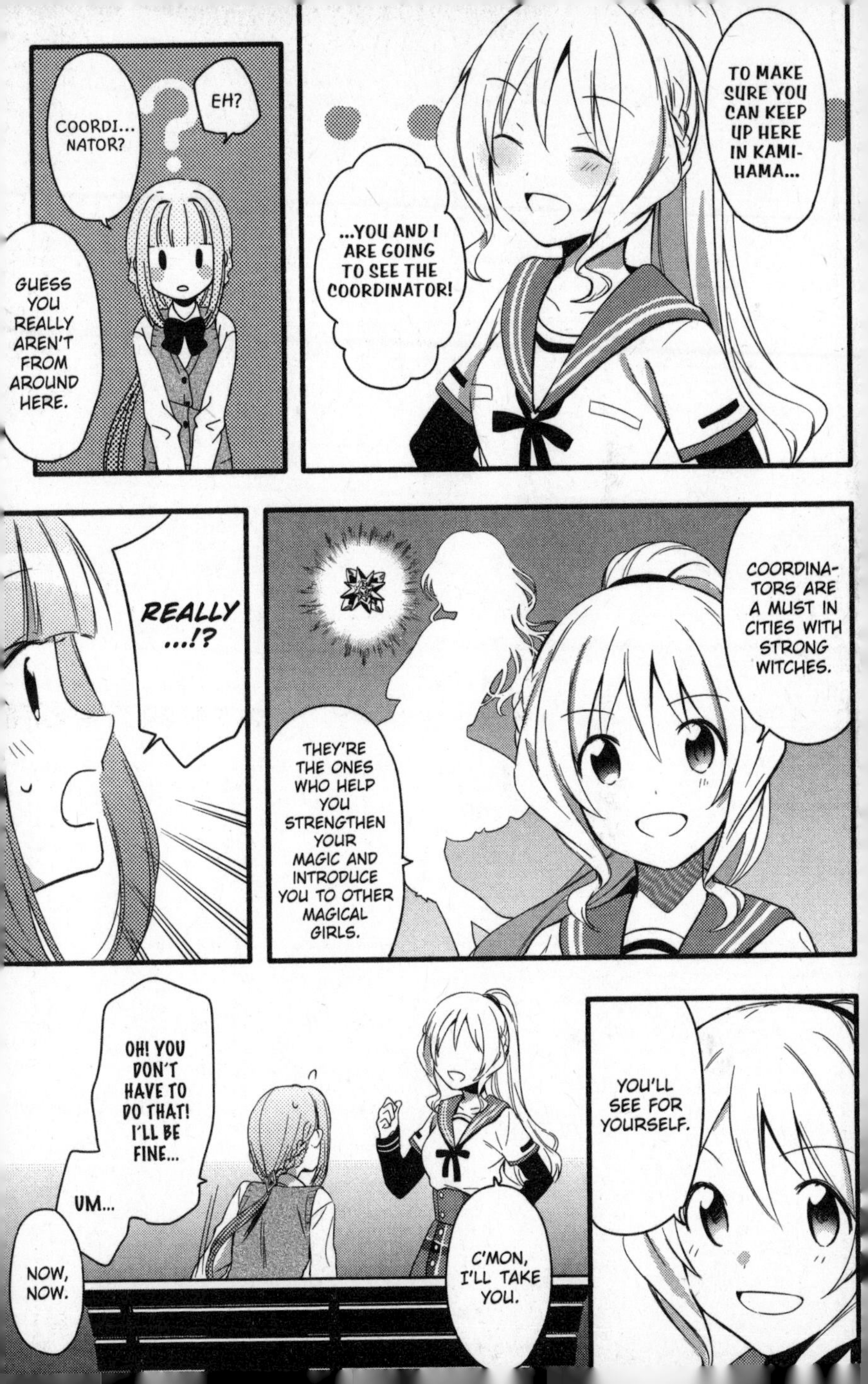
TO MAKE SURE YOU CAN KEEP UP HERE IN KAMI-HAMA...
...YOU AND I ARE GOING TO SEE THE COORDINATOR!
EH?
COORDI... NATOR?
GUESS YOU REALLY AREN'T FROM AROUND HERE.
COORDINA-TORS ARE A MUST IN CITIES WITH STRONG WITCHES.
THEY'RE THE ONES WHO HELP YOU STRENGTHEN YOUR MAGIC AND INTRODUCE YOU TO OTHER MAGICAL GIRLS.
REALLY ...!?
YOU'LL SEE FOR YOURSELF.
C'MON, I'LL TAKE YOU.
OH! YOU DON'T HAVE TO DO THAT! I'LL BE FINE...
UM...
NOW, NOW.

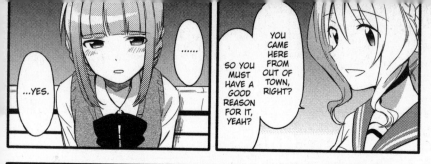

......

...YES.

SO YOU MUST HAVE A GOOD REASON FOR IT, YEAH?

YOU CAME HERE FROM OUT OF TOWN, RIGHT?

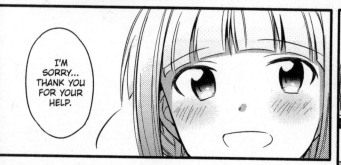

I'M SORRY... THANK YOU FOR YOUR HELP.

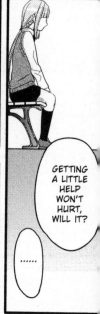

GETTING A LITTLE HELP WON'T HURT, WILL IT?

......

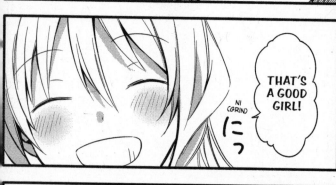

THAT'S A GOOD GIRL!

NI (GRIN)
にっ

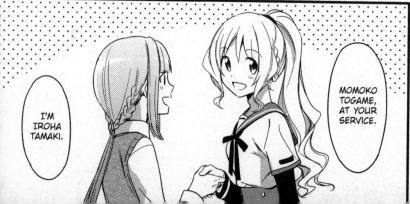

I'M IROHA TAMAKI.

MOMOKO TOGAME, AT YOUR SERVICE.

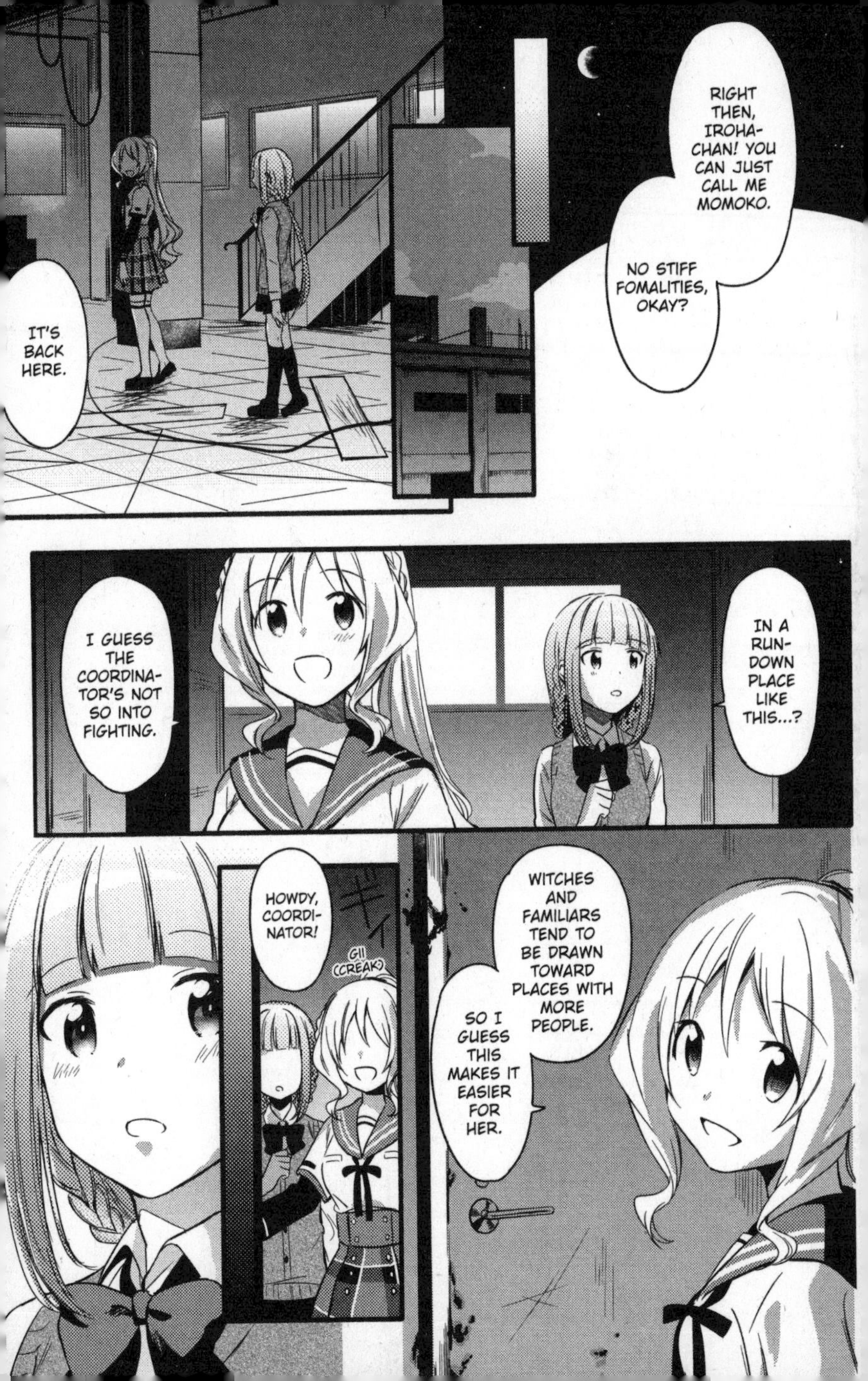
RIGHT THEN, IROHA-CHAN! YOU CAN JUST CALL ME MOMOKO.
NO STIFF FOMALITIES, OKAY?
IT'S BACK HERE.
IN A RUN-DOWN PLACE LIKE THIS...?
I GUESS THE COORDINATOR'S NOT SO INTO FIGHTING.
WITCHES AND FAMILIARS TEND TO BE DRAWN TOWARD PLACES WITH MORE PEOPLE.
SO I GUESS THIS MAKES IT EASIER FOR HER.
HOWDY, COORDINATOR!
GII (CREAK)

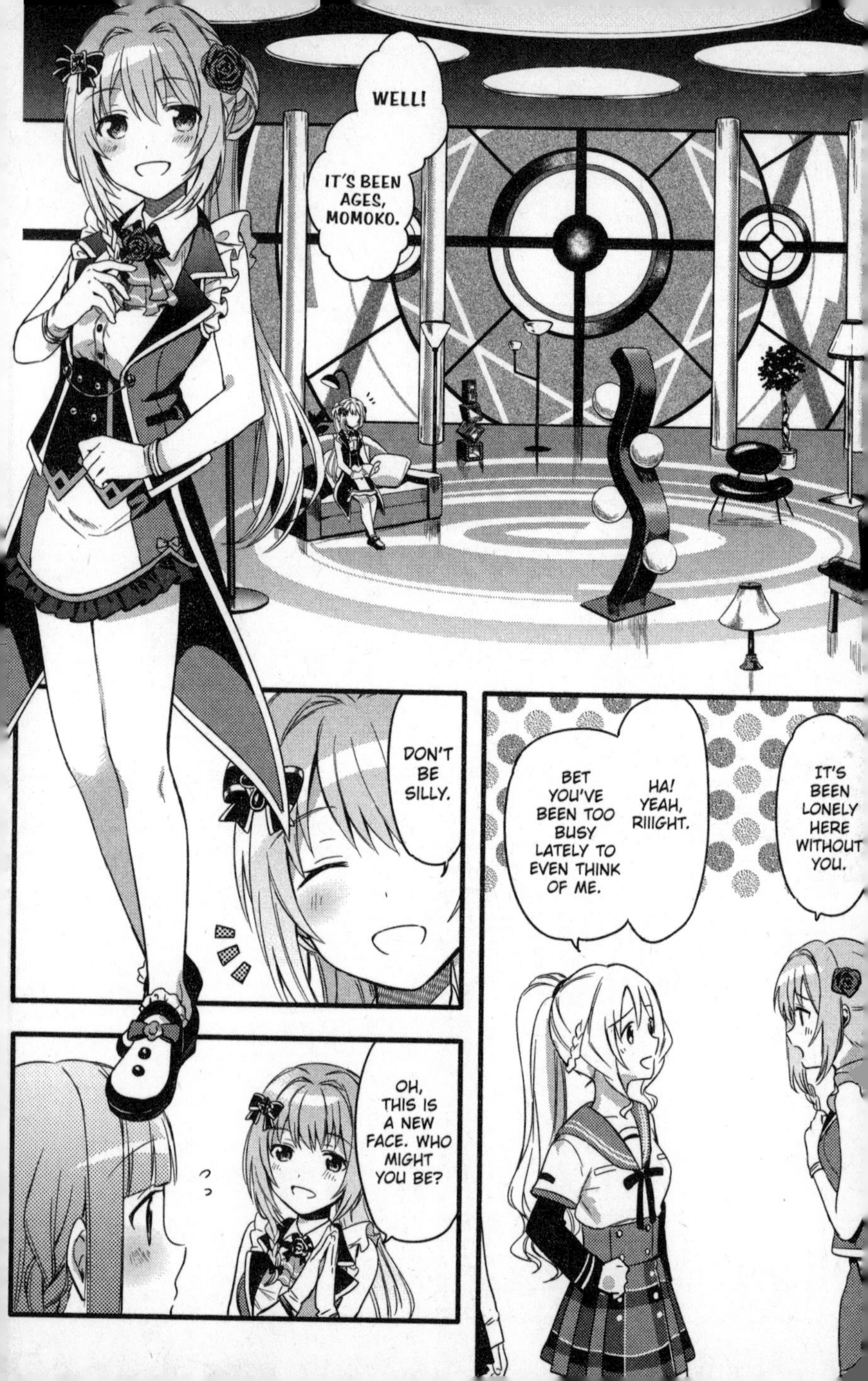
WELL!
IT'S BEEN AGES, MOMOKO.
IT'S BEEN LONELY HERE WITHOUT YOU.
HA! YEAH, RIIIGHT.
BET YOU'VE BEEN TOO BUSY LATELY TO EVEN THINK OF ME.
DON'T BE SILLY.
OH, THIS IS A NEW FACE. WHO MIGHT YOU BE?

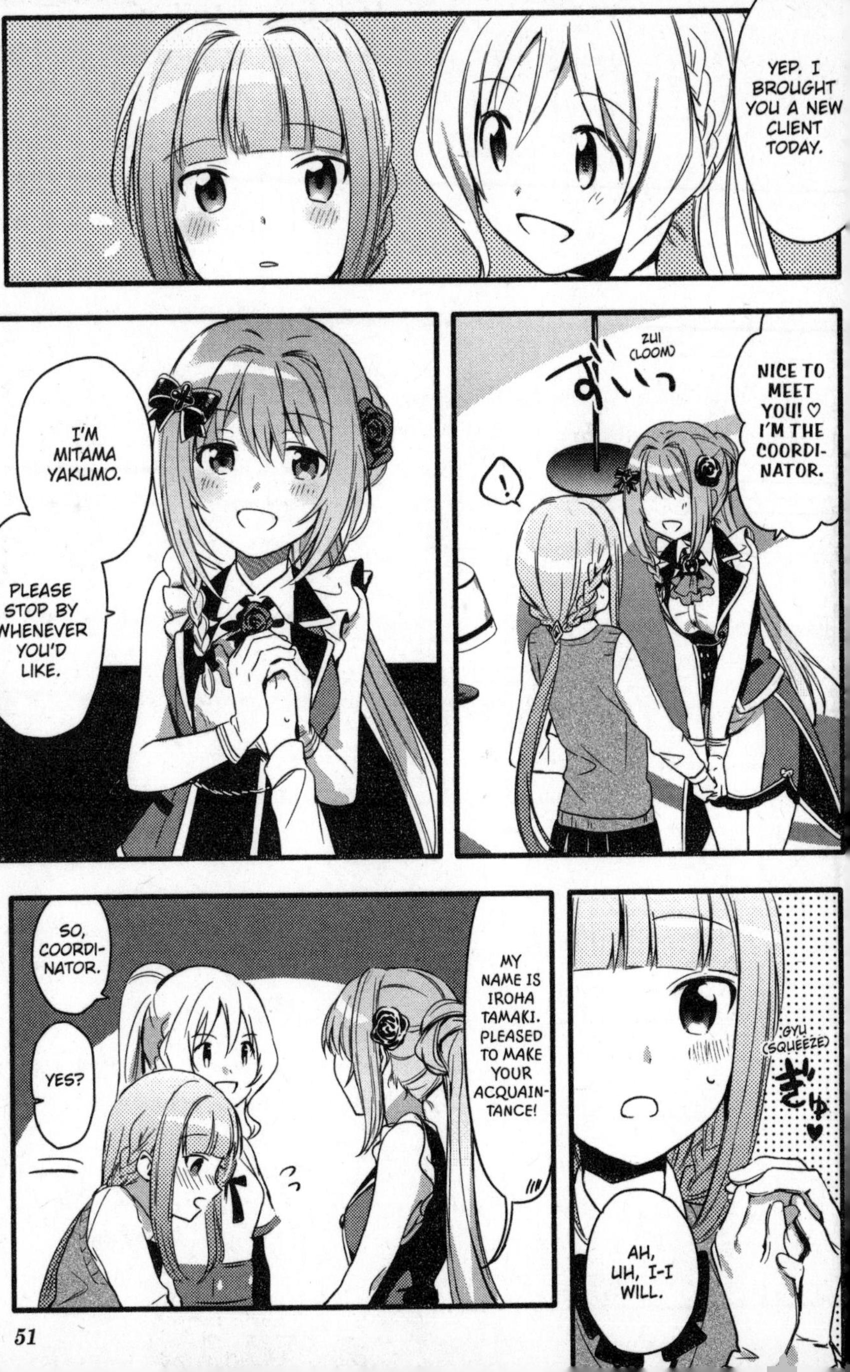
YEP. I BROUGHT YOU A NEW CLIENT TODAY.
ZUI (LOOM)
ずいっ
NICE TO MEET YOU! ♡ I'M THE COORDI-NATOR.
!
I'M MITAMA YAKUMO.
PLEASE STOP BY WHENEVER YOU'D LIKE.
GYU (SQUEEZE)
ぎゅ♥
AH, UH, I-I WILL.
MY NAME IS IROHA TAMAKI. PLEASED TO MAKE YOUR ACQUAIN-TANCE!
SO, COORDI-NATOR.
YES?

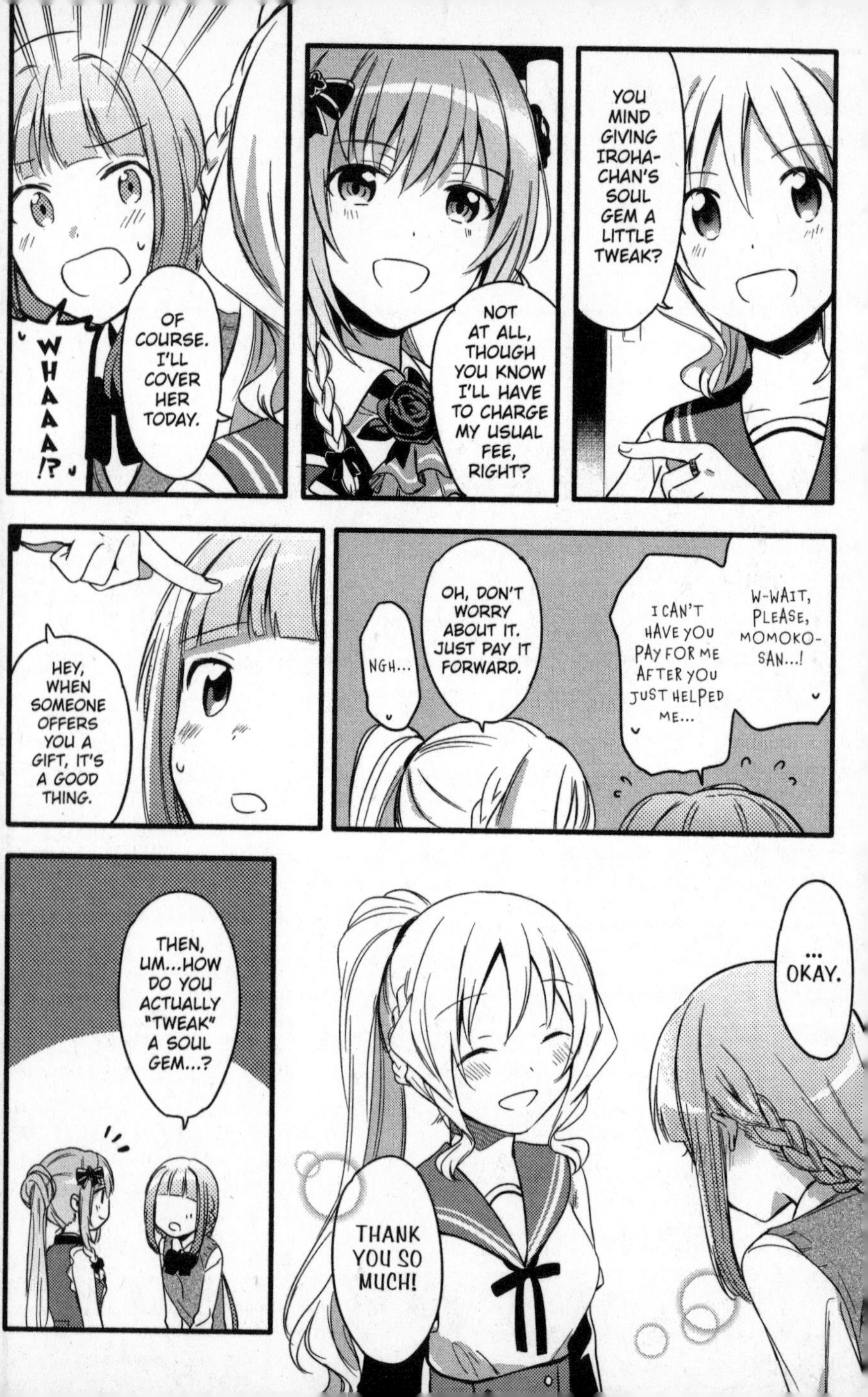
YOU MIND GIVING IROHA-CHAN'S SOUL GEM A LITTLE TWEAK?
NOT AT ALL, THOUGH YOU KNOW I'LL HAVE TO CHARGE MY USUAL FEE, RIGHT?
OF COURSE. I'LL COVER HER TODAY.
WHAAAA!?
W-WAIT, PLEASE, MOMOKO-SAN...!
I CAN'T HAVE YOU PAY FOR ME AFTER YOU JUST HELPED ME...
OH, DON'T WORRY ABOUT IT. JUST PAY IT FORWARD.
NGH...
HEY, WHEN SOMEONE OFFERS YOU A GIFT, IT'S A GOOD THING.
...OKAY.
THANK YOU SO MUCH!
THEN, UM...HOW DO YOU ACTUALLY "TWEAK" A SOUL GEM...?

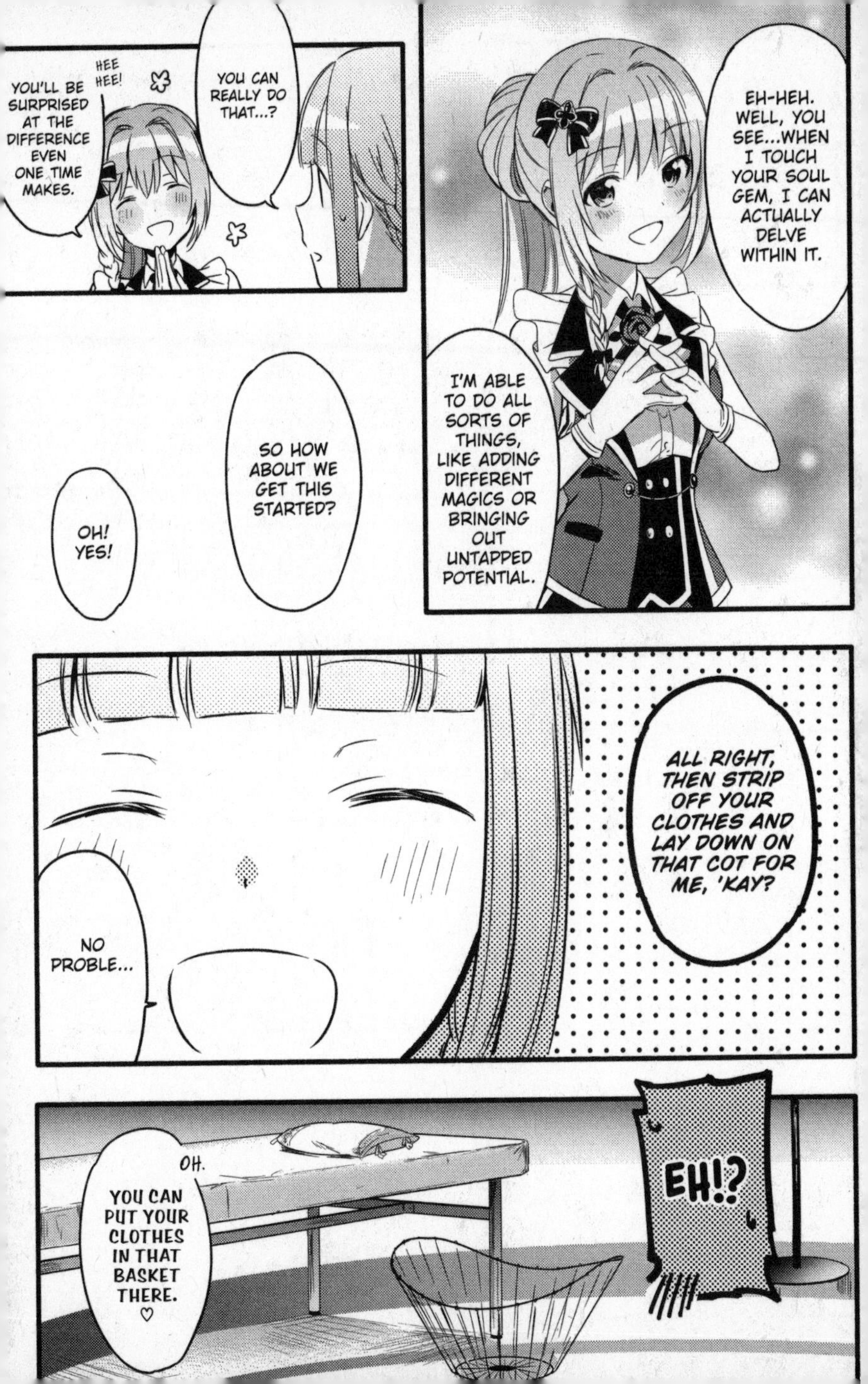
EH-HEH. WELL, YOU SEE...WHEN I TOUCH YOUR SOUL GEM, I CAN ACTUALLY DELVE WITHIN IT.
I'M ABLE TO DO ALL SORTS OF THINGS, LIKE ADDING DIFFERENT MAGICS OR BRINGING OUT UNTAPPED POTENTIAL.
YOU CAN REALLY DO THAT...?
HEE HEE!
YOU'LL BE SURPRISED AT THE DIFFERENCE EVEN ONE TIME MAKES.
SO HOW ABOUT WE GET THIS STARTED?
OH! YES!
ALL RIGHT, THEN STRIP OFF YOUR CLOTHES AND LAY DOWN ON THAT COT FOR ME, 'KAY?
NO PROBLE...
EH!?
OH.
YOU CAN PUT YOUR CLOTHES IN THAT BASKET THERE. ♡

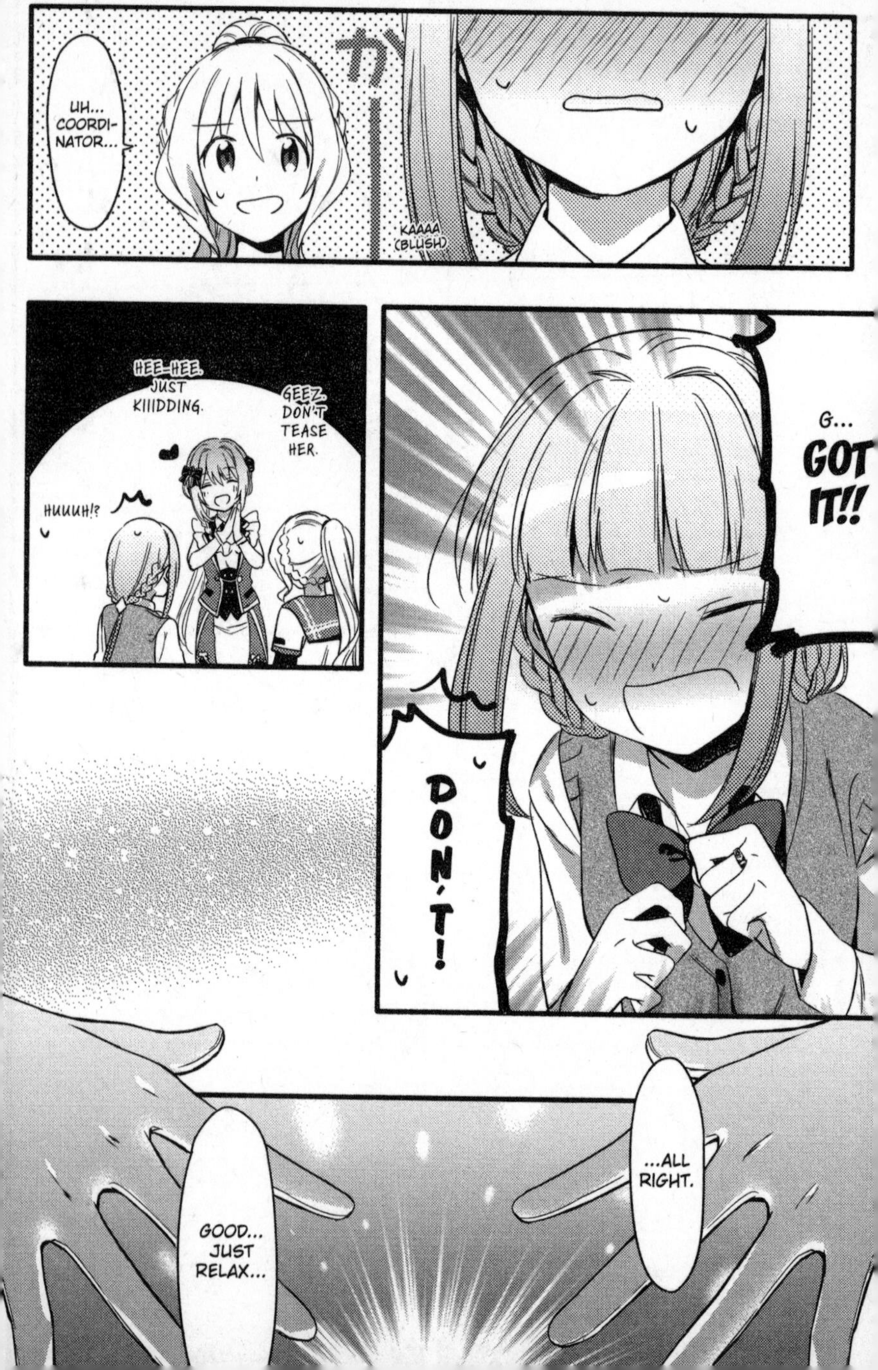
KAAAA (BLUSH)
UH... COORDI-NATOR...
G... GOT IT!!
DON'T!
HEE-HEE. JUST KIIIDDING.
GEEZ. DON'T TEASE HER.
HUUUH!?
...ALL RIGHT.
GOOD... JUST RELAX...

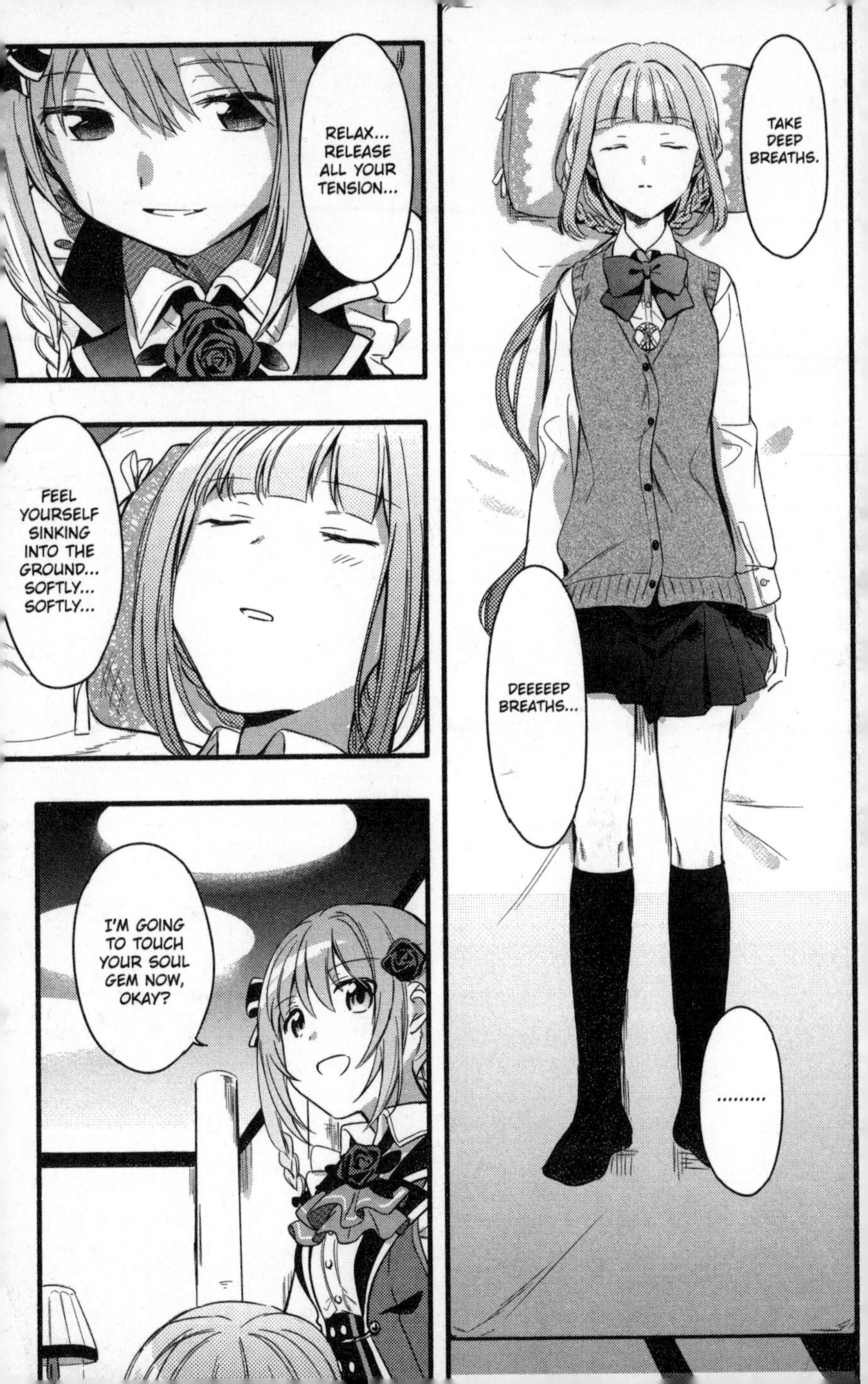
TAKE DEEP BREATHS.
DEEEEEP BREATHS...
....
RELAX... RELEASE ALL YOUR TENSION...
FEEL YOURSELF SINKING INTO THE GROUND... SOFTLY... SOFTLY...
I'M GOING TO TOUCH YOUR SOUL GEM NOW, OKAY?

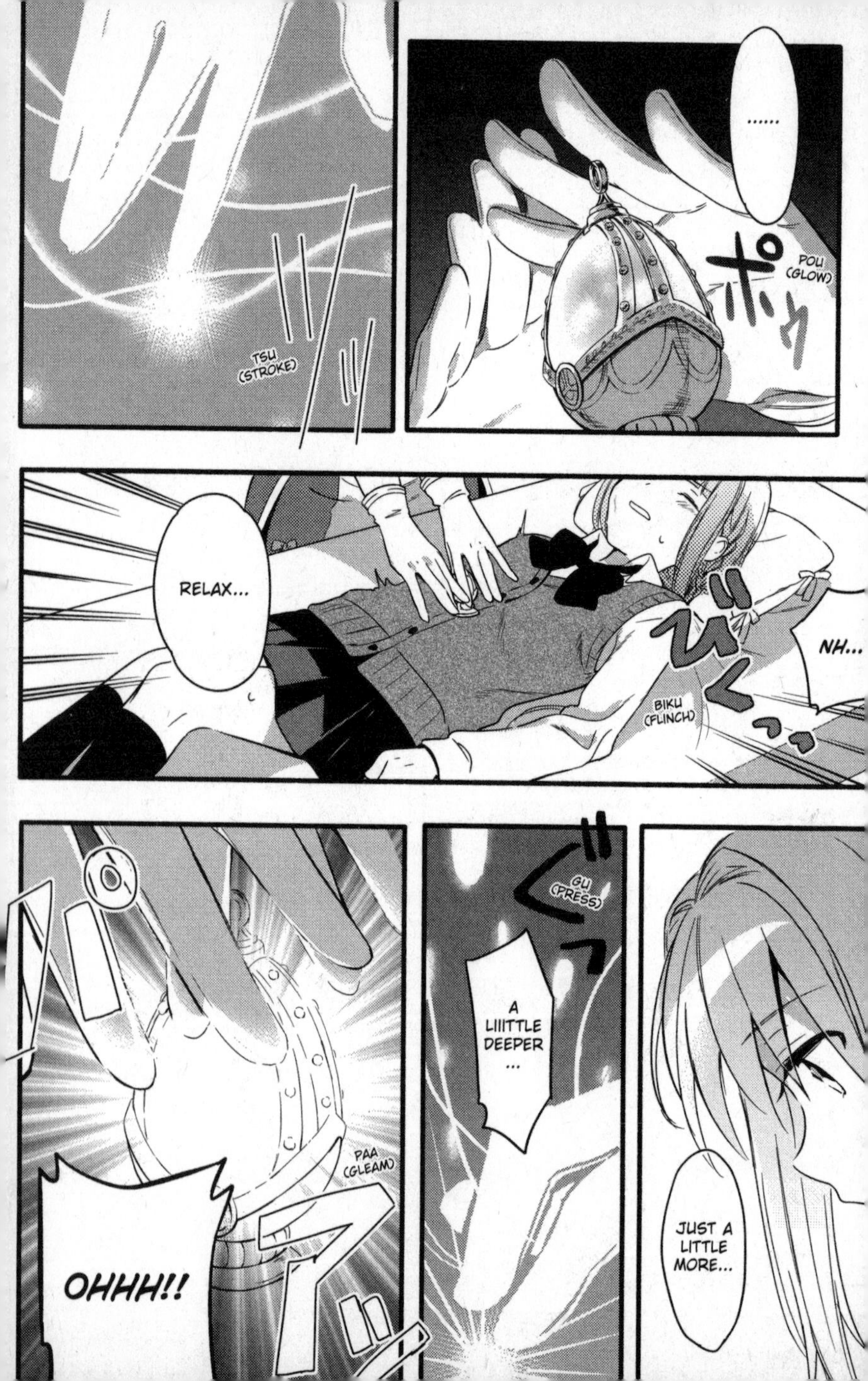
......
POU (GLOW)
TSU (STROKE)
NH...
BIKU (FLINCH)
RELAX...
JUST A LITTLE MORE...
GU (PRESS)
A LIIITTLE DEEPER ...
PAA (GLEAM)
OHHH!!

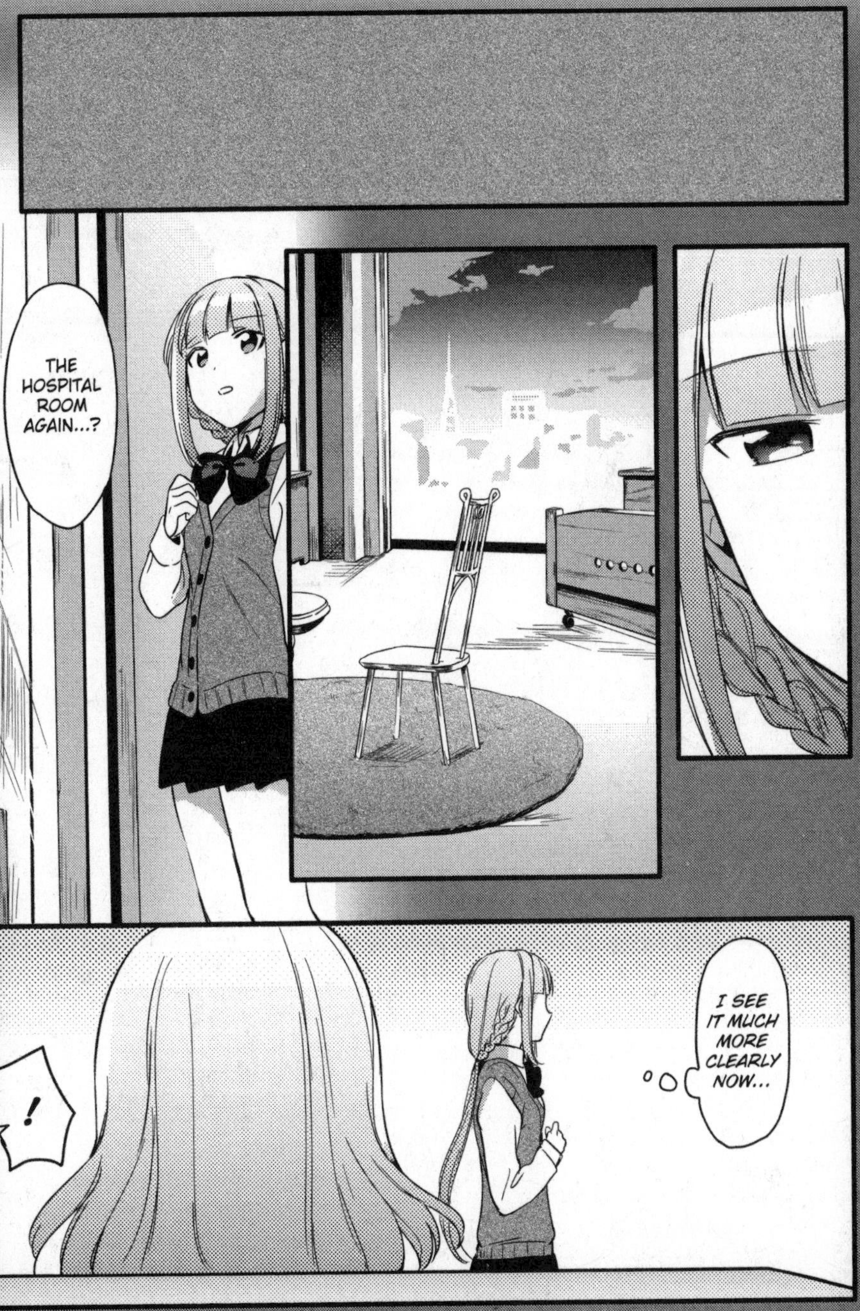
THE HOSPITAL ROOM AGAIN...?
I SEE IT MUCH MORE CLEARLY NOW...
!

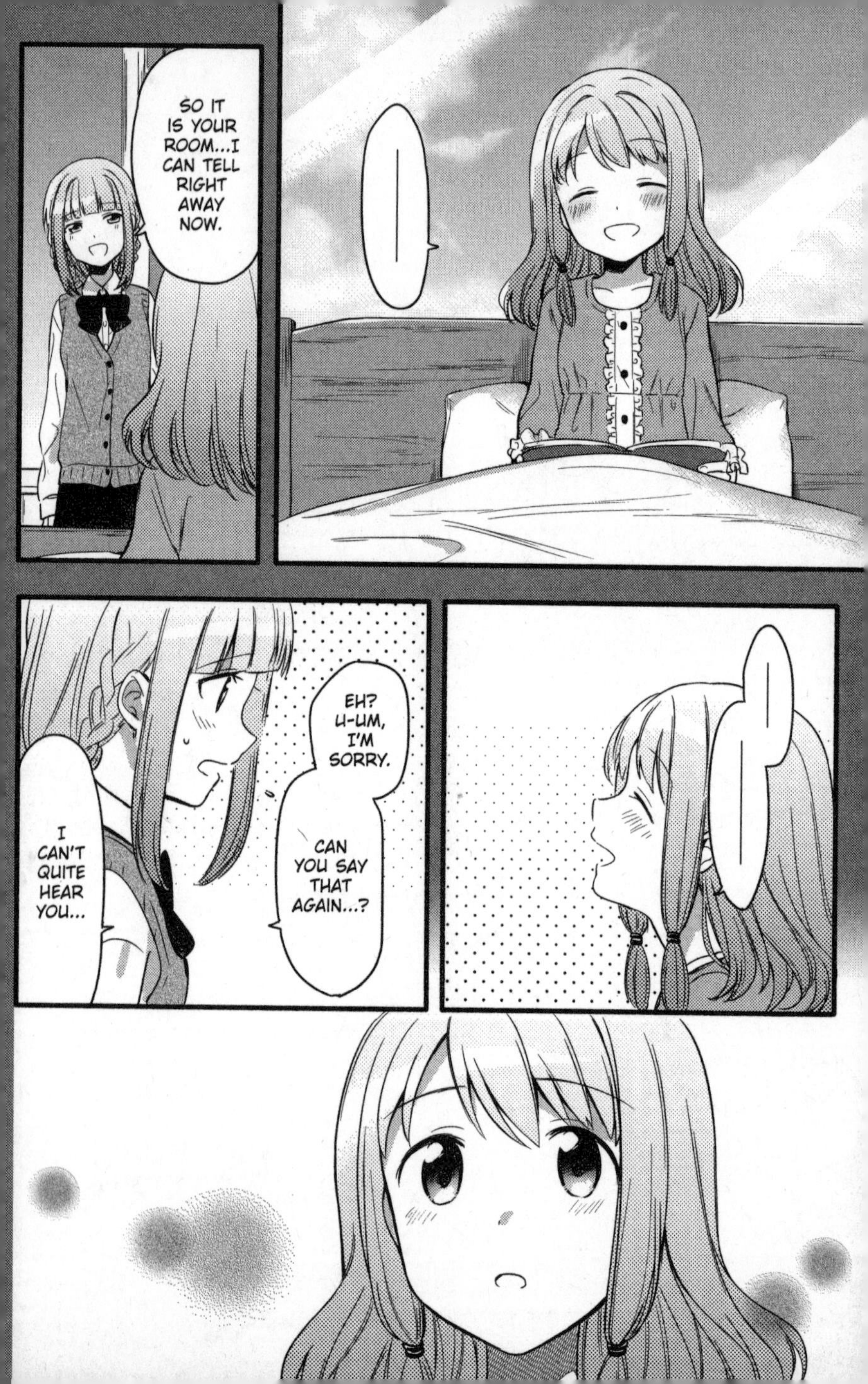
SO IT IS YOUR ROOM...I CAN TELL RIGHT AWAY NOW.
EH? U-UM, I'M SORRY.
CAN YOU SAY THAT AGAIN...?
I CAN'T QUITE HEAR YOU...

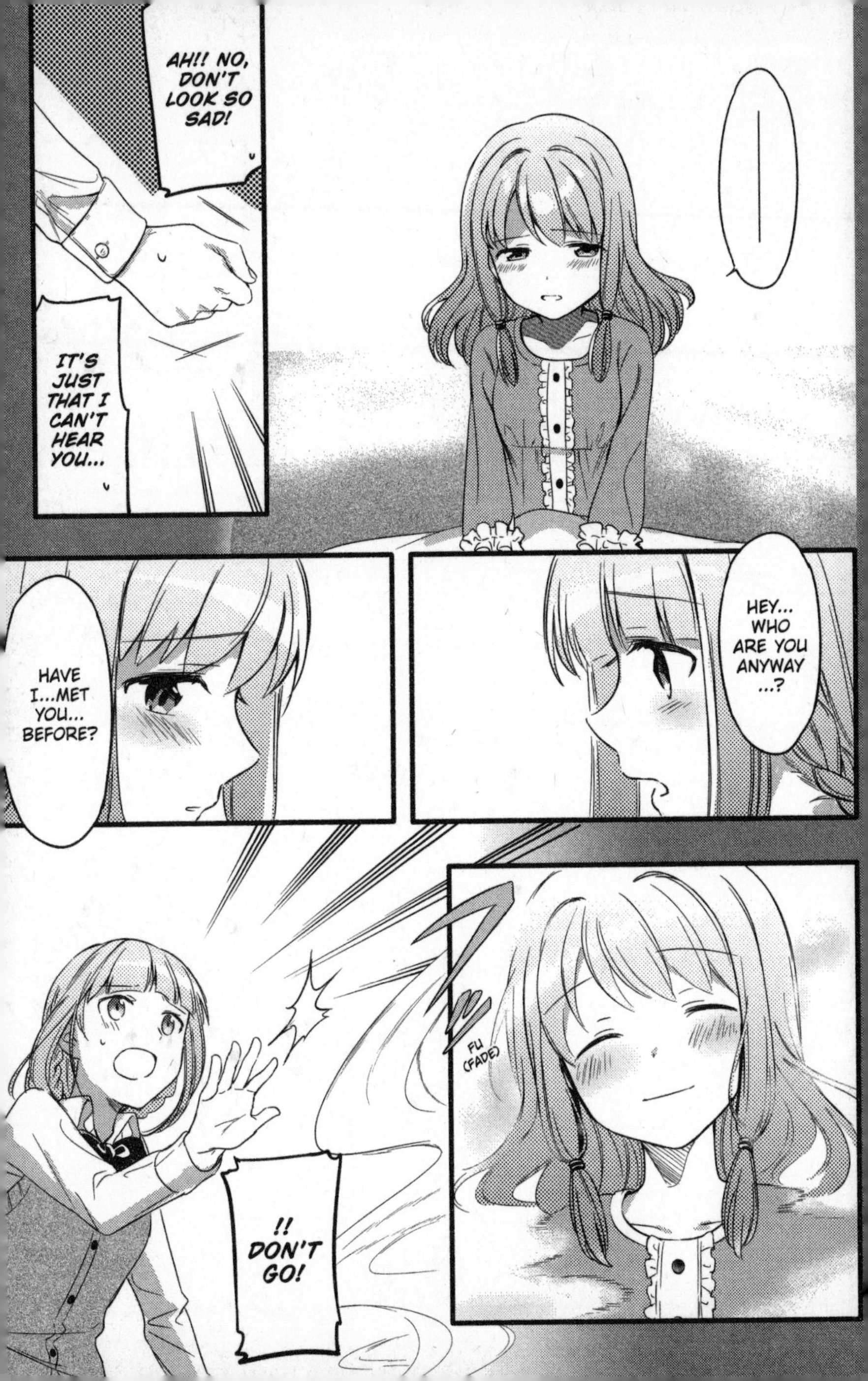
—
AH!! NO, DON'T LOOK SO SAD!
IT'S JUST THAT I CAN'T HEAR YOU...
HEY... WHO ARE YOU ANYWAY ...?
HAVE I...MET YOU... BEFORE?
FU (FADE)
!! DON'T GO!

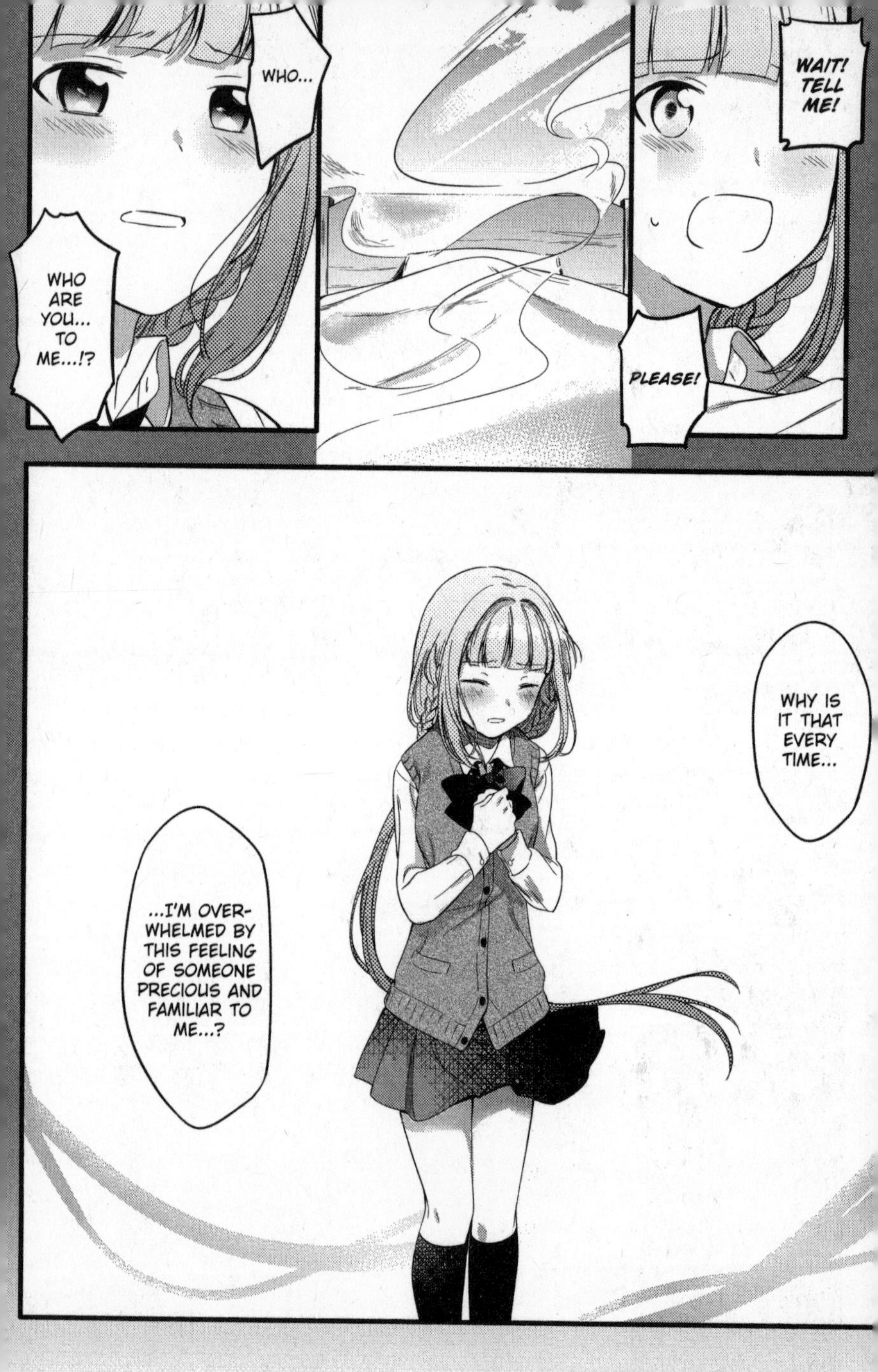
WAIT! TELL ME!
PLEASE!
WHO...
WHO ARE YOU... TO ME...!?
WHY IS IT THAT EVERY TIME...
...I'M OVER-WHELMED BY THIS FEELING OF SOMEONE PRECIOUS AND FAMILIAR TO ME...?

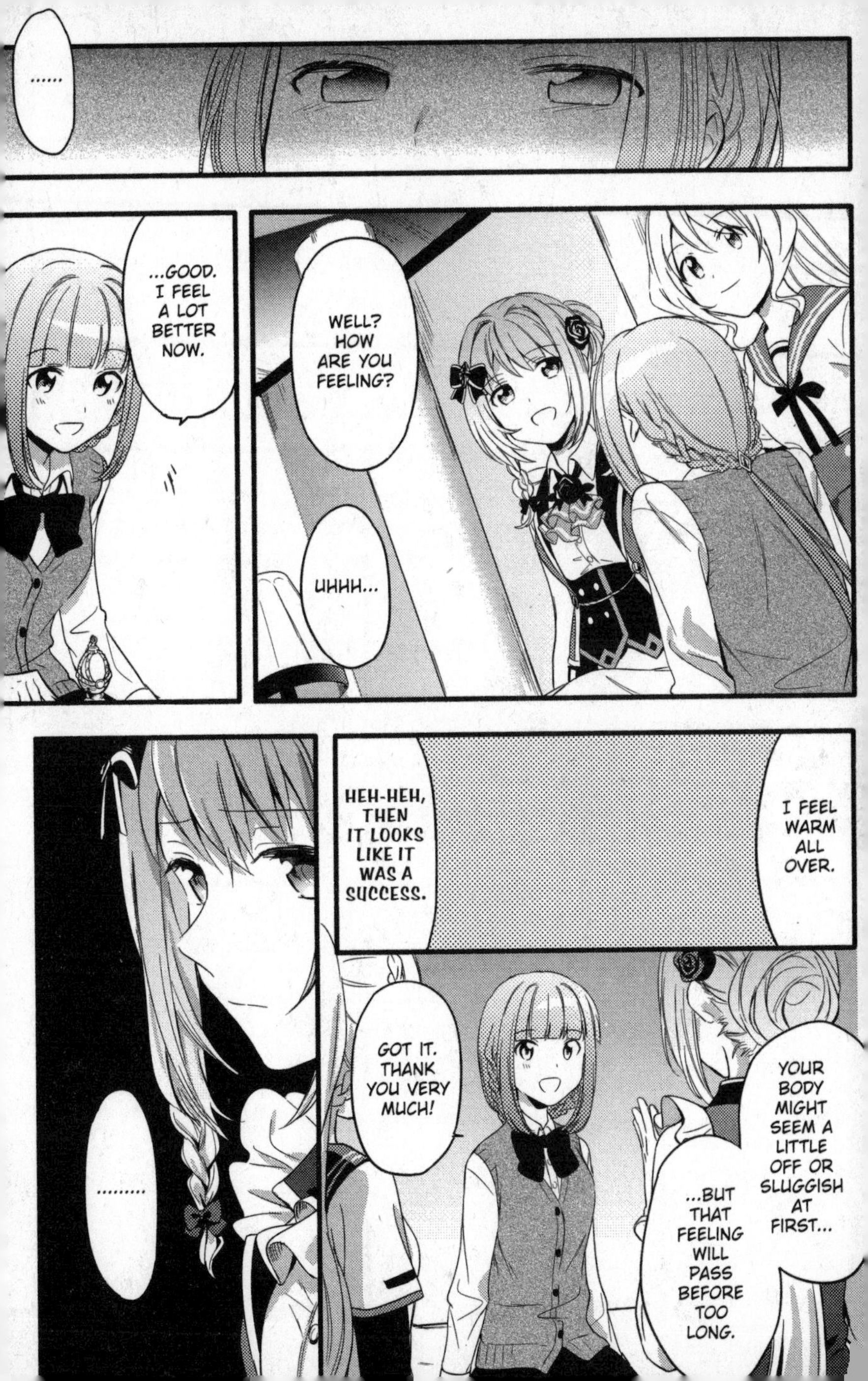
......
WELL? HOW ARE YOU FEELING?
UHHH...
...GOOD. I FEEL A LOT BETTER NOW.
I FEEL WARM ALL OVER.
HEH-HEH, THEN IT LOOKS LIKE IT WAS A SUCCESS.
YOUR BODY MIGHT SEEM A LITTLE OFF OR SLUGGISH AT FIRST...
...BUT THAT FEELING WILL PASS BEFORE TOO LONG.
GOT IT. THANK YOU VERY MUCH!
....

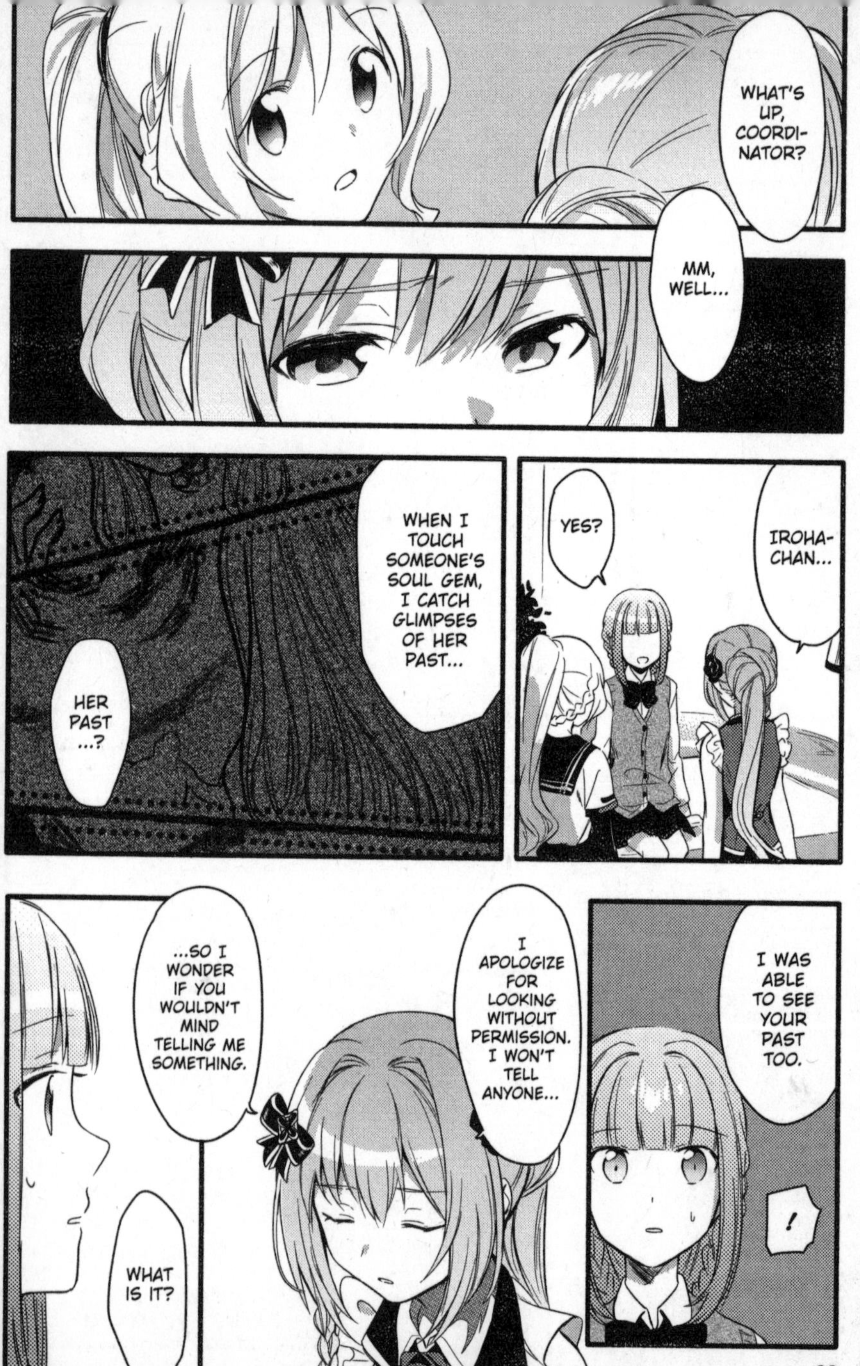
WHAT'S UP, COORDINATOR?
MM, WELL...
IROHA-CHAN...
YES?
WHEN I TOUCH SOMEONE'S SOUL GEM, I CATCH GLIMPSES OF HER PAST...
HER PAST ...?
I WAS ABLE TO SEE YOUR PAST TOO.
!
I APOLOGIZE FOR LOOKING WITHOUT PERMISSION. I WON'T TELL ANYONE...
...SO I WONDER IF YOU WOULDN'T MIND TELLING ME SOMETHING.
WHAT IS IT?

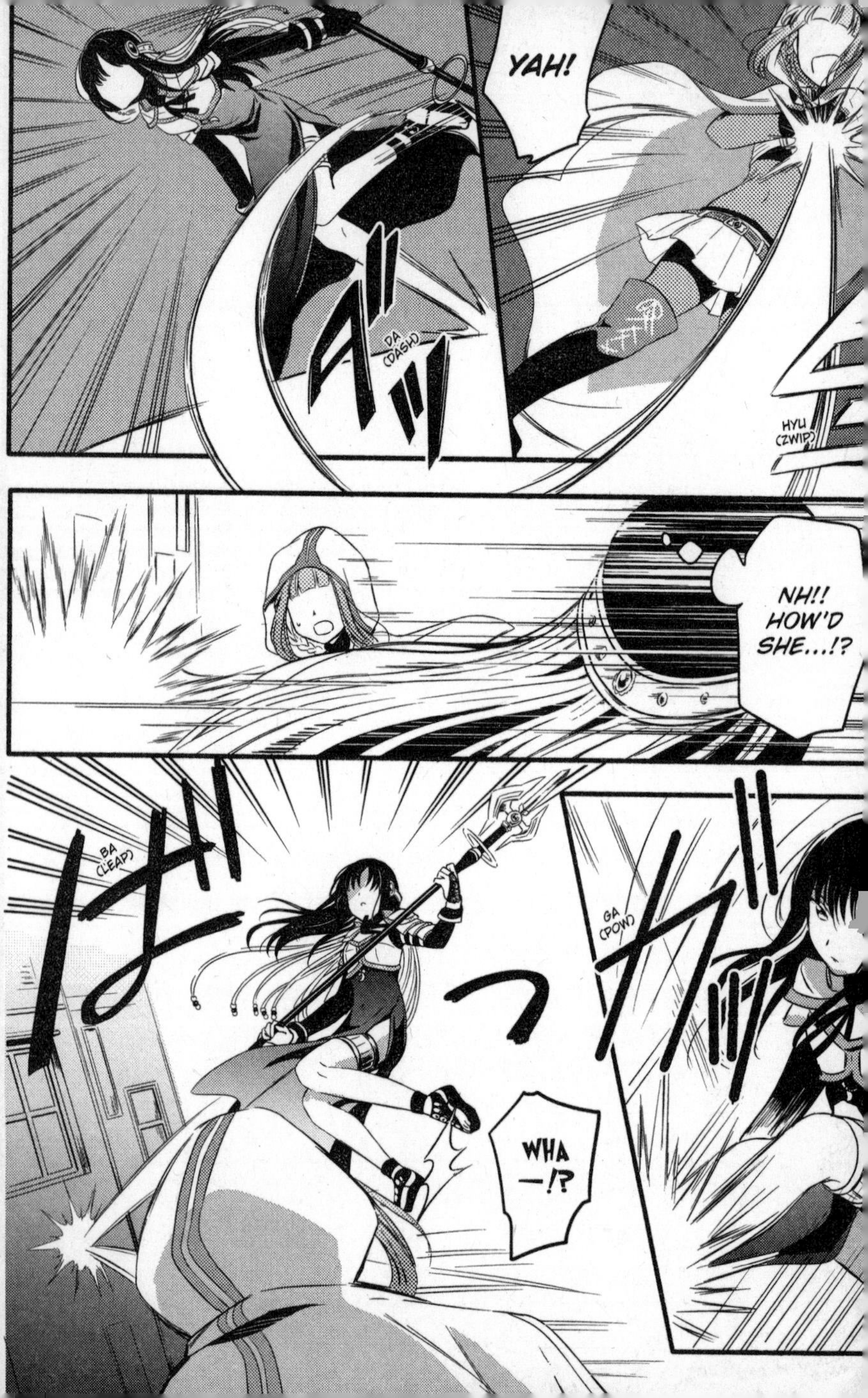
YAH!
HYU (ZWIP)
DA (DASH)
NH!! HOW'D SHE...!?
GA (POW)
BA (LEAP)
WHA—!?

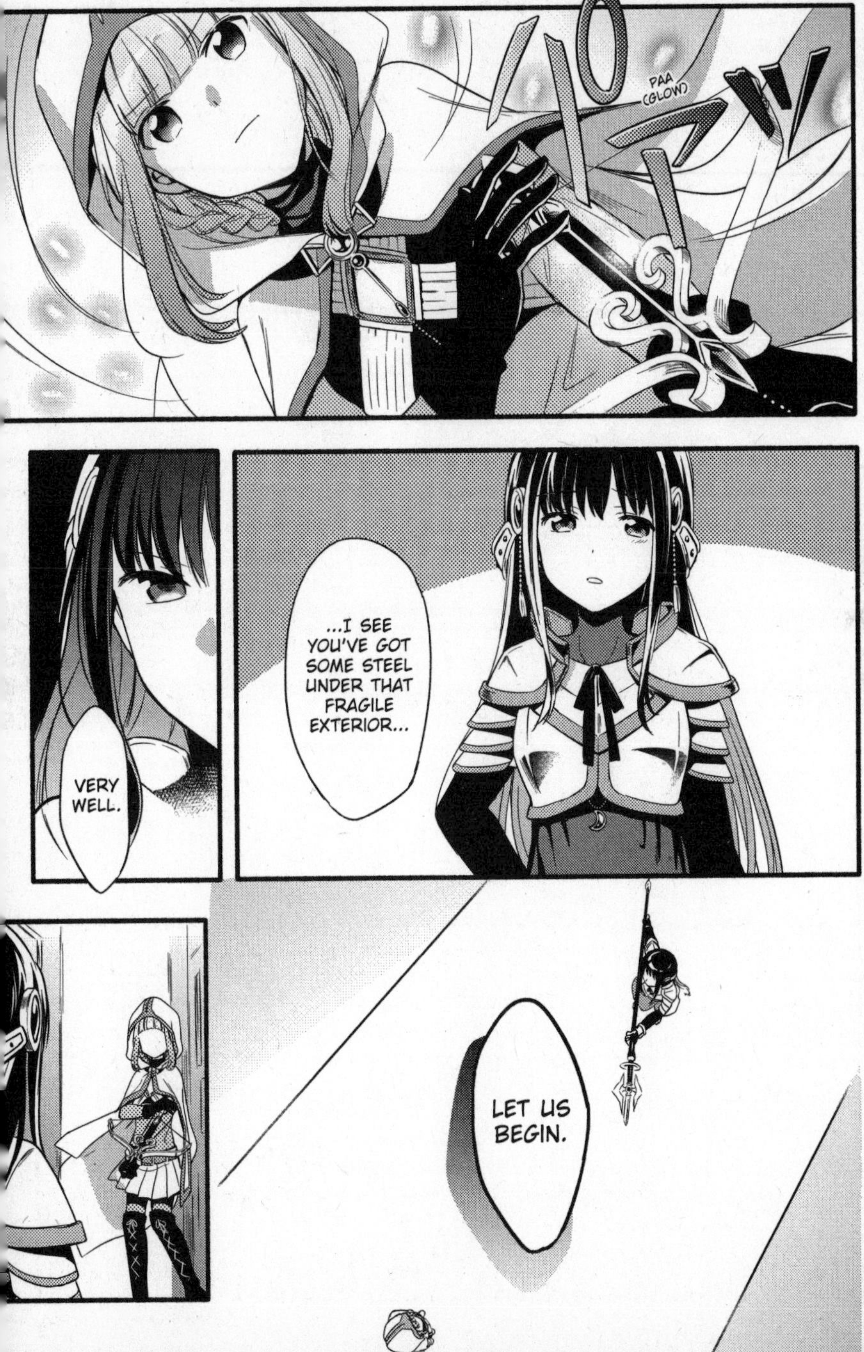
PAA (GLOW)
...I SEE YOU'VE GOT SOME STEEL UNDER THAT FRAGILE EXTERIOR...
VERY WELL.
LET US BEGIN.

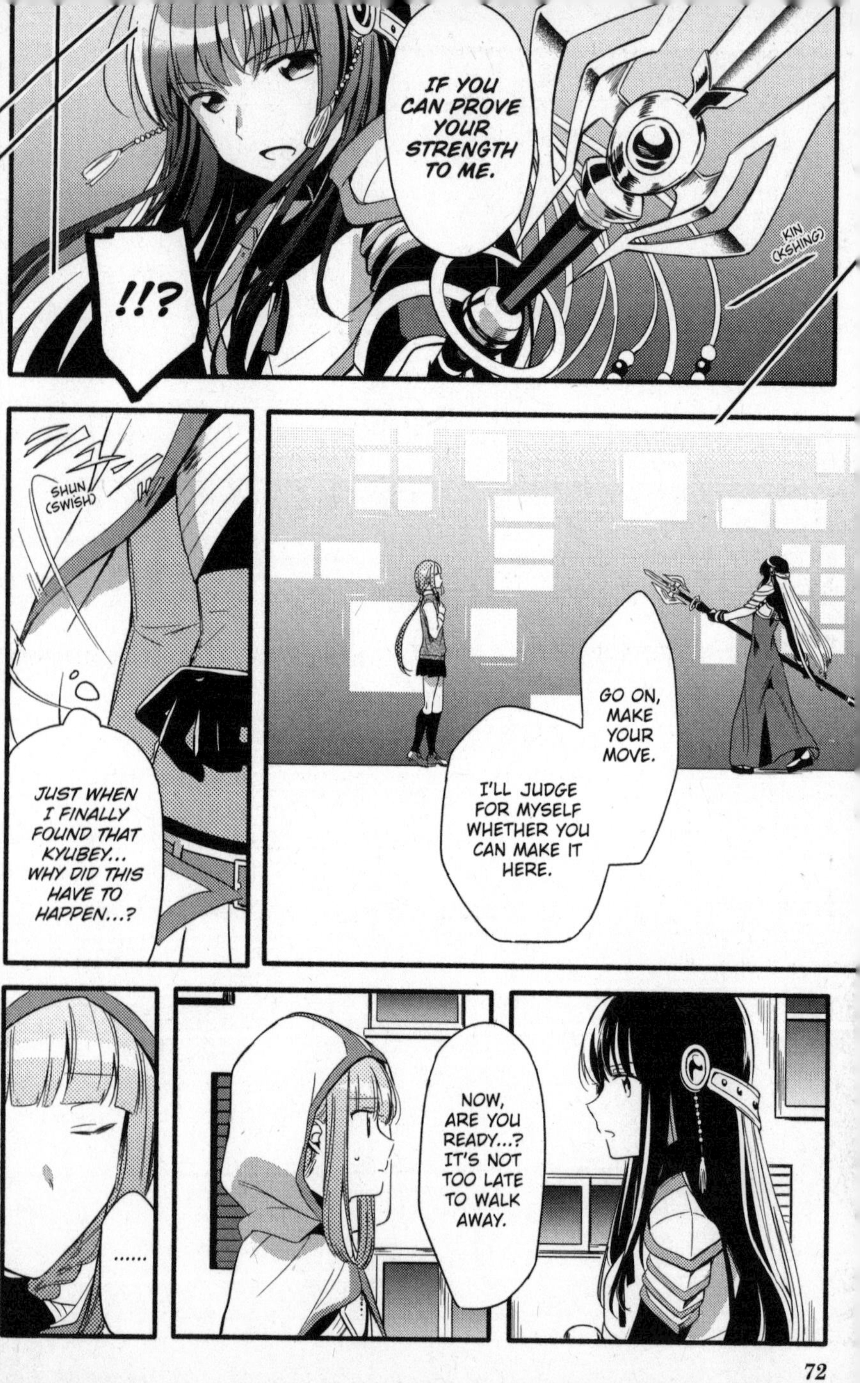
IF YOU CAN PROVE YOUR STRENGTH TO ME.
KIN (KSHING)
!!?
GO ON, MAKE YOUR MOVE.
I'LL JUDGE FOR MYSELF WHETHER YOU CAN MAKE IT HERE.
SHUN (SWISH)
JUST WHEN I FINALLY FOUND THAT KYUBEY... WHY DID THIS HAVE TO HAPPEN...?
NOW, ARE YOU READY...? IT'S NOT TOO LATE TO WALK AWAY.
......

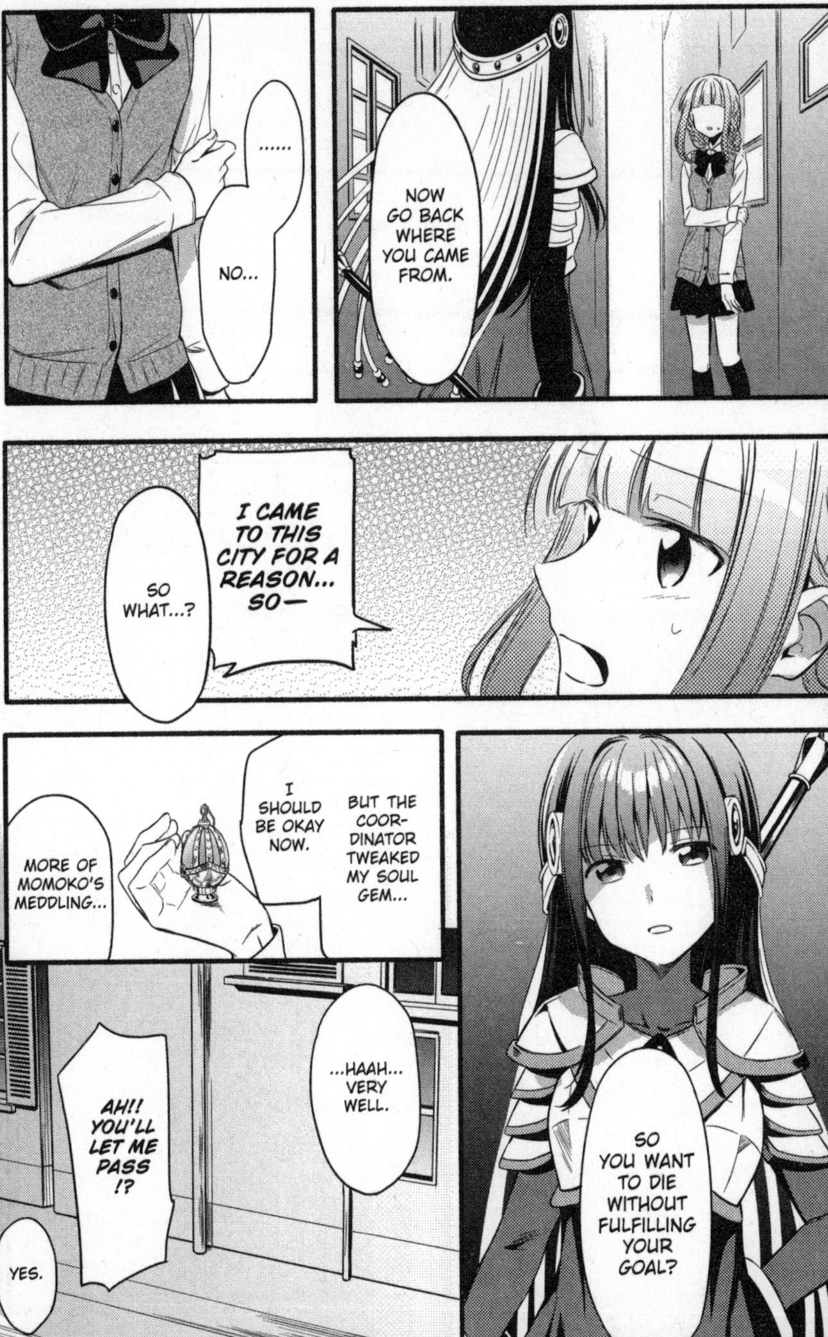
NOW GO BACK WHERE YOU CAME FROM.
......
NO...
I CAME TO THIS CITY FOR A REASON... SO—
SO WHAT...?
SO YOU WANT TO DIE WITHOUT FULFILLING YOUR GOAL?
BUT THE COORDINATOR TWEAKED MY SOUL GEM...
I SHOULD BE OKAY NOW.
MORE OF MOMOKO'S MEDDLING...
...HAAH... VERY WELL.
AH!! YOU'LL LET ME PASS!?
YES.

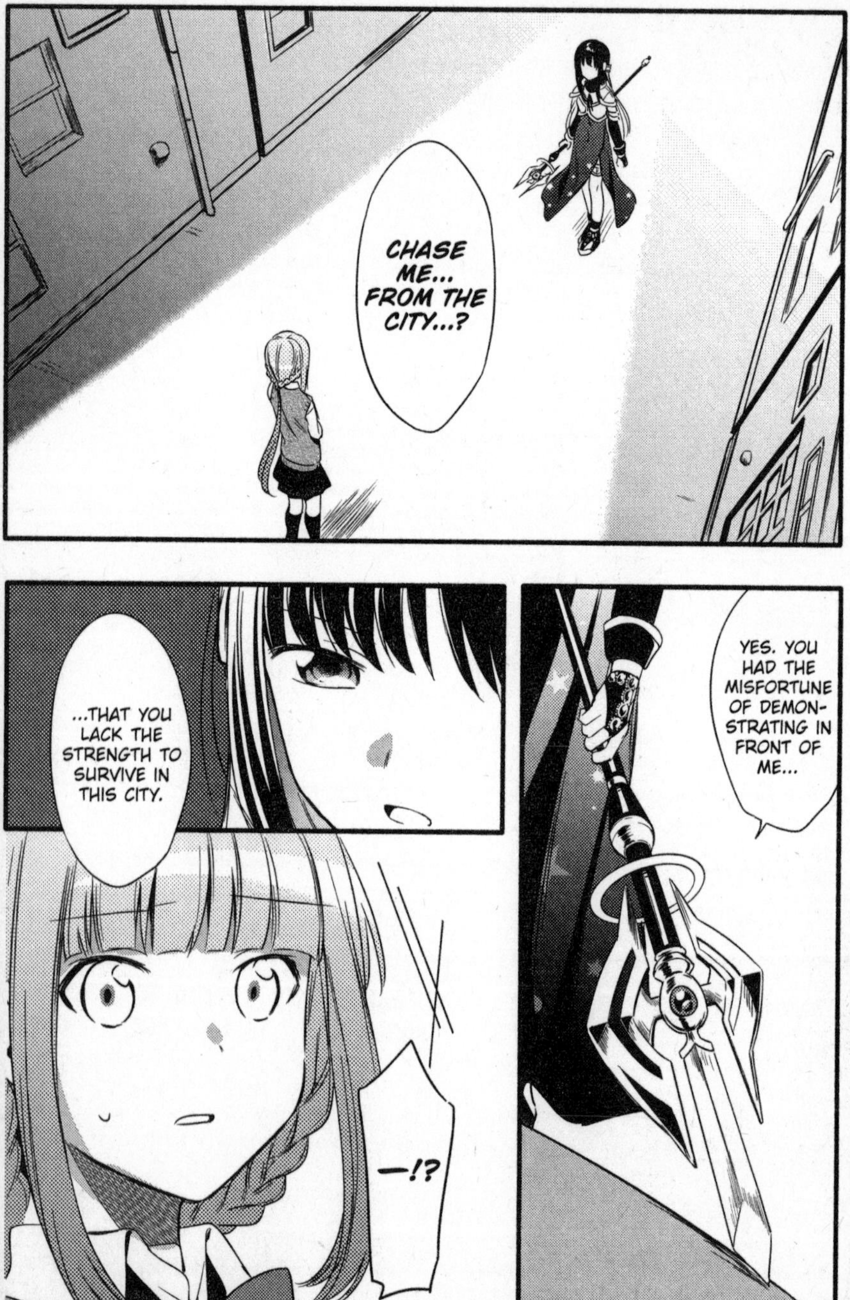
CHASE ME... FROM THE CITY...?
YES. YOU HAD THE MISFORTUNE OF DEMON-STRATING IN FRONT OF ME...
...THAT YOU LACK THE STRENGTH TO SURVIVE IN THIS CITY.
—!?

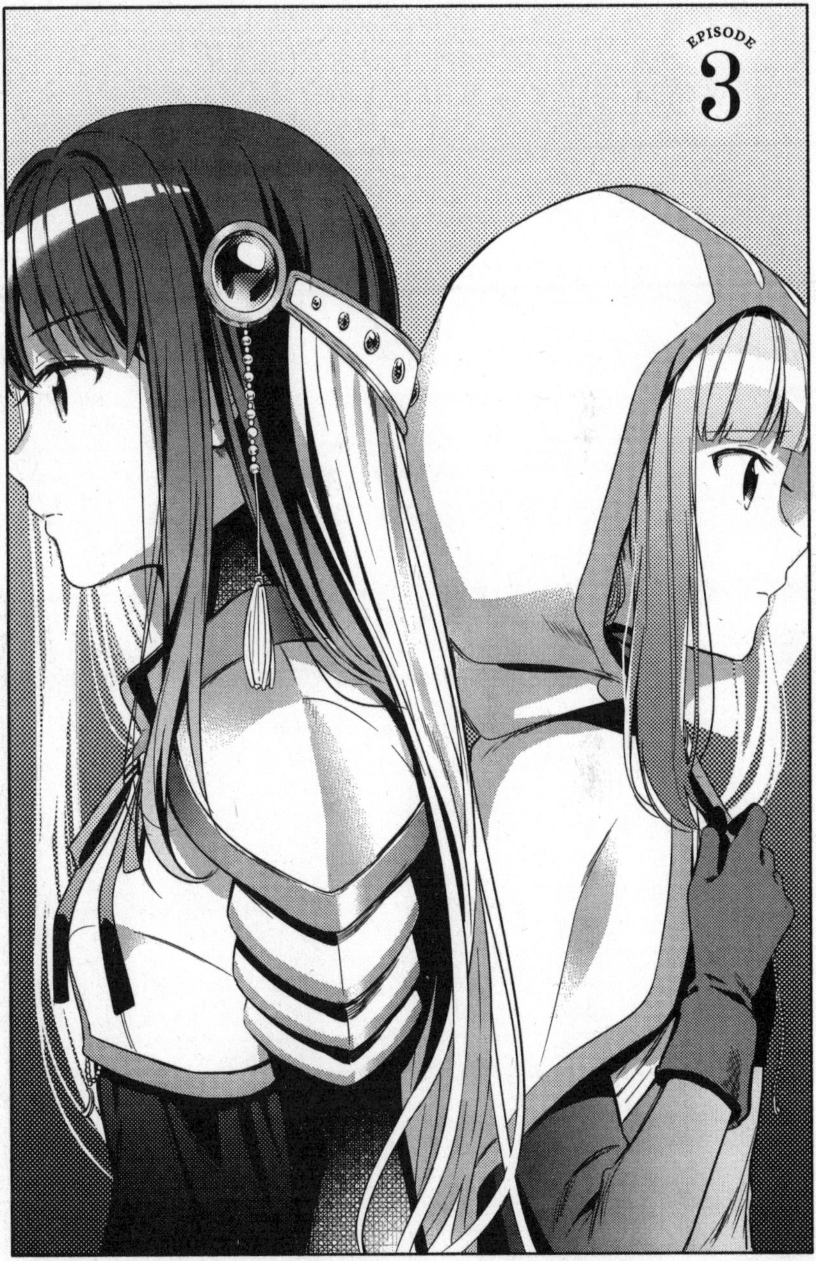
EPISODE
3

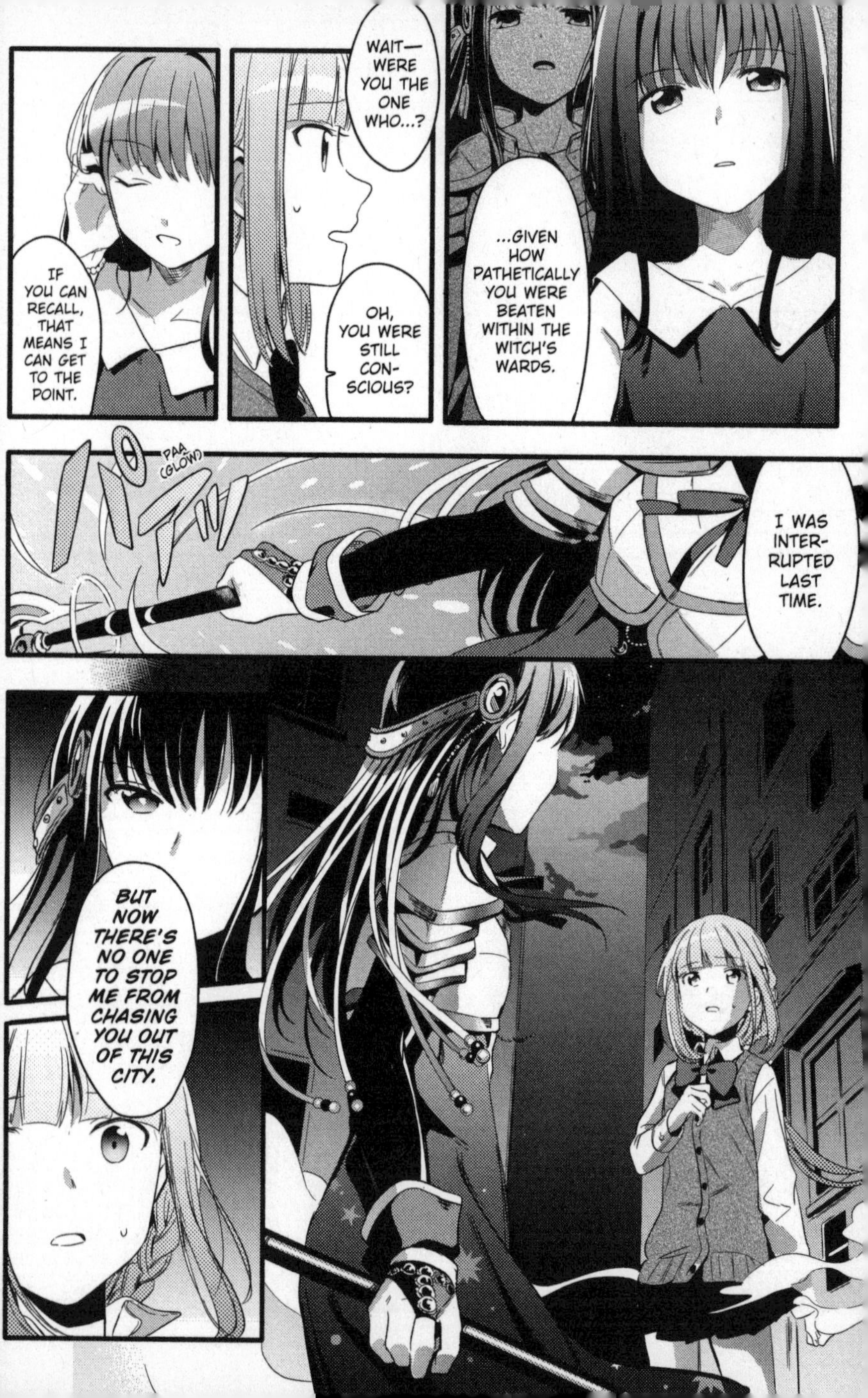
...GIVEN HOW PATHETICALLY YOU WERE BEATEN WITHIN THE WITCH'S WARDS.
WAIT— WERE YOU THE ONE WHO...?
OH, YOU WERE STILL CON-SCIOUS?
IF YOU CAN RECALL, THAT MEANS I CAN GET TO THE POINT.
I WAS INTER-RUPTED LAST TIME.
PAA (GLOW)
BUT NOW THERE'S NO ONE TO STOP ME FROM CHASING YOU OUT OF THIS CITY.

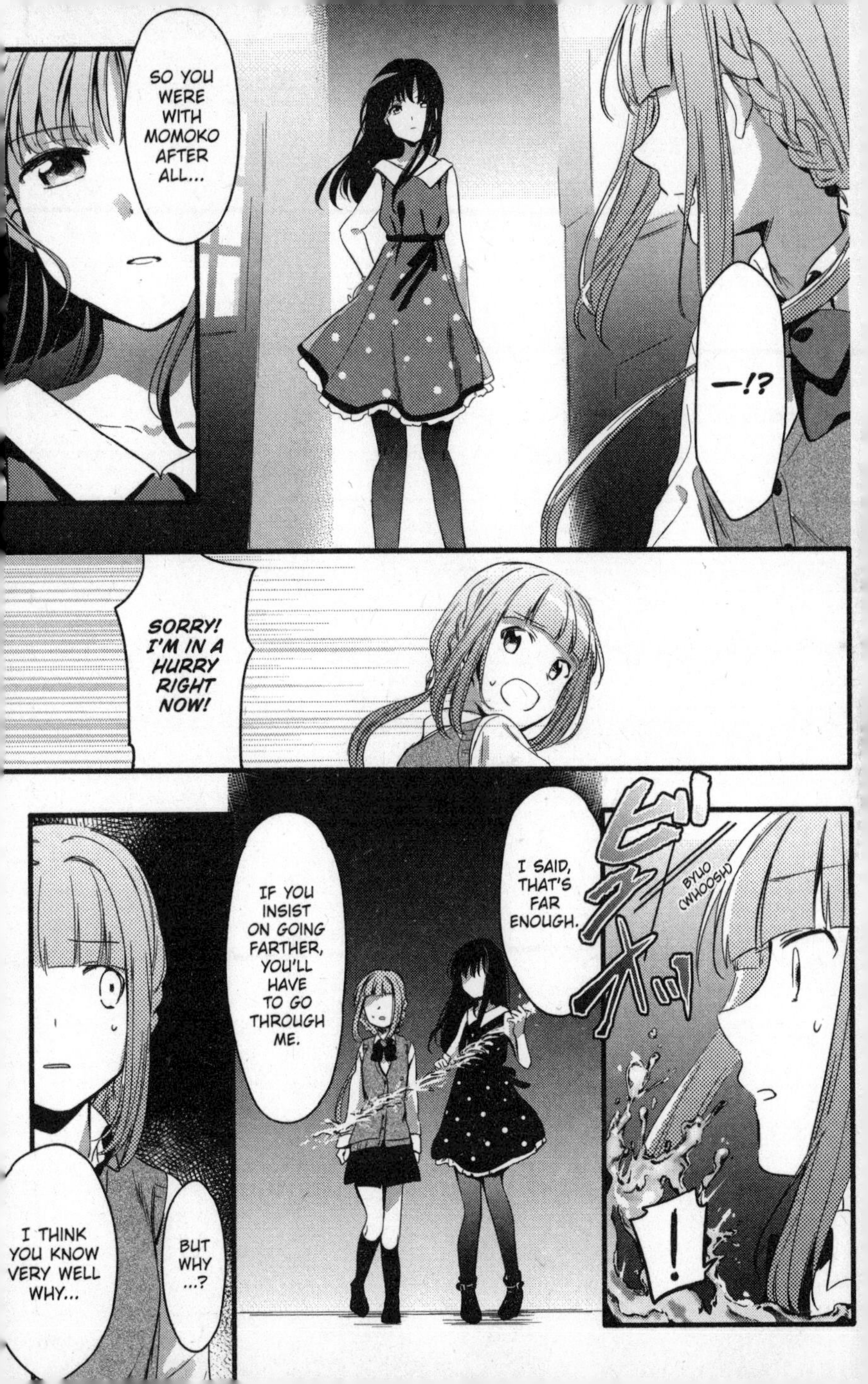
—!?
SO YOU WERE WITH MOMOKO AFTER ALL...
SORRY! I'M IN A HURRY RIGHT NOW!
BYUO (WHOOSH)
!
I SAID, THAT'S FAR ENOUGH.
IF YOU INSIST ON GOING FARTHER, YOU'LL HAVE TO GO THROUGH ME.
BUT WHY ...?
I THINK YOU KNOW VERY WELL WHY...

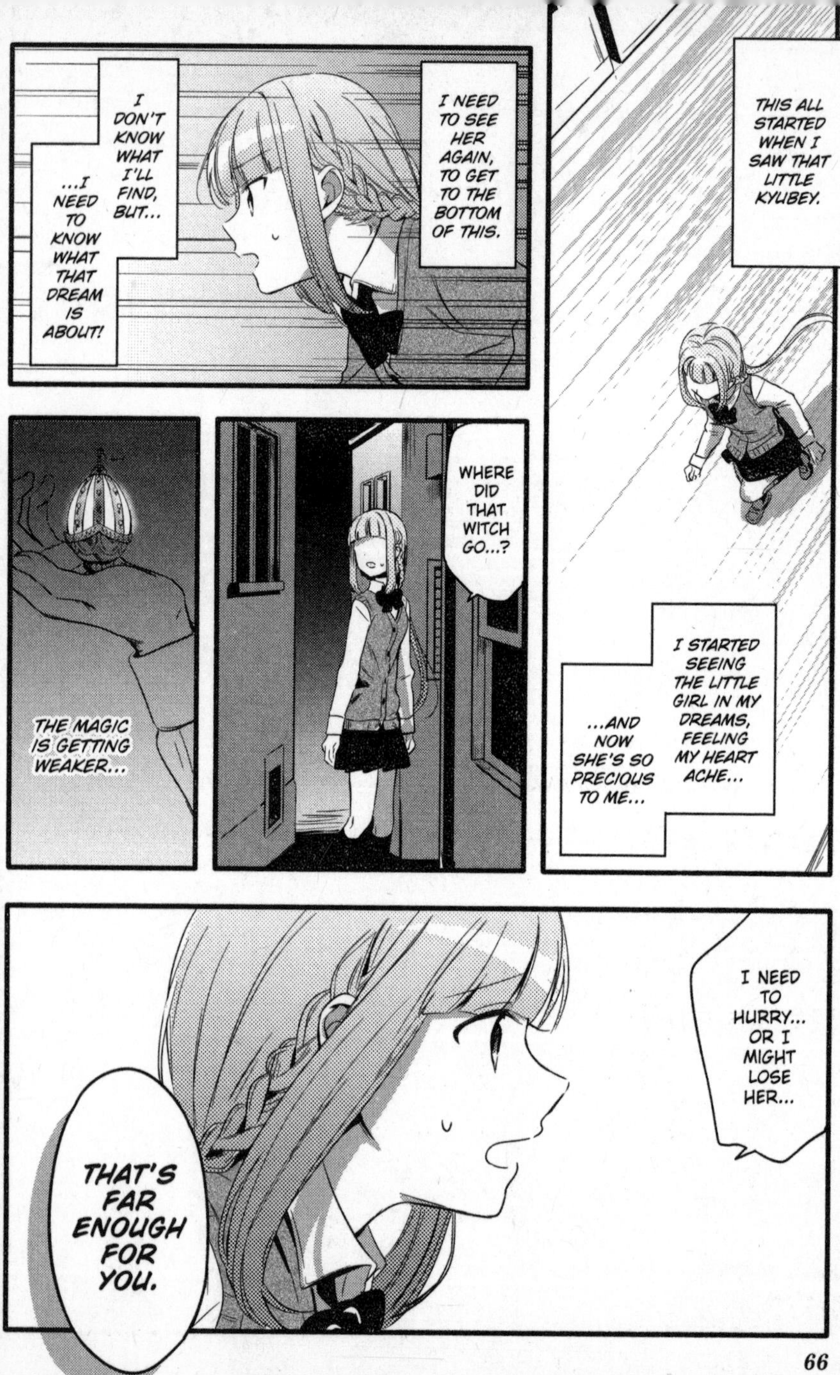
THIS ALL STARTED WHEN I SAW THAT LITTLE KYUBEY.
I STARTED SEEING THE LITTLE GIRL IN MY DREAMS, FEELING MY HEART ACHE...
...AND NOW SHE'S SO PRECIOUS TO ME...
I NEED TO SEE HER AGAIN, TO GET TO THE BOTTOM OF THIS.
I DON'T KNOW WHAT I'LL FIND, BUT...
...I NEED TO KNOW WHAT THAT DREAM IS ABOUT!
WHERE DID THAT WITCH GO...?
THE MAGIC IS GETTING WEAKER...
I NEED TO HURRY... OR I MIGHT LOSE HER...
THAT'S FAR ENOUGH FOR YOU.

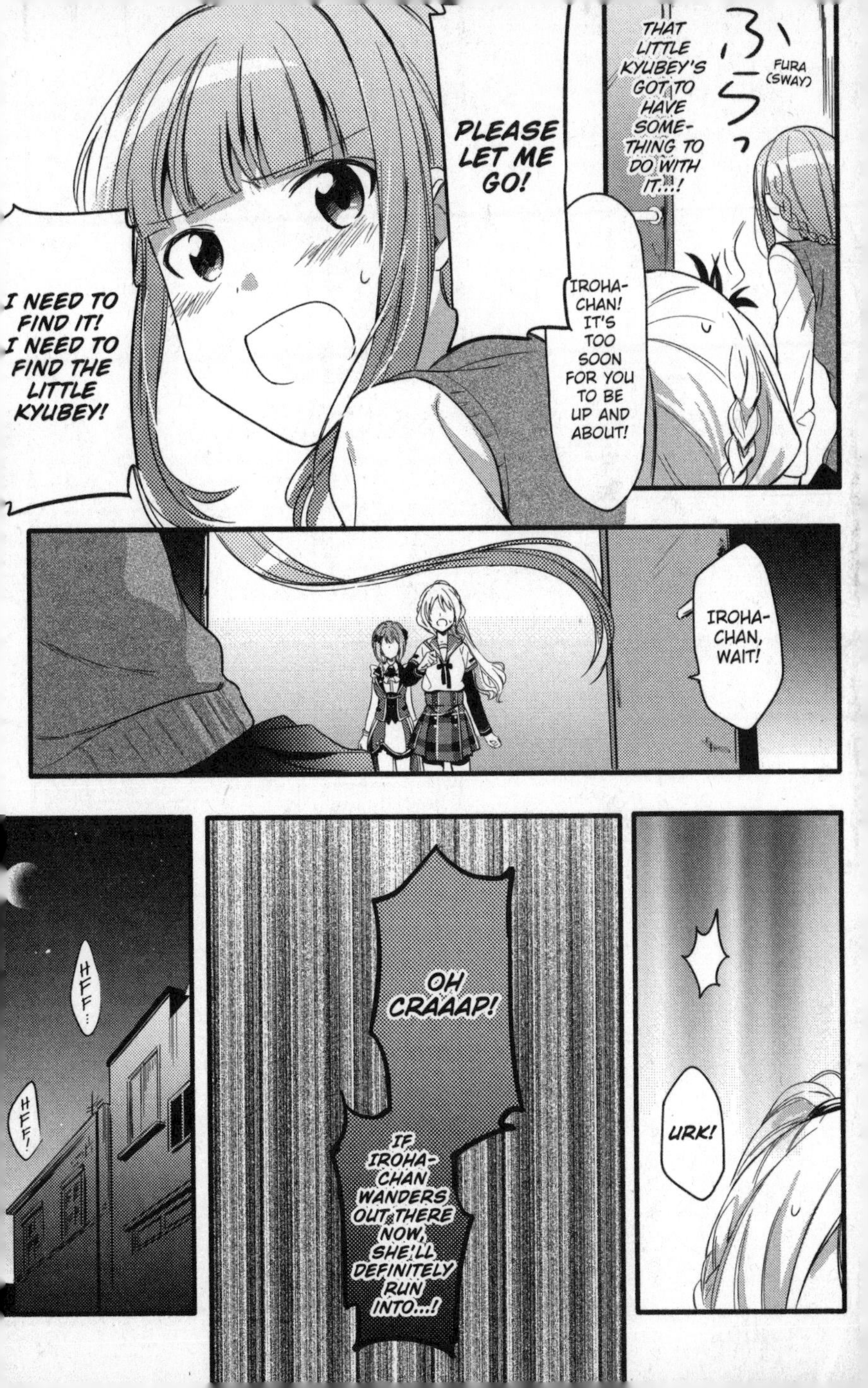
THAT LITTLE KYUBEY'S GOT TO HAVE SOME-THING TO DO WITH IT...!
FURA (SWAY)
IROHA-CHAN! IT'S TOO SOON FOR YOU TO BE UP AND ABOUT!
PLEASE LET ME GO!
I NEED TO FIND IT! I NEED TO FIND THE LITTLE KYUBEY!
IROHA-CHAN, WAIT!
URK!
OH CRAAAP!
IF IROHA-CHAN WANDERS OUT THERE NOW, SHE'LL DEFINITELY RUN INTO...!
HFF...
HFF!

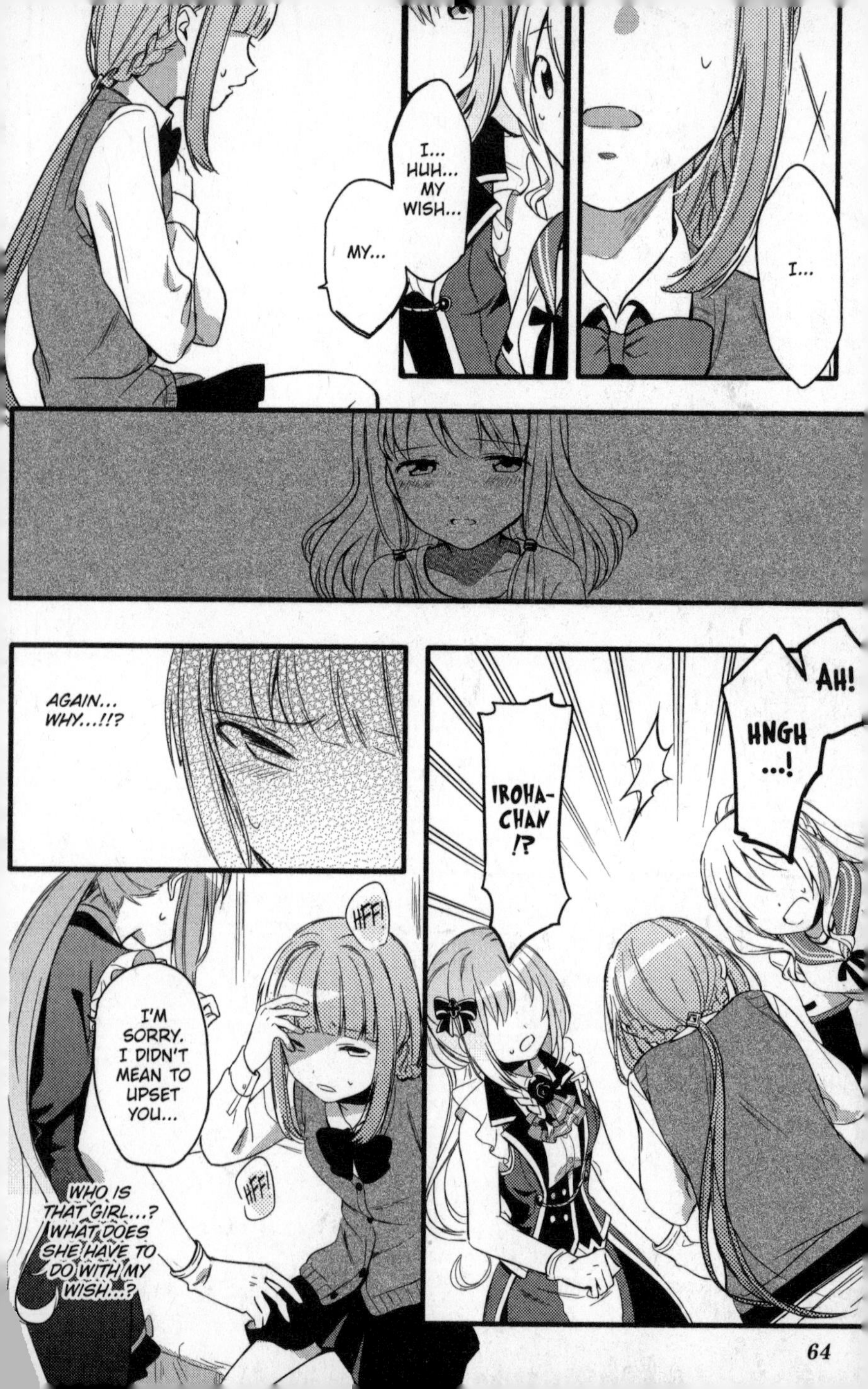
I...
I... HUH... MY WISH... MY...
AH! HNGH...!
IROHA-CHAN!?
AGAIN... WHY...!!?
HFF!
I'M SORRY. I DIDN'T MEAN TO UPSET YOU...
HFF!
WHO IS THAT GIRL...? WHAT DOES SHE HAVE TO DO WITH MY WISH...?

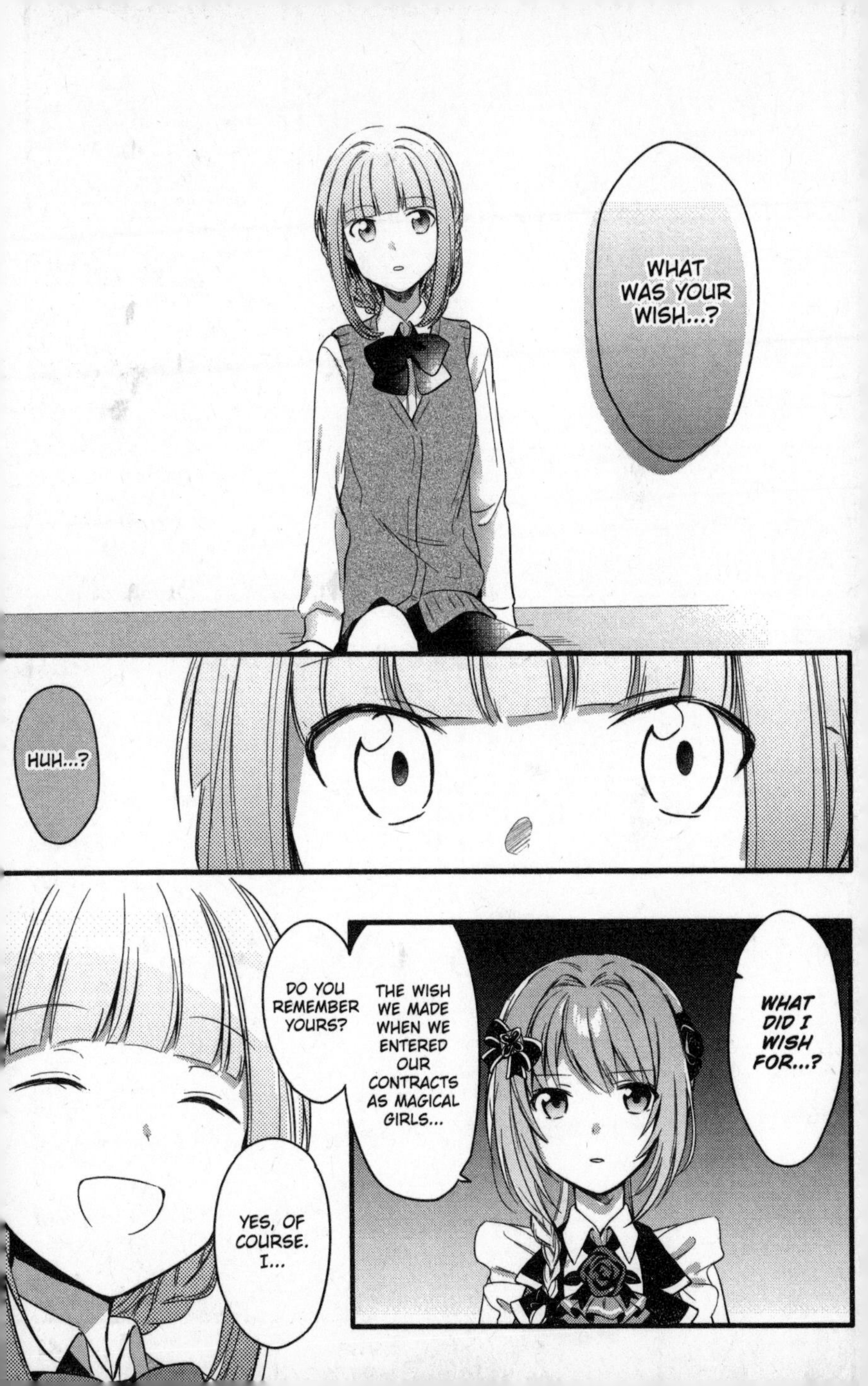
WHAT WAS YOUR WISH...?
HUH...?
WHAT DID I WISH FOR...?
THE WISH WE MADE WHEN WE ENTERED OUR CONTRACTS AS MAGICAL GIRLS...
DO YOU REMEMBER YOURS?
YES, OF COURSE. I...

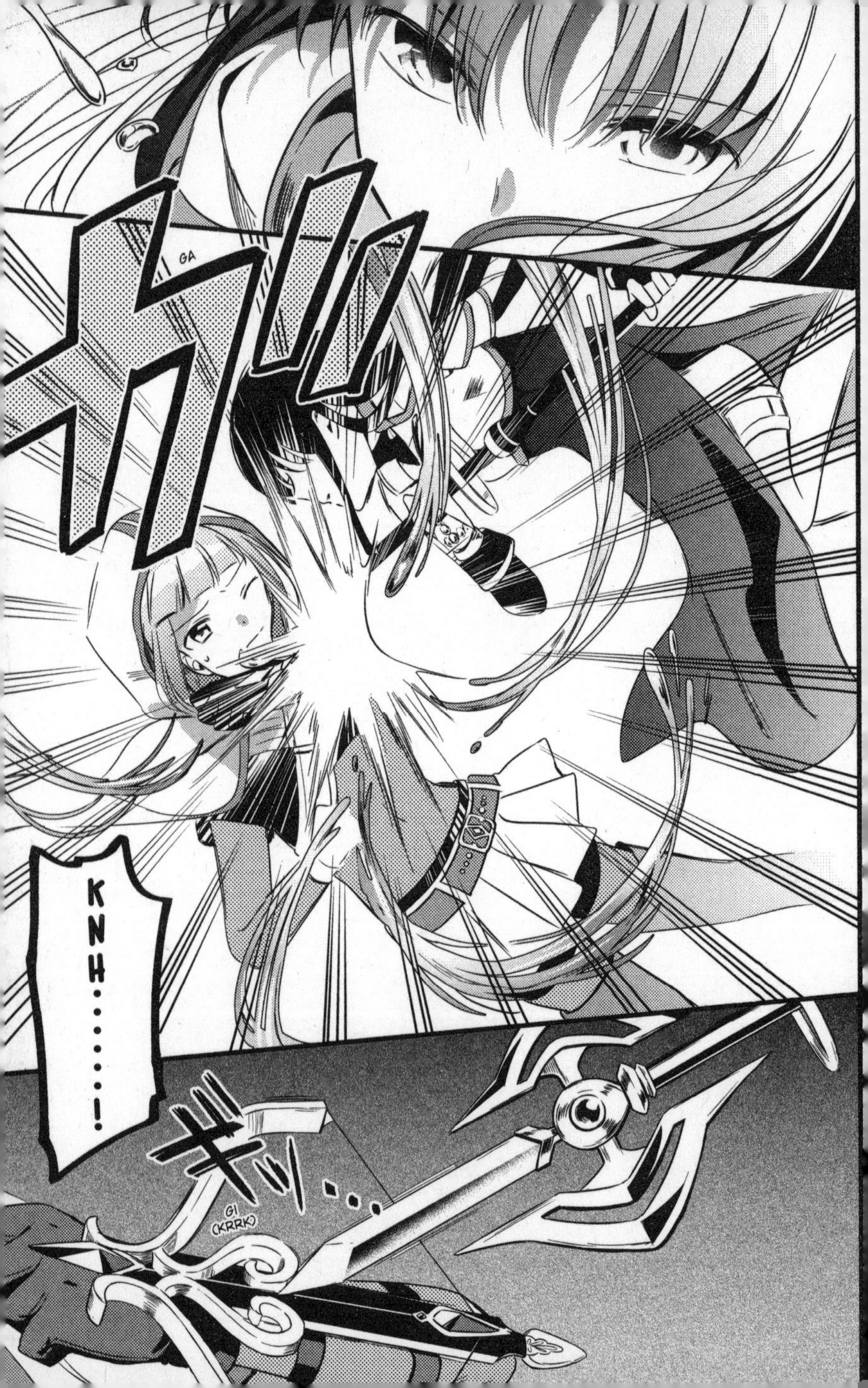
GA
KNH......!
GI
(KRRK)

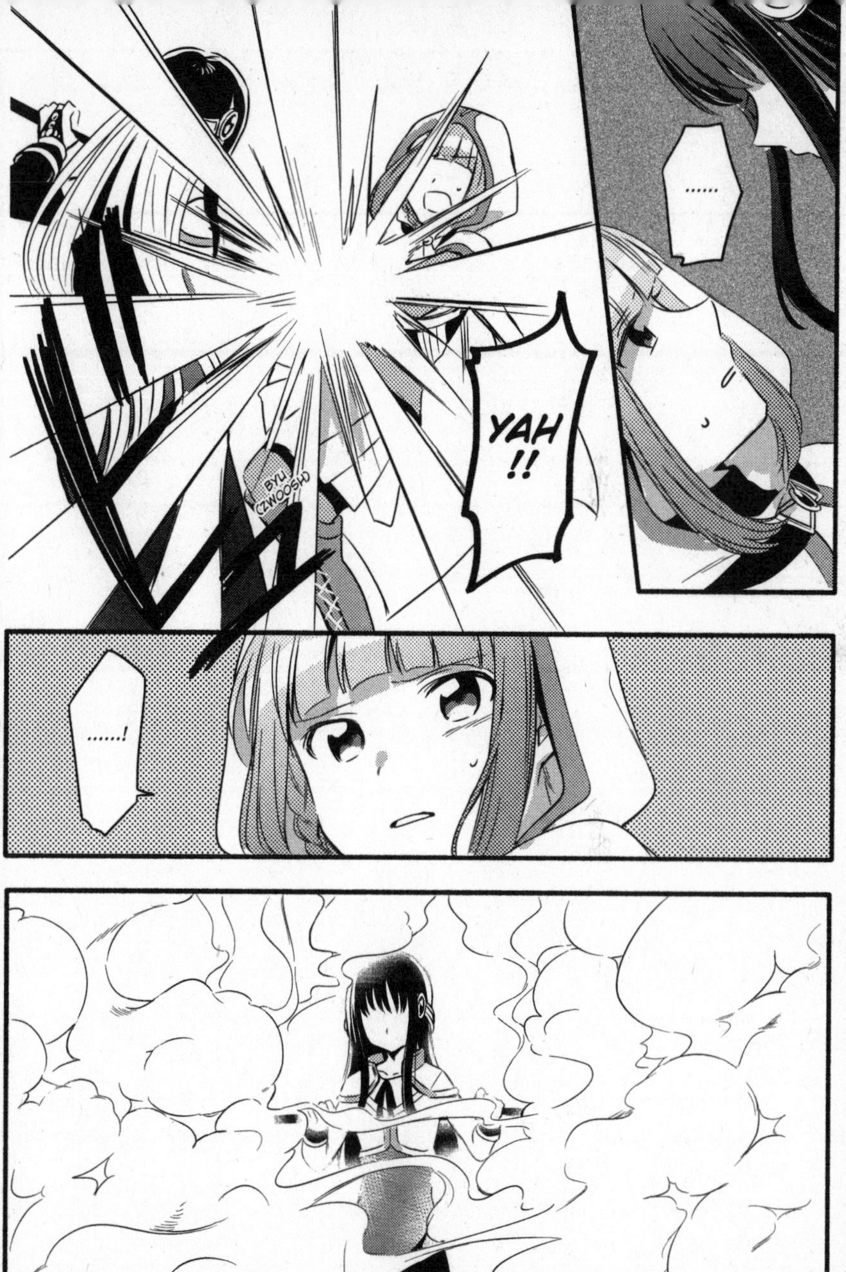
......
YAH!!
BYU (ZWOOSH)
......!

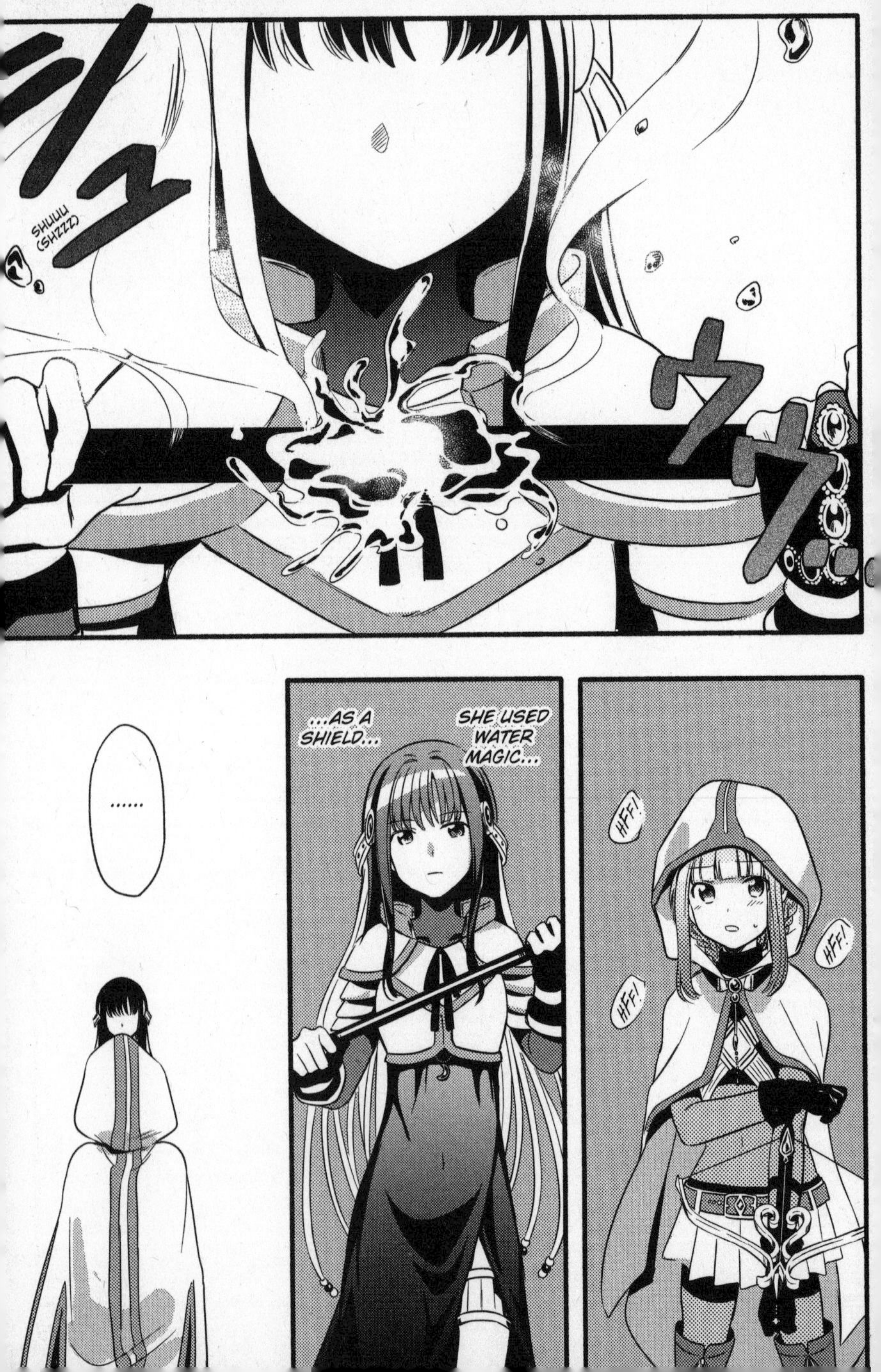
シュ
SHUUU (SHZZZ)
ウウ…
HFF!
HFF!
HFF!
SHE USED WATER MAGIC...
...AS A SHIELD...
......

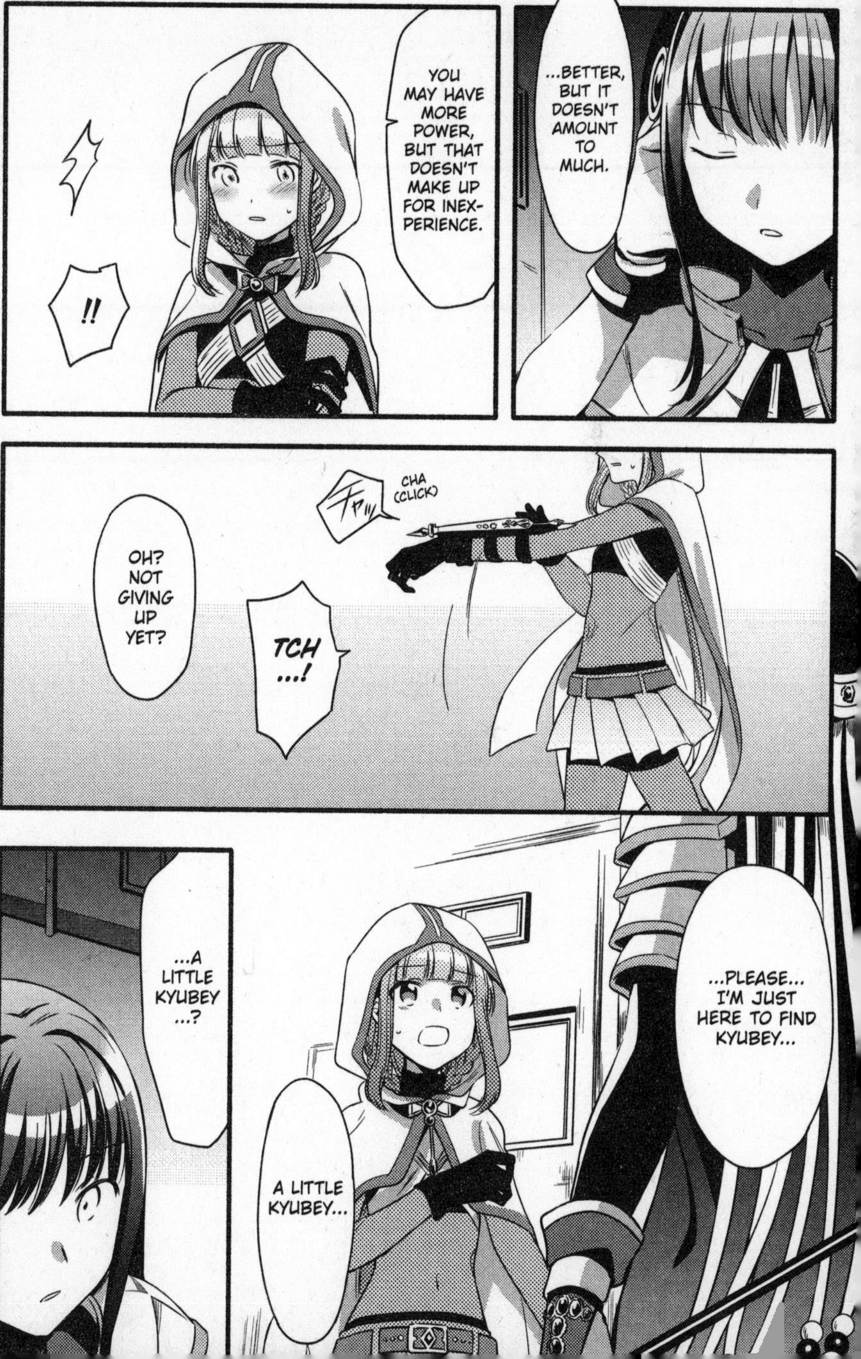

...BETTER, BUT IT DOESN'T AMOUNT TO MUCH.
YOU MAY HAVE MORE POWER, BUT THAT DOESN'T MAKE UP FOR INEXPERIENCE.
!!
チャッ
CHA (CLICK)
TCH ...!
OH? NOT GIVING UP YET?
...PLEASE... I'M JUST HERE TO FIND KYUBEY...
A LITTLE KYUBEY...
...A LITTLE KYUBEY ...?

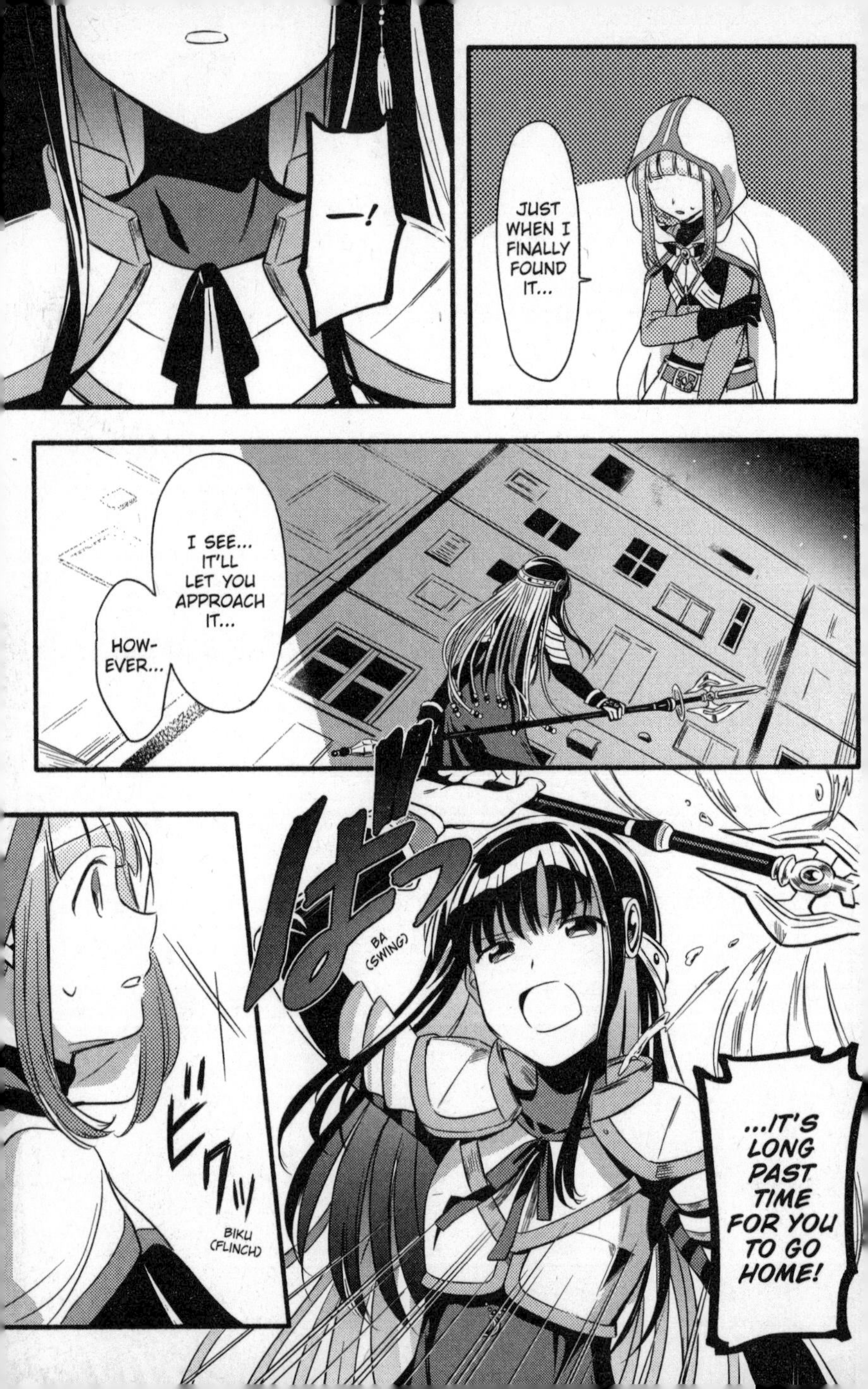
JUST WHEN I FINALLY FOUND IT...
—!
I SEE... IT'LL LET YOU APPROACH IT...
HOW-EVER...
BA (SWING)
...IT'S LONG PAST TIME FOR YOU TO GO HOME!
BIKU (FLINCH)

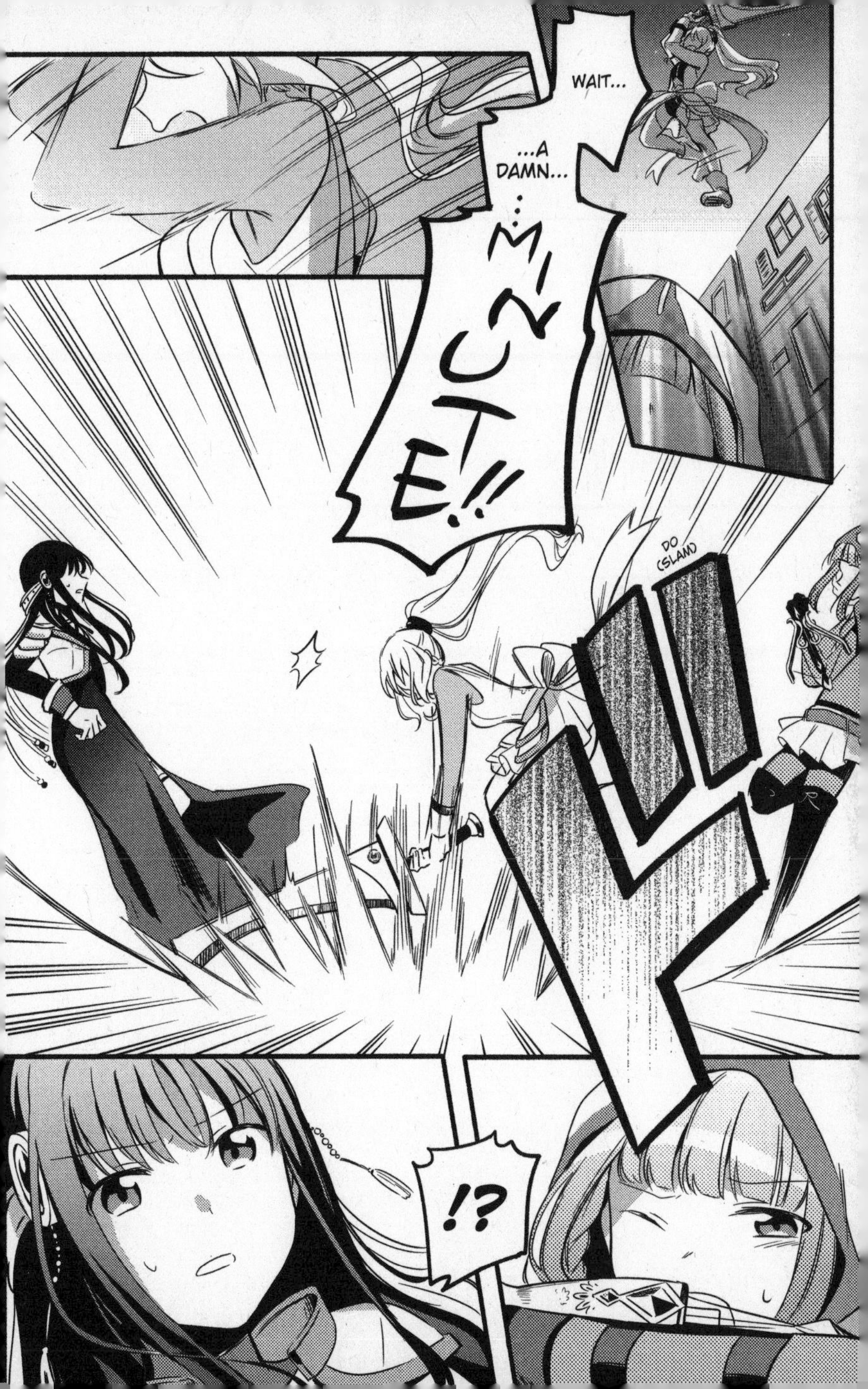
WAIT...
...A DAMN...
...MINUTE!!
DO (SLAM)
!?

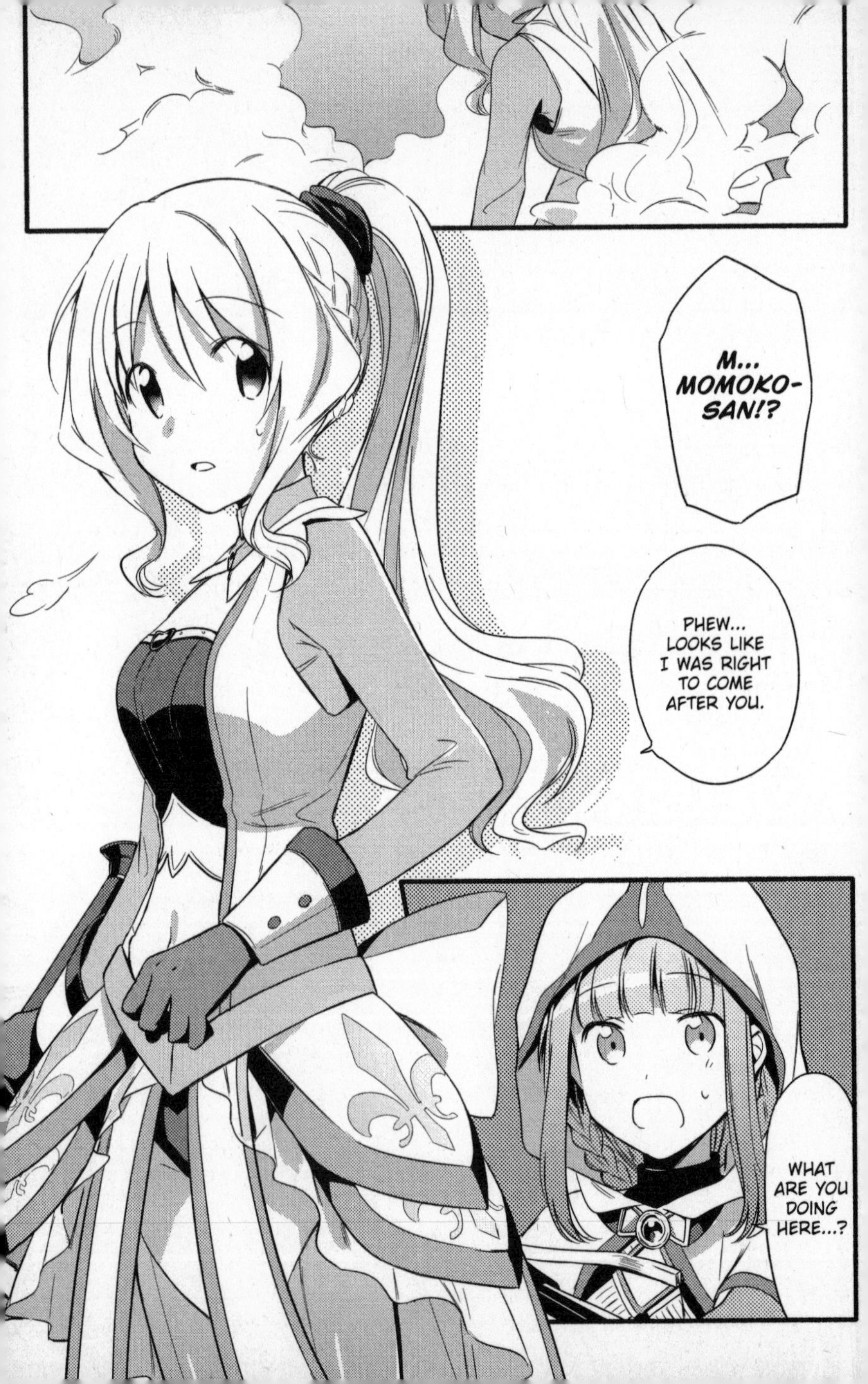
M... MOMOKO-SAN!?
PHEW... LOOKS LIKE I WAS RIGHT TO COME AFTER YOU.
WHAT ARE YOU DOING HERE...?

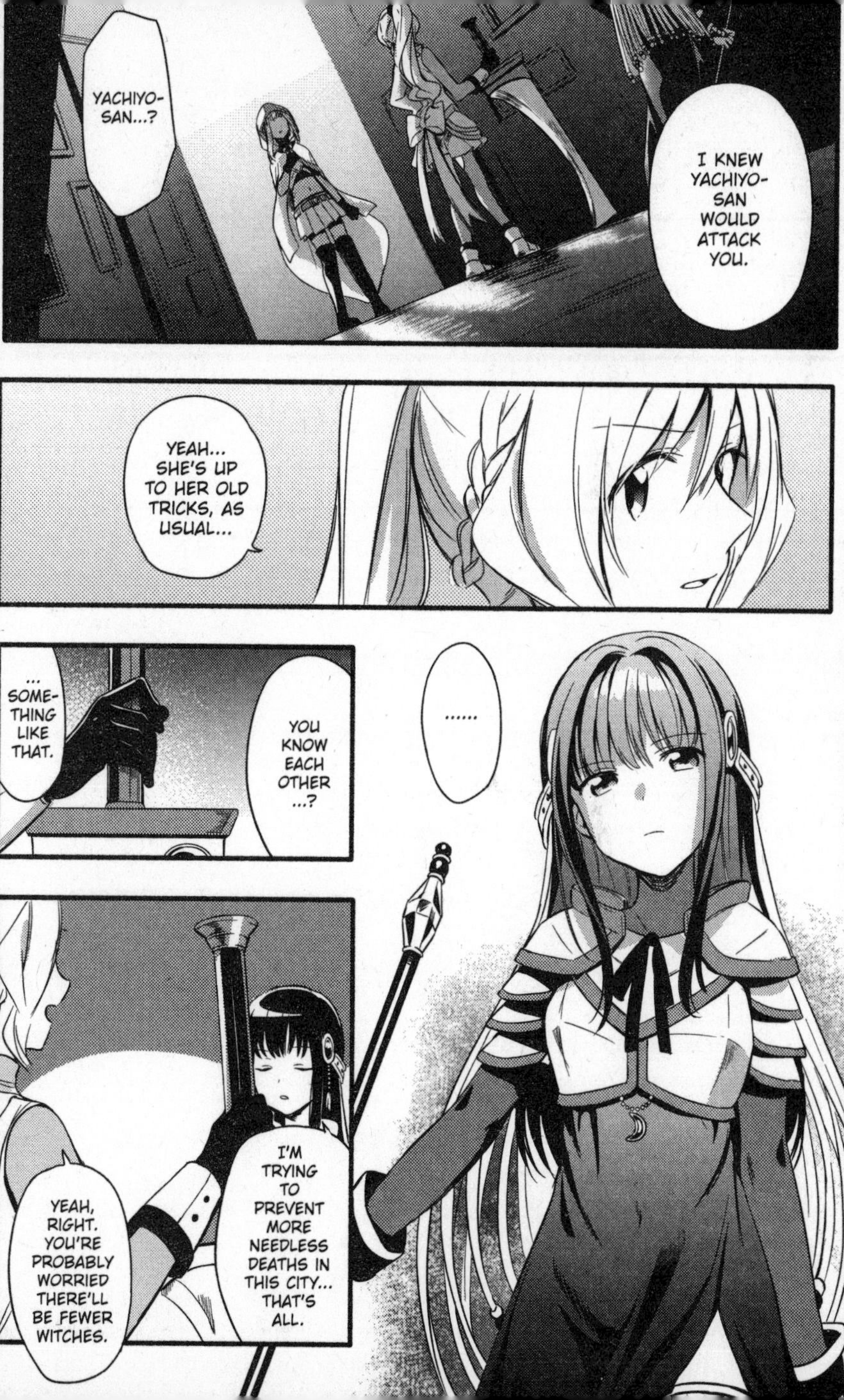
I KNEW YACHIYO-SAN WOULD ATTACK YOU.
YACHIYO-SAN...?
YEAH... SHE'S UP TO HER OLD TRICKS, AS USUAL...
......
YOU KNOW EACH OTHER ...?
... SOMETHING LIKE THAT.
I'M TRYING TO PREVENT MORE NEEDLESS DEATHS IN THIS CITY... THAT'S ALL.
YEAH, RIGHT. YOU'RE PROBABLY WORRIED THERE'LL BE FEWER WITCHES.

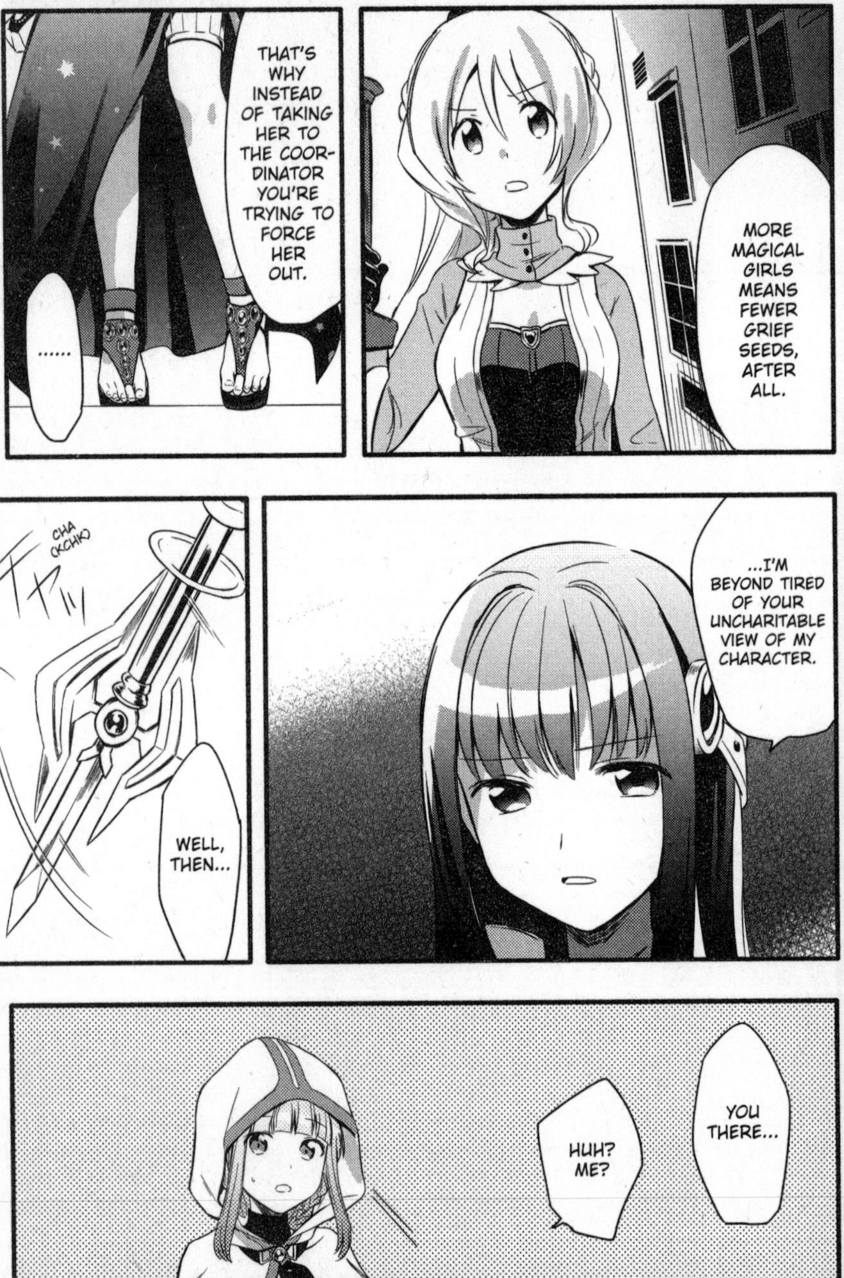
MORE MAGICAL GIRLS MEANS FEWER GRIEF SEEDS, AFTER ALL.
THAT'S WHY INSTEAD OF TAKING HER TO THE COOR-DINATOR YOU'RE TRYING TO FORCE HER OUT.
......
...I'M BEYOND TIRED OF YOUR UNCHARITABLE VIEW OF MY CHARACTER.
CHA (KCHK)
WELL, THEN...
YOU THERE...
HUH? ME?

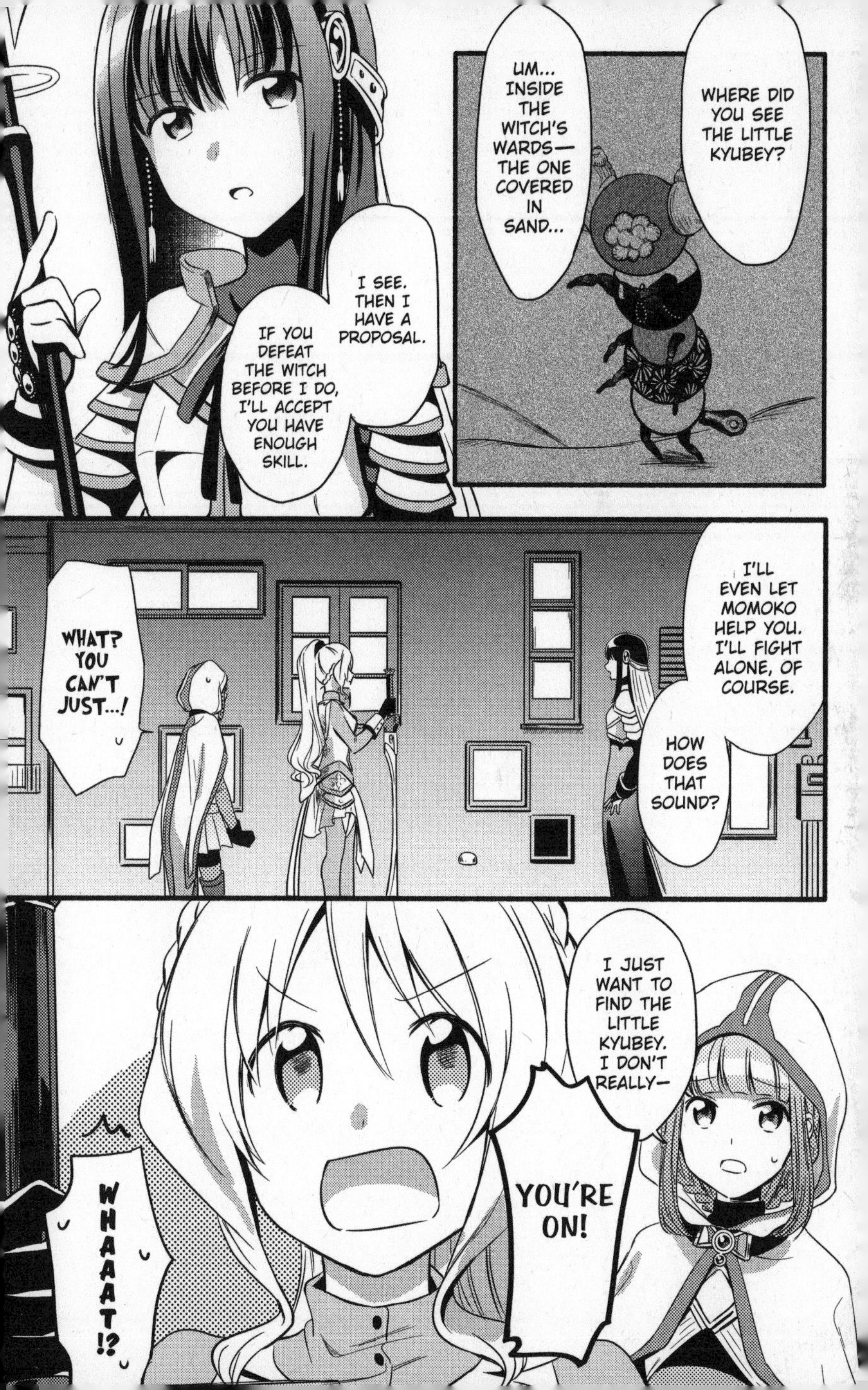
WHERE DID YOU SEE THE LITTLE KYUBEY?
UM... INSIDE THE WITCH'S WARDS—THE ONE COVERED IN SAND...
I SEE. THEN I HAVE A PROPOSAL.
IF YOU DEFEAT THE WITCH BEFORE I DO, I'LL ACCEPT YOU HAVE ENOUGH SKILL.
I'LL EVEN LET MOMOKO HELP YOU. I'LL FIGHT ALONE, OF COURSE.
HOW DOES THAT SOUND?
WHAT? YOU CAN'T JUST...!
I JUST WANT TO FIND THE LITTLE KYUBEY. I DON'T REALLY—
YOU'RE ON!
WHAAAT!?

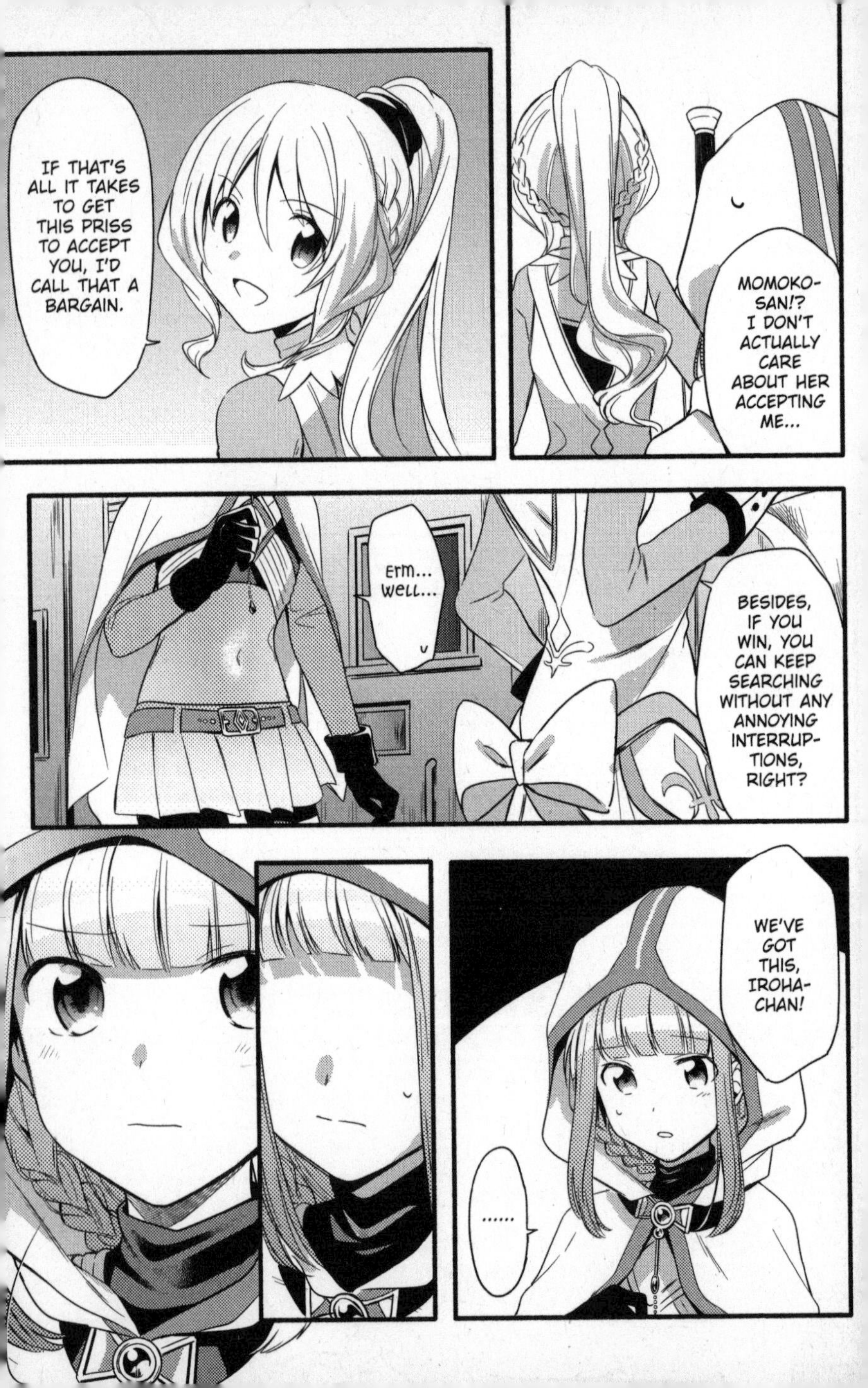
MOMOKO-SAN!? I DON'T ACTUALLY CARE ABOUT HER ACCEPTING ME...
IF THAT'S ALL IT TAKES TO GET THIS PRISS TO ACCEPT YOU, I'D CALL THAT A BARGAIN.
BESIDES, IF YOU WIN, YOU CAN KEEP SEARCHING WITHOUT ANY ANNOYING INTERRUP-TIONS, RIGHT?
Erm... well...
WE'VE GOT THIS, IROHA-CHAN!
......

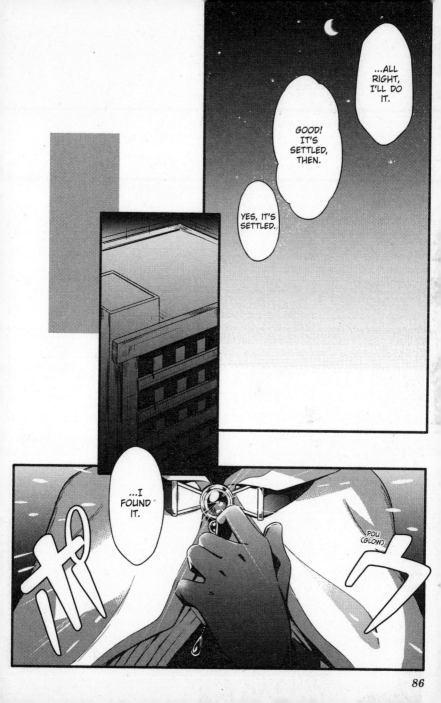

...ALL RIGHT, I'LL DO IT.

GOOD! IT'S SETTLED, THEN.

YES, IT'S SETTLED.

...I FOUND IT.

POU (GLOW)

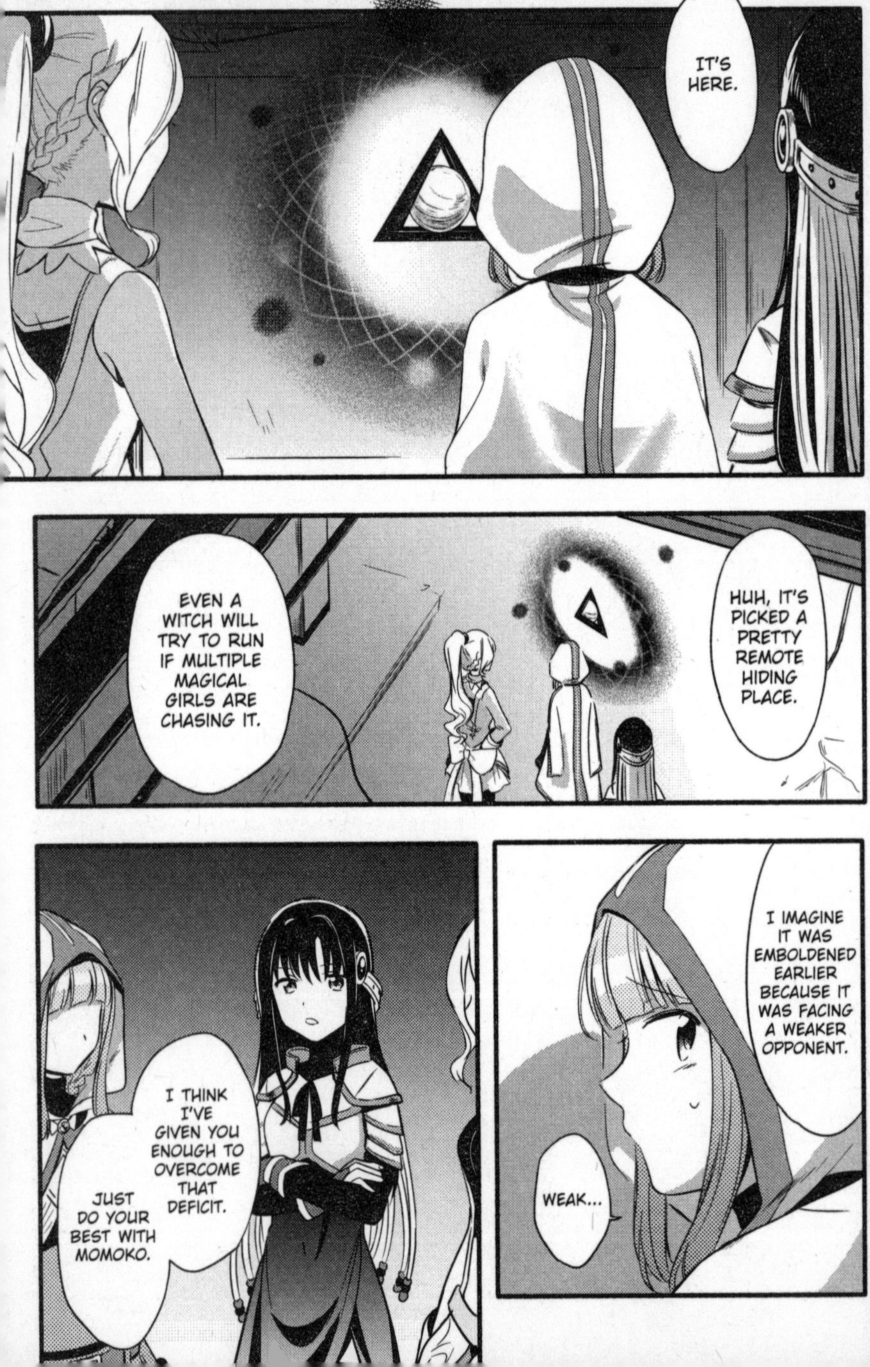
IT'S HERE.
HUH, IT'S PICKED A PRETTY REMOTE HIDING PLACE.
EVEN A WITCH WILL TRY TO RUN IF MULTIPLE MAGICAL GIRLS ARE CHASING IT.
I IMAGINE IT WAS EMBOLDENED EARLIER BECAUSE IT WAS FACING A WEAKER OPPONENT.
WEAK...
I THINK I'VE GIVEN YOU ENOUGH TO OVERCOME THAT DEFICIT.
JUST DO YOUR BEST WITH MOMOKO.

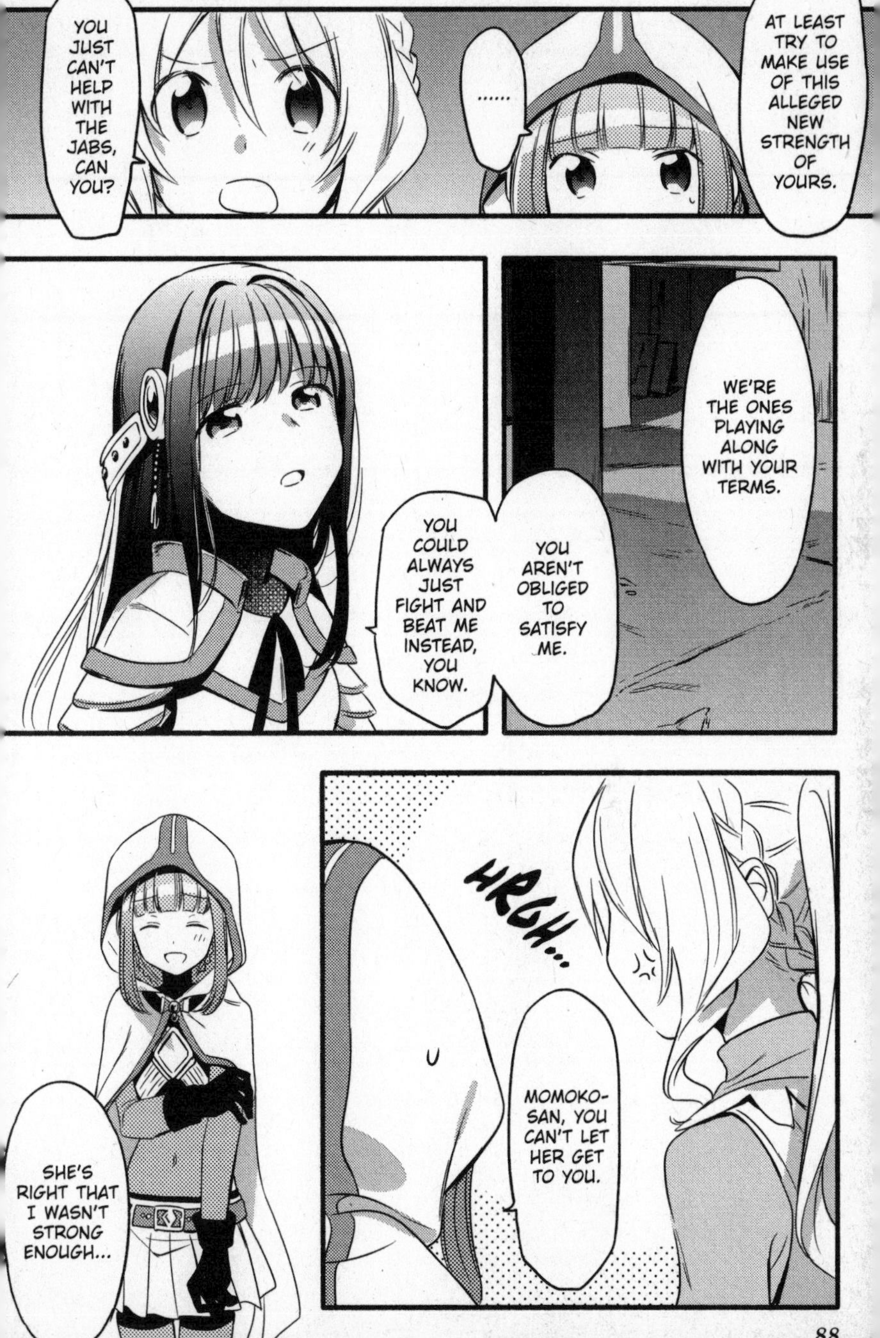
AT LEAST TRY TO MAKE USE OF THIS ALLEGED NEW STRENGTH OF YOURS.
......
YOU JUST CAN'T HELP WITH THE JABS, CAN YOU?
WE'RE THE ONES PLAYING ALONG WITH YOUR TERMS.
YOU AREN'T OBLIGED TO SATISFY ME.
YOU COULD ALWAYS JUST FIGHT AND BEAT ME INSTEAD, YOU KNOW.
HRGH...
MOMOKO-SAN, YOU CAN'T LET HER GET TO YOU.
SHE'S RIGHT THAT I WASN'T STRONG ENOUGH...

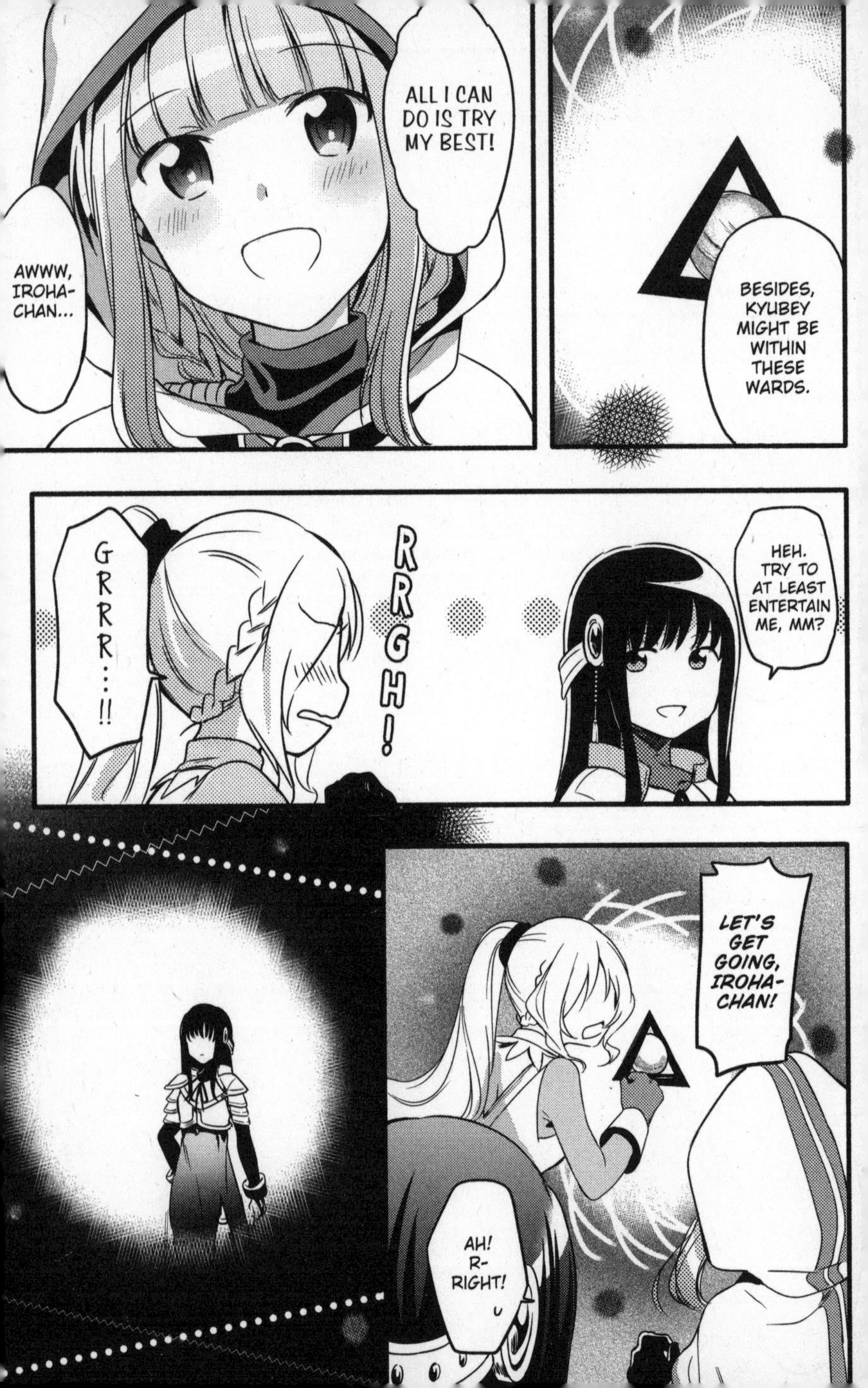
BESIDES, KYUBEY MIGHT BE WITHIN THESE WARDS.
ALL I CAN DO IS TRY MY BEST!
AWWW, IROHA-CHAN...
HEH. TRY TO AT LEAST ENTERTAIN ME, MM?
RRRGH!
GRRR...!!
LET'S GET GOING, IROHA-CHAN!
AH! R-RIGHT!

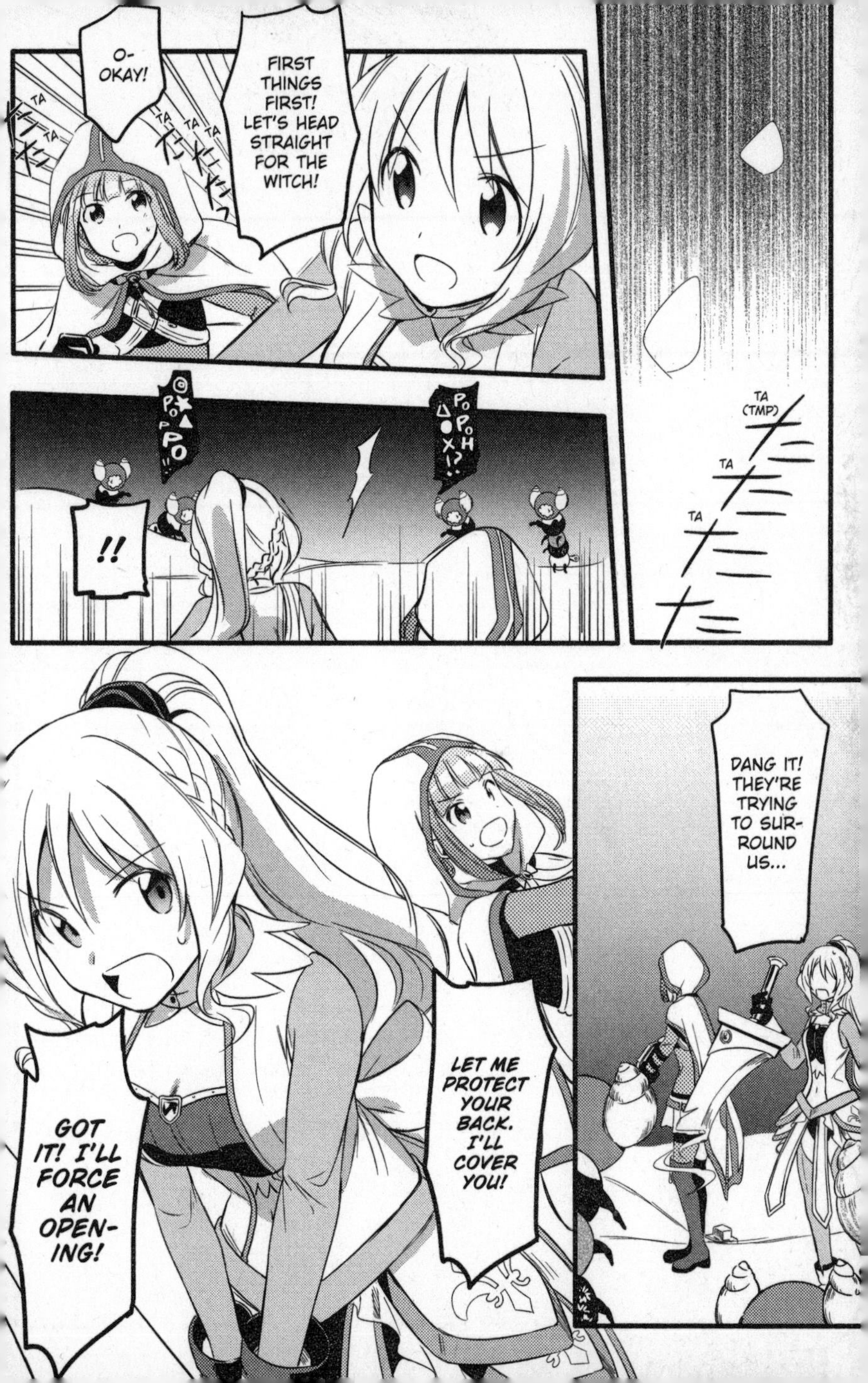
TA (TMP)
TA
TA
FIRST THINGS FIRST! LET'S HEAD STRAIGHT FOR THE WITCH!
O-OKAY!
TA TA TA TA TA
POPOH △○×!?!
©☆▲ POPPO!!
!!
DANG IT! THEY'RE TRYING TO SUR-ROUND US...
LET ME PROTECT YOUR BACK. I'LL COVER YOU!
GOT IT! I'LL FORCE AN OPEN-ING!

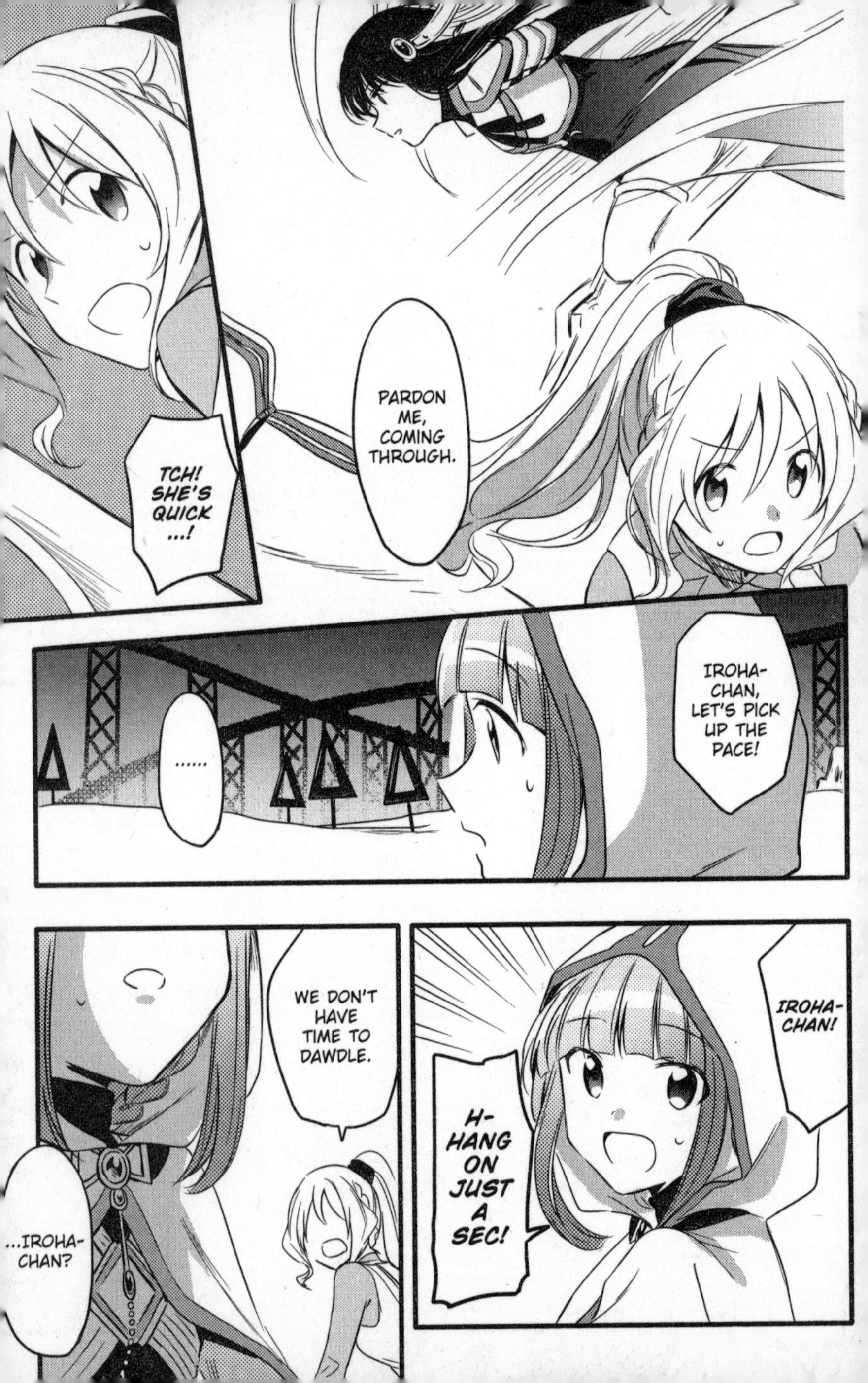
PARDON ME, COMING THROUGH.
TCH! SHE'S QUICK ...!
IROHA-CHAN, LET'S PICK UP THE PACE!
......
IROHA-CHAN!
H-HANG ON JUST A SEC!
WE DON'T HAVE TIME TO DAWDLE.
...IROHA-CHAN?

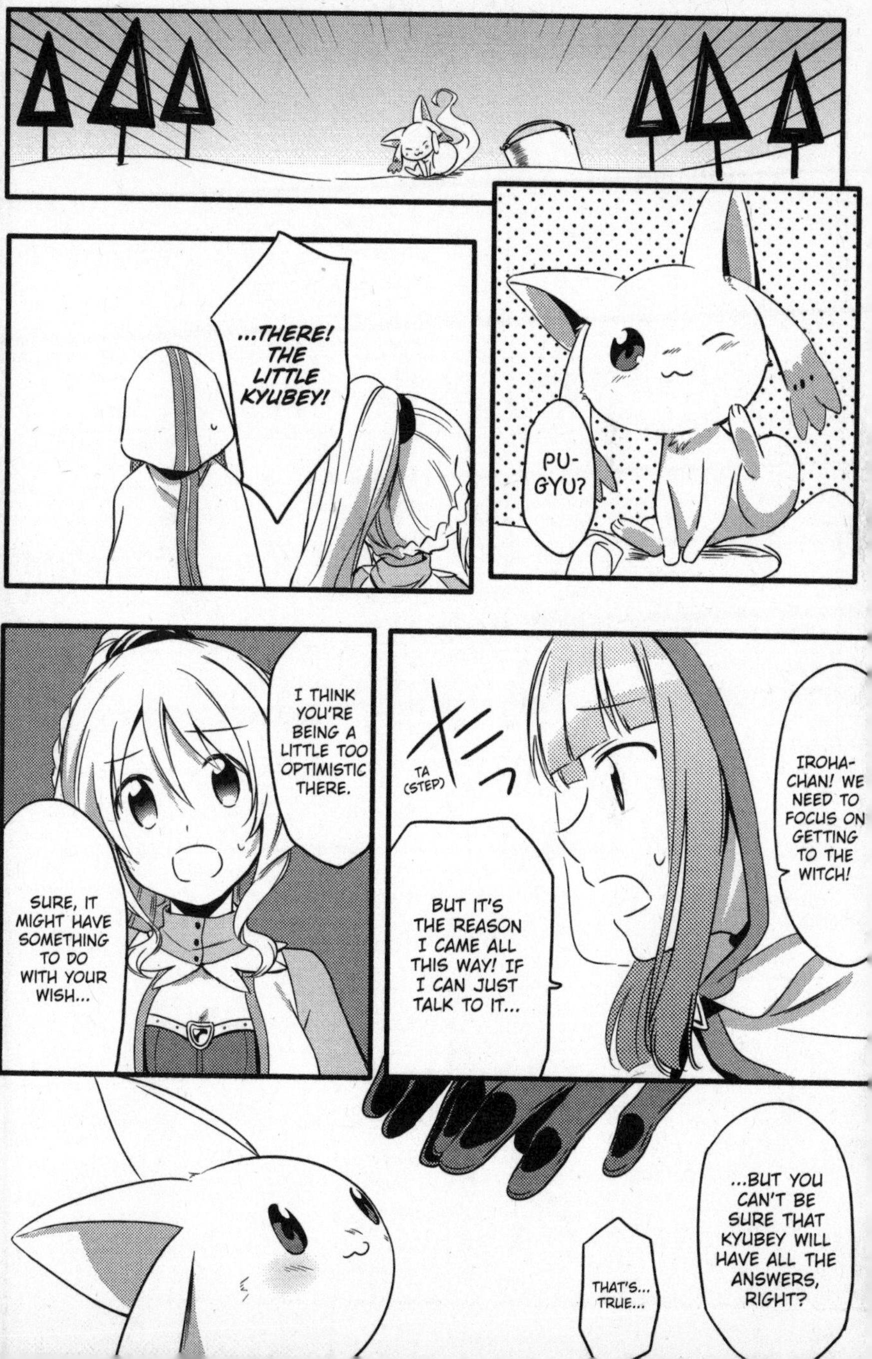
PU-GYU?
...THERE! THE LITTLE KYUBEY!
IROHA-CHAN! WE NEED TO FOCUS ON GETTING TO THE WITCH!
TA (STEP)
BUT IT'S THE REASON I CAME ALL THIS WAY! IF I CAN JUST TALK TO IT...
I THINK YOU'RE BEING A LITTLE TOO OPTIMISTIC THERE.
SURE, IT MIGHT HAVE SOMETHING TO DO WITH YOUR WISH...
...BUT YOU CAN'T BE SURE THAT KYUBEY WILL HAVE ALL THE ANSWERS, RIGHT?
THAT'S... TRUE...

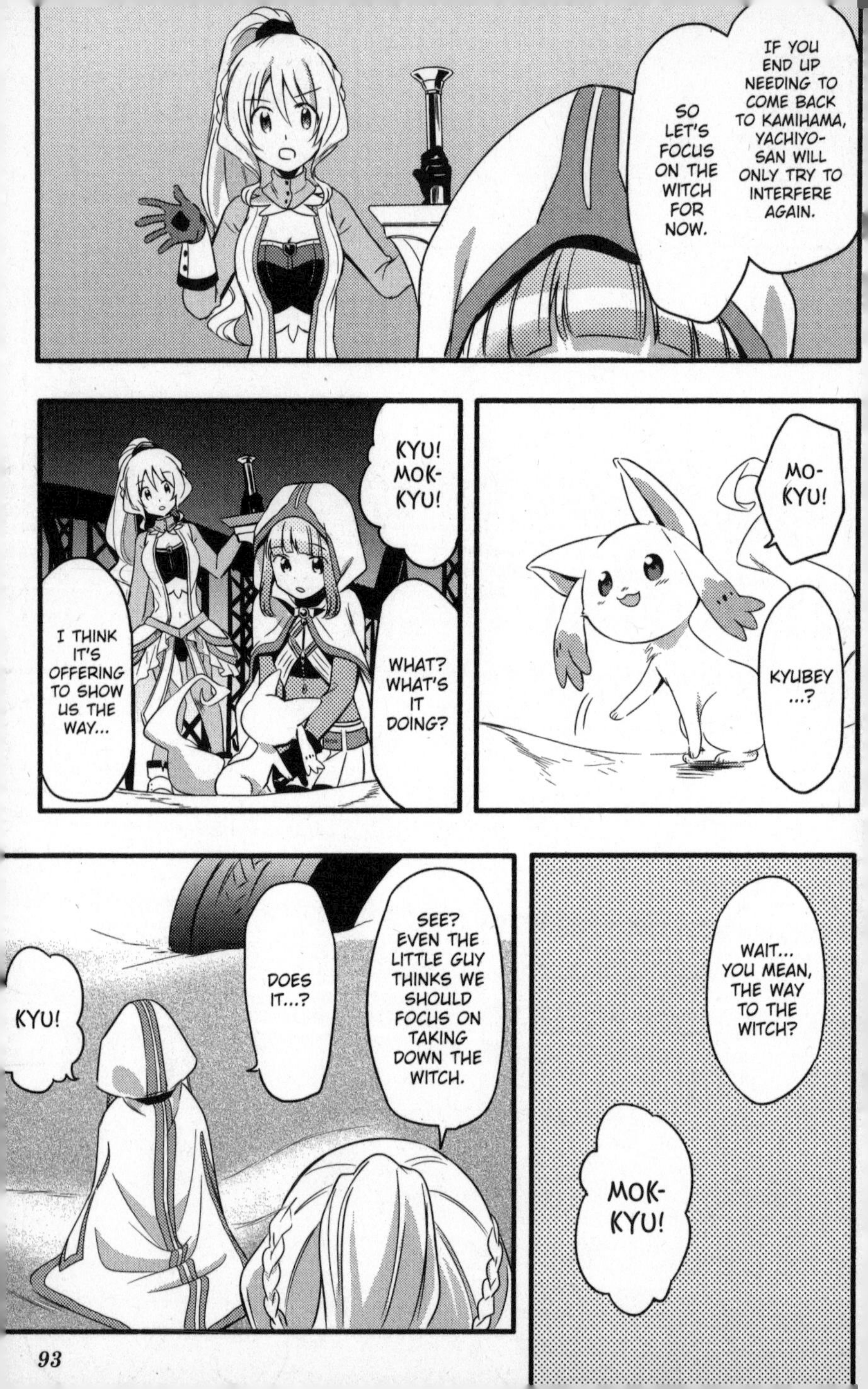
IF YOU END UP NEEDING TO COME BACK TO KAMIHAMA, YACHIYO-SAN WILL ONLY TRY TO INTERFERE AGAIN.
SO LET'S FOCUS ON THE WITCH FOR NOW.
MO-KYU!
KYUBEY ...?
KYU! MOK-KYU!
WHAT? WHAT'S IT DOING?
I THINK IT'S OFFERING TO SHOW US THE WAY...
WAIT... YOU MEAN, THE WAY TO THE WITCH?
MOK-KYU!
SEE? EVEN THE LITTLE GUY THINKS WE SHOULD FOCUS ON TAKING DOWN THE WITCH.
DOES IT...?
KYU!

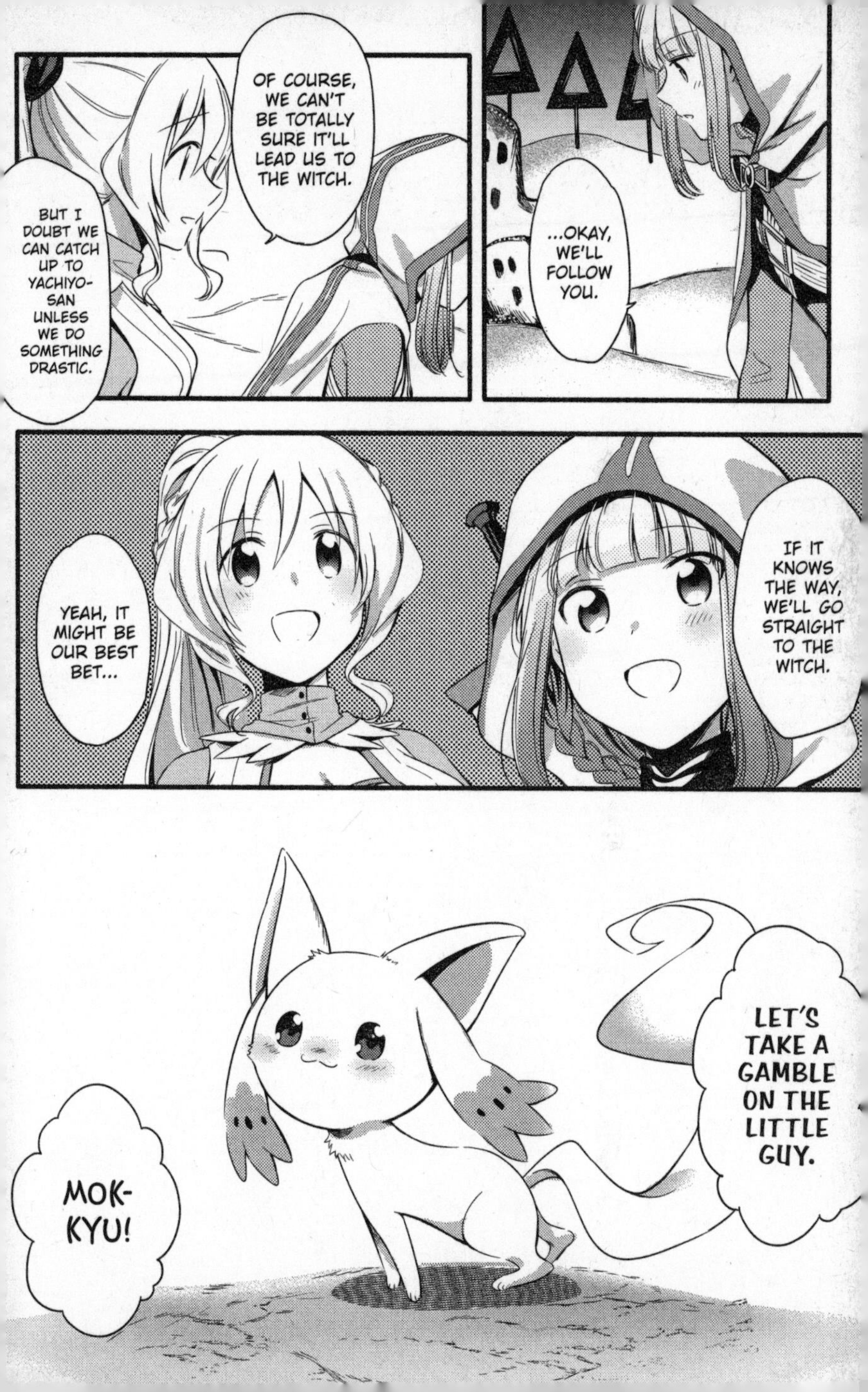
...OKAY, WE'LL FOLLOW YOU.
OF COURSE, WE CAN'T BE TOTALLY SURE IT'LL LEAD US TO THE WITCH.
BUT I DOUBT WE CAN CATCH UP TO YACHIYO-SAN UNLESS WE DO SOMETHING DRASTIC.
IF IT KNOWS THE WAY, WE'LL GO STRAIGHT TO THE WITCH.
YEAH, IT MIGHT BE OUR BEST BET...
LET'S TAKE A GAMBLE ON THE LITTLE GUY.
MOK-KYU!

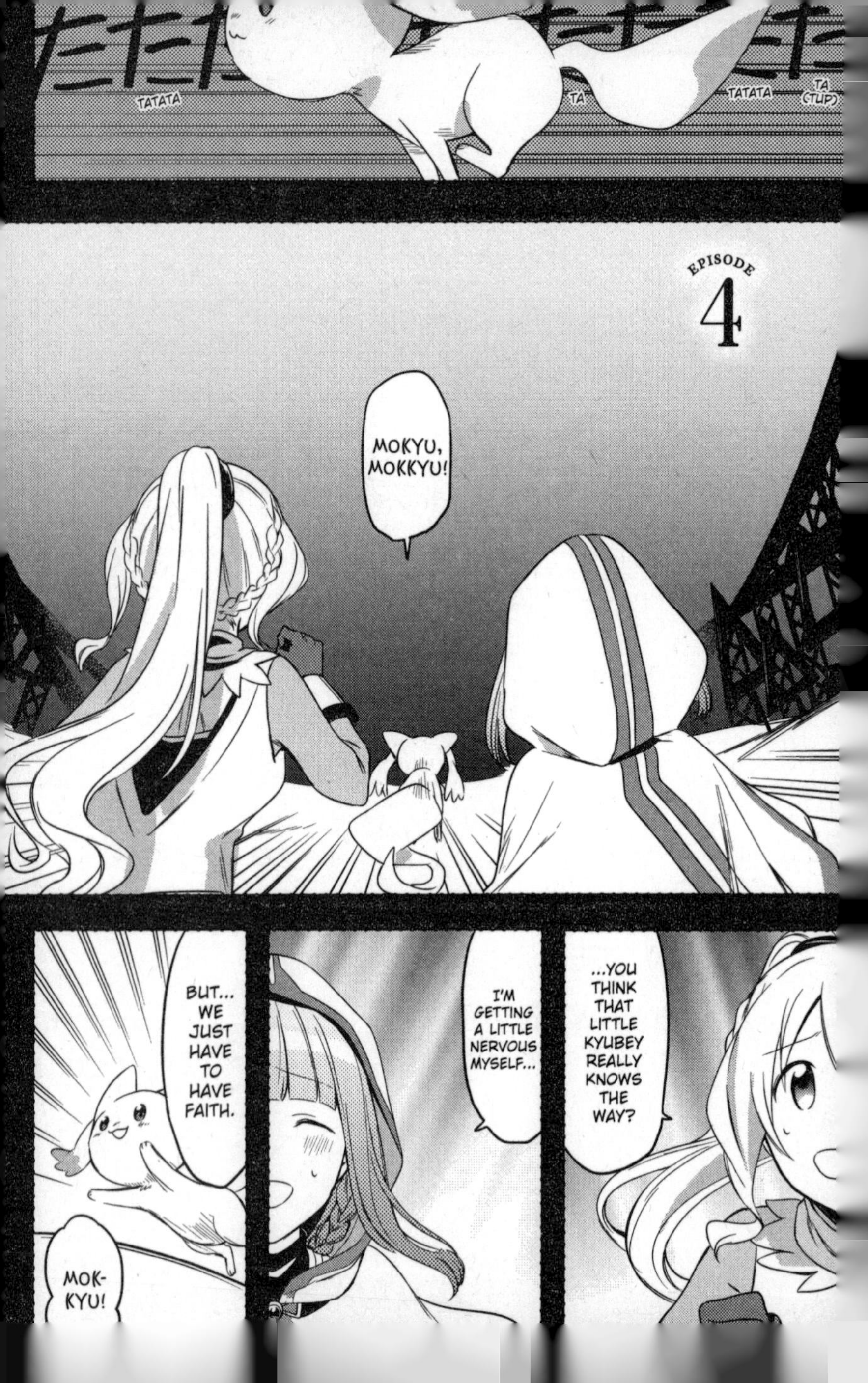
TA (TUP)
TATATA
TA
TATATA
EPISODE 4
MOKYU, MOKKYU!
...YOU THINK THAT LITTLE KYUBEY REALLY KNOWS THE WAY?
I'M GETTING A LITTLE NERVOUS MYSELF...
BUT... WE JUST HAVE TO HAVE FAITH.
MOK-KYU!

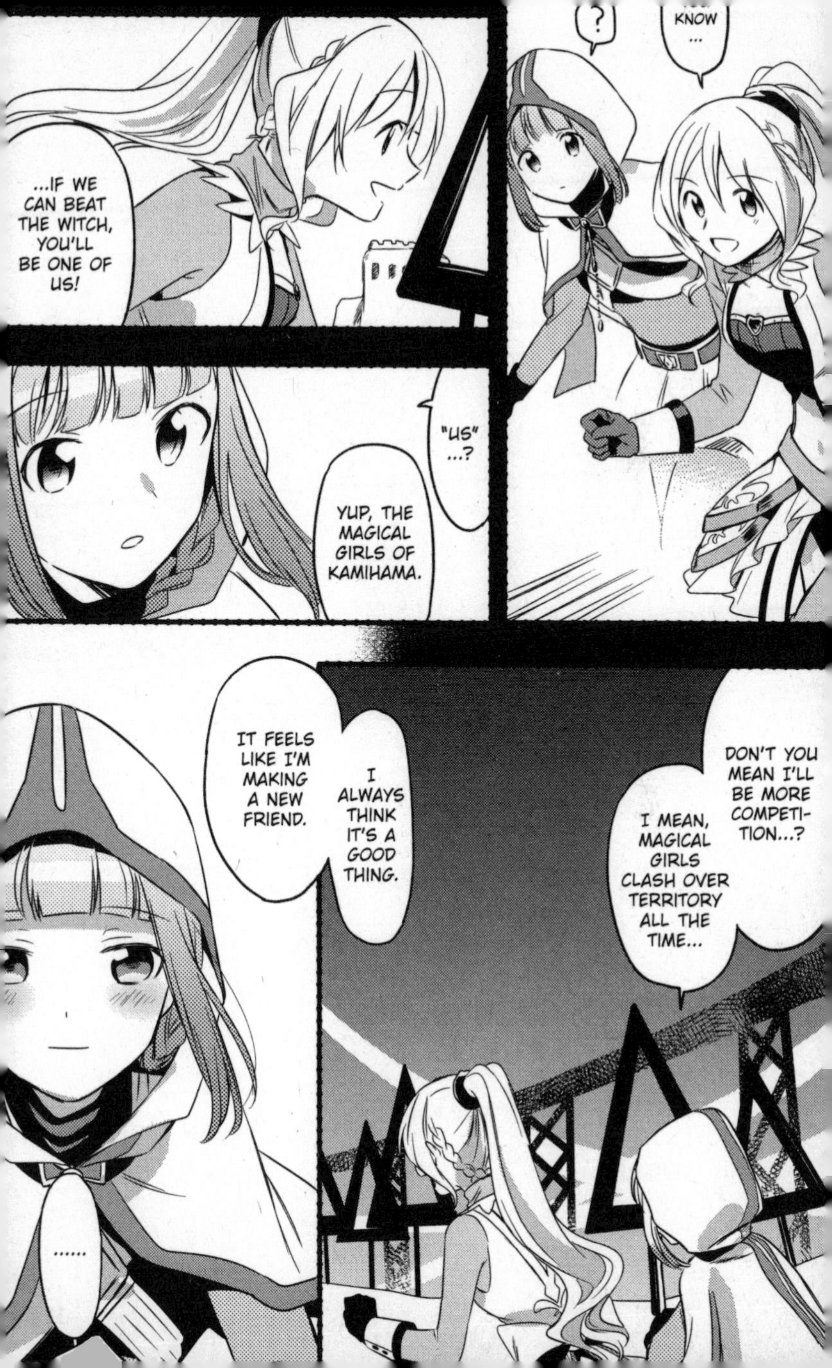
?
KNOW ...
...IF WE CAN BEAT THE WITCH, YOU'LL BE ONE OF US!
"US" ...?
YUP, THE MAGICAL GIRLS OF KAMIHAMA.
DON'T YOU MEAN I'LL BE MORE COMPETITION...?
I MEAN, MAGICAL GIRLS CLASH OVER TERRITORY ALL THE TIME...
I ALWAYS THINK IT'S A GOOD THING.
IT FEELS LIKE I'M MAKING A NEW FRIEND.
......

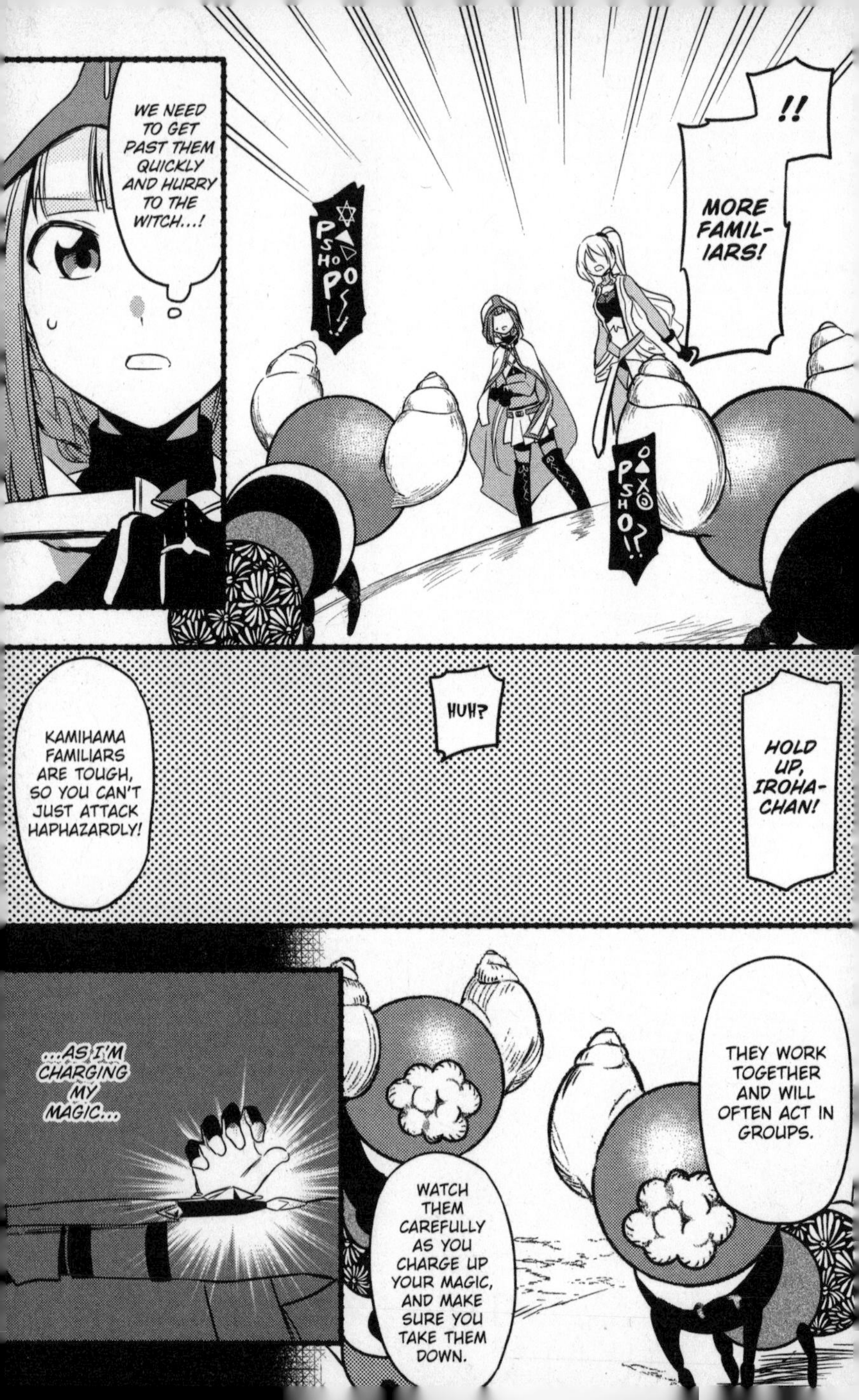
!!
MORE FAMIL-IARS!
WE NEED TO GET PAST THEM QUICKLY AND HURRY TO THE WITCH...!
HOLD UP, IROHA-CHAN!
HUH?
KAMIHAMA FAMILIARS ARE TOUGH, SO YOU CAN'T JUST ATTACK HAPHAZARDLY!
THEY WORK TOGETHER AND WILL OFTEN ACT IN GROUPS.
WATCH THEM CAREFULLY AS YOU CHARGE UP YOUR MAGIC, AND MAKE SURE YOU TAKE THEM DOWN.
...AS I'M CHARGING MY MAGIC...

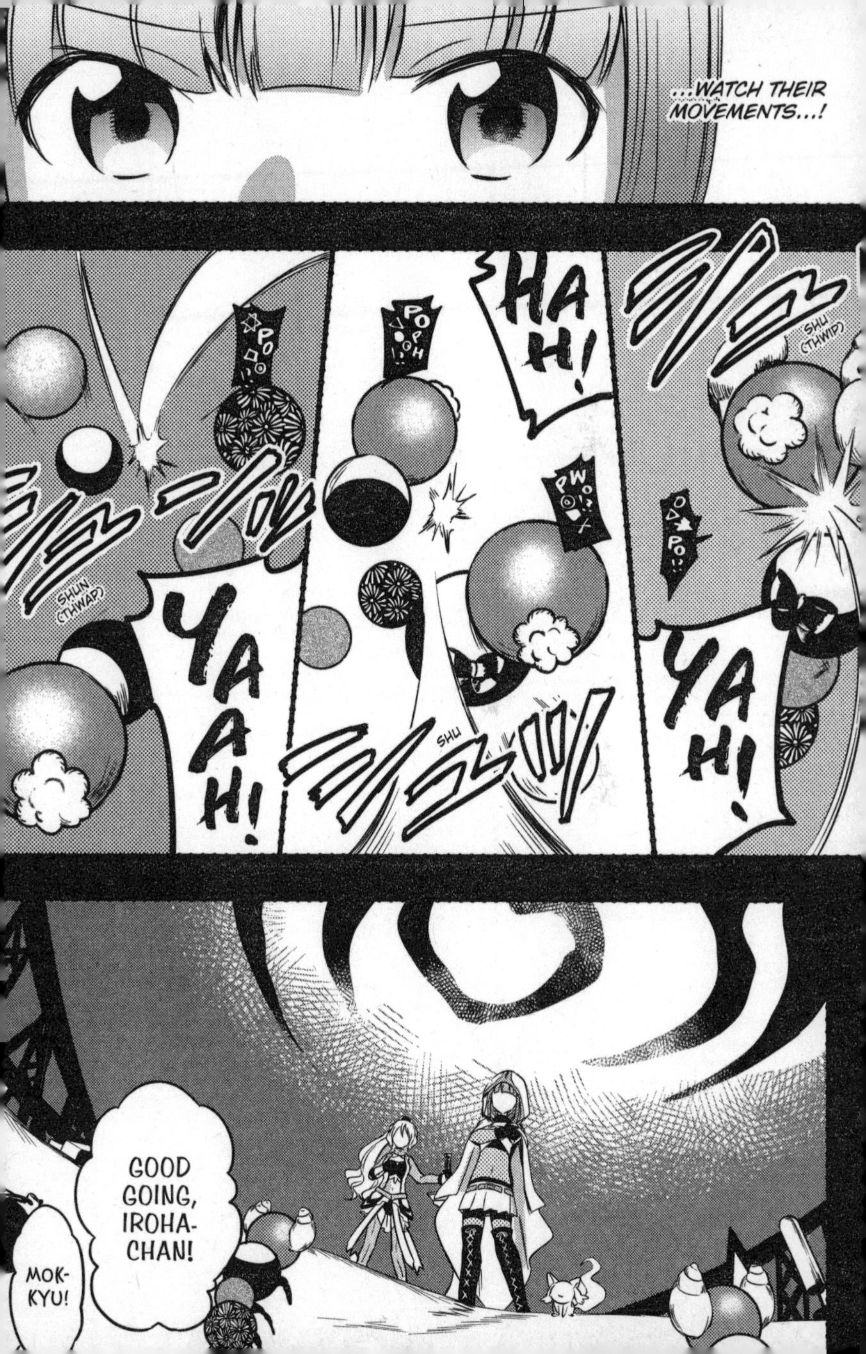
...WATCH THEIR MOVEMENTS...!
SHU (THWIP)
PO!!
YAH!
HAH!
PWO!!
SHU
POPOH!!
PO!!
SHUN (THWAP)
YAAAH!
GOOD GOING, IROHA-CHAN!
MOK-KYU!

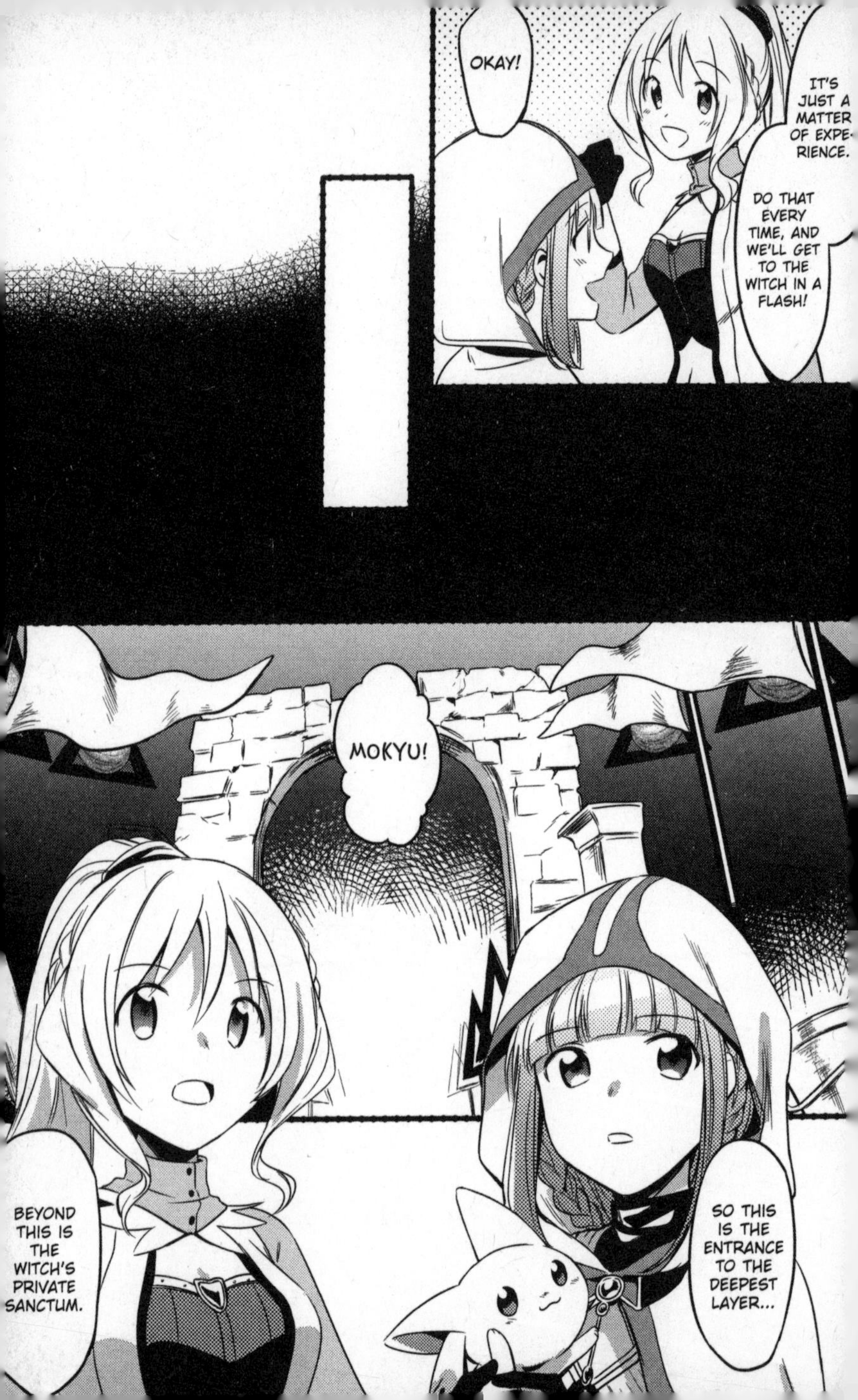
IT'S JUST A MATTER OF EXPERIENCE.
DO THAT EVERY TIME, AND WE'LL GET TO THE WITCH IN A FLASH!
OKAY!
MOKYU!
SO THIS IS THE ENTRANCE TO THE DEEPEST LAYER...
BEYOND THIS IS THE WITCH'S PRIVATE SANCTUM.

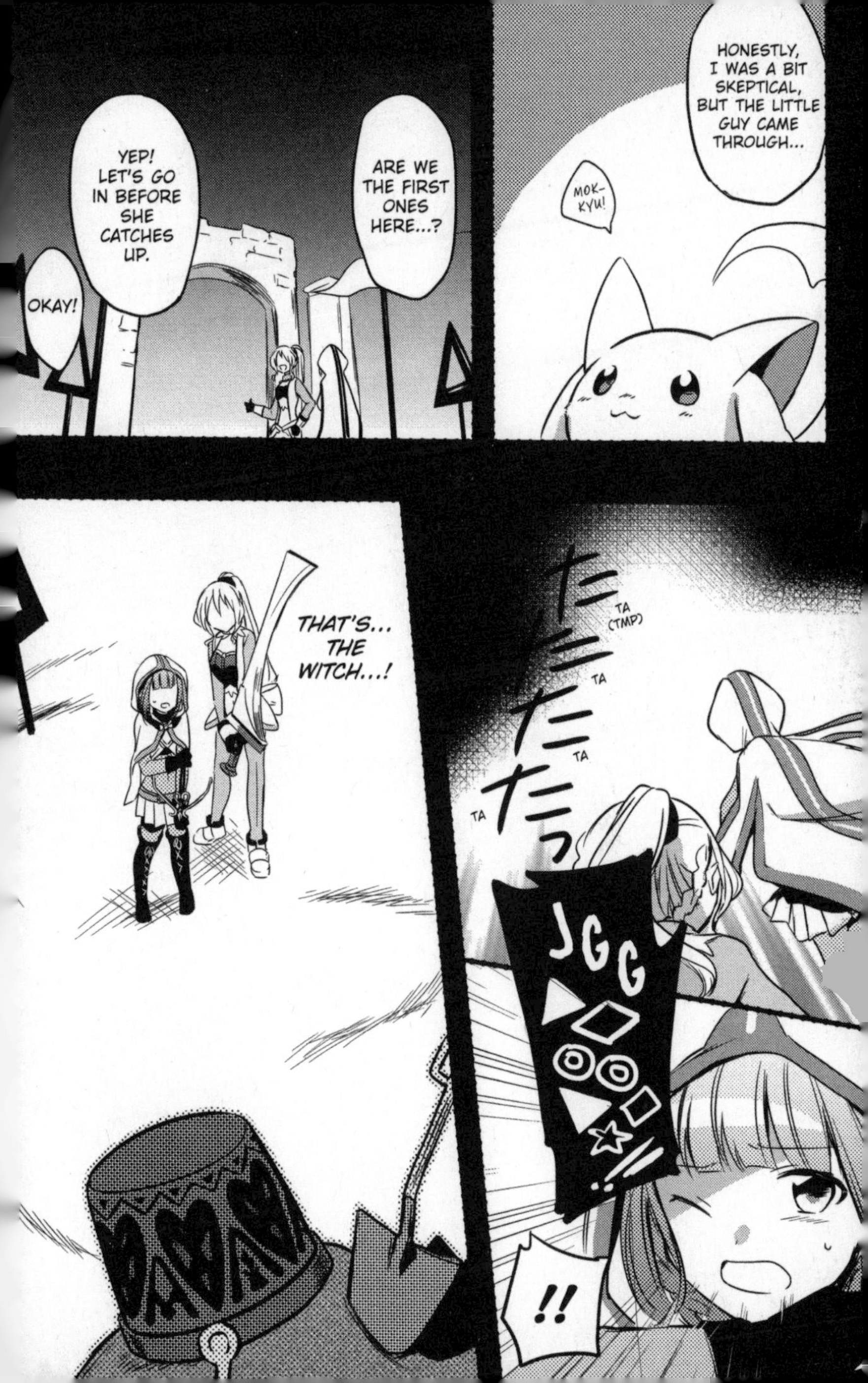
HONESTLY, I WAS A BIT SKEPTICAL, BUT THE LITTLE GUY CAME THROUGH...
MOK-KYU!
ARE WE THE FIRST ONES HERE...?
YEP! LET'S GO IN BEFORE SHE CATCHES UP.
OKAY!
TA (TMP)
TA
TA
TA
JGG
!!
THAT'S... THE WITCH...!

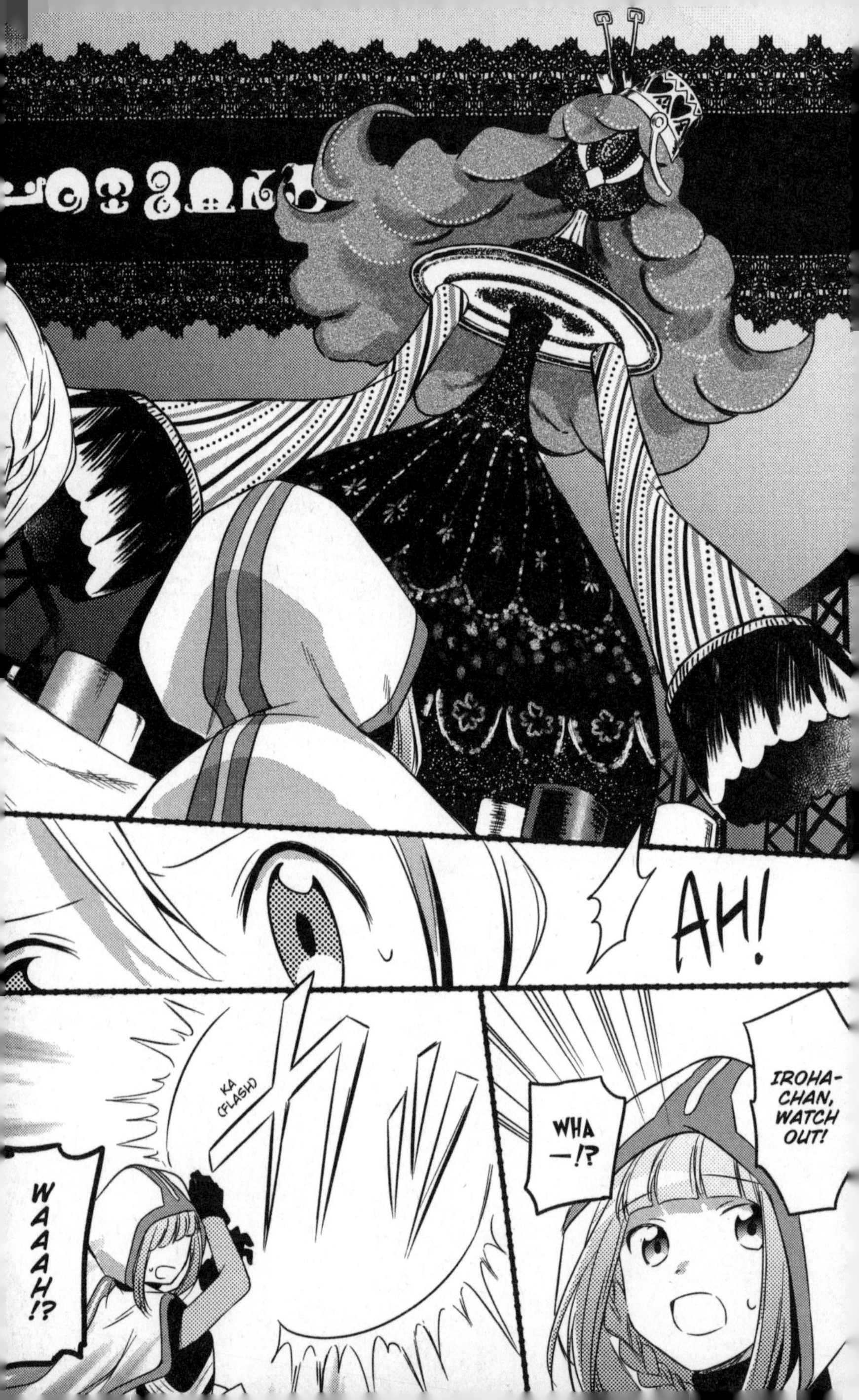
AH!
IROHA-CHAN, WATCH OUT!
WHA—!?
KA (FLASH)
WAAAAH!?

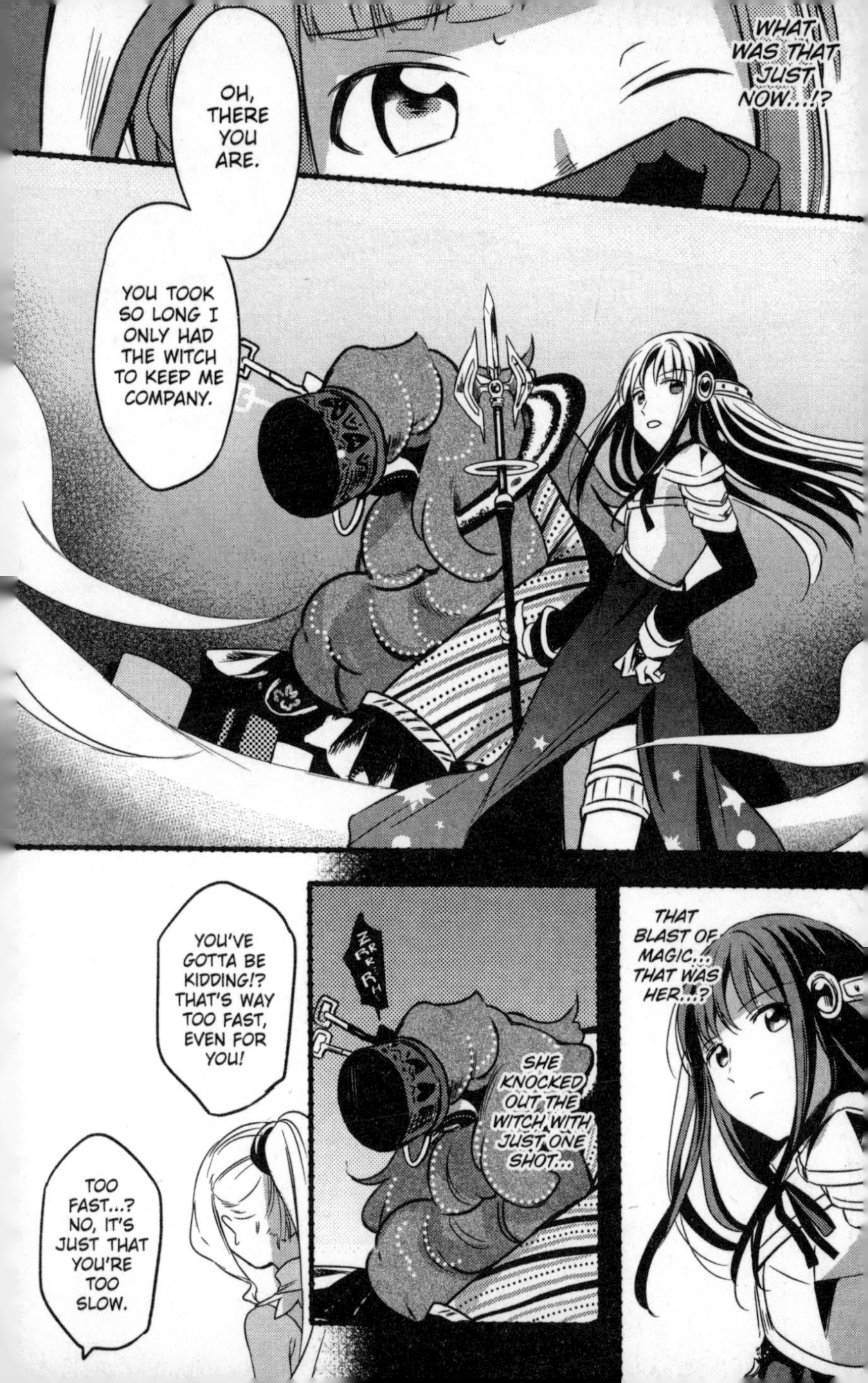
WHAT WAS THAT JUST NOW...!?
OH, THERE YOU ARE.
YOU TOOK SO LONG I ONLY HAD THE WITCH TO KEEP ME COMPANY.
THAT BLAST OF MAGIC... THAT WAS HER...?
ZRRRH
SHE KNOCKED OUT THE WITCH WITH JUST ONE SHOT...
YOU'VE GOTTA BE KIDDING!? THAT'S WAY TOO FAST, EVEN FOR YOU!
TOO FAST...? NO, IT'S JUST THAT YOU'RE TOO SLOW.

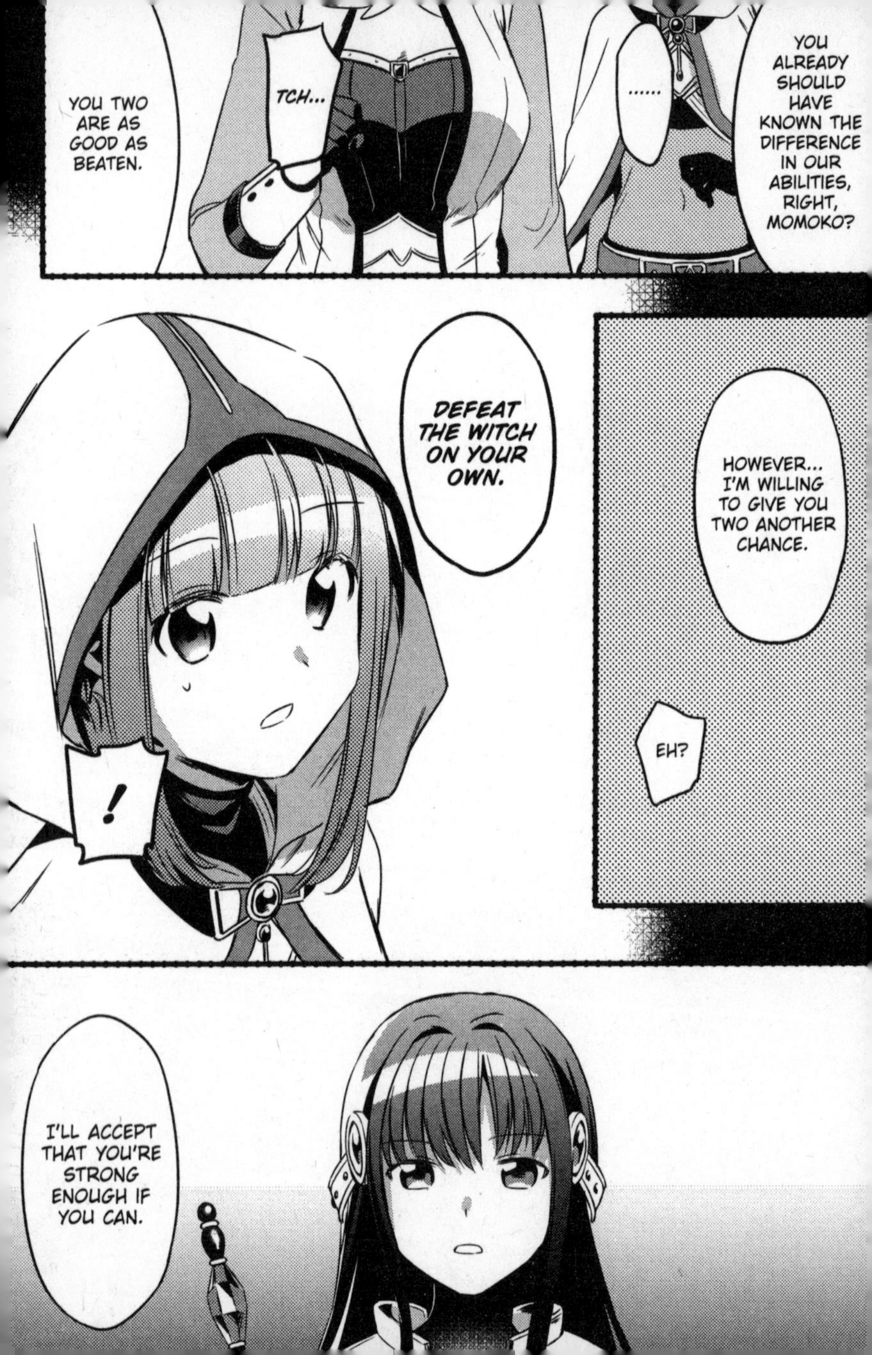
YOU ALREADY SHOULD HAVE KNOWN THE DIFFERENCE IN OUR ABILITIES, RIGHT, MOMOKO?
......
TCH...
YOU TWO ARE AS GOOD AS BEATEN.
HOWEVER... I'M WILLING TO GIVE YOU TWO ANOTHER CHANCE.
EH?
DEFEAT THE WITCH ON YOUR OWN.
!
I'LL ACCEPT THAT YOU'RE STRONG ENOUGH IF YOU CAN.

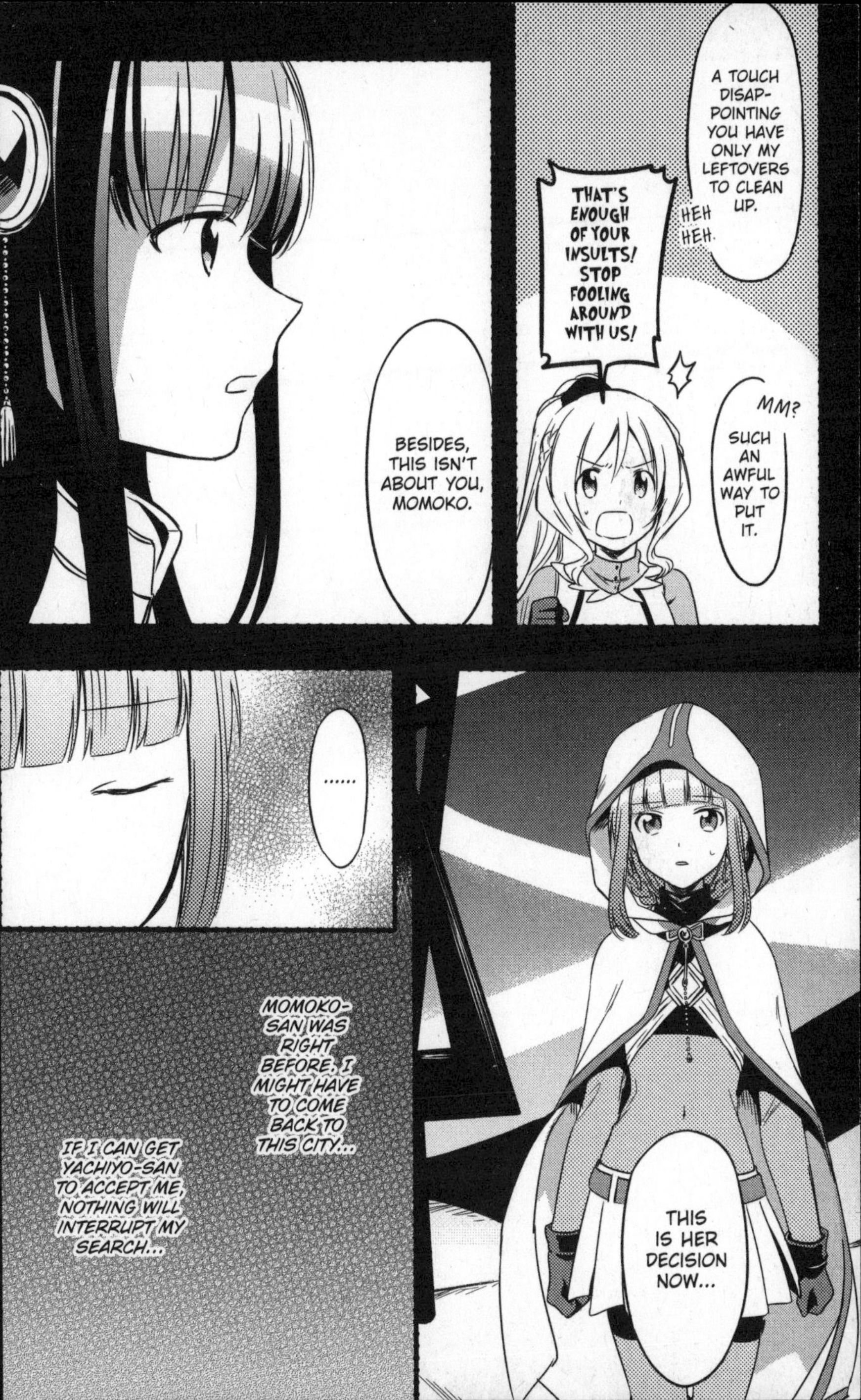
A TOUCH DISAPPOINTING YOU HAVE ONLY MY LEFTOVERS TO CLEAN UP.
HEH HEH.
THAT'S ENOUGH OF YOUR INSULTS! STOP FOOLING AROUND WITH US!
MM? SUCH AN AWFUL WAY TO PUT IT.
BESIDES, THIS ISN'T ABOUT YOU, MOMOKO.
THIS IS HER DECISION NOW...
......
MOMOKO-SAN WAS RIGHT BEFORE. I MIGHT HAVE TO COME BACK TO THIS CITY...
IF I CAN GET YACHIYO-SAN TO ACCEPT ME, NOTHING WILL INTERRUPT MY SEARCH...

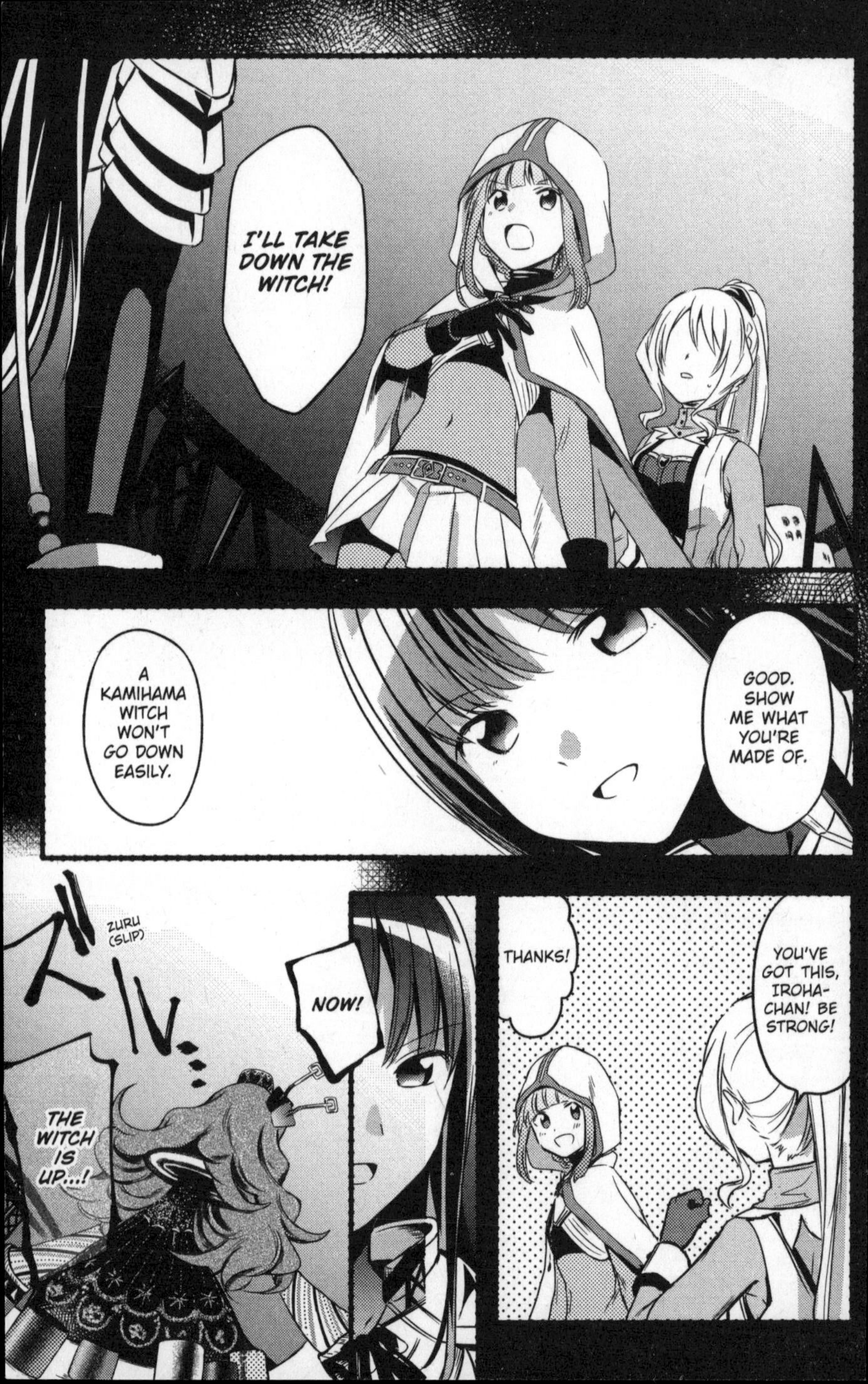
I'LL TAKE DOWN THE WITCH!
GOOD. SHOW ME WHAT YOU'RE MADE OF.
A KAMIHAMA WITCH WON'T GO DOWN EASILY.
YOU'VE GOT THIS, IROHA-CHAN! BE STRONG!
THANKS!
NOW!
ZURU (SLIP)
THE WITCH IS UP...!

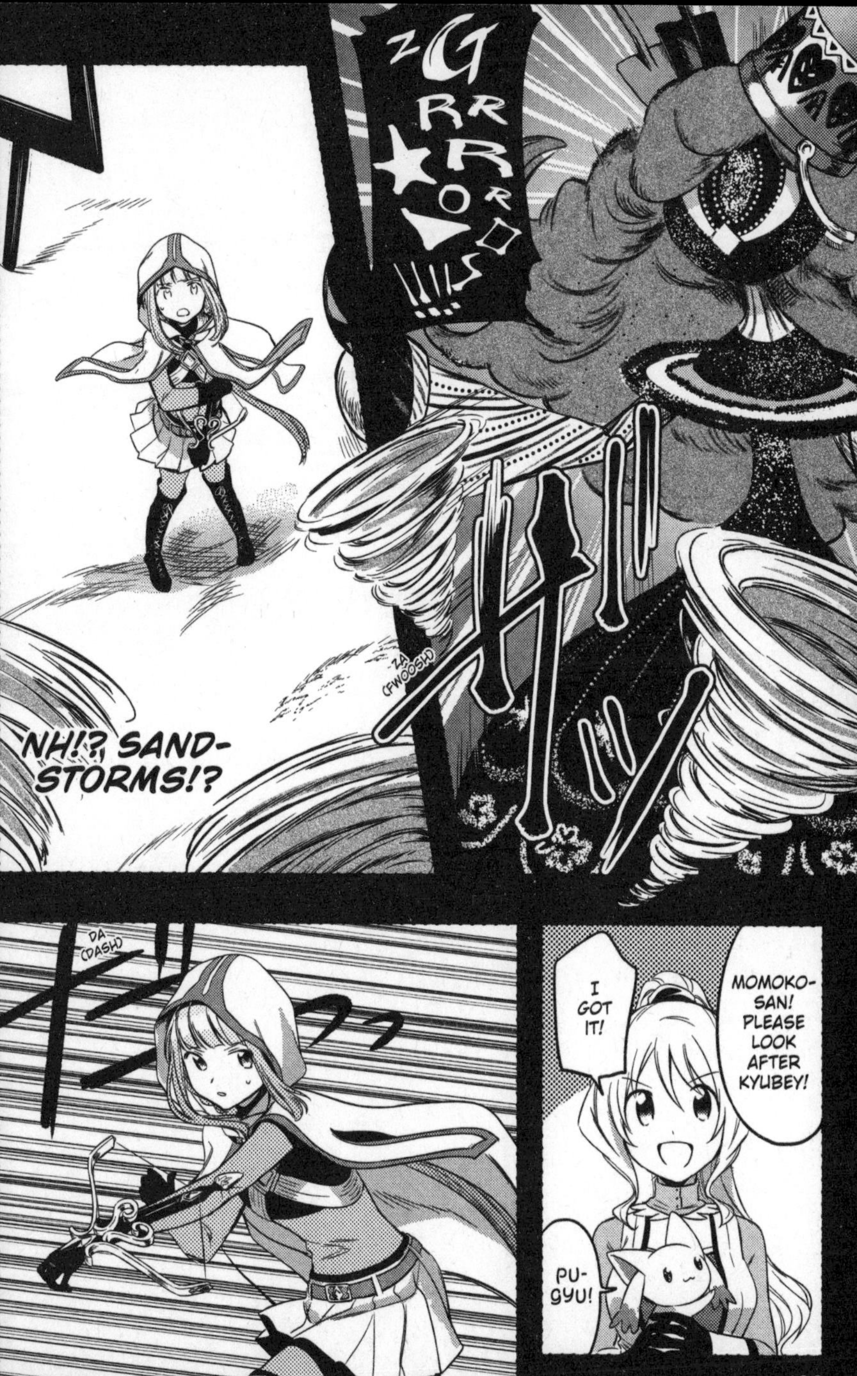
ZGRRRORS!!!
ZA (FWOOSH)
NH!?, SAND-STORMS!?
MOMOKO-SAN! PLEASE LOOK AFTER KYUBEY!
I GOT IT!
PU-GYU!
DA (DASH)

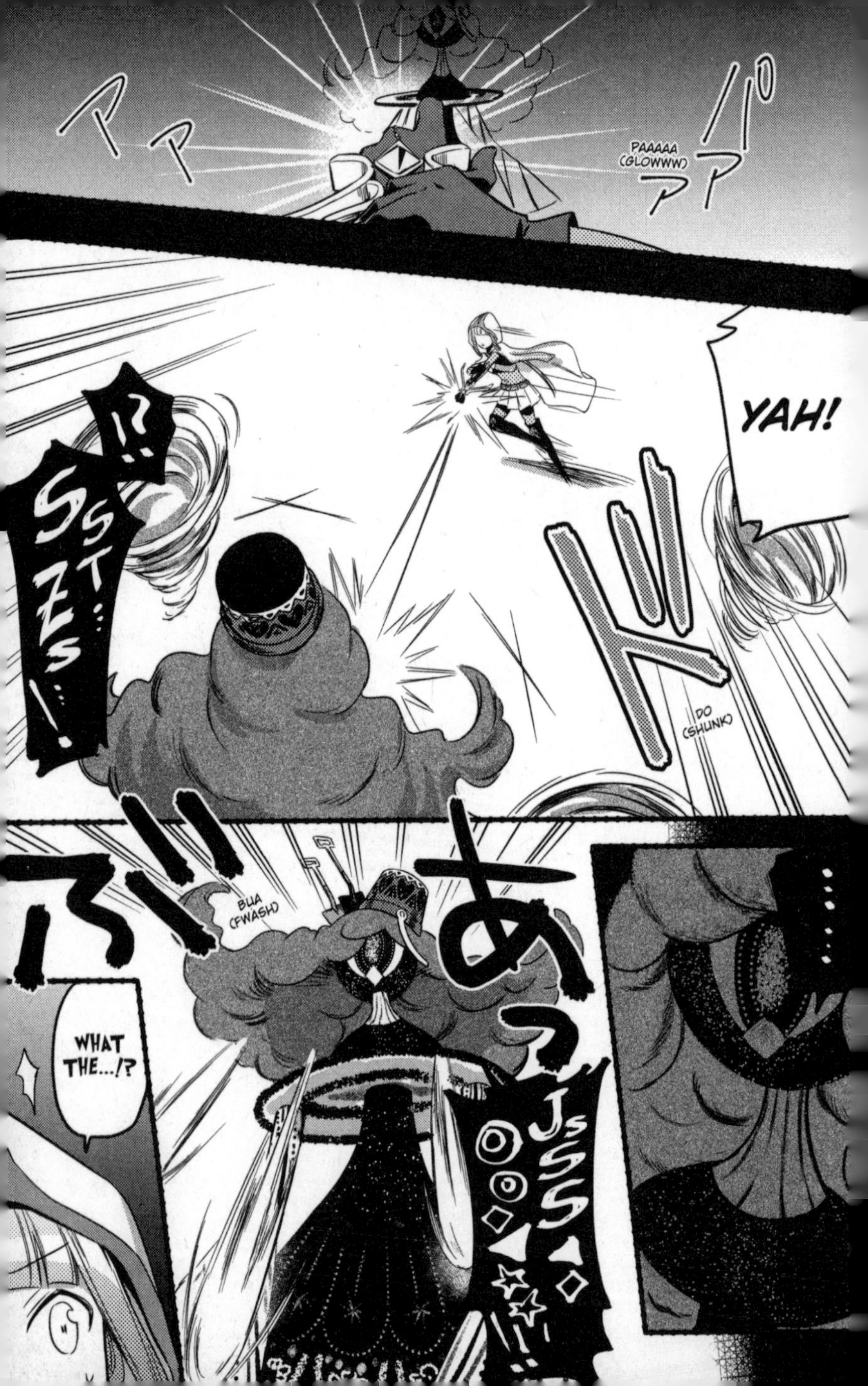
PAAAAA (GLOWWW)
YAH!
DO (SHUNK)
SSST... ZZS...!
!?
......
BUA (FWASH)
WHAT THE...!?
JSSS...!!

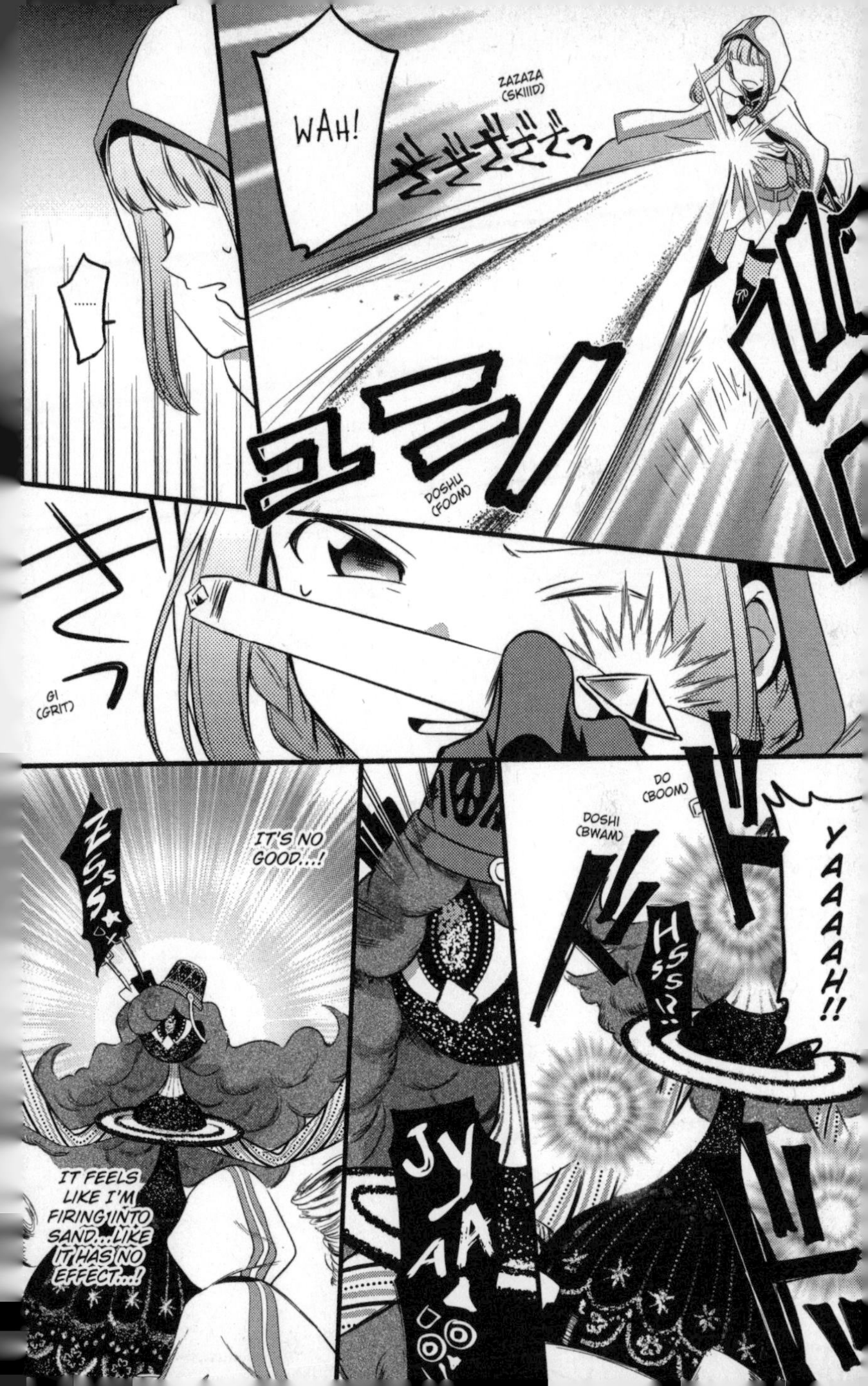

WAH!
ZAZAZA (SKIIID)
DOSHU (FOOM)
......
GI (GRIT)
DO (BOOM)
DOSHI (BWAM)
YAAAAAH!!
HSSS?!
JYA
IT'S NO GOOD...!
IT FEELS LIKE I'M FIRING INTO SAND... LIKE IT HAS NO EFFECT...!
ZSSS

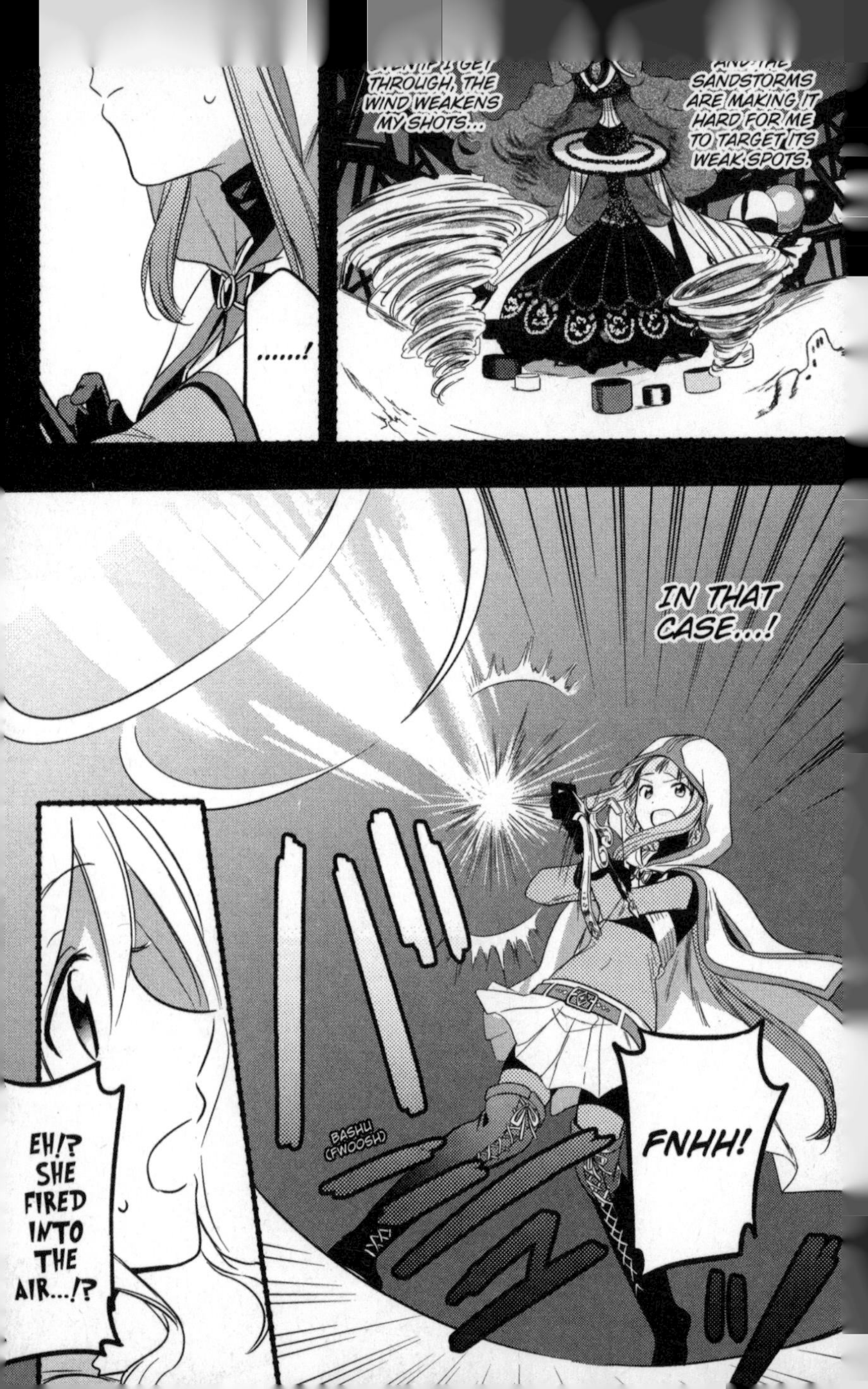
THROUGH, THE WIND WEAKENS MY SHOTS...
SANDSTORMS ARE MAKING IT HARD FOR ME TO TARGET ITS WEAK SPOTS.
......!
IN THAT CASE...!
FNHH!
BASHU (FWOOSH)
EH!? SHE FIRED INTO THE AIR...!?

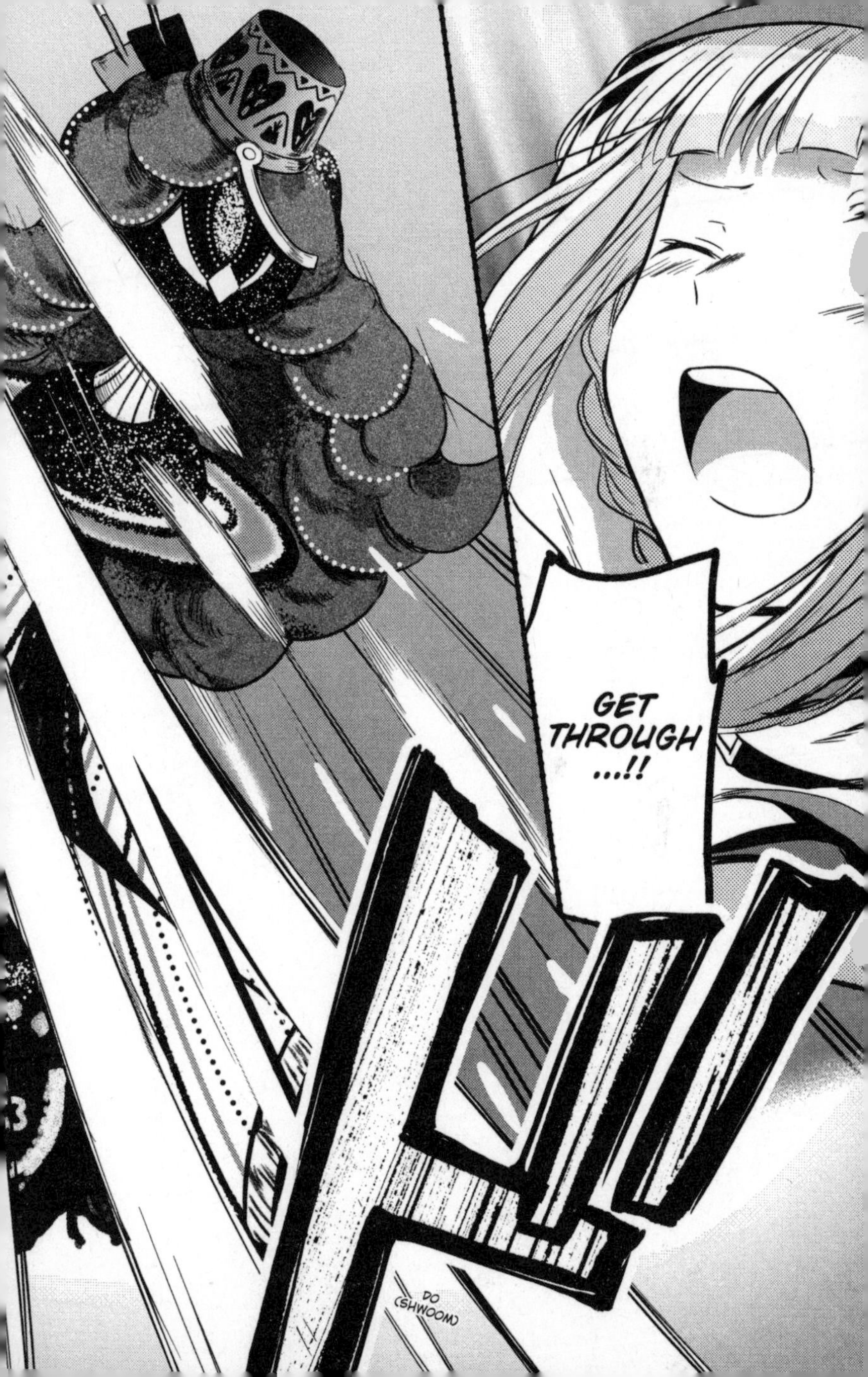
GET THROUGH ...!!
DO (SHWOOM)

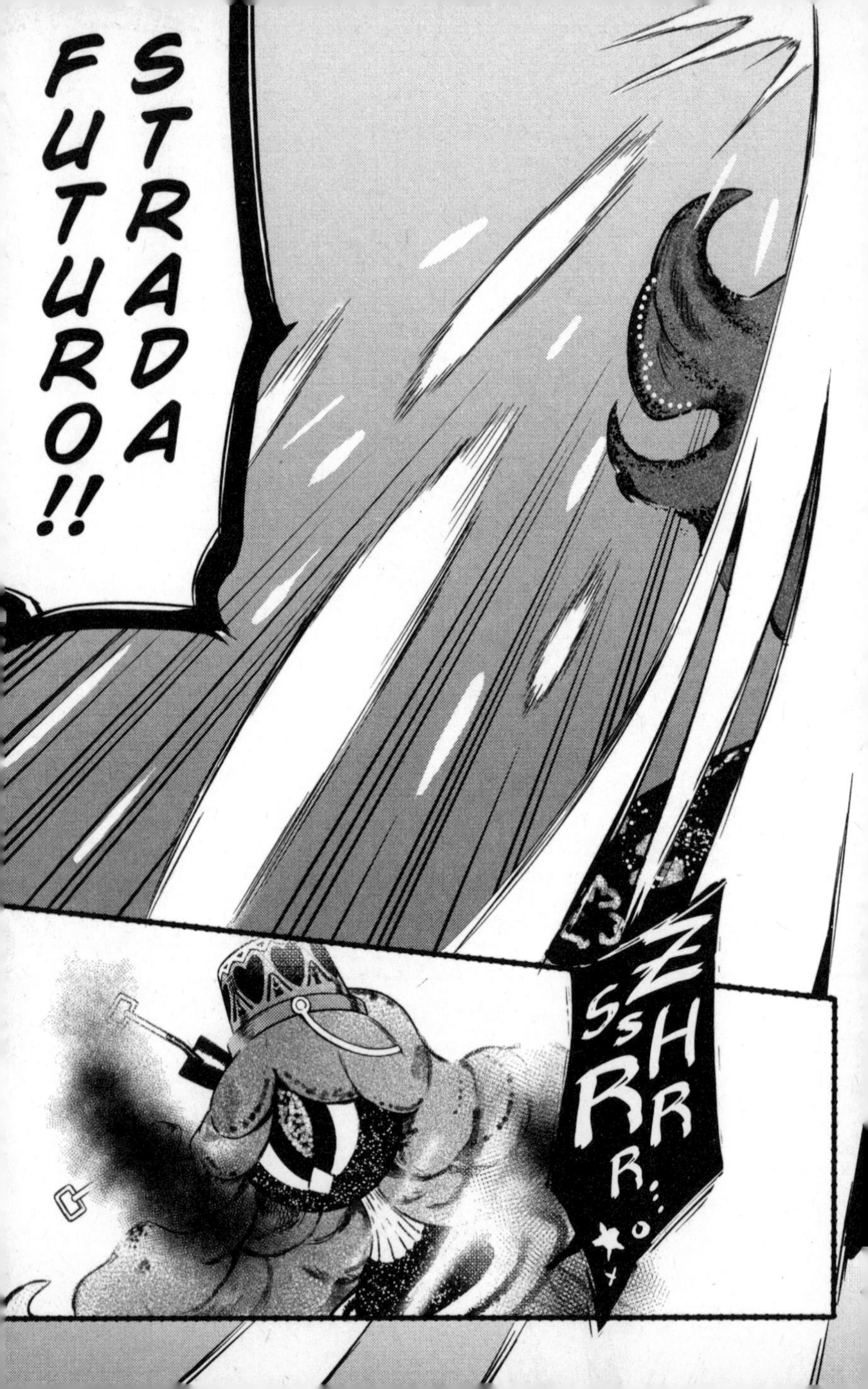
STRADA FUTURO!!
ZSHRRR...

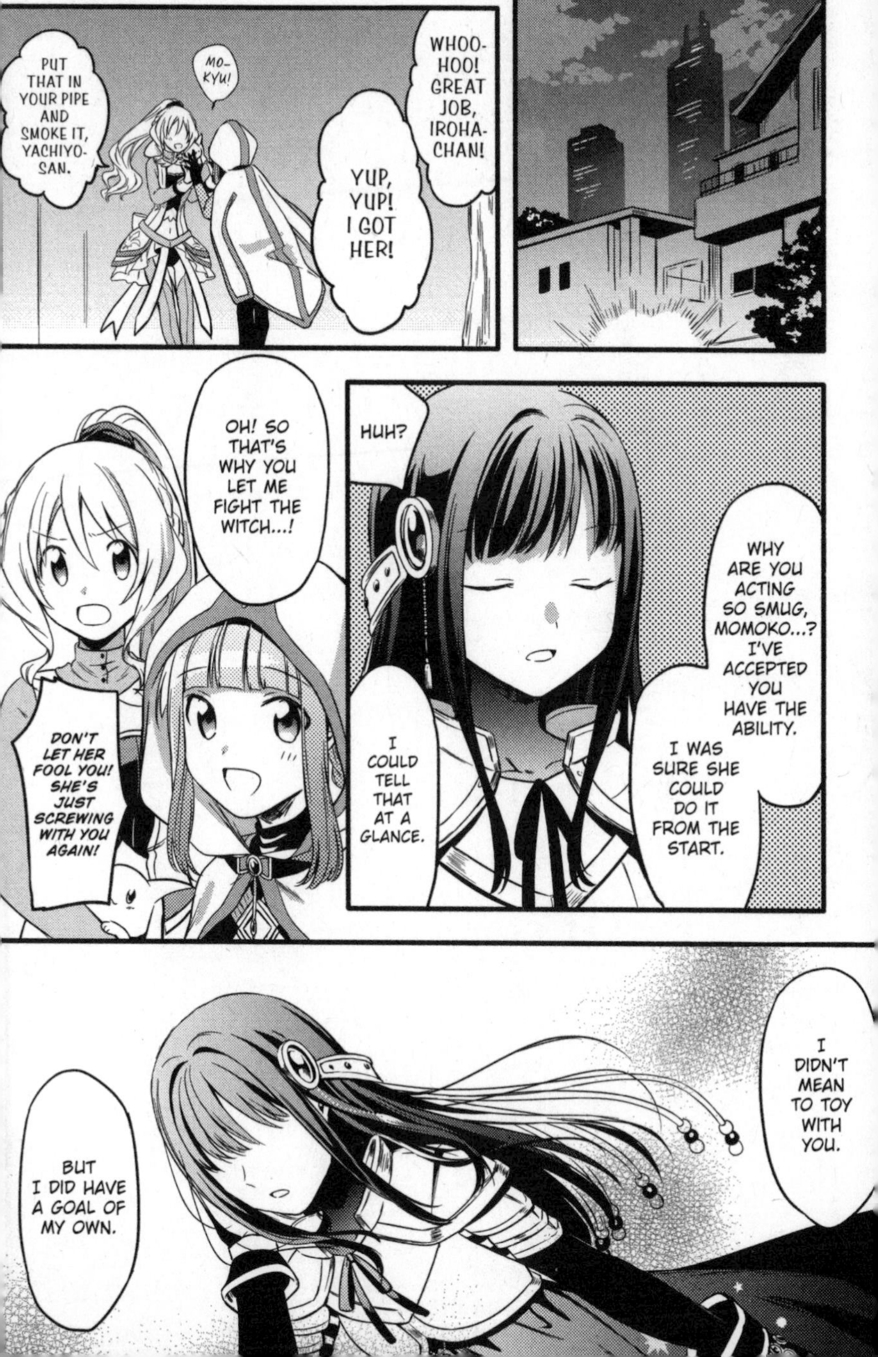
WHOO-HOO! GREAT JOB, IROHA-CHAN!
YUP, YUP! I GOT HER!
MO-KYU!
PUT THAT IN YOUR PIPE AND SMOKE IT, YACHIYO-SAN.
HUH?
WHY ARE YOU ACTING SO SMUG, MOMOKO...? I'VE ACCEPTED YOU HAVE THE ABILITY.
I WAS SURE SHE COULD DO IT FROM THE START.
I COULD TELL THAT AT A GLANCE.
OH! SO THAT'S WHY YOU LET ME FIGHT THE WITCH...!
DON'T LET HER FOOL YOU! SHE'S JUST SCREWING WITH YOU AGAIN!
I DIDN'T MEAN TO TOY WITH YOU.
BUT I DID HAVE A GOAL OF MY OWN.

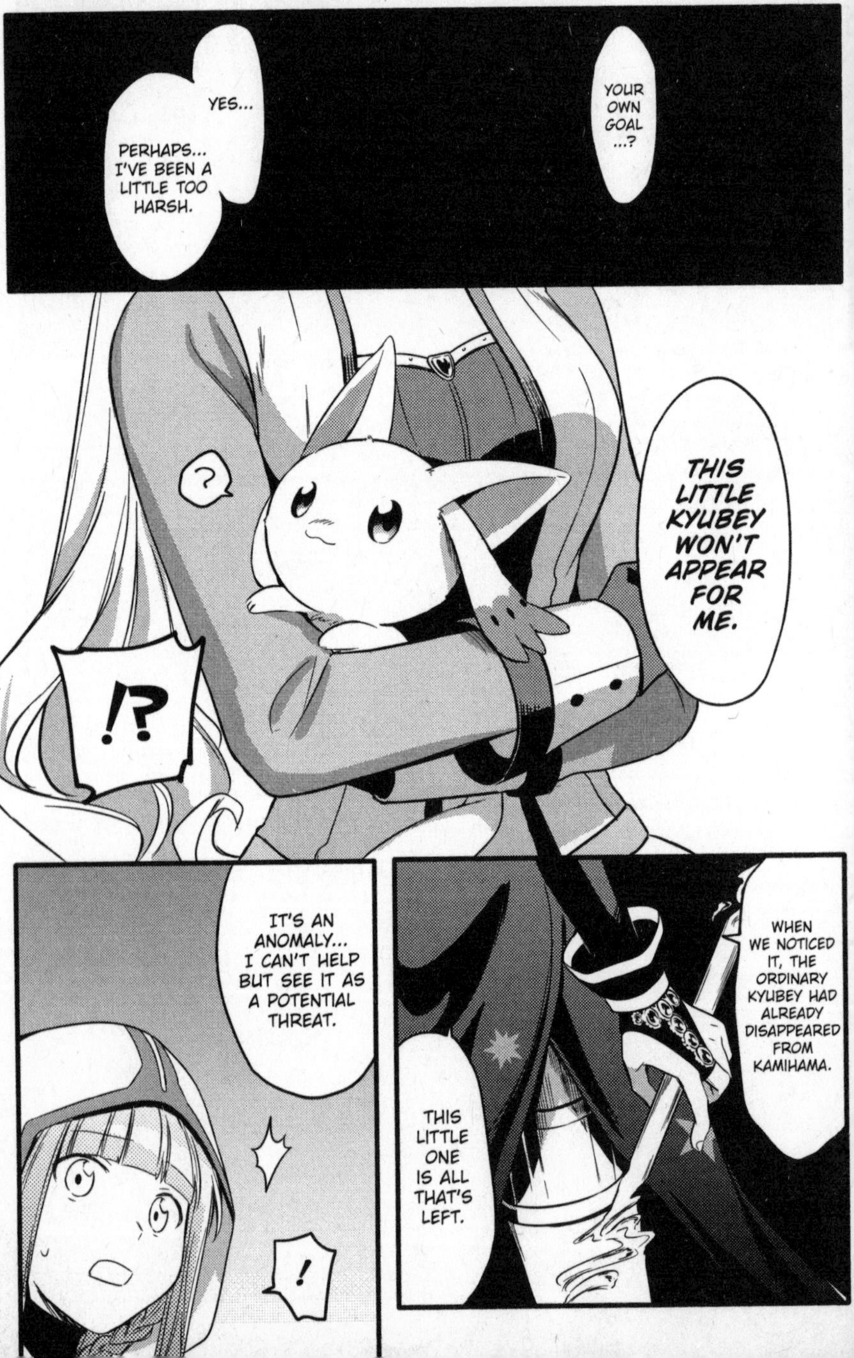
YOUR OWN GOAL ...?
YES...
PERHAPS... I'VE BEEN A LITTLE TOO HARSH.
THIS LITTLE KYUBEY WON'T APPEAR FOR ME.
?
!?
WHEN WE NOTICED IT, THE ORDINARY KYUBEY HAD ALREADY DISAPPEARED FROM KAMIHAMA.
THIS LITTLE ONE IS ALL THAT'S LEFT.
IT'S AN ANOMALY... I CAN'T HELP BUT SEE IT AS A POTENTIAL THREAT.
!

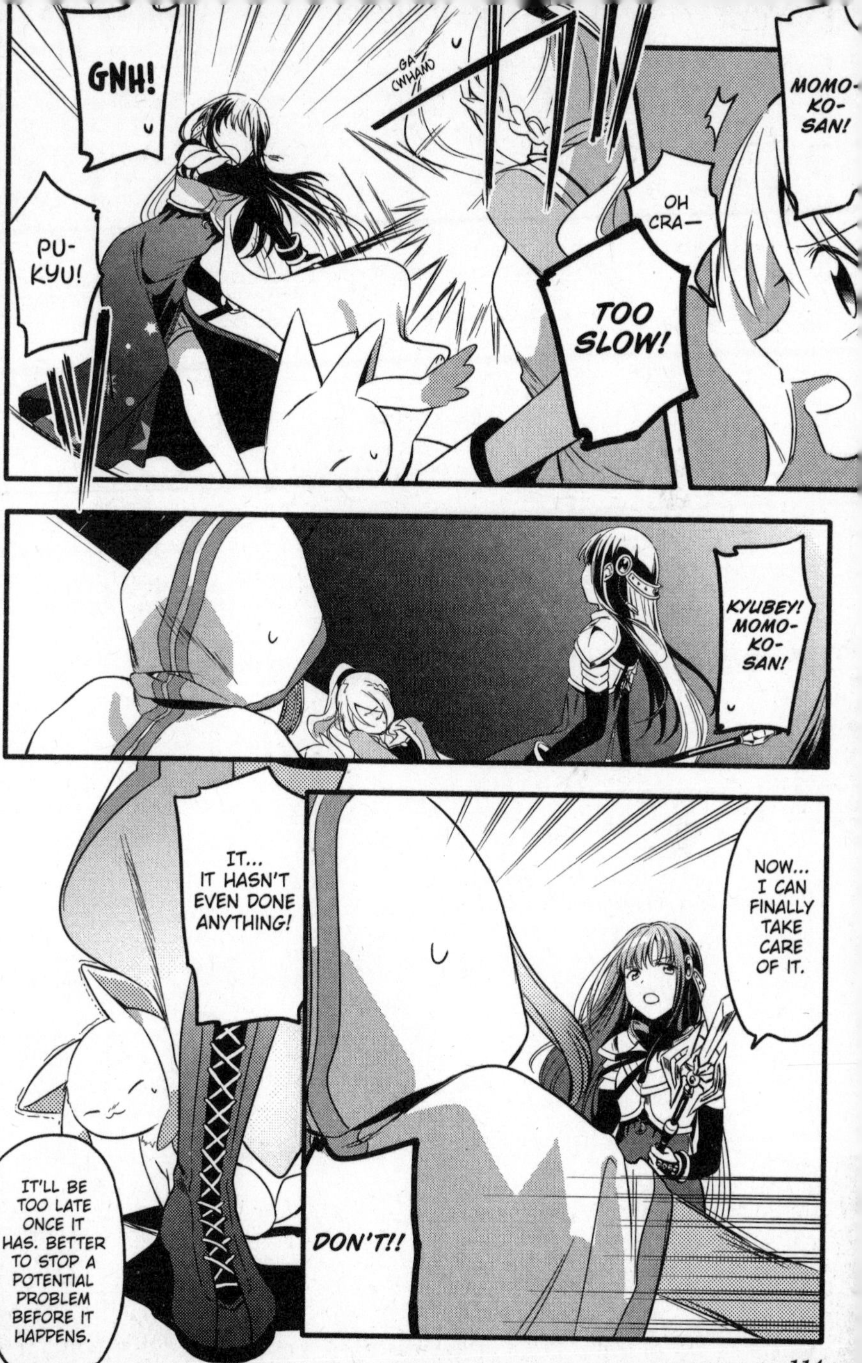
MOMO-KO-SAN!
OH CRA—
TOO SLOW!
GA CWHAM
GNH!
PU-KYU!
KYUBEY! MOMO-KO-SAN!
NOW... I CAN FINALLY TAKE CARE OF IT.
DON'T!!
IT... IT HASN'T EVEN DONE ANYTHING!
IT'LL BE TOO LATE ONCE IT HAS. BETTER TO STOP A POTENTIAL PROBLEM BEFORE IT HAPPENS.

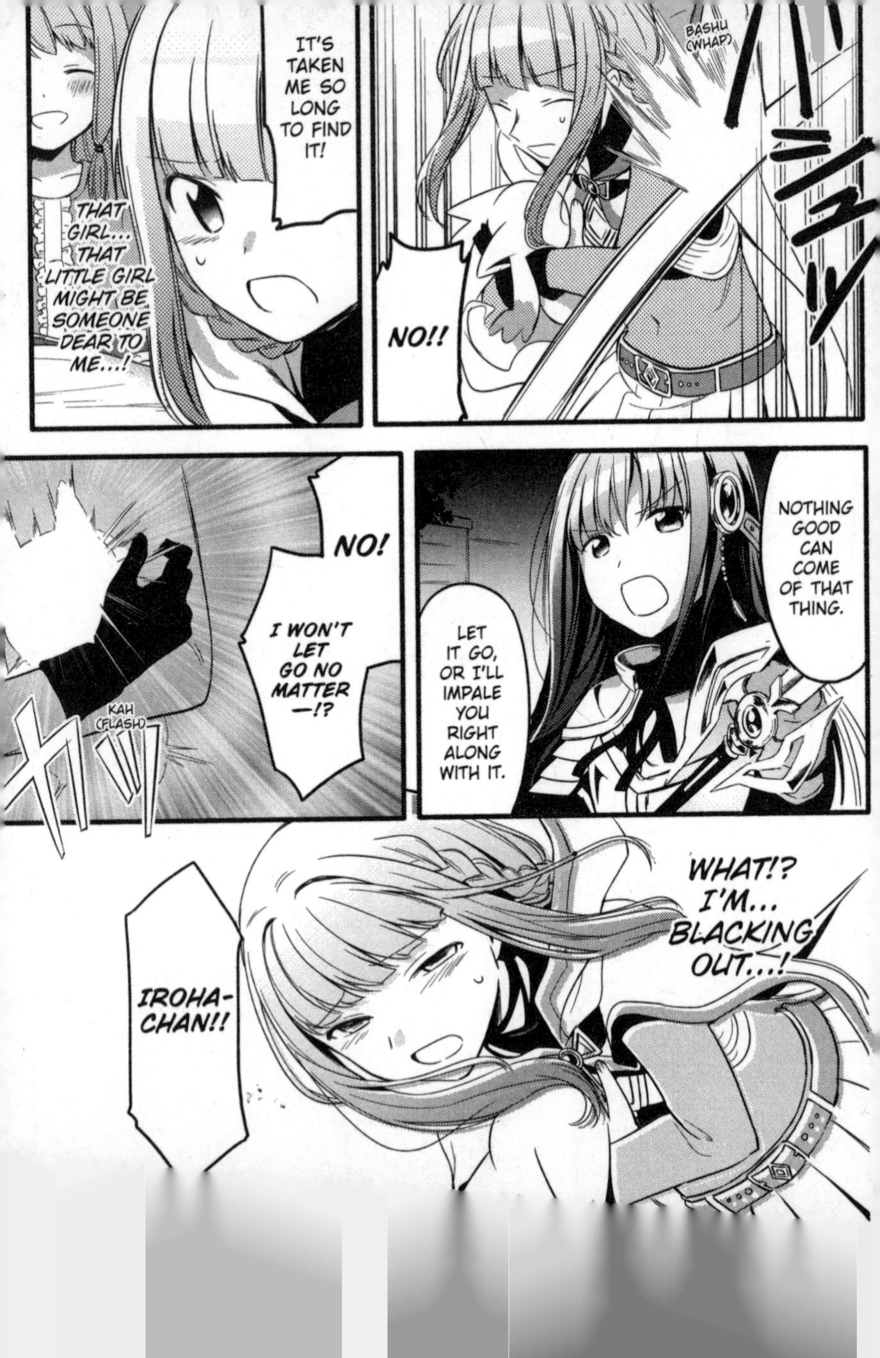
BASHU (WHAP)
NO!!
IT'S TAKEN ME SO LONG TO FIND IT!
THAT GIRL... THAT LITTLE GIRL MIGHT BE SOMEONE DEAR TO ME...!
NOTHING GOOD CAN COME OF THAT THING.
LET IT GO, OR I'LL IMPALE YOU RIGHT ALONG WITH IT.
NO!
I WON'T LET GO NO MATTER—!?
KAH (FLASH)
WHAT!? I'M... BLACKING OUT...!
IROHA-CHAN!!

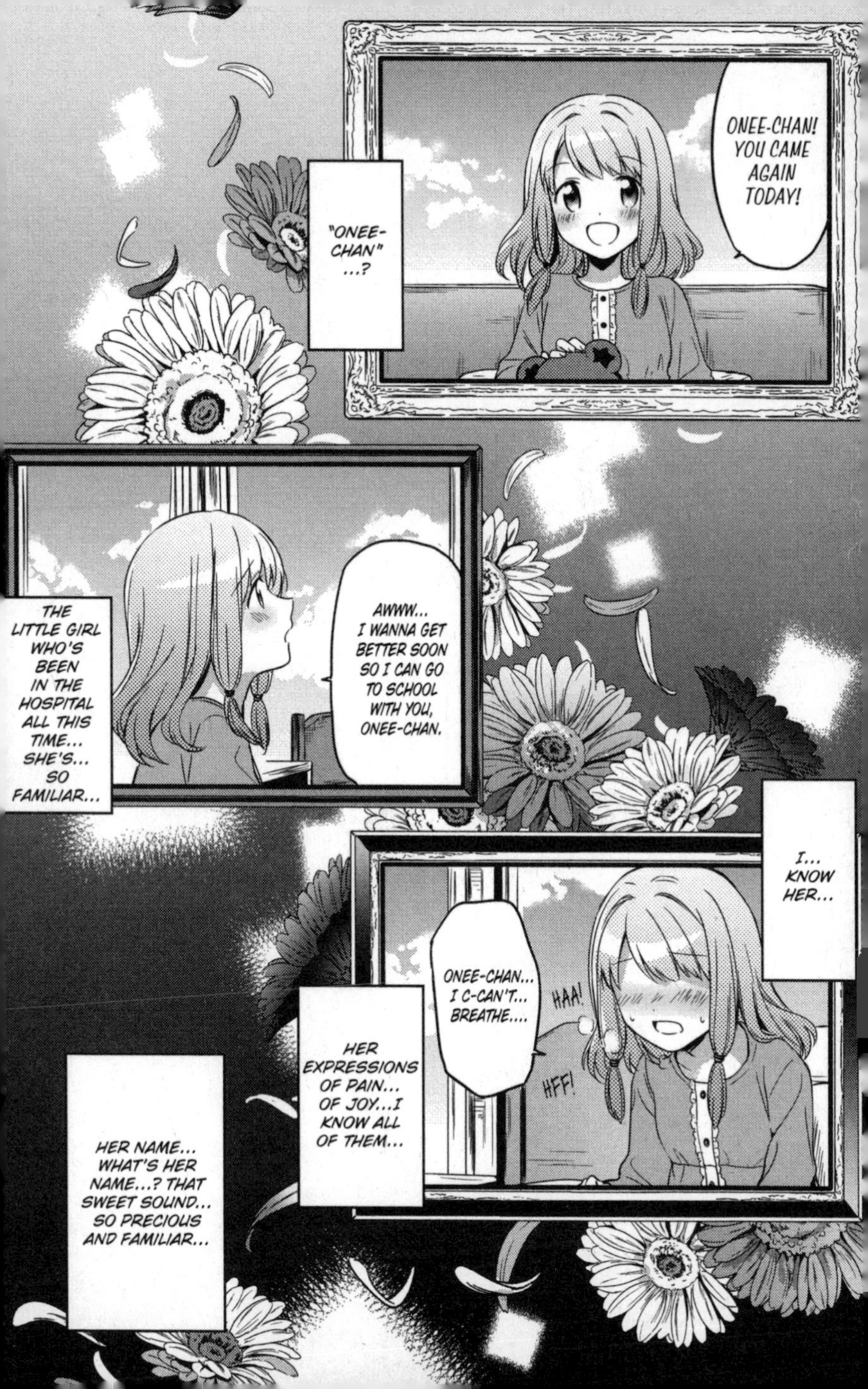
ONEE-CHAN! YOU CAME AGAIN TODAY!
"ONEE-CHAN" ...?
AWWW... I WANNA GET BETTER SOON SO I CAN GO TO SCHOOL WITH YOU, ONEE-CHAN.
THE LITTLE GIRL WHO'S BEEN IN THE HOSPITAL ALL THIS TIME... SHE'S... SO FAMILIAR...
I... KNOW HER...
HAA!
HFF!
ONEE-CHAN... I C-CAN'T... BREATHE....
HER EXPRESSIONS OF PAIN... OF JOY... I KNOW ALL OF THEM...
HER NAME... WHAT'S HER NAME...? THAT SWEET SOUND... SO PRECIOUS AND FAMILIAR...

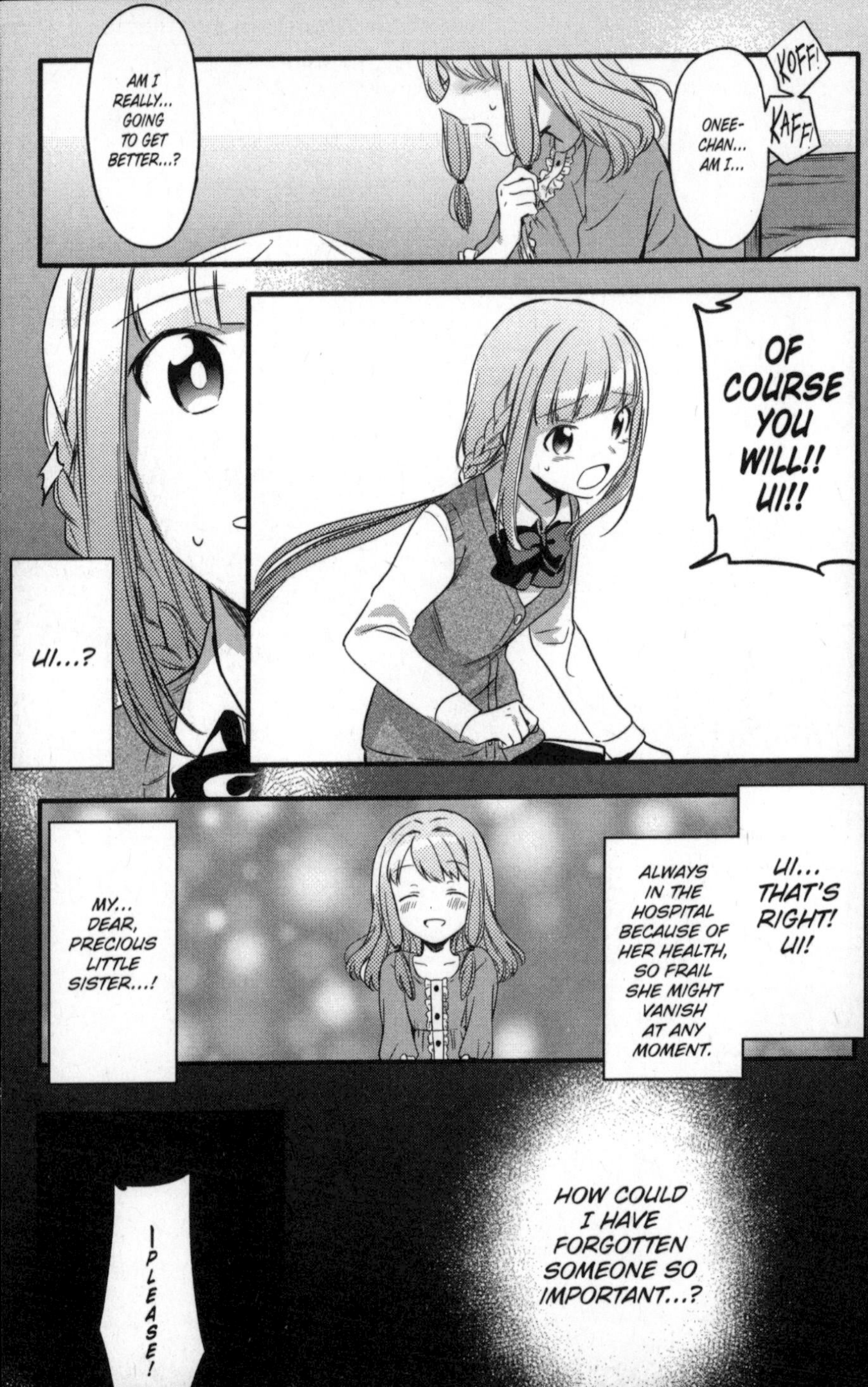
KOFF!
KAFF!
ONEE-CHAN... AM I...
AM I REALLY... GOING TO GET BETTER...?
OF COURSE YOU WILL!! UI!!
UI...?
UI... THAT'S RIGHT! UI!
ALWAYS IN THE HOSPITAL BECAUSE OF HER HEALTH, SO FRAIL SHE MIGHT VANISH AT ANY MOMENT.
MY... DEAR, PRECIOUS LITTLE SISTER...!
HOW COULD I HAVE FORGOTTEN SOMEONE SO IMPORTANT...?
PLEASE!

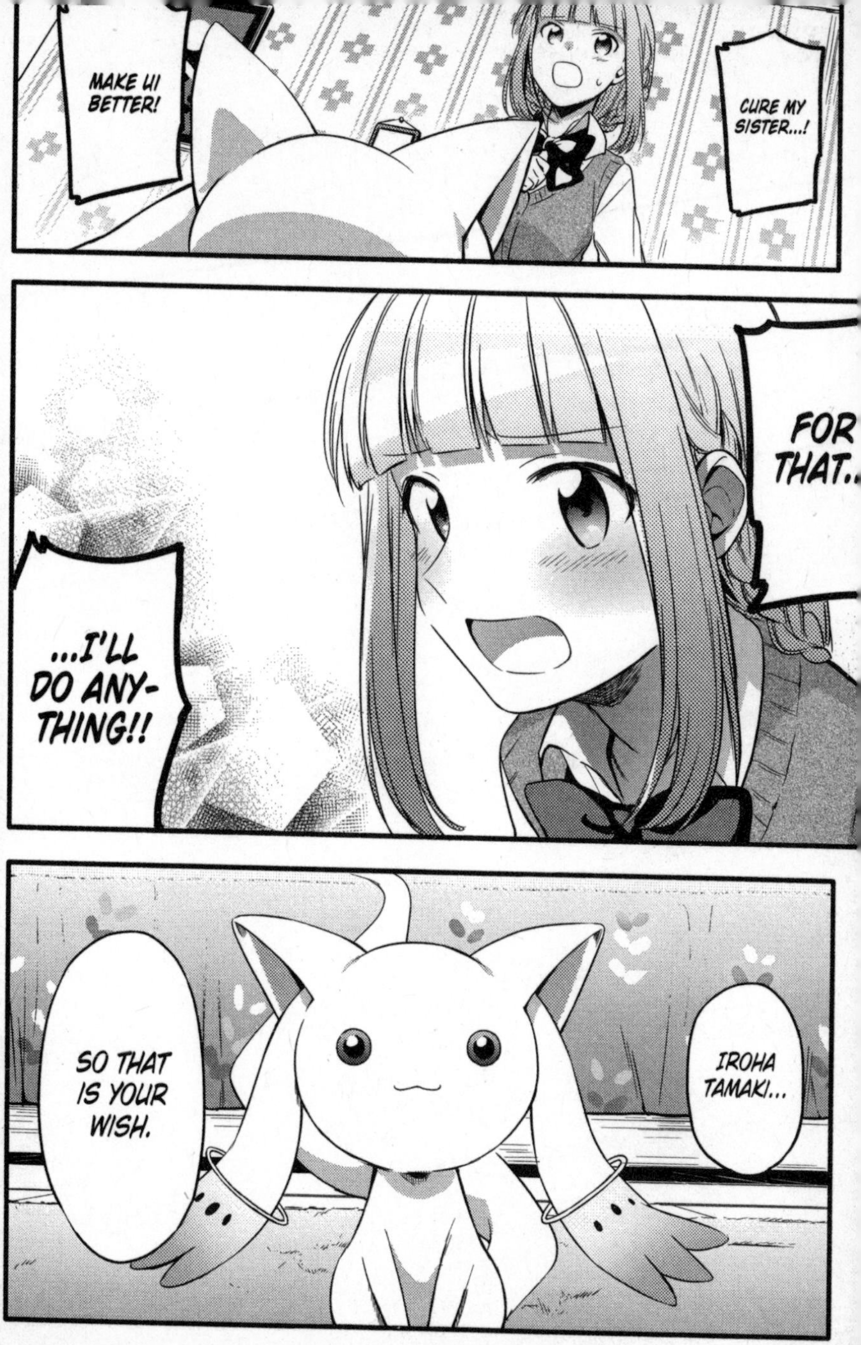
CURE MY SISTER...!
MAKE UI BETTER!
FOR THAT...
...I'LL DO ANY-THING!!
IROHA TAMAKI...
SO THAT IS YOUR WISH.

EPISODE 5

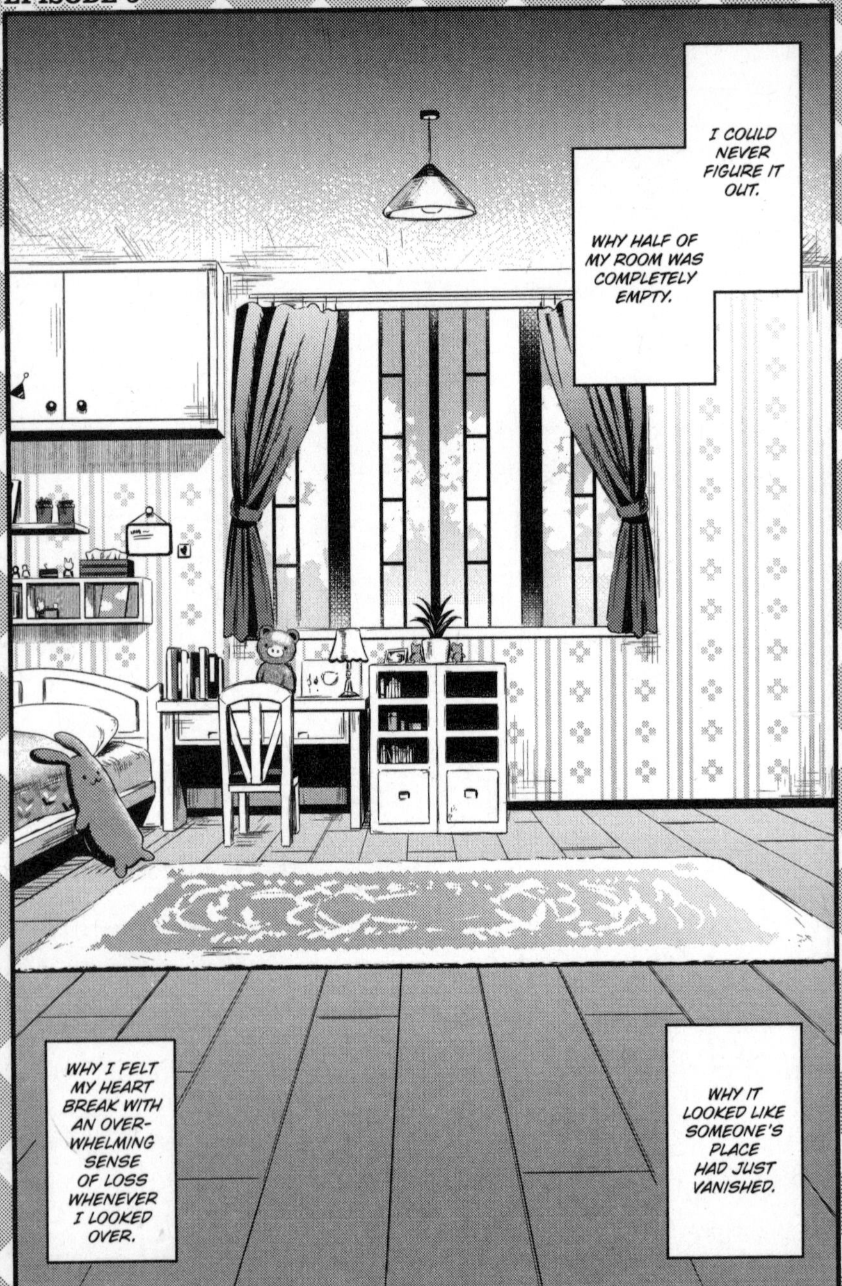
I COULD NEVER FIGURE IT OUT.
WHY HALF OF MY ROOM WAS COMPLETELY EMPTY.
WHY IT LOOKED LIKE SOMEONE'S PLACE HAD JUST VANISHED.
WHY I FELT MY HEART BREAK WITH AN OVER-WHELMING SENSE OF LOSS WHENEVER I LOOKED OVER.

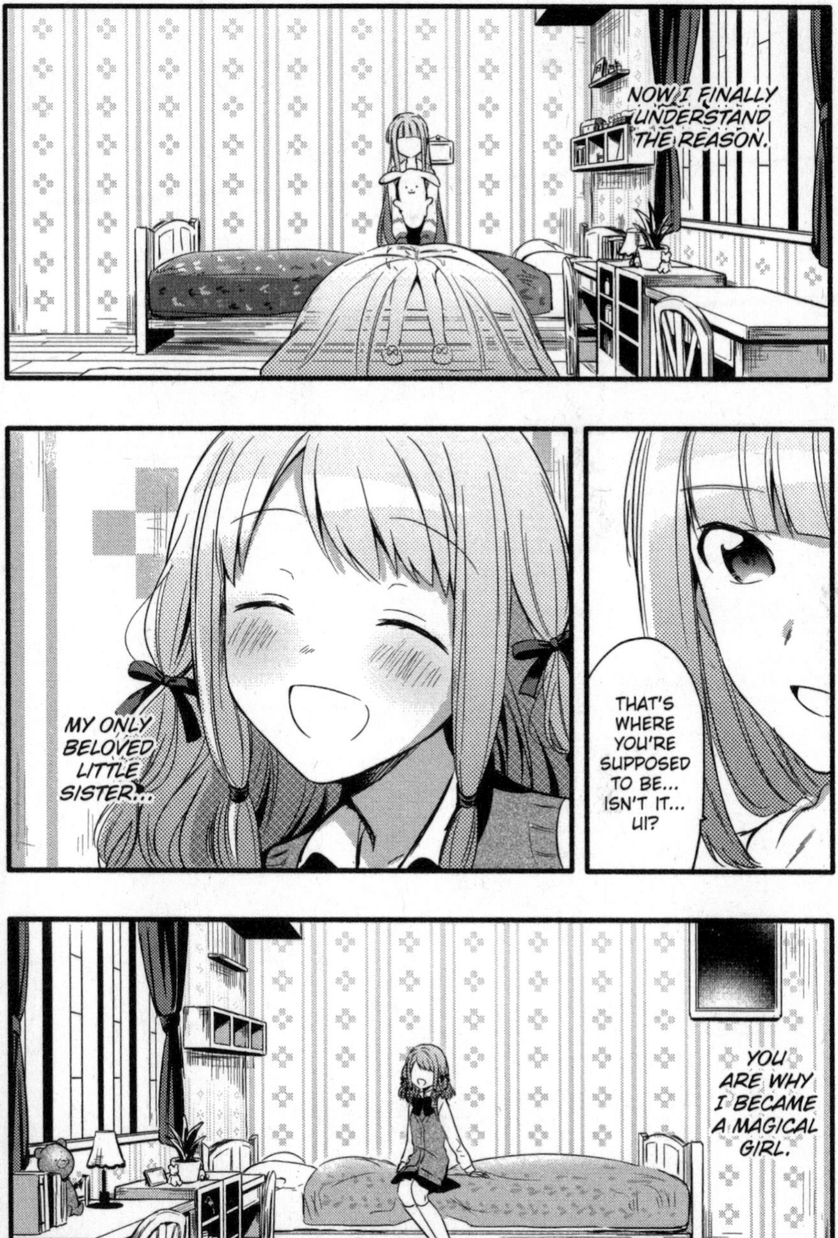
NOW I FINALLY UNDERSTAND THE REASON.
THAT'S WHERE YOU'RE SUPPOSED TO BE... ISN'T IT... UI?
MY ONLY BELOVED LITTLE SISTER...
YOU ARE WHY I BECAME A MAGICAL GIRL.

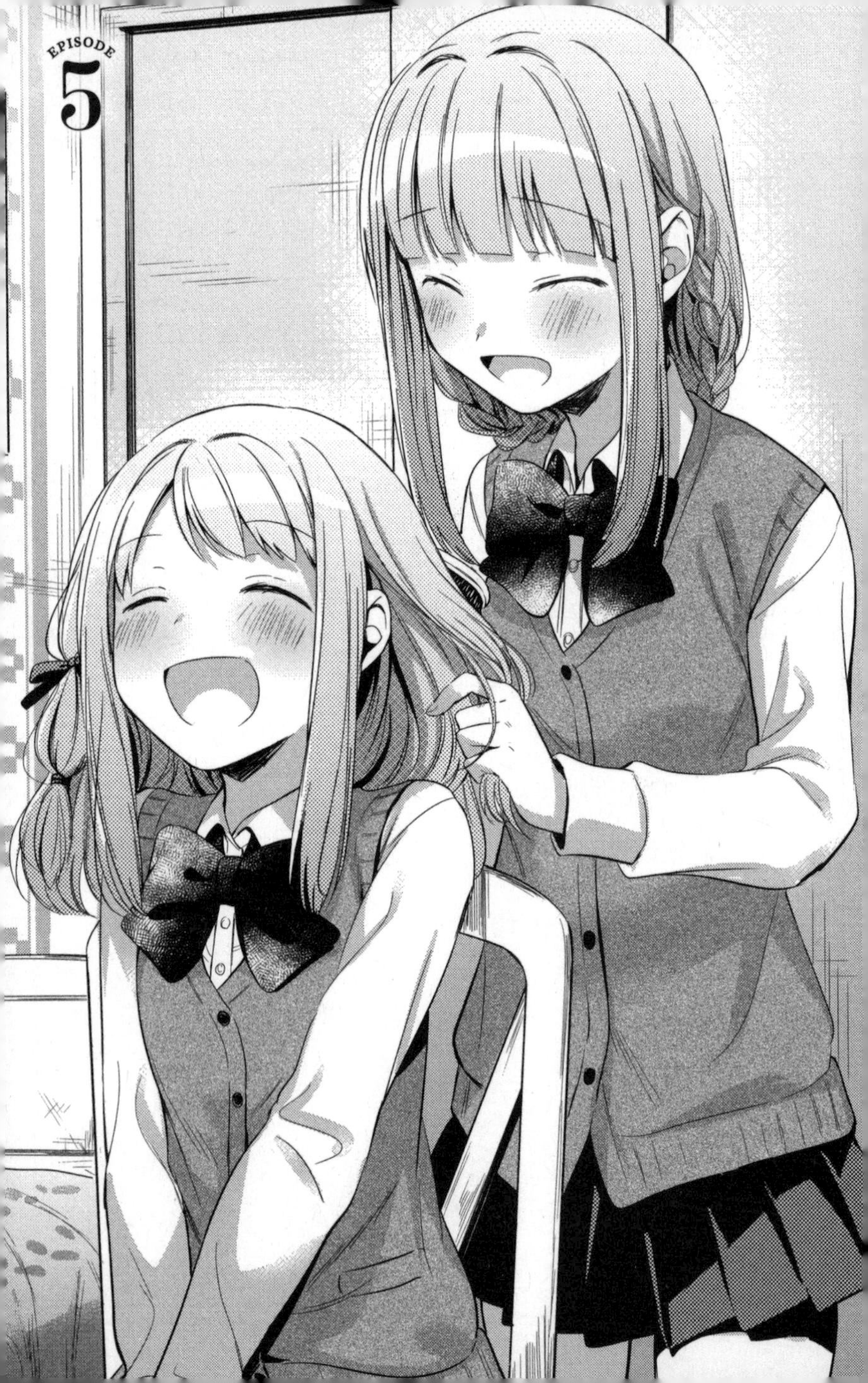
EPISODE
5

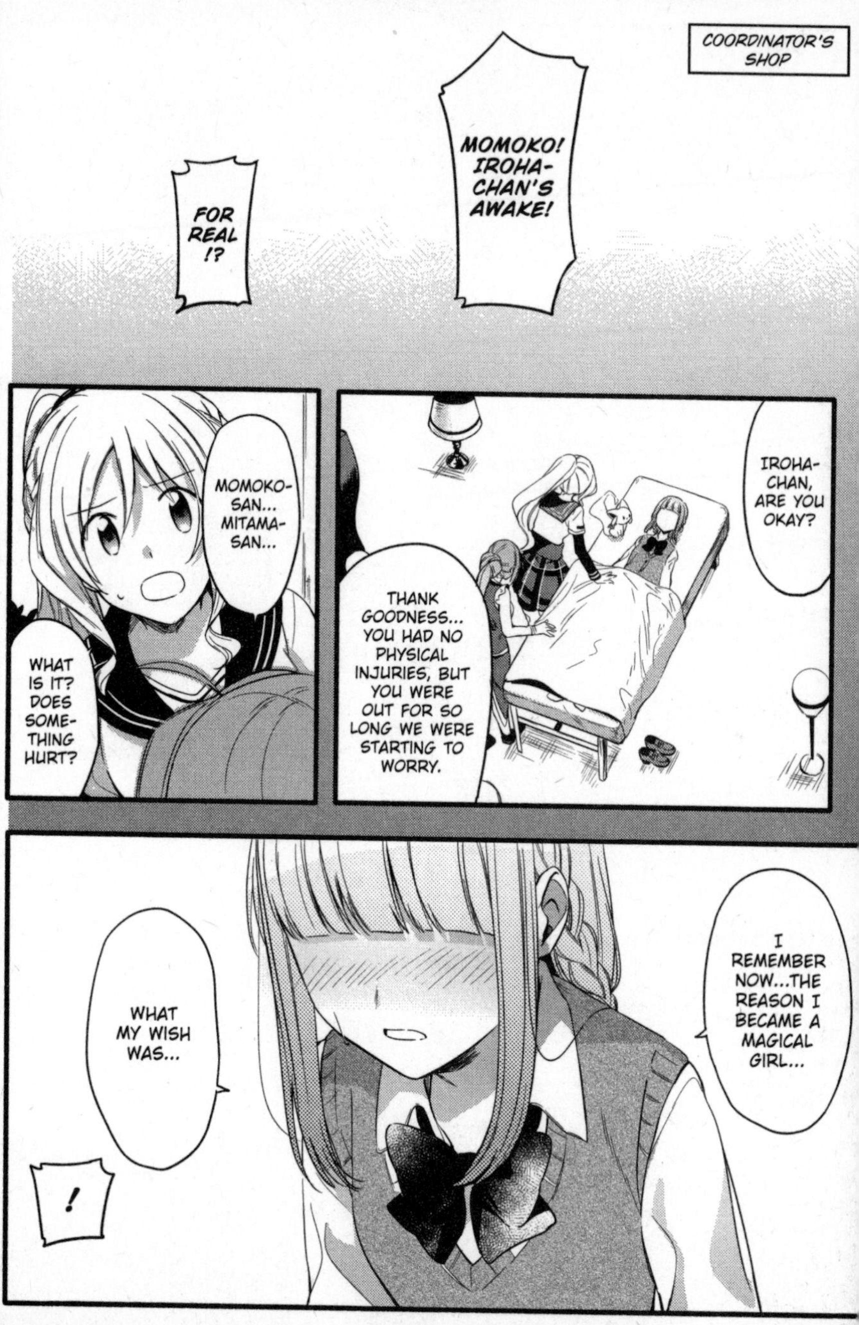
COORDINATOR'S SHOP
MOMOKO! IROHA-CHAN'S AWAKE!
FOR REAL !?
IROHA-CHAN, ARE YOU OKAY?
THANK GOODNESS... YOU HAD NO PHYSICAL INJURIES, BUT YOU WERE OUT FOR SO LONG WE WERE STARTING TO WORRY.
MOMOKO-SAN... MITAMA-SAN...
WHAT IS IT? DOES SOMETHING HURT?
I REMEMBER NOW...THE REASON I BECAME A MAGICAL GIRL...
WHAT MY WISH WAS...
!

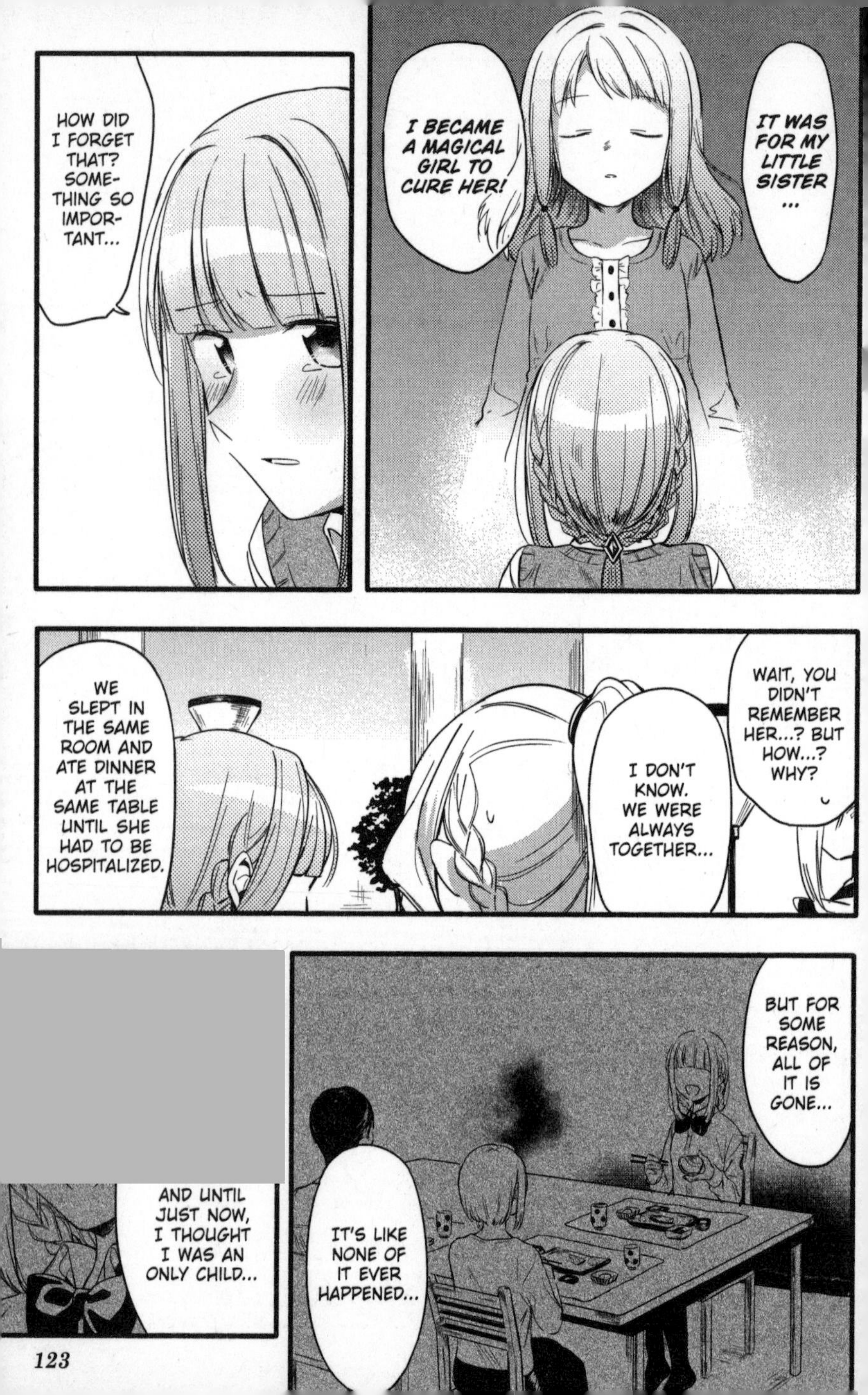
IT WAS FOR MY LITTLE SISTER...
I BECAME A MAGICAL GIRL TO CURE HER!
HOW DID I FORGET THAT? SOME-THING SO IMPOR-TANT...
WAIT, YOU DIDN'T REMEMBER HER...? BUT HOW...? WHY?
I DON'T KNOW. WE WERE ALWAYS TOGETHER...
WE SLEPT IN THE SAME ROOM AND ATE DINNER AT THE SAME TABLE UNTIL SHE HAD TO BE HOSPITALIZED.
BUT FOR SOME REASON, ALL OF IT IS GONE...
IT'S LIKE NONE OF IT EVER HAPPENED...
AND UNTIL JUST NOW, I THOUGHT I WAS AN ONLY CHILD...

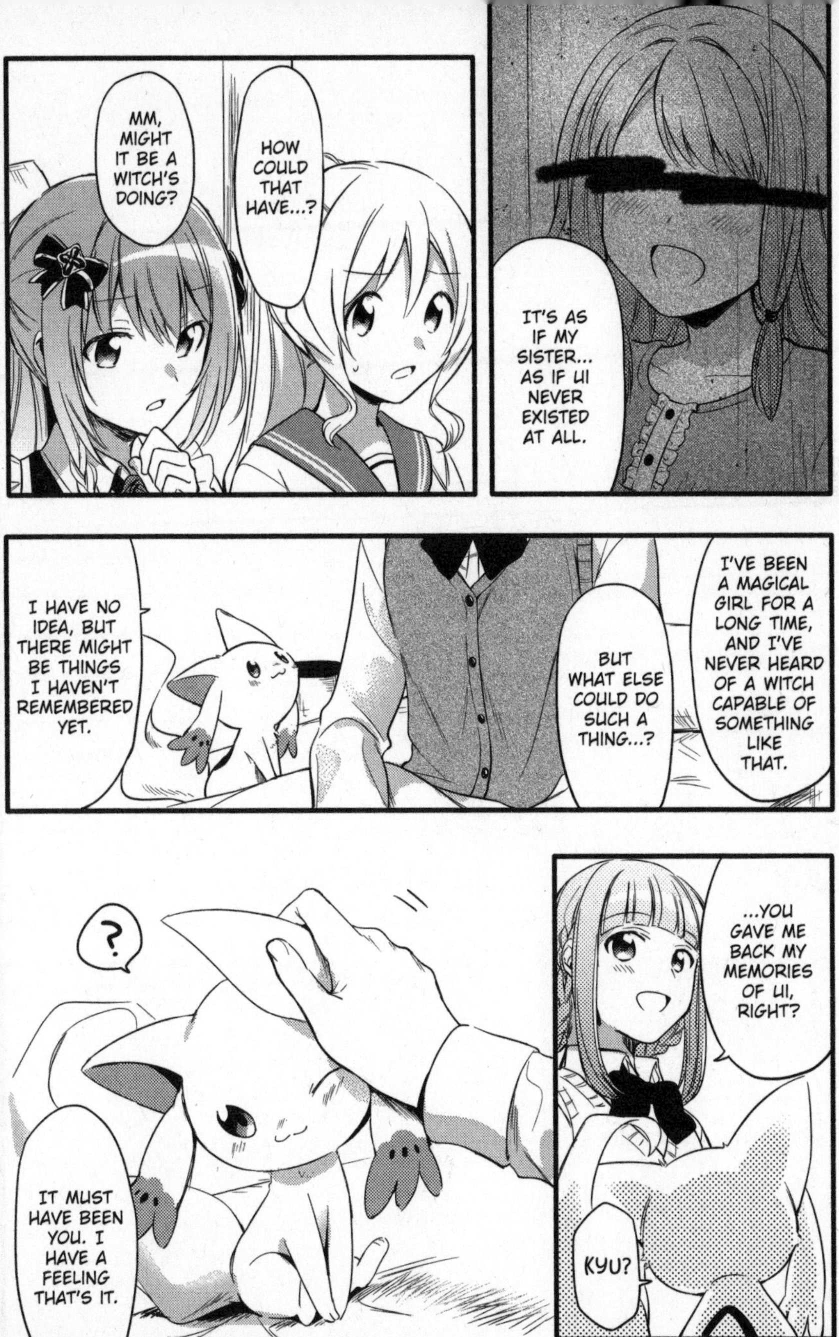
IT'S AS IF MY SISTER... AS IF UI NEVER EXISTED AT ALL.
HOW COULD THAT HAVE...?
MM, MIGHT IT BE A WITCH'S DOING?
I'VE BEEN A MAGICAL GIRL FOR A LONG TIME, AND I'VE NEVER HEARD OF A WITCH CAPABLE OF SOMETHING LIKE THAT.
BUT WHAT ELSE COULD DO SUCH A THING...?
I HAVE NO IDEA, BUT THERE MIGHT BE THINGS I HAVEN'T REMEMBERED YET.
...YOU GAVE ME BACK MY MEMORIES OF UI, RIGHT?
KYU?
?
IT MUST HAVE BEEN YOU. I HAVE A FEELING THAT'S IT.

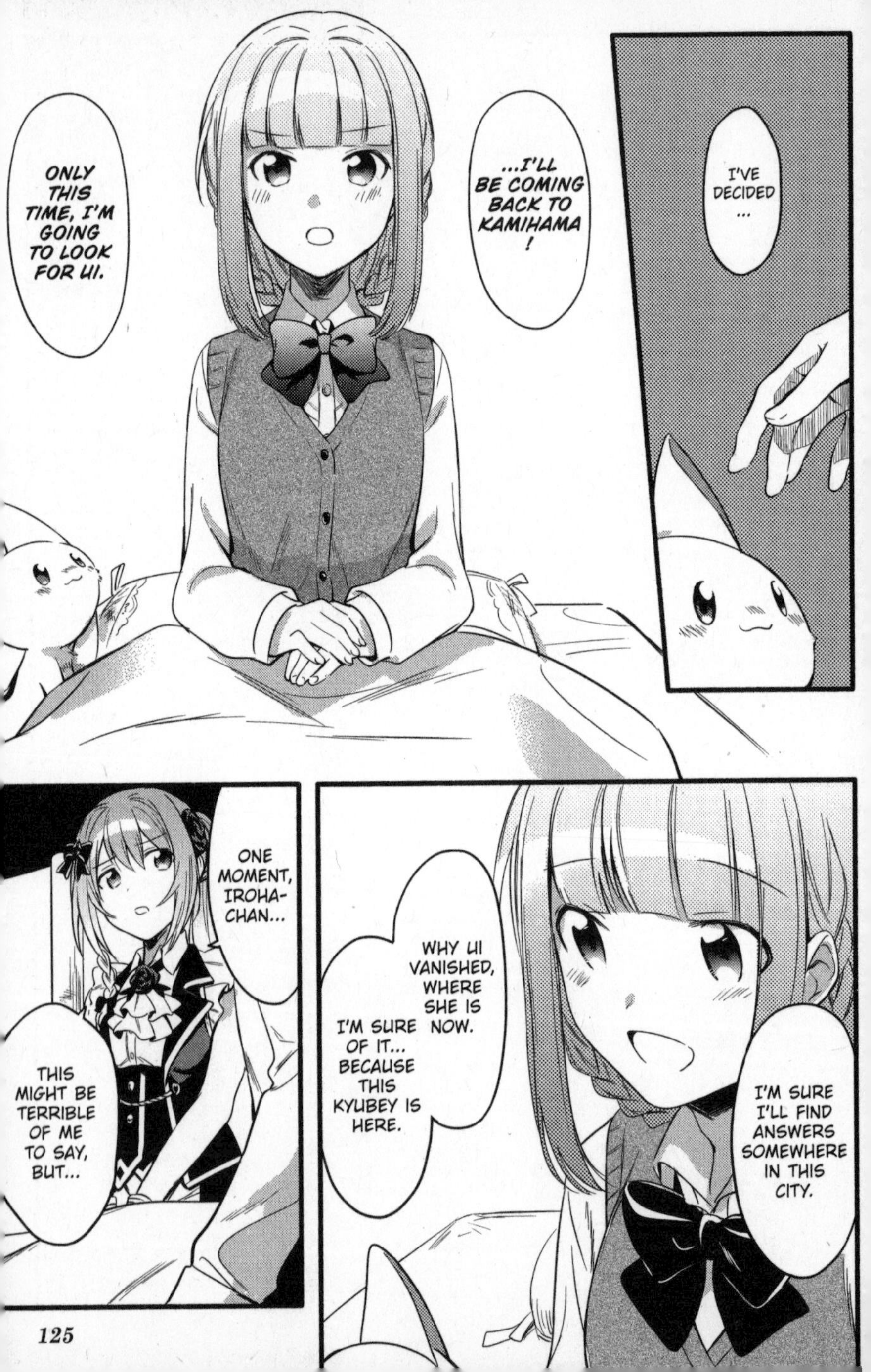
I'VE DECIDED...
...I'LL BE COMING BACK TO KAMIHAMA!
ONLY THIS TIME, I'M GOING TO LOOK FOR UI.
I'M SURE I'LL FIND ANSWERS SOMEWHERE IN THIS CITY.
WHY UI VANISHED, WHERE SHE IS NOW.
I'M SURE OF IT... BECAUSE THIS KYUBEY IS HERE.
ONE MOMENT, IROHA-CHAN...
THIS MIGHT BE TERRIBLE OF ME TO SAY, BUT...

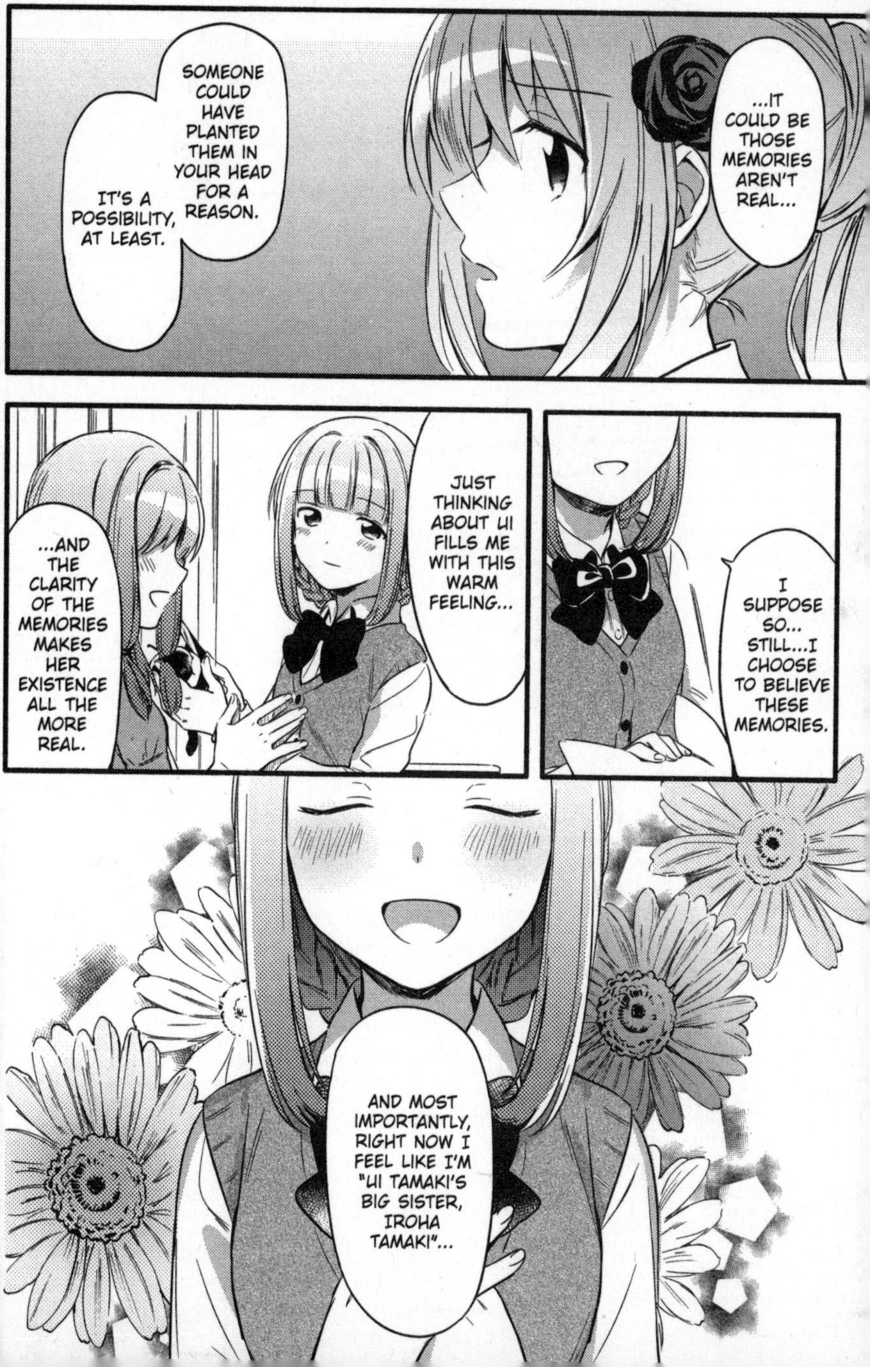
...IT COULD BE THOSE MEMORIES AREN'T REAL...
SOMEONE COULD HAVE PLANTED THEM IN YOUR HEAD FOR A REASON.
IT'S A POSSIBILITY, AT LEAST.
I SUPPOSE SO... STILL...I CHOOSE TO BELIEVE THESE MEMORIES.
JUST THINKING ABOUT UI FILLS ME WITH THIS WARM FEELING...
...AND THE CLARITY OF THE MEMORIES MAKES HER EXISTENCE ALL THE MORE REAL.
AND MOST IMPORTANTLY, RIGHT NOW I FEEL LIKE I'M "UI TAMAKI'S BIG SISTER, IROHA TAMAKI"...

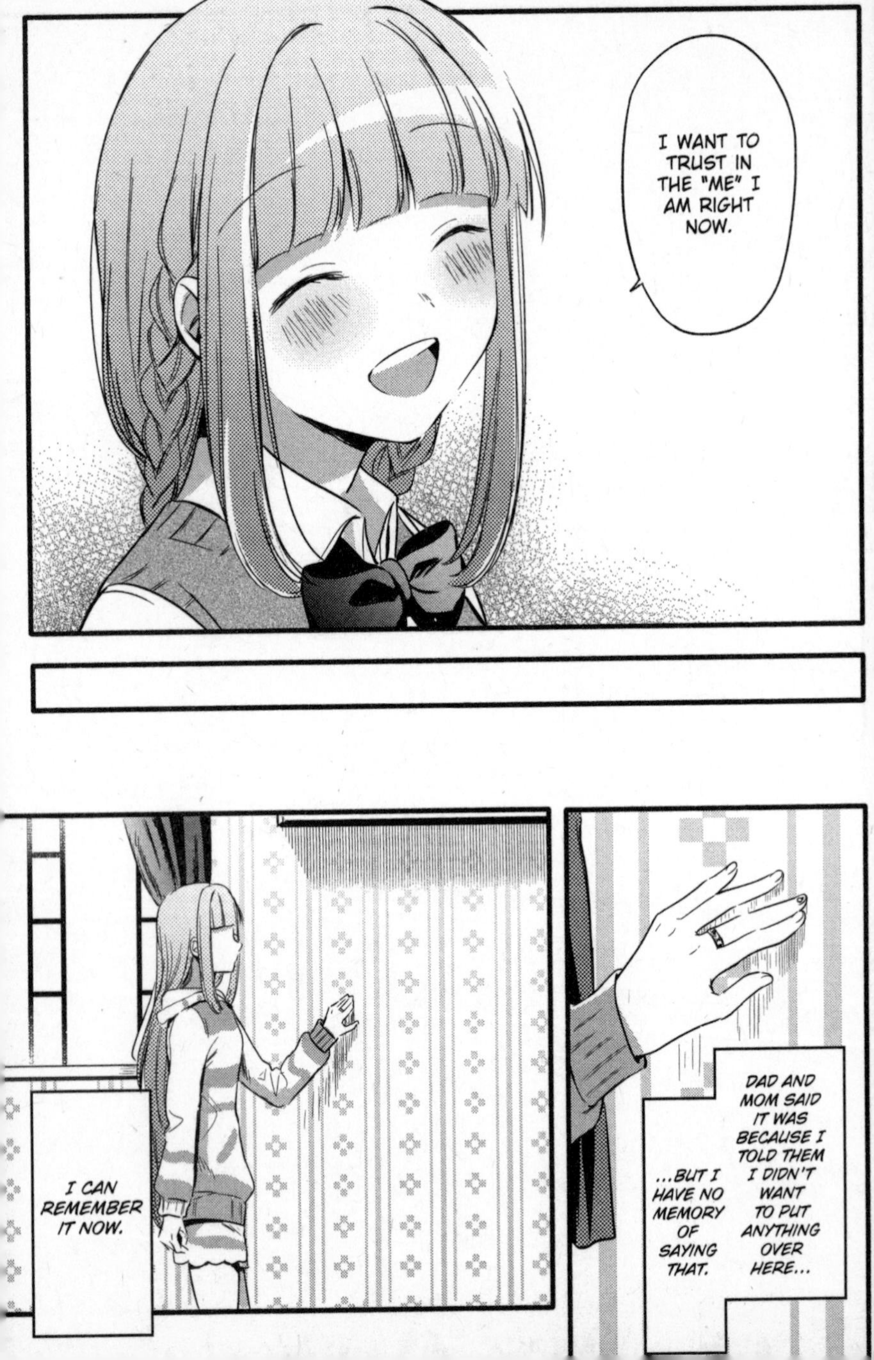
I WANT TO TRUST IN THE "ME" I AM RIGHT NOW.
DAD AND MOM SAID IT WAS BECAUSE I TOLD THEM I DIDN'T WANT TO PUT ANYTHING OVER HERE...
...BUT I HAVE NO MEMORY OF SAYING THAT.
I CAN REMEMBER IT NOW.

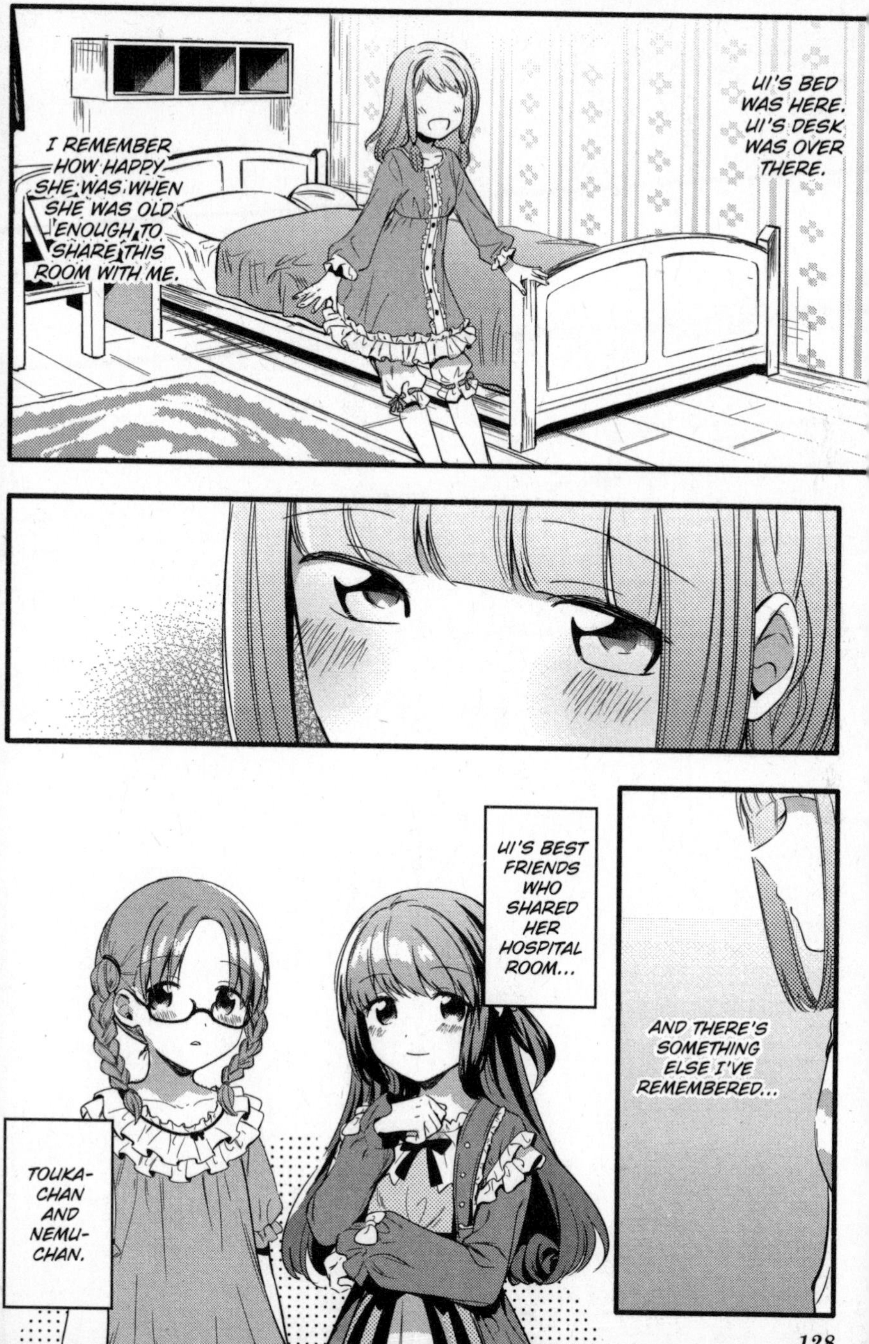
UI'S BED WAS HERE. UI'S DESK WAS OVER THERE.
I REMEMBER HOW HAPPY SHE WAS WHEN SHE WAS OLD ENOUGH TO SHARE THIS ROOM WITH ME.
AND THERE'S SOMETHING ELSE I'VE REMEMBERED...
UI'S BEST FRIENDS WHO SHARED HER HOSPITAL ROOM...
TOUKA-CHAN AND NEMU-CHAN.

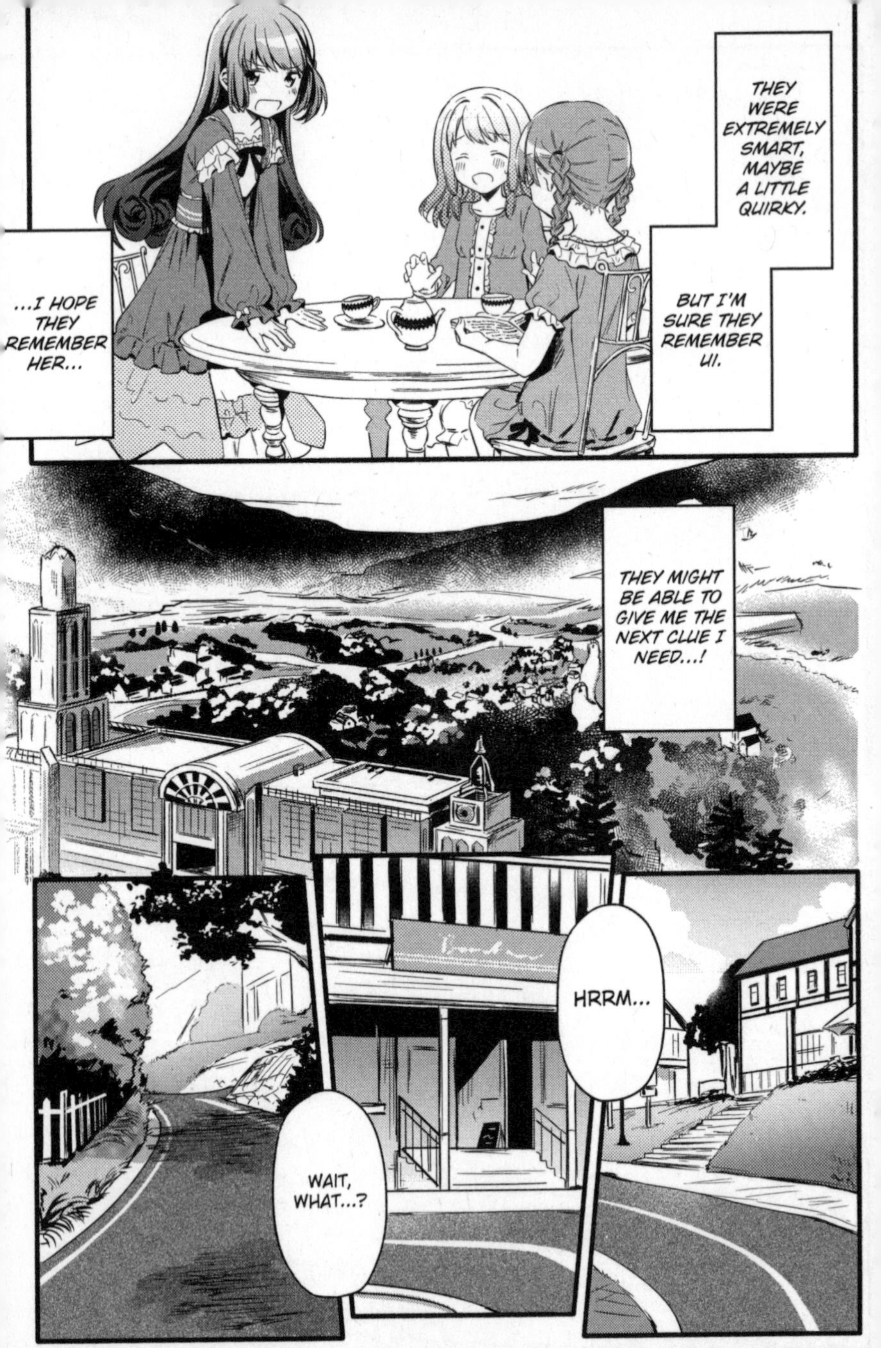
THEY WERE EXTREMELY SMART, MAYBE A LITTLE QUIRKY.
BUT I'M SURE THEY REMEMBER UI.
...I HOPE THEY REMEMBER HER...
THEY MIGHT BE ABLE TO GIVE ME THE NEXT CLUE I NEED...!
HRRM...
WAIT, WHAT...?

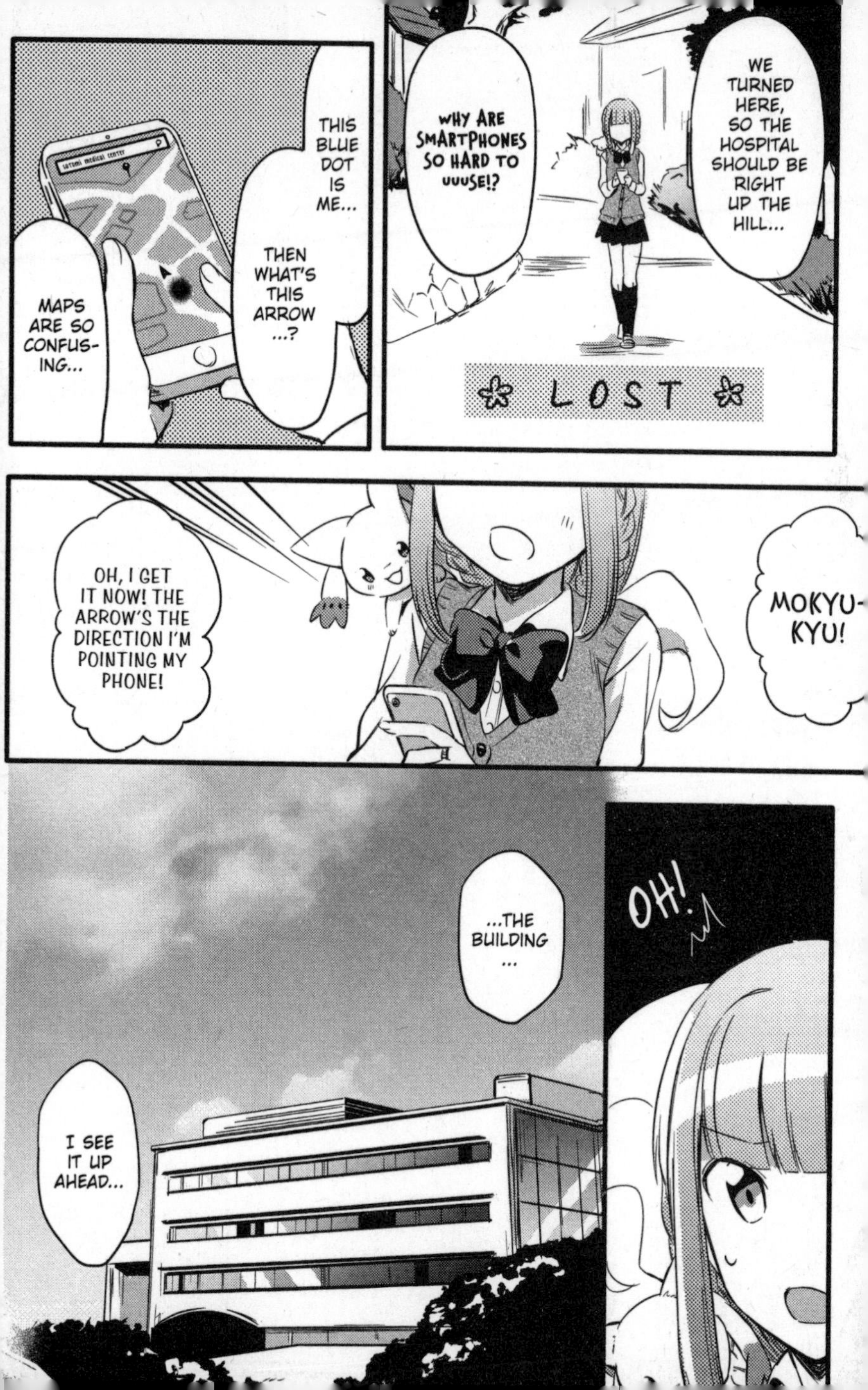
WE TURNED HERE, SO THE HOSPITAL SHOULD BE RIGHT UP THE HILL...
WHY ARE SMARTPHONES SO HARD TO UUUSE!?
LOST
THIS BLUE DOT IS ME...
THEN WHAT'S THIS ARROW ...?
MAPS ARE SO CONFUS-ING...
MOKYU-KYU!
OH, I GET IT NOW! THE ARROW'S THE DIRECTION I'M POINTING MY PHONE!
OH!
...THE BUILDING ...
I SEE IT UP AHEAD...

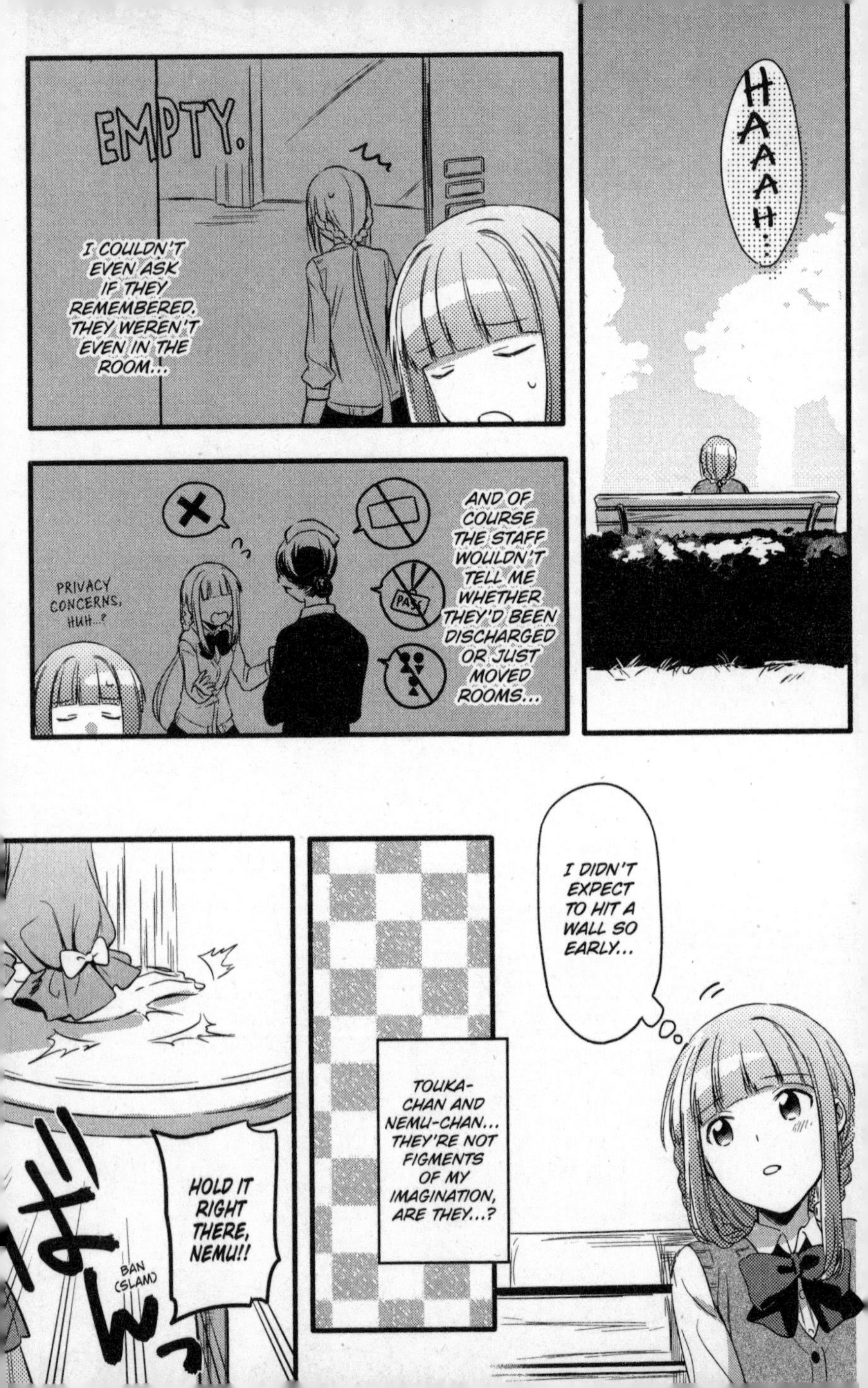
HAAAH...
EMPTY.
I COULDN'T EVEN ASK IF THEY REMEMBERED. THEY WEREN'T EVEN IN THE ROOM...
AND OF COURSE THE STAFF WOULDN'T TELL ME WHETHER THEY'D BEEN DISCHARGED OR JUST MOVED ROOMS...
PASS
PRIVACY CONCERNS, HUH...?
I DIDN'T EXPECT TO HIT A WALL SO EARLY...
TOUKA-CHAN AND NEMU-CHAN... THEY'RE NOT FIGMENTS OF MY IMAGINATION, ARE THEY...?
HOLD IT RIGHT THERE, NEMU!!
ばんっ
BAN (SLAM)

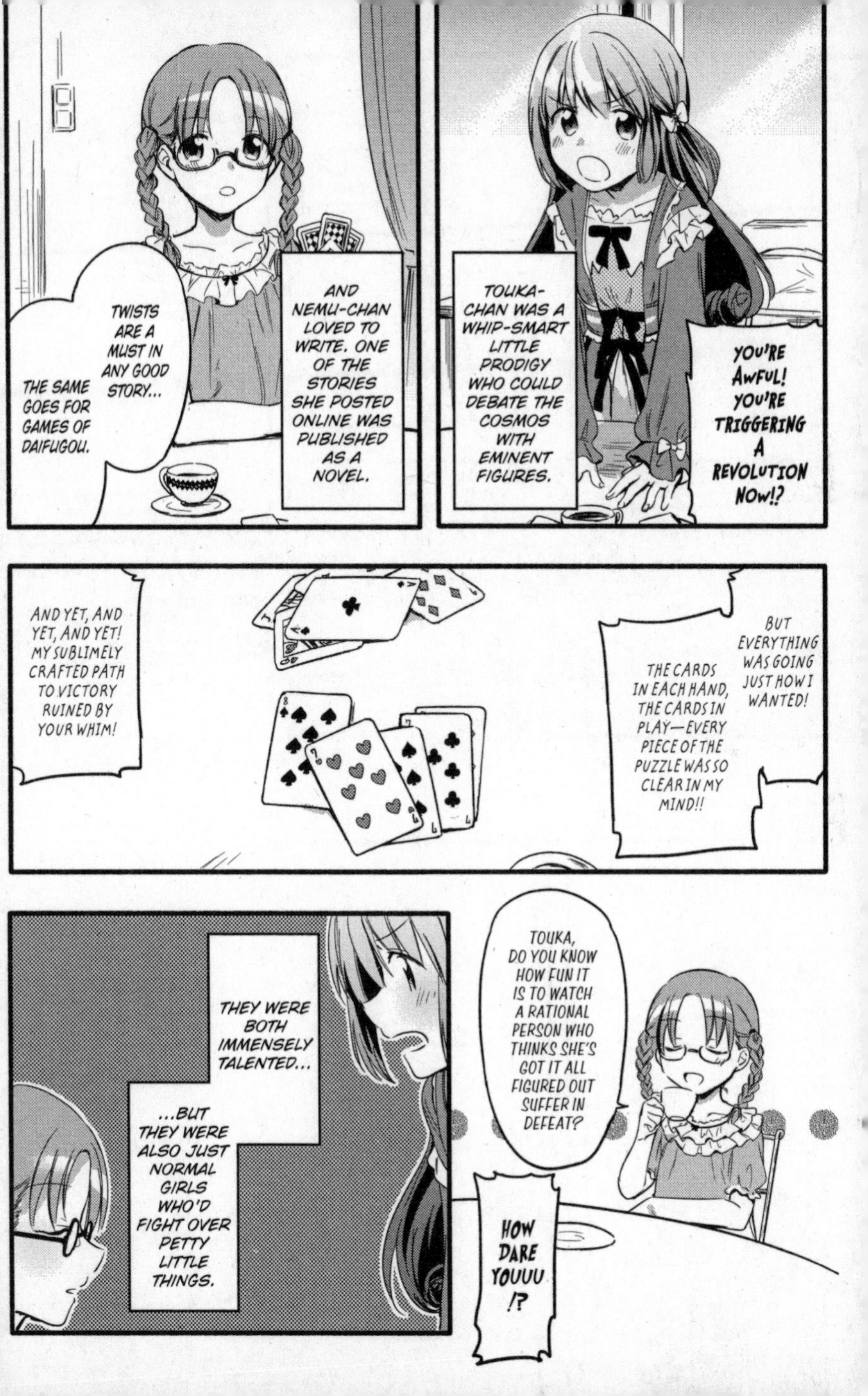
TOUKA-CHAN WAS A WHIP-SMART LITTLE PRODIGY WHO COULD DEBATE THE COSMOS WITH EMINENT FIGURES.
YOU'RE AWFUL! YOU'RE TRIGGERING A REVOLUTION NOW!?
AND NEMU-CHAN LOVED TO WRITE. ONE OF THE STORIES SHE POSTED ONLINE WAS PUBLISHED AS A NOVEL.
TWISTS ARE A MUST IN ANY GOOD STORY...
THE SAME GOES FOR GAMES OF DAIFUGOU.
BUT EVERYTHING WAS GOING JUST HOW I WANTED!
THE CARDS IN EACH HAND, THE CARDS IN PLAY—EVERY PIECE OF THE PUZZLE WAS SO CLEAR IN MY MIND!!
AND YET, AND YET, AND YET! MY SUBLIMELY CRAFTED PATH TO VICTORY RUINED BY YOUR WHIM!
TOUKA, DO YOU KNOW HOW FUN IT IS TO WATCH A RATIONAL PERSON WHO THINKS SHE'S GOT IT ALL FIGURED OUT SUFFER IN DEFEAT?
HOW DARE YOUUU!?
THEY WERE BOTH IMMENSELY TALENTED...
...BUT THEY WERE ALSO JUST NORMAL GIRLS WHO'D FIGHT OVER PETTY LITTLE THINGS.

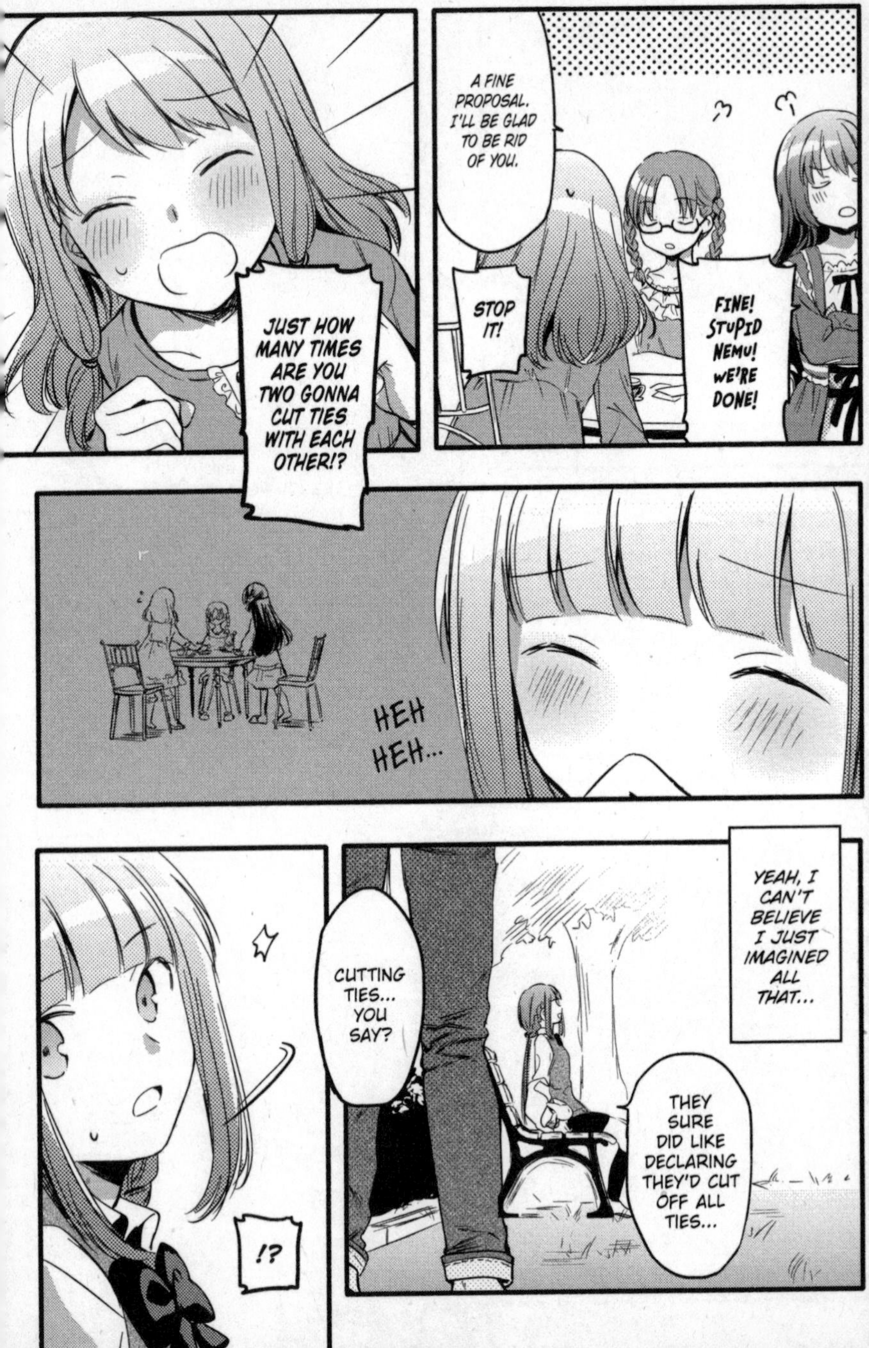
FINE! STUPID NEMU! WE'RE DONE!
A FINE PROPOSAL. I'LL BE GLAD TO BE RID OF YOU.
STOP IT!
JUST HOW MANY TIMES ARE YOU TWO GONNA CUT TIES WITH EACH OTHER!?
HEH HEH...
YEAH, I CAN'T BELIEVE I JUST IMAGINED ALL THAT...
THEY SURE DID LIKE DECLARING THEY'D CUT OFF ALL TIES...
CUTTING TIES... YOU SAY?
!?

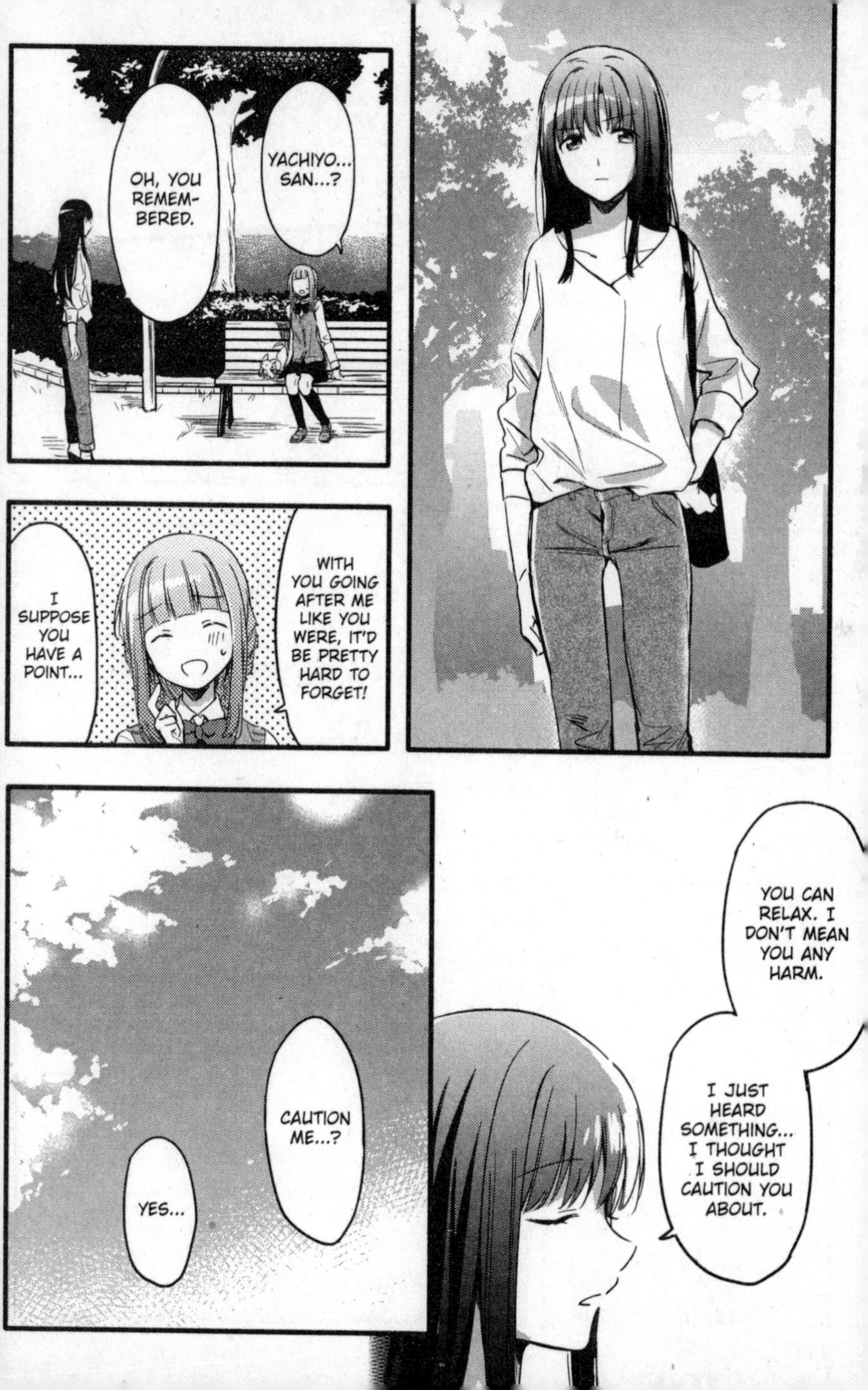
YACHIYO... SAN...?
OH, YOU REMEMBERED.
WITH YOU GOING AFTER ME LIKE YOU WERE, IT'D BE PRETTY HARD TO FORGET!
I SUPPOSE YOU HAVE A POINT...
YOU CAN RELAX. I DON'T MEAN YOU ANY HARM.
I JUST HEARD SOMETHING... I THOUGHT I SHOULD CAUTION YOU ABOUT.
CAUTION ME...?
YES...

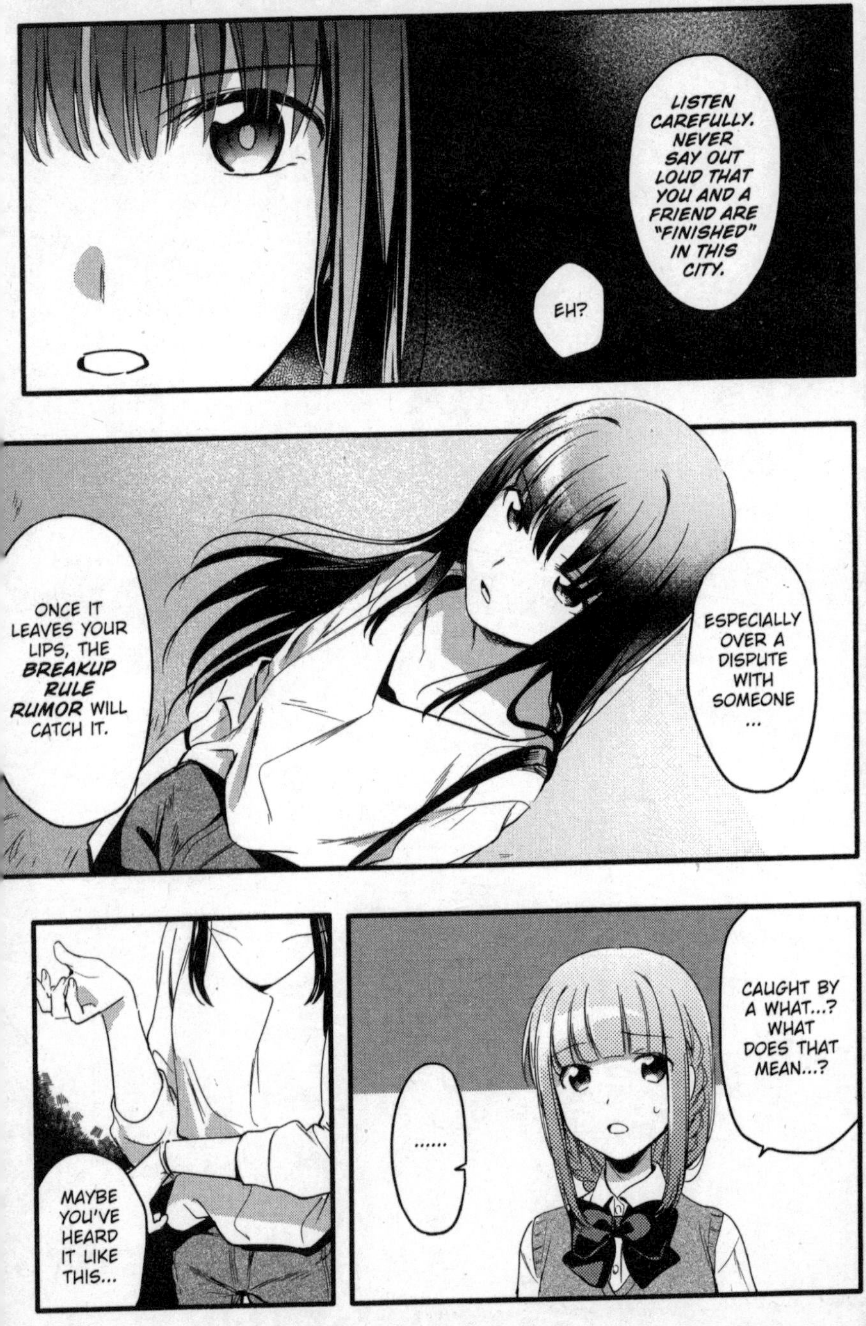
LISTEN CAREFULLY. NEVER SAY OUT LOUD THAT YOU AND A FRIEND ARE "FINISHED" IN THIS CITY.
EH?
ESPECIALLY OVER A DISPUTE WITH SOMEONE ...
ONCE IT LEAVES YOUR LIPS, THE BREAKUP RULE RUMOR WILL CATCH IT.
CAUGHT BY A WHAT...? WHAT DOES THAT MEAN...?
......
MAYBE YOU'VE HEARD IT LIKE THIS...

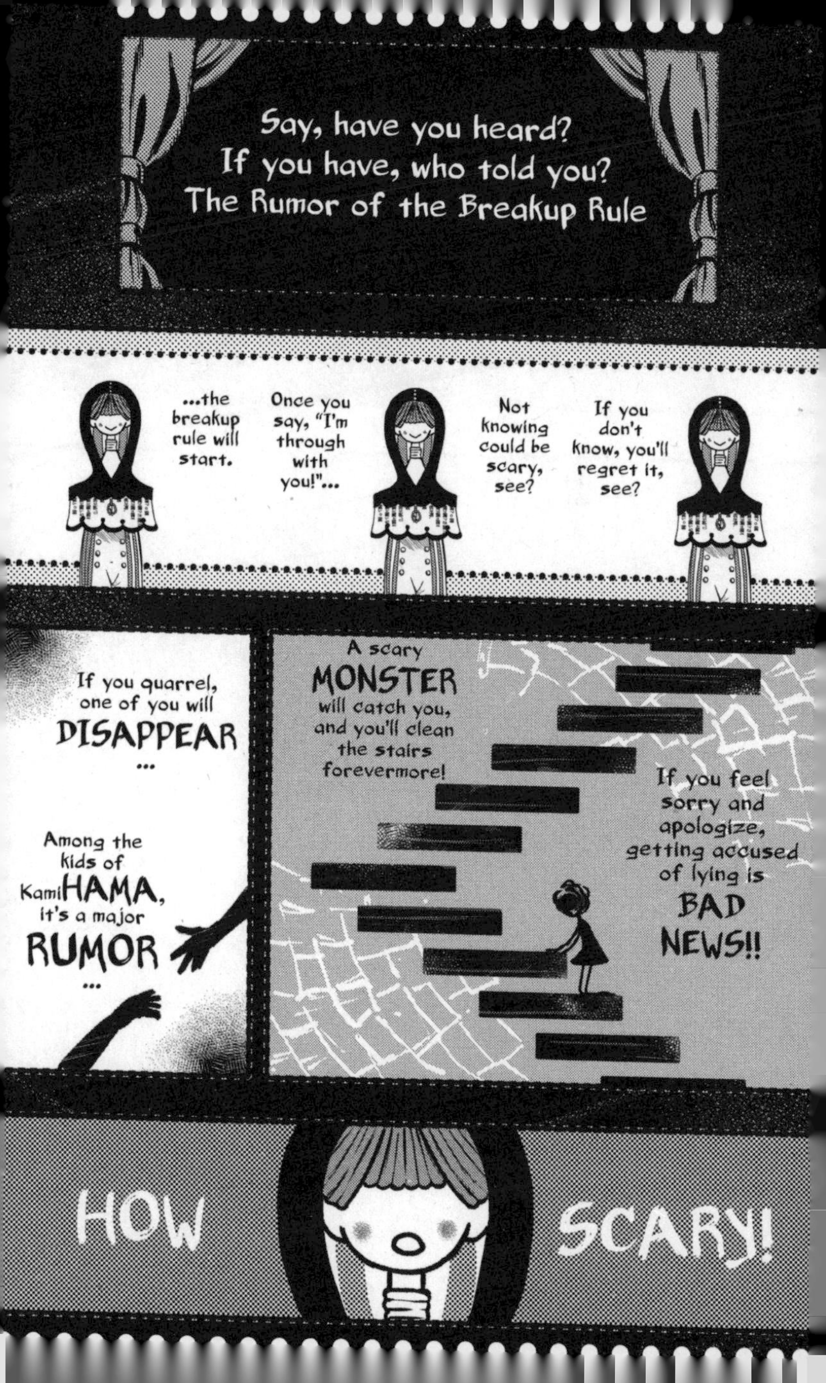
Say, have you heard?
If you have, who told you?
The Rumor of the Breakup Rule
If you don't know, you'll regret it, see?
Not knowing could be scary, see?
Once you say, "I'm through with you!"...
...the breakup rule will start.
A scary MONSTER will catch you, and you'll clean the stairs forevermore!
If you feel sorry and apologize, getting accused of lying is BAD NEWS!!
If you quarrel, one of you will DISAPPEAR...
Among the kids of KamiHAMA, it's a major RUMOR...
HOW SCARY!

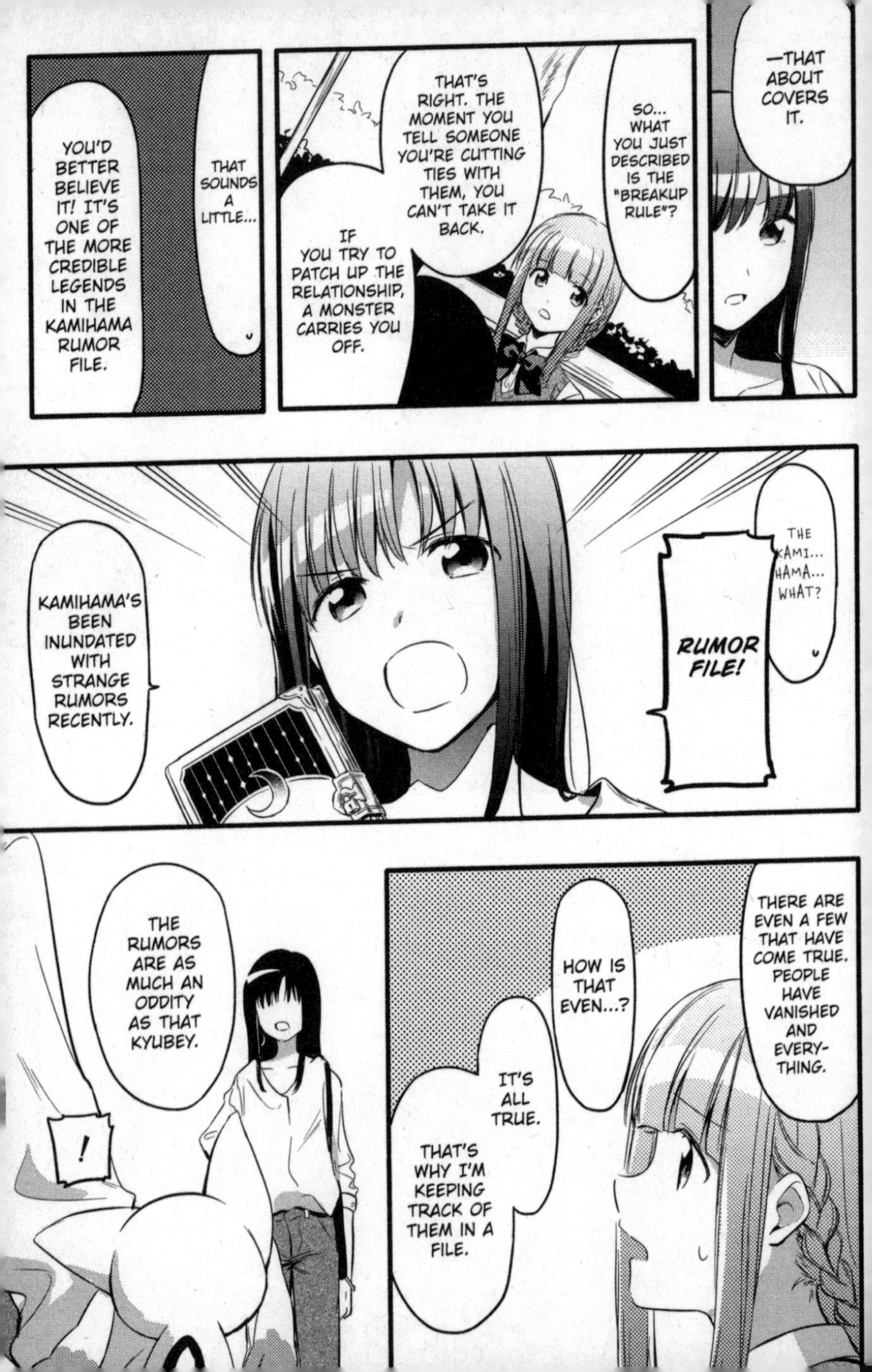
—THAT ABOUT COVERS IT.
SO... WHAT YOU JUST DESCRIBED IS THE "BREAKUP RULE"?
THAT'S RIGHT. THE MOMENT YOU TELL SOMEONE YOU'RE CUTTING TIES WITH THEM, YOU CAN'T TAKE IT BACK.
IF YOU TRY TO PATCH UP THE RELATIONSHIP, A MONSTER CARRIES YOU OFF.
THAT SOUNDS A LITTLE...
YOU'D BETTER BELIEVE IT! IT'S ONE OF THE MORE CREDIBLE LEGENDS IN THE KAMIHAMA RUMOR FILE.
THE KAMI... HAMA... WHAT?
RUMOR FILE!
KAMIHAMA'S BEEN INUNDATED WITH STRANGE RUMORS RECENTLY.
THERE ARE EVEN A FEW THAT HAVE COME TRUE. PEOPLE HAVE VANISHED AND EVERYTHING.
HOW IS THAT EVEN...?
IT'S ALL TRUE.
THAT'S WHY I'M KEEPING TRACK OF THEM IN A FILE.
THE RUMORS ARE AS MUCH AN ODDITY AS THAT KYUBEY.
!

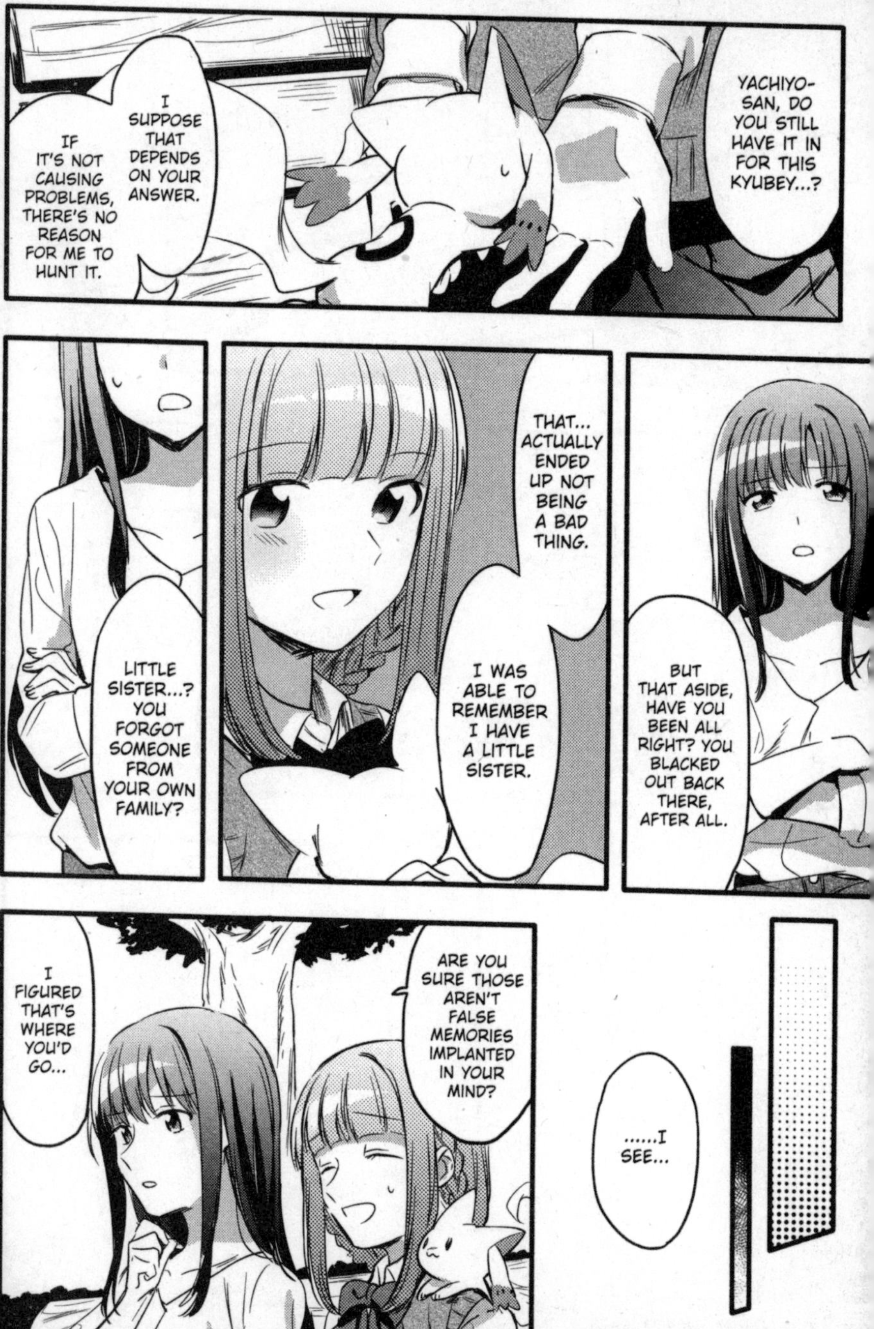
YACHIYO-SAN, DO YOU STILL HAVE IT IN FOR THIS KYUBEY...?
I SUPPOSE THAT DEPENDS ON YOUR ANSWER.
IF IT'S NOT CAUSING PROBLEMS, THERE'S NO REASON FOR ME TO HUNT IT.
BUT THAT ASIDE, HAVE YOU BEEN ALL RIGHT? YOU BLACKED OUT BACK THERE, AFTER ALL.
THAT... ACTUALLY ENDED UP NOT BEING A BAD THING.
I WAS ABLE TO REMEMBER I HAVE A LITTLE SISTER.
LITTLE SISTER...? YOU FORGOT SOMEONE FROM YOUR OWN FAMILY?
......I SEE...
ARE YOU SURE THOSE AREN'T FALSE MEMORIES IMPLANTED IN YOUR MIND?
I FIGURED THAT'S WHERE YOU'D GO...

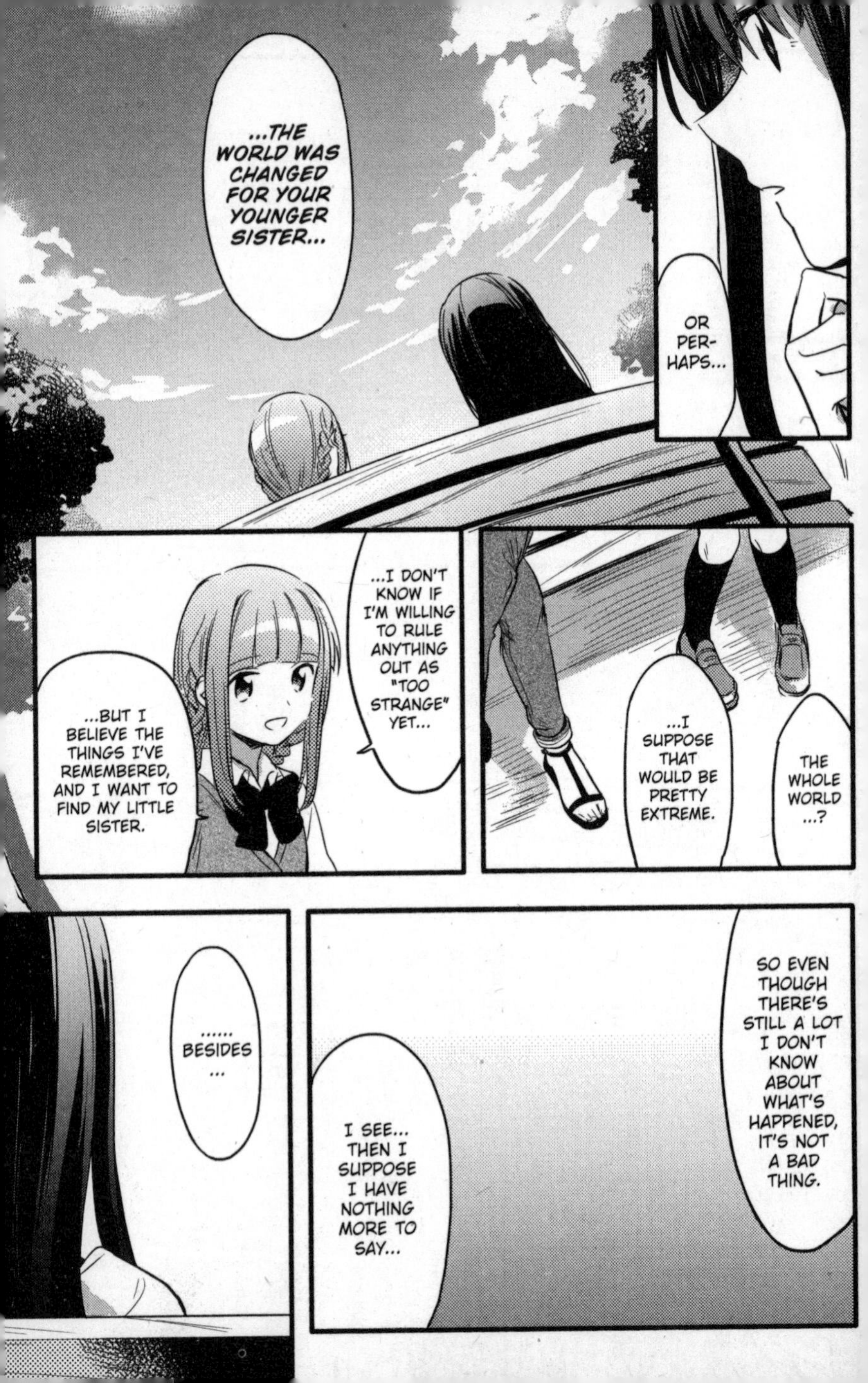
OR PER-HAPS...
...THE WORLD WAS CHANGED FOR YOUR YOUNGER SISTER...
THE WHOLE WORLD ...?
...I SUPPOSE THAT WOULD BE PRETTY EXTREME.
...I DON'T KNOW IF I'M WILLING TO RULE ANYTHING OUT AS "TOO STRANGE" YET...
...BUT I BELIEVE THE THINGS I'VE REMEMBERED, AND I WANT TO FIND MY LITTLE SISTER.
SO EVEN THOUGH THERE'S STILL A LOT I DON'T KNOW ABOUT WHAT'S HAPPENED, IT'S NOT A BAD THING.
I SEE... THEN I SUPPOSE I HAVE NOTHING MORE TO SAY...
...... BESIDES ...

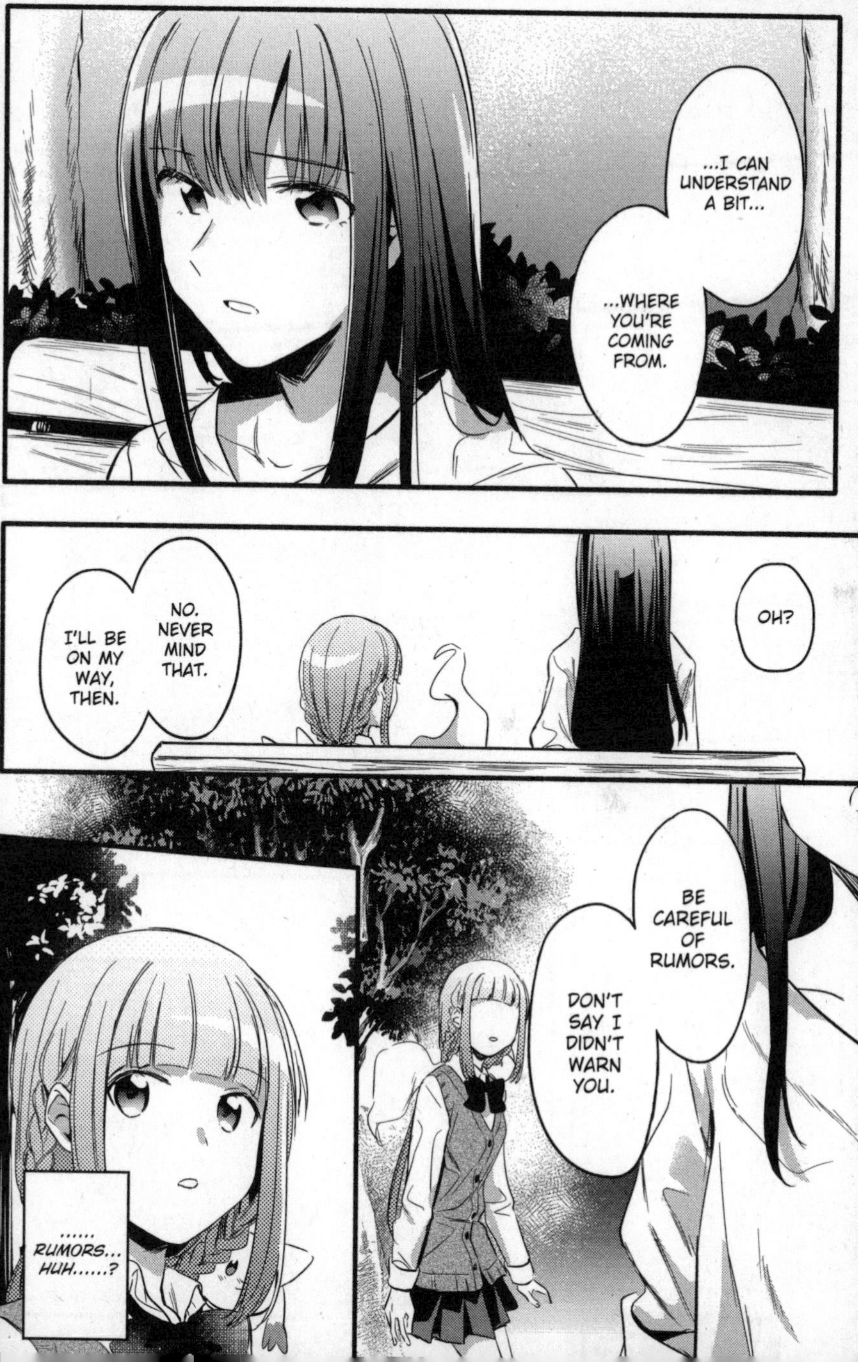
...I CAN UNDERSTAND A BIT...
...WHERE YOU'RE COMING FROM.
OH?
NO. NEVER MIND THAT.
I'LL BE ON MY WAY, THEN.
BE CAREFUL OF RUMORS.
DON'T SAY I DIDN'T WARN YOU.
......RUMORS... HUH......?

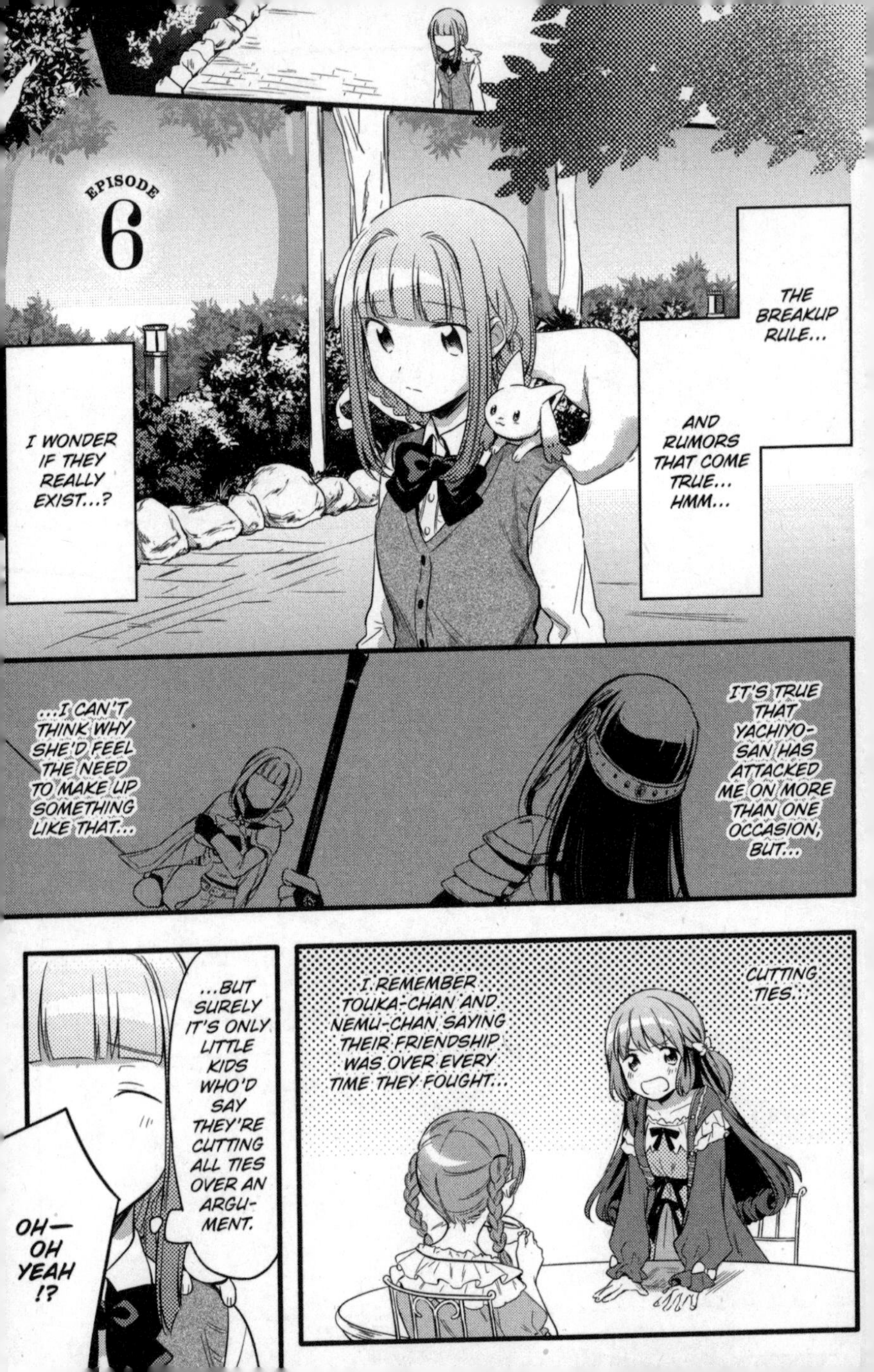
EPISODE 6
THE BREAKUP RULE...
AND RUMORS THAT COME TRUE... HMM...
I WONDER IF THEY REALLY EXIST...?
IT'S TRUE THAT YACHIYO-SAN HAS ATTACKED ME ON MORE THAN ONE OCCASION, BUT...
...I CAN'T THINK WHY SHE'D FEEL THE NEED TO MAKE UP SOMETHING LIKE THAT...
CUTTING TIES.
I REMEMBER TOUKA-CHAN AND NEMU-CHAN SAYING THEIR FRIENDSHIP WAS OVER EVERY TIME THEY FOUGHT...
...BUT SURELY IT'S ONLY LITTLE KIDS WHO'D SAY THEY'RE CUTTING ALL TIES OVER AN ARGUMENT.
OH— OH YEAH!?

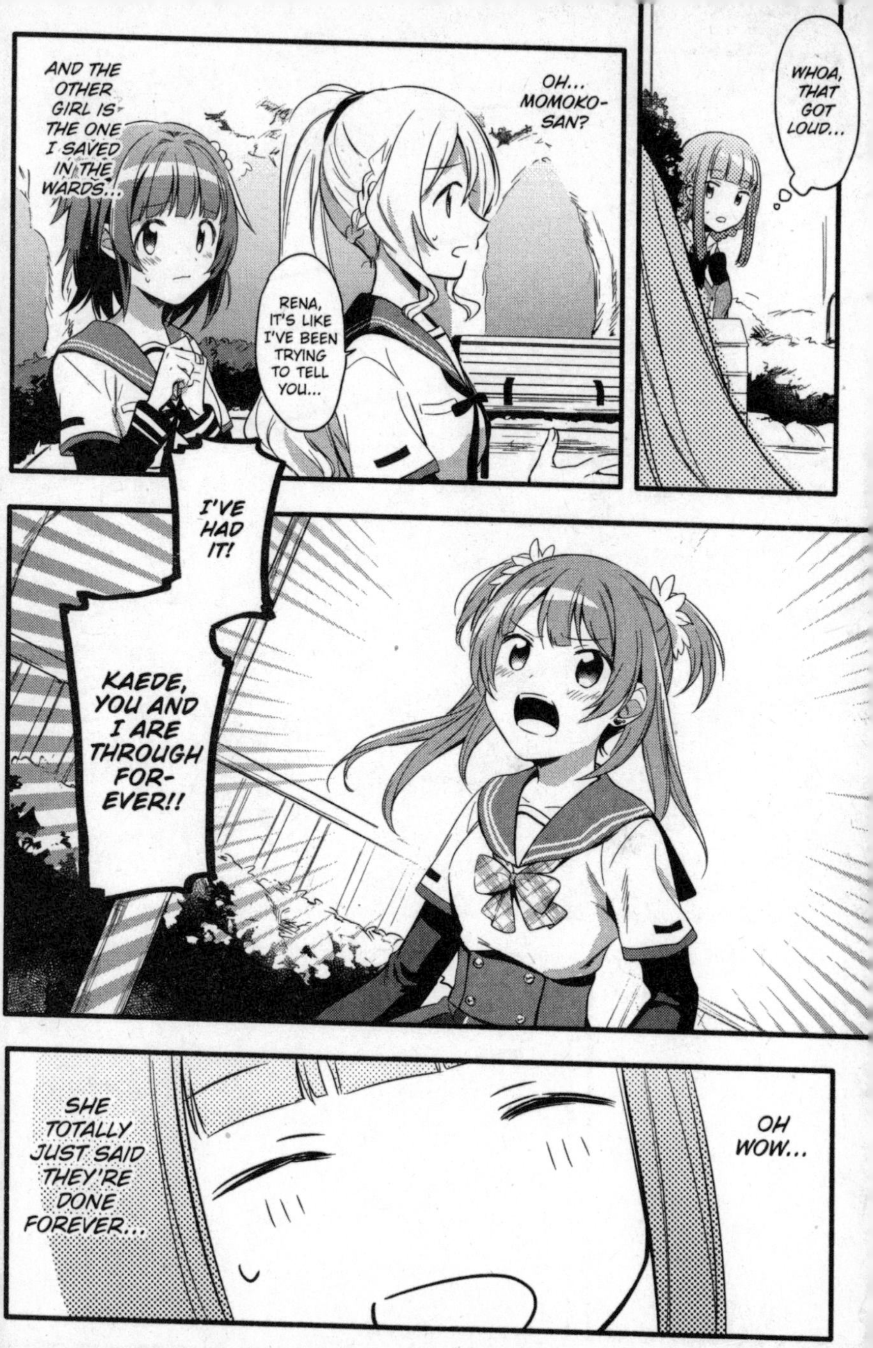
WHOA, THAT GOT LOUD...
OH... MOMOKO-SAN?
AND THE OTHER GIRL IS THE ONE I SAVED IN THE WARDS...
RENA, IT'S LIKE I'VE BEEN TRYING TO TELL YOU...
I'VE HAD IT!
KAEDE, YOU AND I ARE THROUGH FOR-EVER!!
OH WOW...
SHE TOTALLY JUST SAID THEY'RE DONE FOREVER...

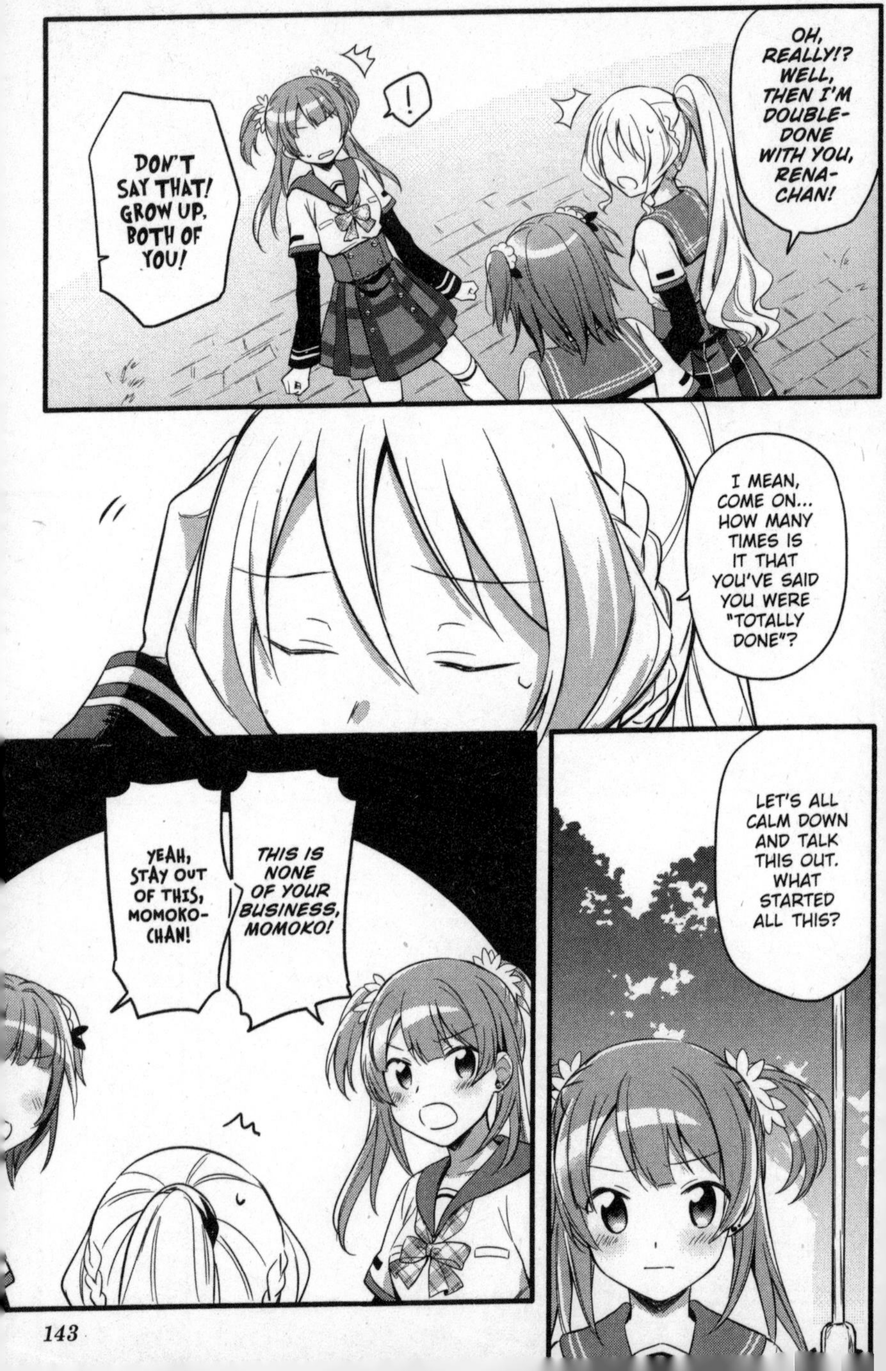
OH, REALLY!? WELL, THEN I'M DOUBLE-DONE WITH YOU, RENA-CHAN!
!
DON'T SAY THAT! GROW UP, BOTH OF YOU!
I MEAN, COME ON... HOW MANY TIMES IS IT THAT YOU'VE SAID YOU WERE "TOTALLY DONE"?
LET'S ALL CALM DOWN AND TALK THIS OUT. WHAT STARTED ALL THIS?
THIS IS NONE OF YOUR BUSINESS, MOMOKO!
YEAH, STAY OUT OF THIS, MOMOKO-CHAN!

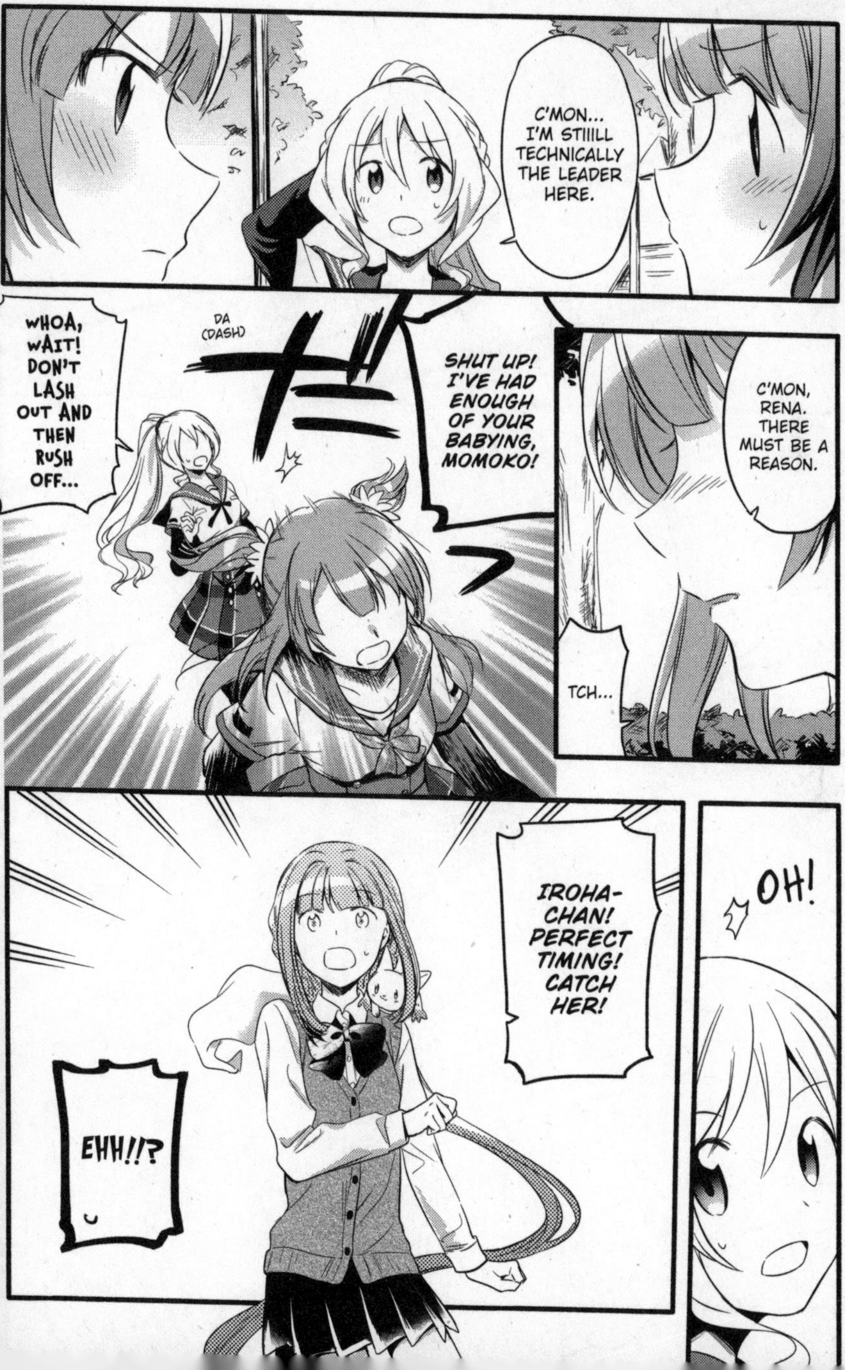
C'MON... I'M STIIIILL TECHNICALLY THE LEADER HERE.
C'MON, RENA. THERE MUST BE A REASON.
TCH...
SHUT UP! I'VE HAD ENOUGH OF YOUR BABYING, MOMOKO!
DA (DASH)
WHOA, WAIT! DON'T LASH OUT AND THEN RUSH OFF...
OH!
IROHA-CHAN! PERFECT TIMING! CATCH HER!
EHH!!?

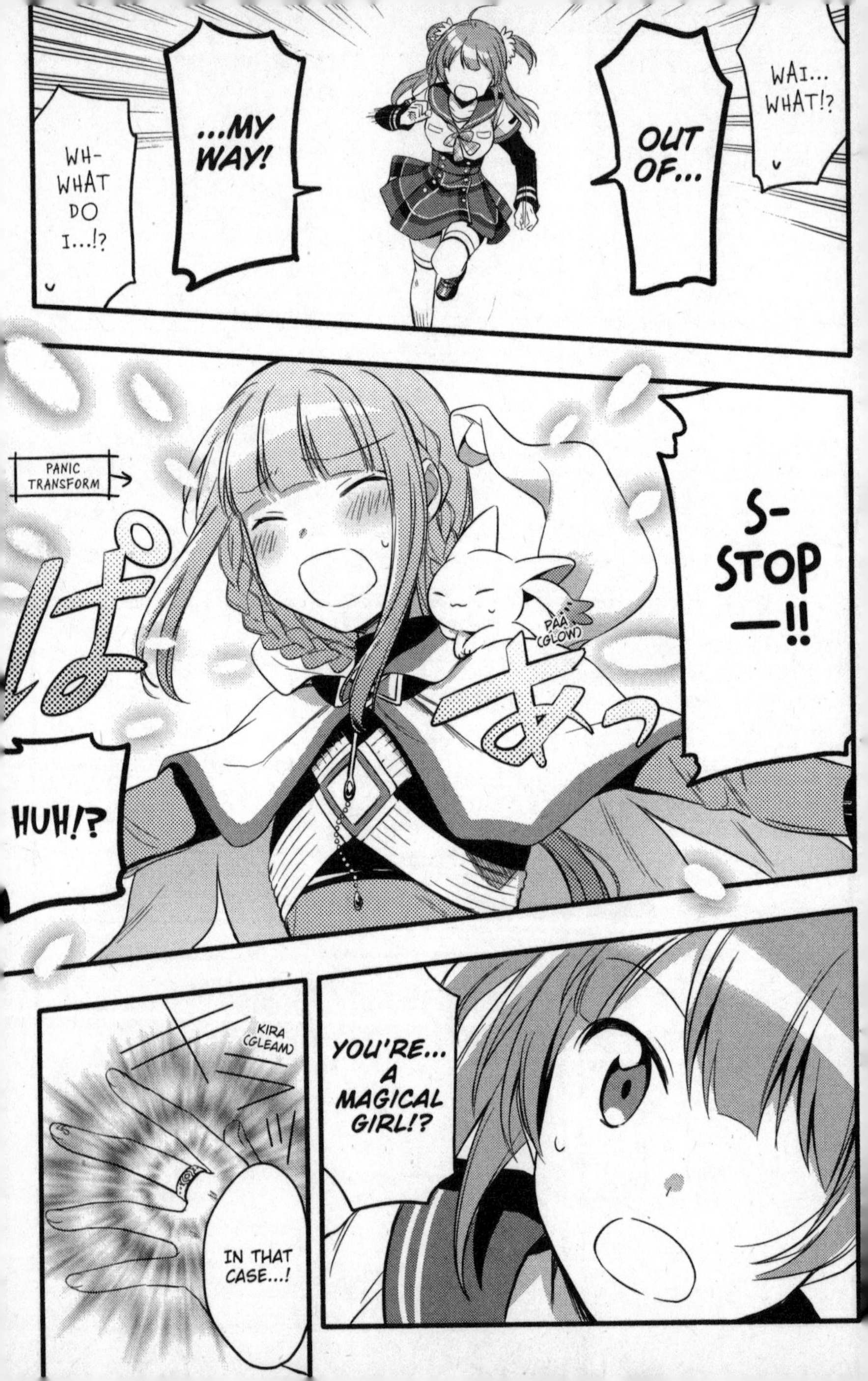
WAI... WHAT!?
OUT OF...
...MY WAY!
WH-WHAT DO I...!?
S-STOP—!!
PAA (GLOW)
ぱあっ
PANIC TRANSFORM
HUH!?
YOU'RE... A MAGICAL GIRL!?
KIRA (GLEAM)
IN THAT CASE...!

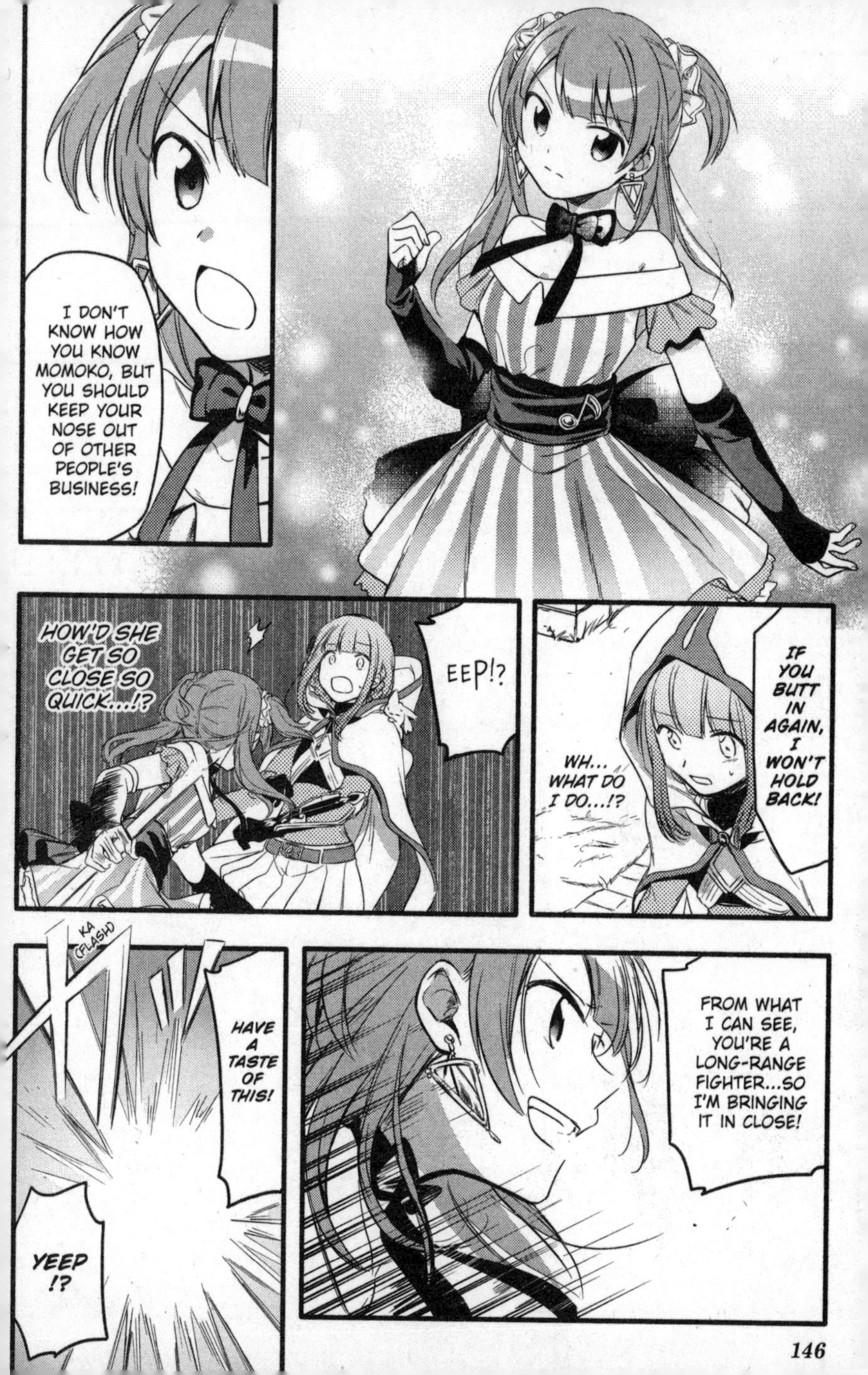
I DON'T KNOW HOW YOU KNOW MOMOKO, BUT YOU SHOULD KEEP YOUR NOSE OUT OF OTHER PEOPLE'S BUSINESS!
IF YOU BUTT IN AGAIN, I WON'T HOLD BACK!
WH... WHAT DO I DO...!?
EEP!?
HOW'D SHE GET SO CLOSE SO QUICK...!?
FROM WHAT I CAN SEE, YOU'RE A LONG-RANGE FIGHTER...SO I'M BRINGING IT IN CLOSE!
KA (FLASH)
HAVE A TASTE OF THIS!
YEEP !?

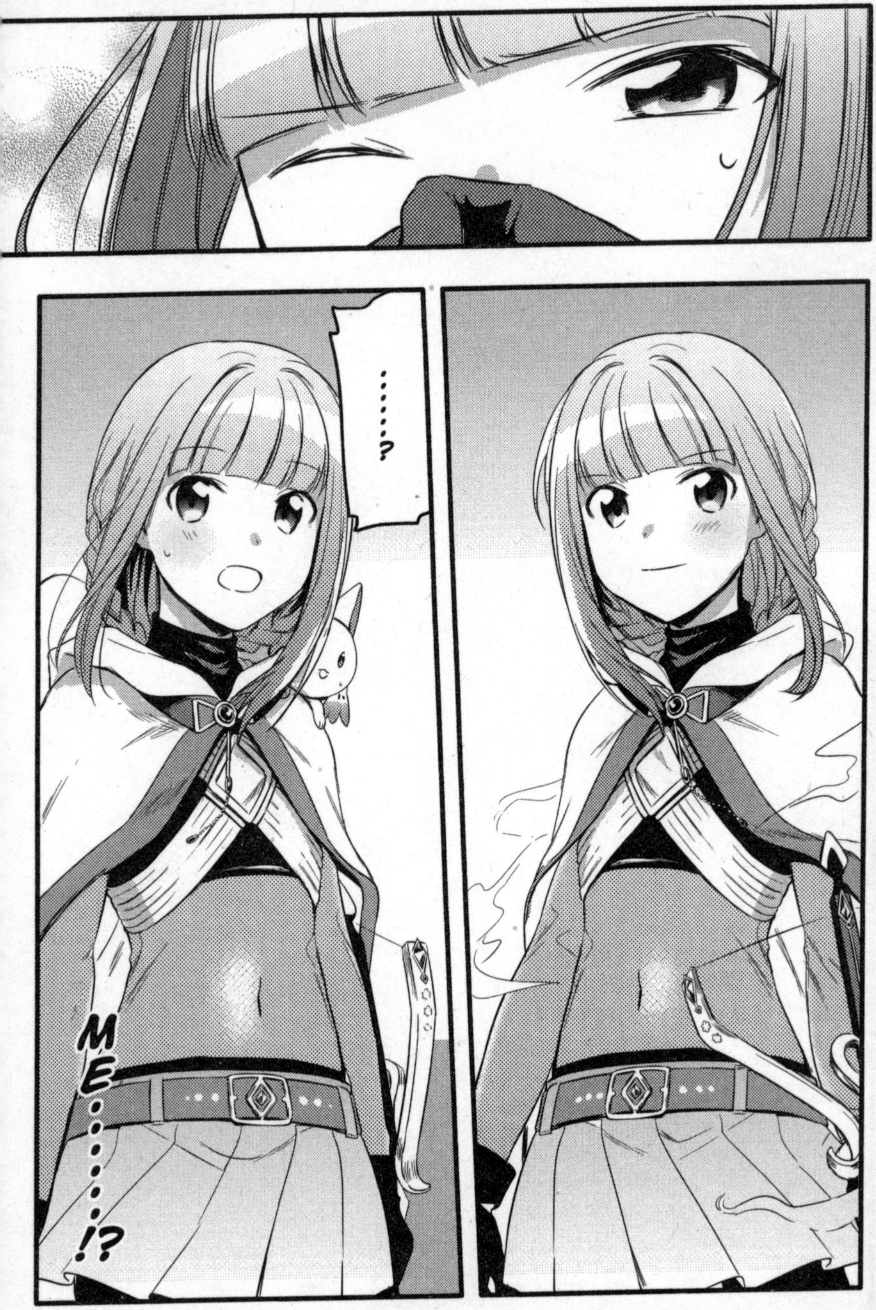
......?
ME......!?

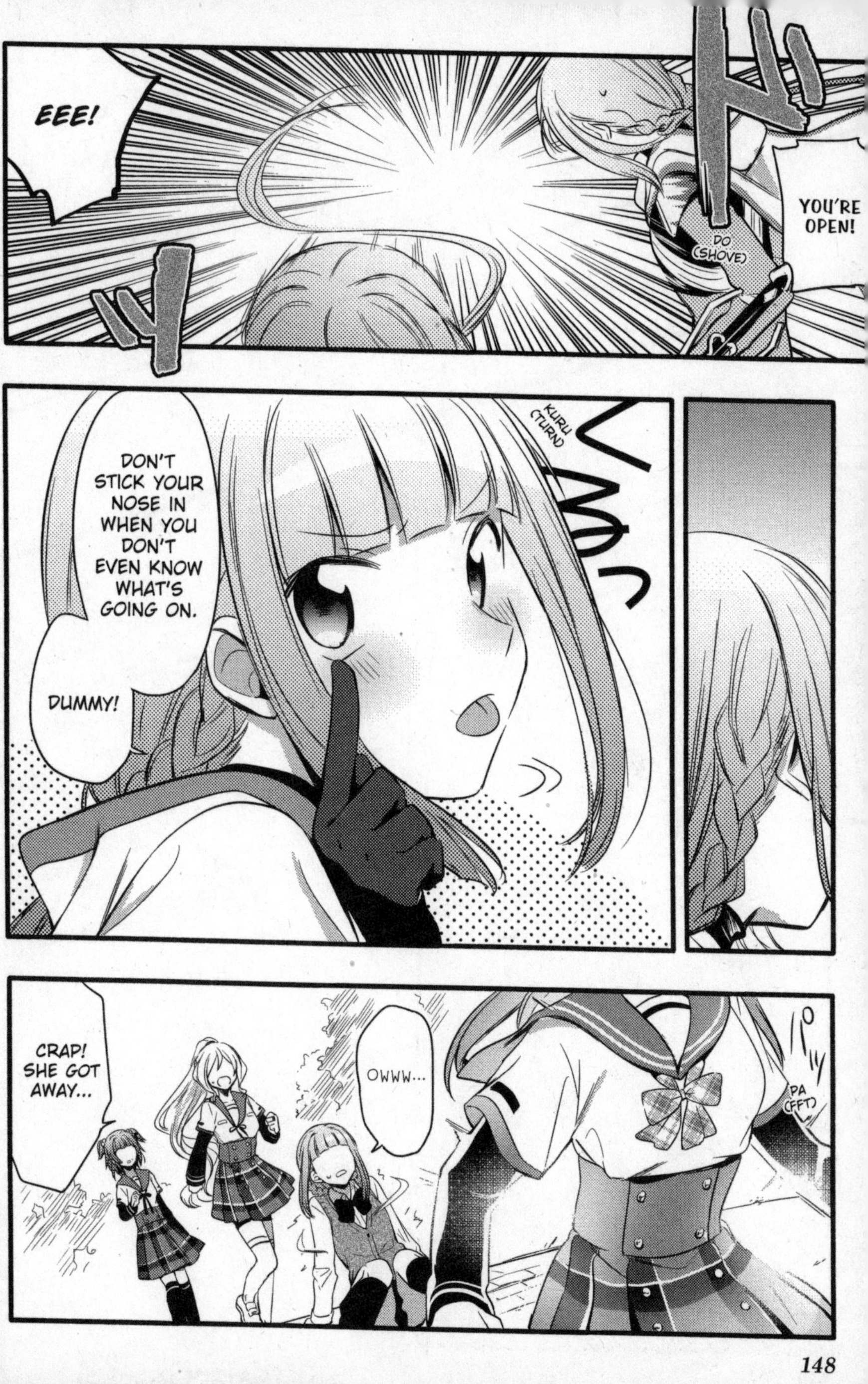
YOU'RE OPEN!
DO (SHOVE)
EEE!
KURU (TURN)
DON'T STICK YOUR NOSE IN WHEN YOU DON'T EVEN KNOW WHAT'S GOING ON.
DUMMY!
PA (FFT)
OWWW...
CRAP! SHE GOT AWAY...

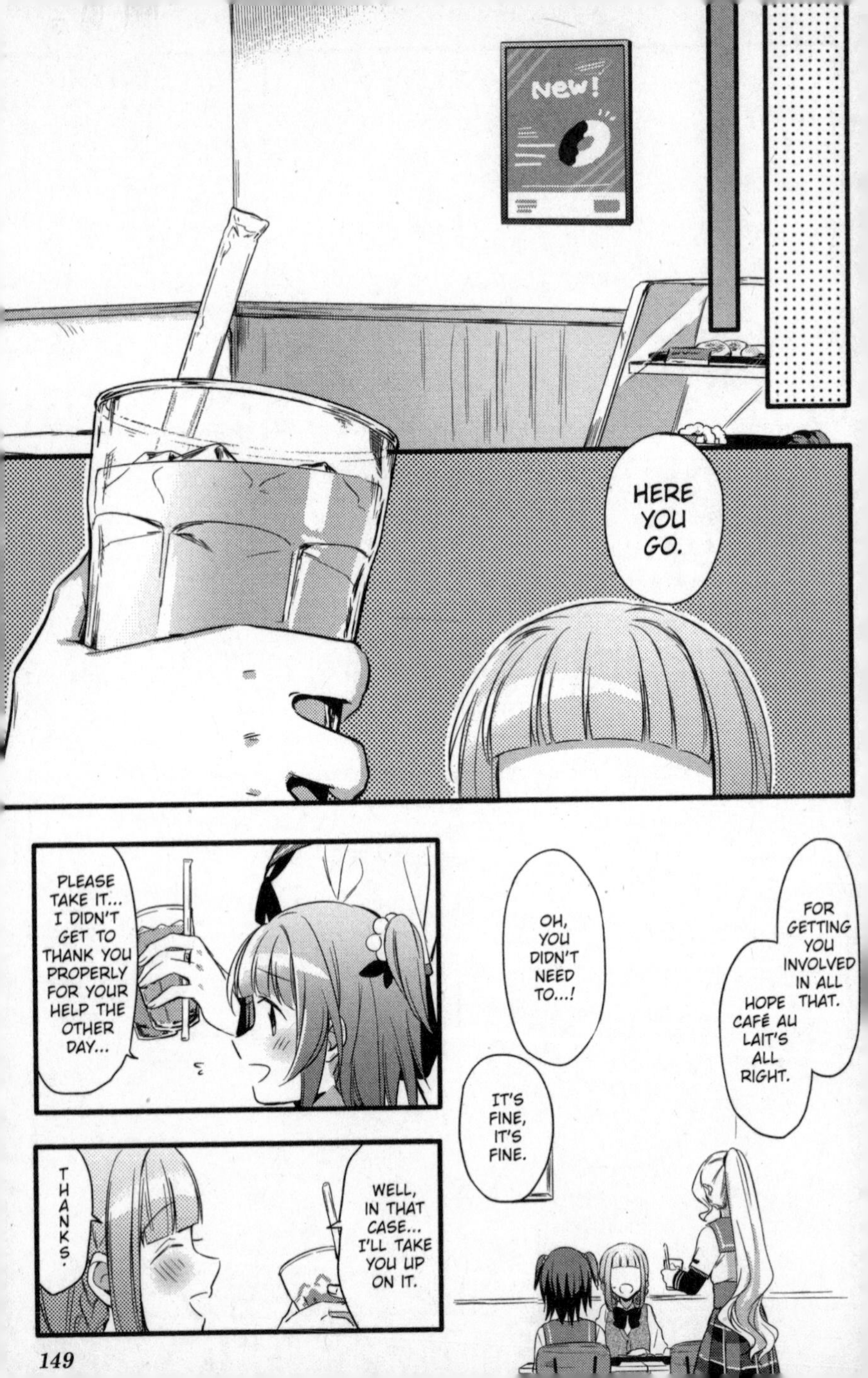
HERE YOU GO.
FOR GETTING YOU INVOLVED IN ALL THAT.
HOPE CAFÉ AU LAIT'S ALL RIGHT.
OH, YOU DIDN'T NEED TO...!
IT'S FINE, IT'S FINE.
PLEASE TAKE IT... I DIDN'T GET TO THANK YOU PROPERLY FOR YOUR HELP THE OTHER DAY...
WELL, IN THAT CASE... I'LL TAKE YOU UP ON IT.
THANKS.

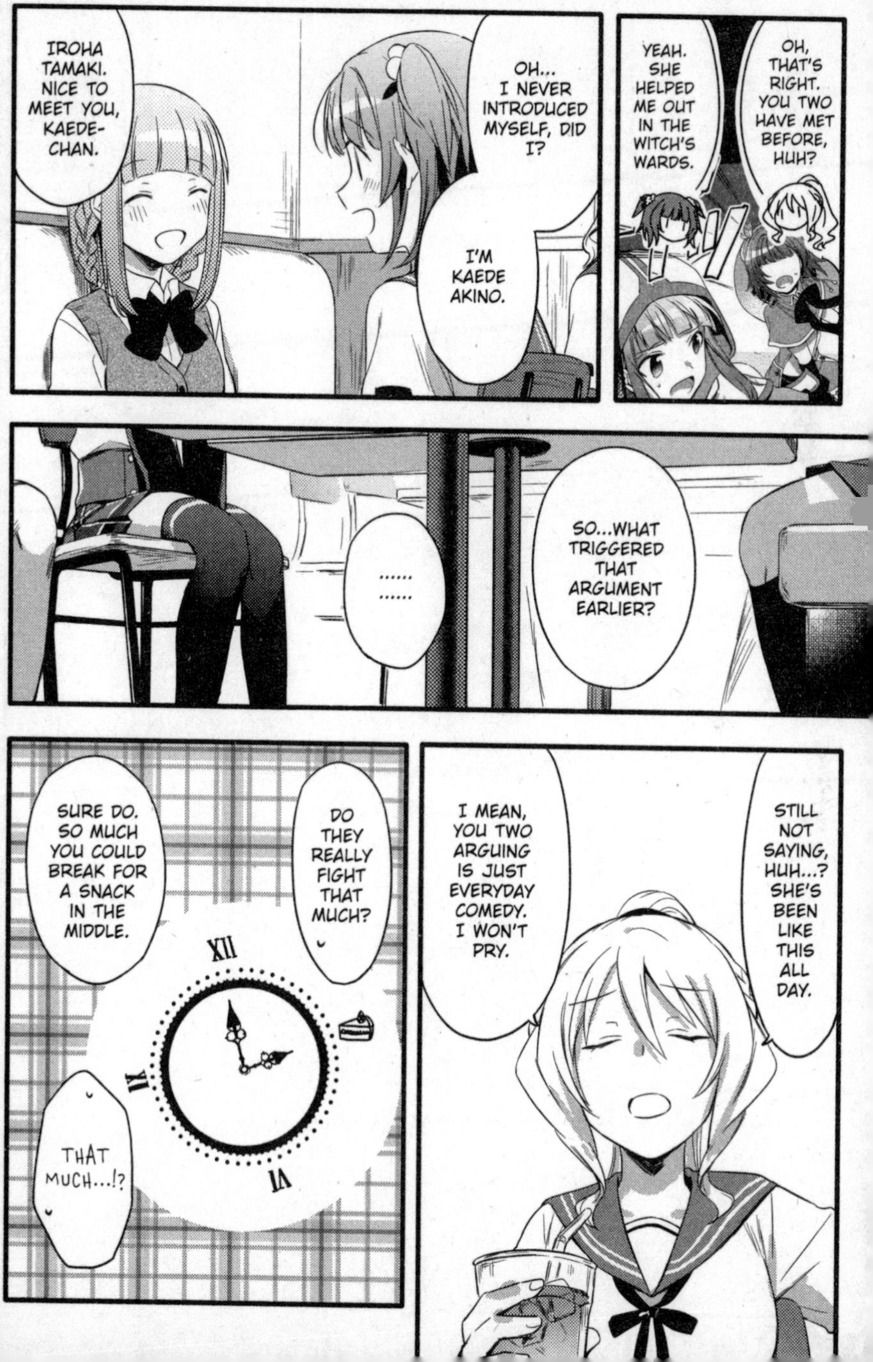
OH, THAT'S RIGHT. YOU TWO HAVE MET BEFORE, HUH?
YEAH. SHE HELPED ME OUT IN THE WITCH'S WARDS.
OH... I NEVER INTRODUCED MYSELF, DID I?
I'M KAEDE AKINO.
IROHA TAMAKI. NICE TO MEET YOU, KAEDE-CHAN.
SO...WHAT TRIGGERED THAT ARGUMENT EARLIER?
....
STILL NOT SAYING, HUH...? SHE'S BEEN LIKE THIS ALL DAY.
I MEAN, YOU TWO ARGUING IS JUST EVERYDAY COMEDY. I WON'T PRY.
DO THEY REALLY FIGHT THAT MUCH?
SURE DO. SO MUCH YOU COULD BREAK FOR A SNACK IN THE MIDDLE.
THAT MUCH...!?

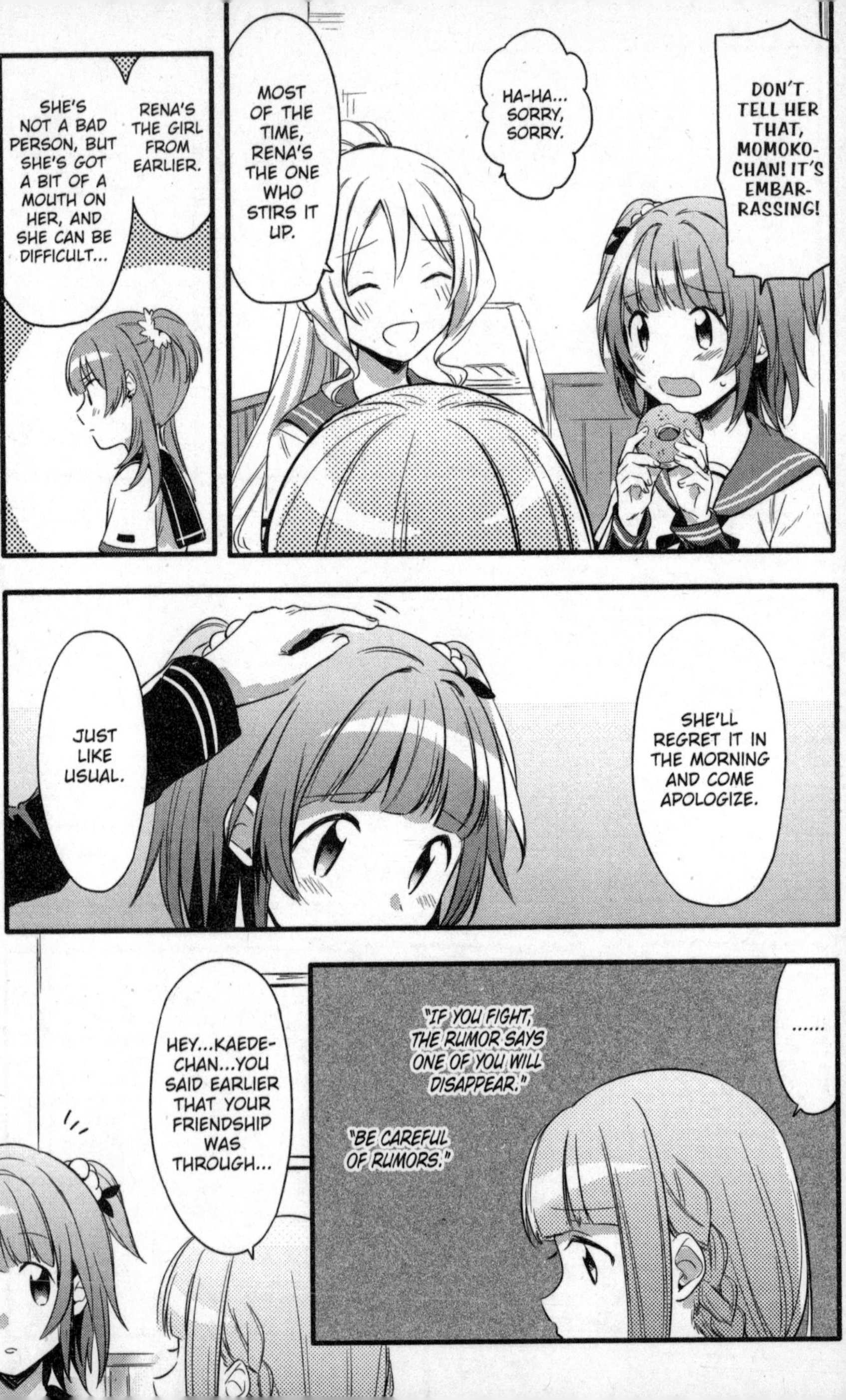
DON'T TELL HER THAT, MOMOKO-CHAN! IT'S EMBARRASSING!
HA-HA... SORRY, SORRY.
MOST OF THE TIME, RENA'S THE ONE WHO STIRS IT UP.
RENA'S THE GIRL FROM EARLIER.
SHE'S NOT A BAD PERSON, BUT SHE'S GOT A BIT OF A MOUTH ON HER, AND SHE CAN BE DIFFICULT...
SHE'LL REGRET IT IN THE MORNING AND COME APOLOGIZE.
JUST LIKE USUAL.
......
"IF YOU FIGHT, THE RUMOR SAYS ONE OF YOU WILL DISAPPEAR."
"BE CAREFUL OF RUMORS."
HEY...KAEDE-CHAN...YOU SAID EARLIER THAT YOUR FRIENDSHIP WAS THROUGH...

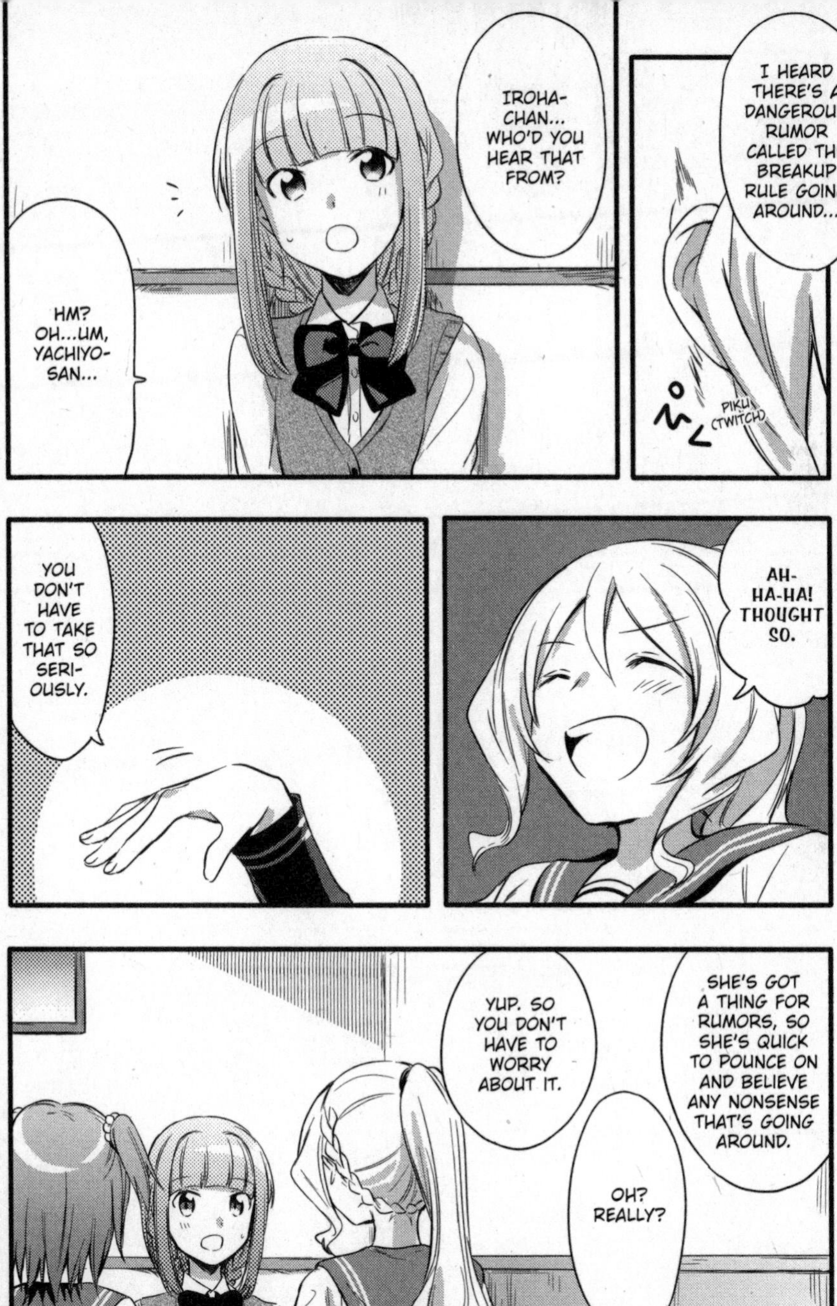
I HEARD THERE'S A DANGEROUS RUMOR CALLED THE BREAKUP RULE GOING AROUND...
PIKU (TWITCH)
IROHA-CHAN... WHO'D YOU HEAR THAT FROM?
HM? OH...UM, YACHIYO-SAN...
AH-HA-HA! THOUGHT SO.
YOU DON'T HAVE TO TAKE THAT SO SERI-OUSLY.
SHE'S GOT A THING FOR RUMORS, SO SHE'S QUICK TO POUNCE ON AND BELIEVE ANY NONSENSE THAT'S GOING AROUND.
YUP. SO YOU DON'T HAVE TO WORRY ABOUT IT.
OH? REALLY?

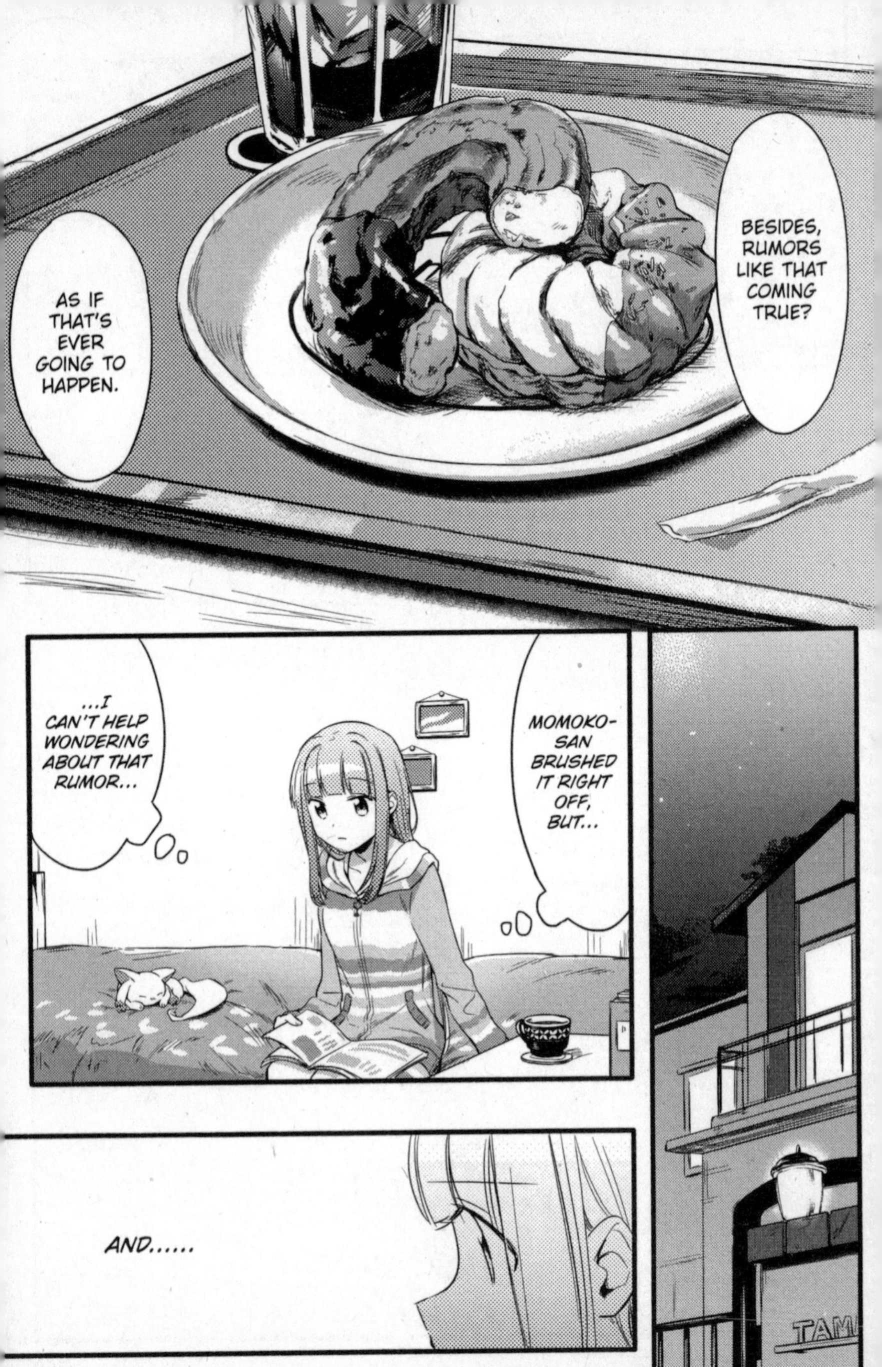
BESIDES, RUMORS LIKE THAT COMING TRUE?
AS IF THAT'S EVER GOING TO HAPPEN.
TAM
MOMOKO-SAN BRUSHED IT RIGHT OFF, BUT...
...I CAN'T HELP WONDERING ABOUT THAT RUMOR...
AND......

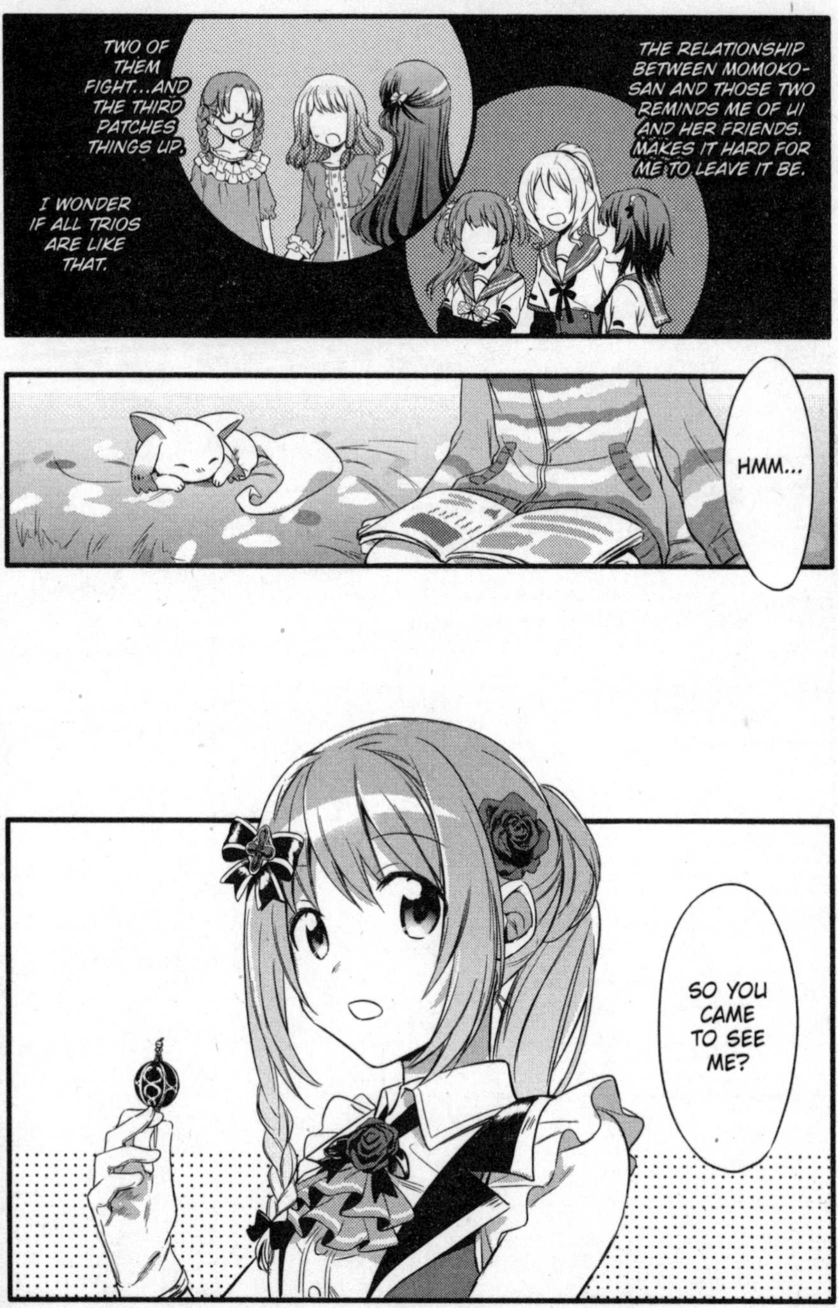
THE RELATIONSHIP BETWEEN MOMOKO-SAN AND THOSE TWO REMINDS ME OF UI AND HER FRIENDS. MAKES IT HARD FOR ME TO LEAVE IT BE.
TWO OF THEM FIGHT...AND THE THIRD PATCHES THINGS UP.
I WONDER IF ALL TRIOS ARE LIKE THAT.
HMM...
SO YOU CAME TO SEE ME?

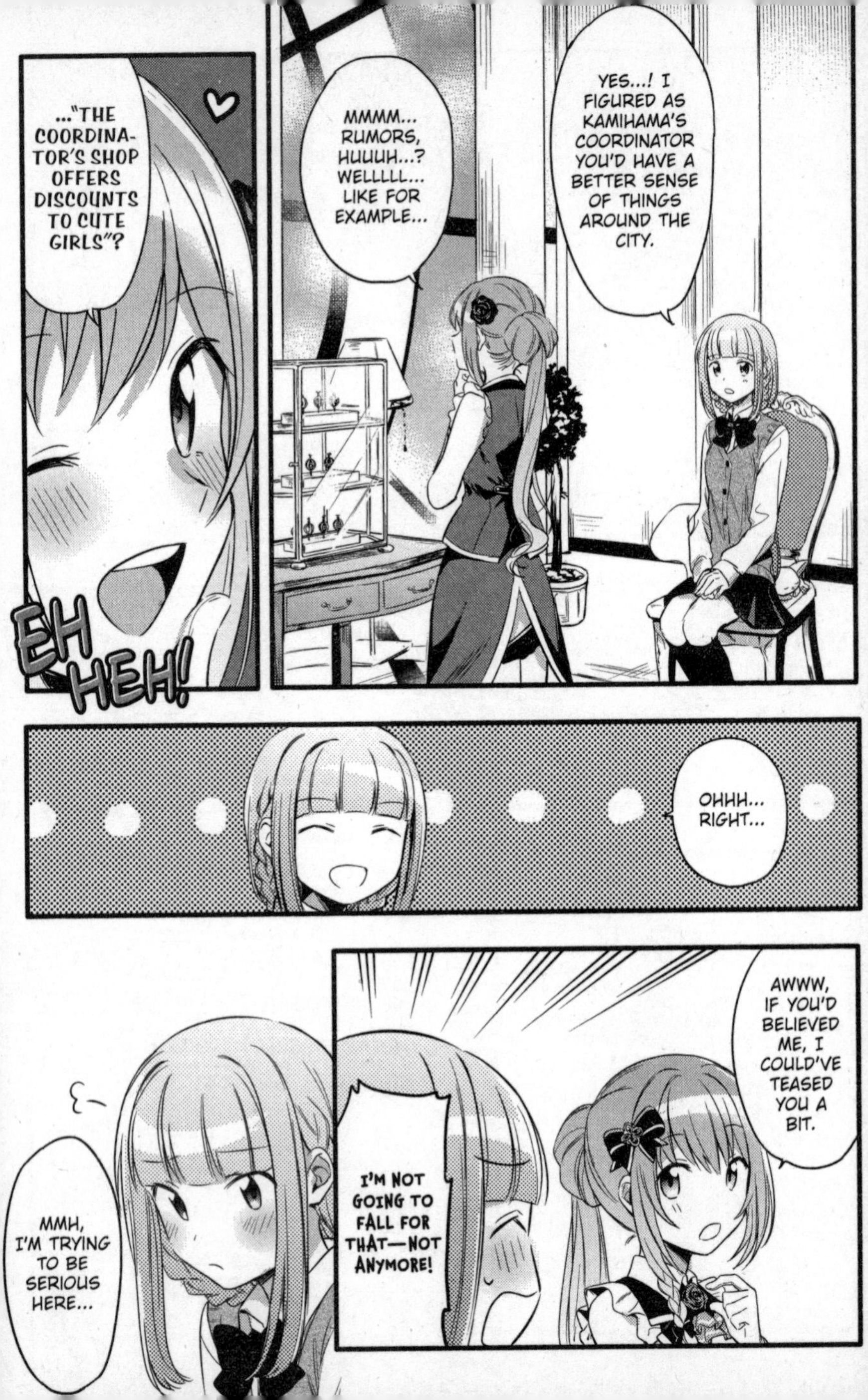
YES...! I FIGURED AS KAMIHAMA'S COORDINATOR YOU'D HAVE A BETTER SENSE OF THINGS AROUND THE CITY.
MMMM... RUMORS, HUUUH...? WELLLLL... LIKE FOR EXAMPLE...
..."THE COORDINATOR'S SHOP OFFERS DISCOUNTS TO CUTE GIRLS"?
EH HEH!
OHHH... RIGHT...
AWWW, IF YOU'D BELIEVED ME, I COULD'VE TEASED YOU A BIT.
I'M NOT GOING TO FALL FOR THAT—NOT ANYMORE!
MMH, I'M TRYING TO BE SERIOUS HERE...

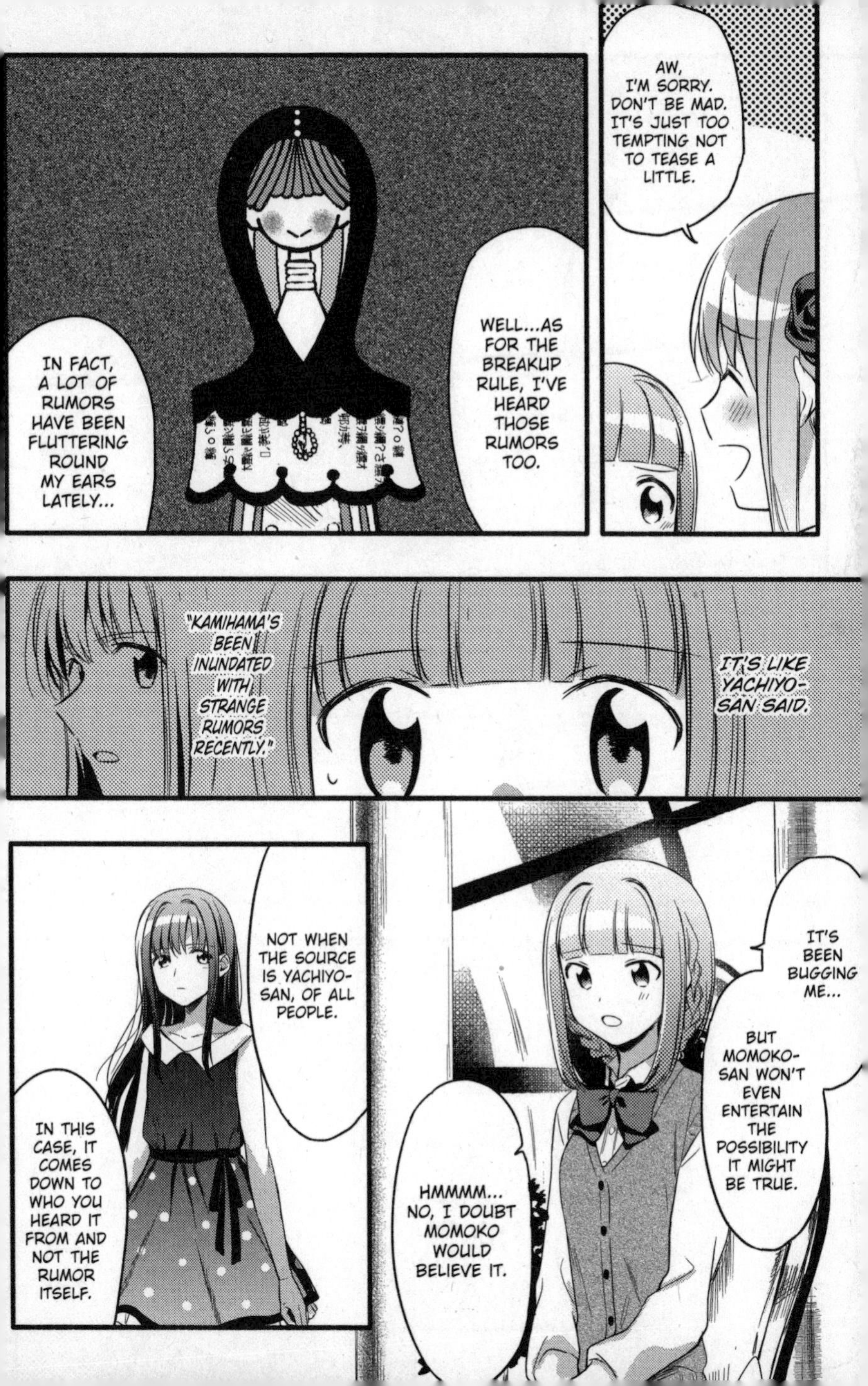
AW, I'M SORRY. DON'T BE MAD. IT'S JUST TOO TEMPTING NOT TO TEASE A LITTLE.
WELL...AS FOR THE BREAKUP RULE, I'VE HEARD THOSE RUMORS TOO.
IN FACT, A LOT OF RUMORS HAVE BEEN FLUTTERING ROUND MY EARS LATELY...
IT'S LIKE YACHIYO-SAN SAID.
"KAMIHAMA'S BEEN INUNDATED WITH STRANGE RUMORS RECENTLY."
IT'S BEEN BUGGING ME...
BUT MOMOKO-SAN WON'T EVEN ENTERTAIN THE POSSIBILITY IT MIGHT BE TRUE.
HMMMM... NO, I DOUBT MOMOKO WOULD BELIEVE IT.
NOT WHEN THE SOURCE IS YACHIYO-SAN, OF ALL PEOPLE.
IN THIS CASE, IT COMES DOWN TO WHO YOU HEARD IT FROM AND NOT THE RUMOR ITSELF.

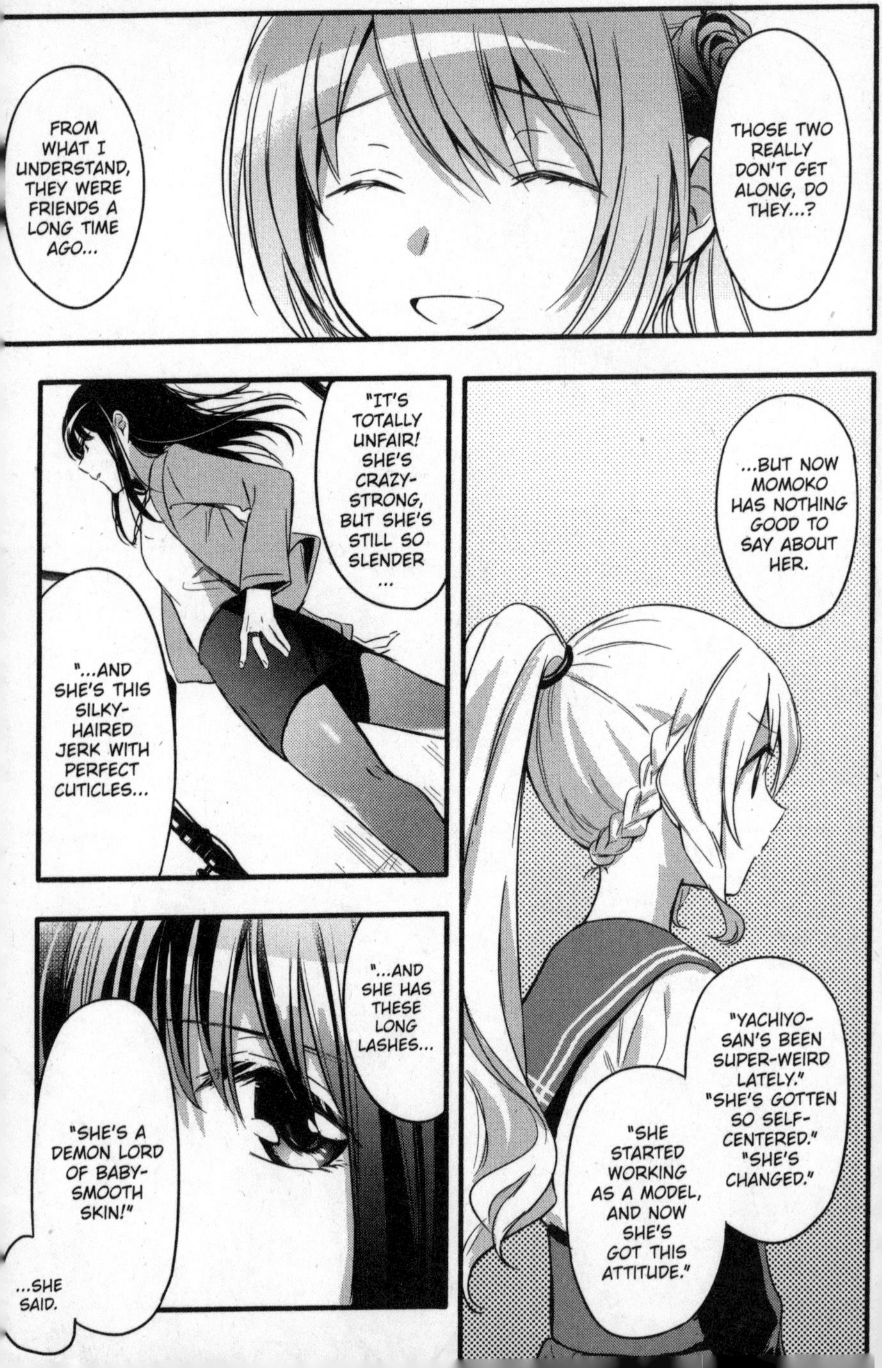
THOSE TWO REALLY DON'T GET ALONG, DO THEY...?
FROM WHAT I UNDERSTAND, THEY WERE FRIENDS A LONG TIME AGO...
...BUT NOW MOMOKO HAS NOTHING GOOD TO SAY ABOUT HER.
"YACHIYO-SAN'S BEEN SUPER-WEIRD LATELY." "SHE'S GOTTEN SO SELF-CENTERED." "SHE'S CHANGED."
"SHE STARTED WORKING AS A MODEL, AND NOW SHE'S GOT THIS ATTITUDE."
"IT'S TOTALLY UNFAIR! SHE'S CRAZY-STRONG, BUT SHE'S STILL SO SLENDER...
"...AND SHE'S THIS SILKY-HAIRED JERK WITH PERFECT CUTICLES...
"...AND SHE HAS THESE LONG LASHES...
"SHE'S A DEMON LORD OF BABY-SMOOTH SKIN!"
...SHE SAID.

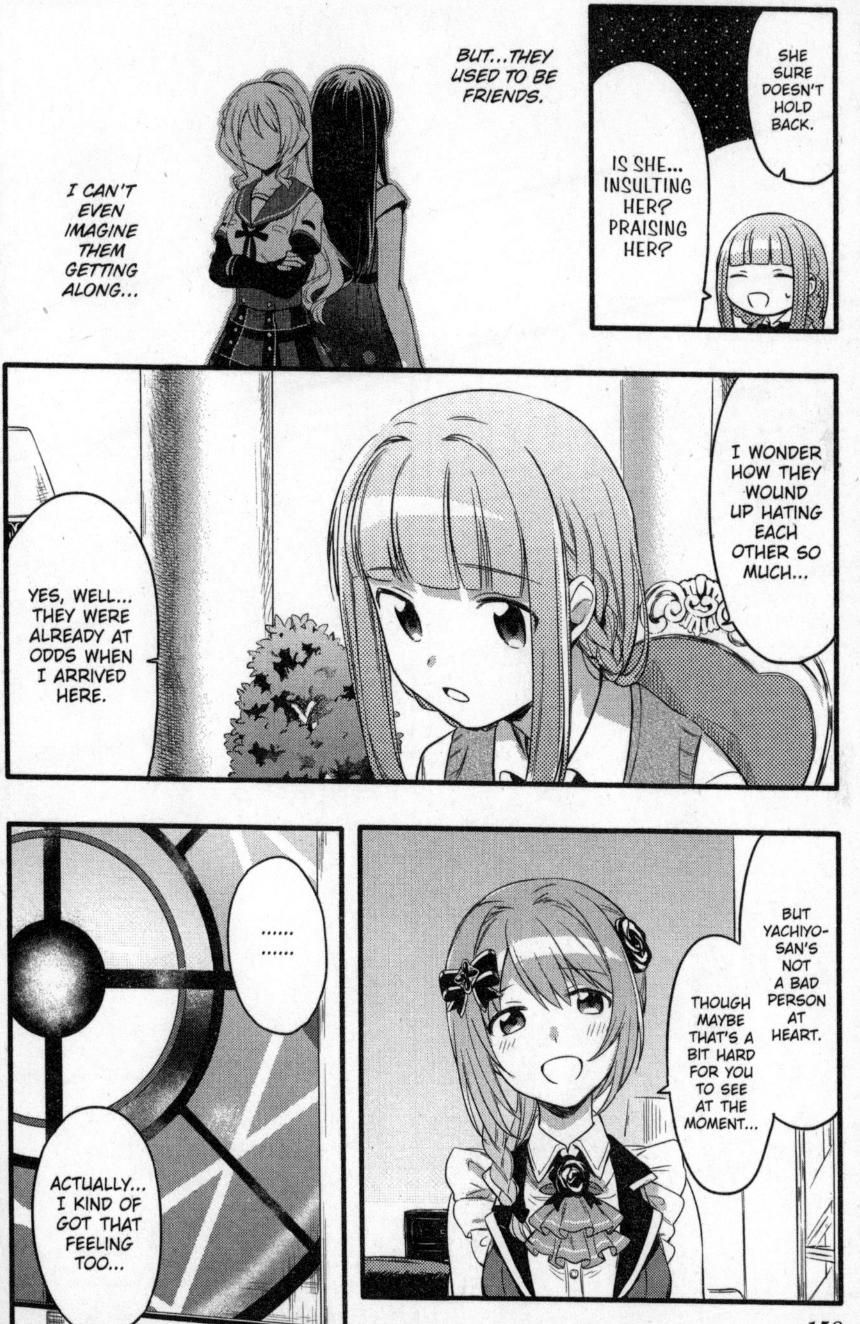
SHE SURE DOESN'T HOLD BACK.
IS SHE... INSULTING HER? PRAISING HER?
BUT...THEY USED TO BE FRIENDS.
I CAN'T EVEN IMAGINE THEM GETTING ALONG...
I WONDER HOW THEY WOUND UP HATING EACH OTHER SO MUCH...
YES, WELL... THEY WERE ALREADY AT ODDS WHEN I ARRIVED HERE.
BUT YACHIYO-SAN'S NOT A BAD PERSON AT HEART.
THOUGH MAYBE THAT'S A BIT HARD FOR YOU TO SEE AT THE MOMENT...
....
ACTUALLY... I KIND OF GOT THAT FEELING TOO...

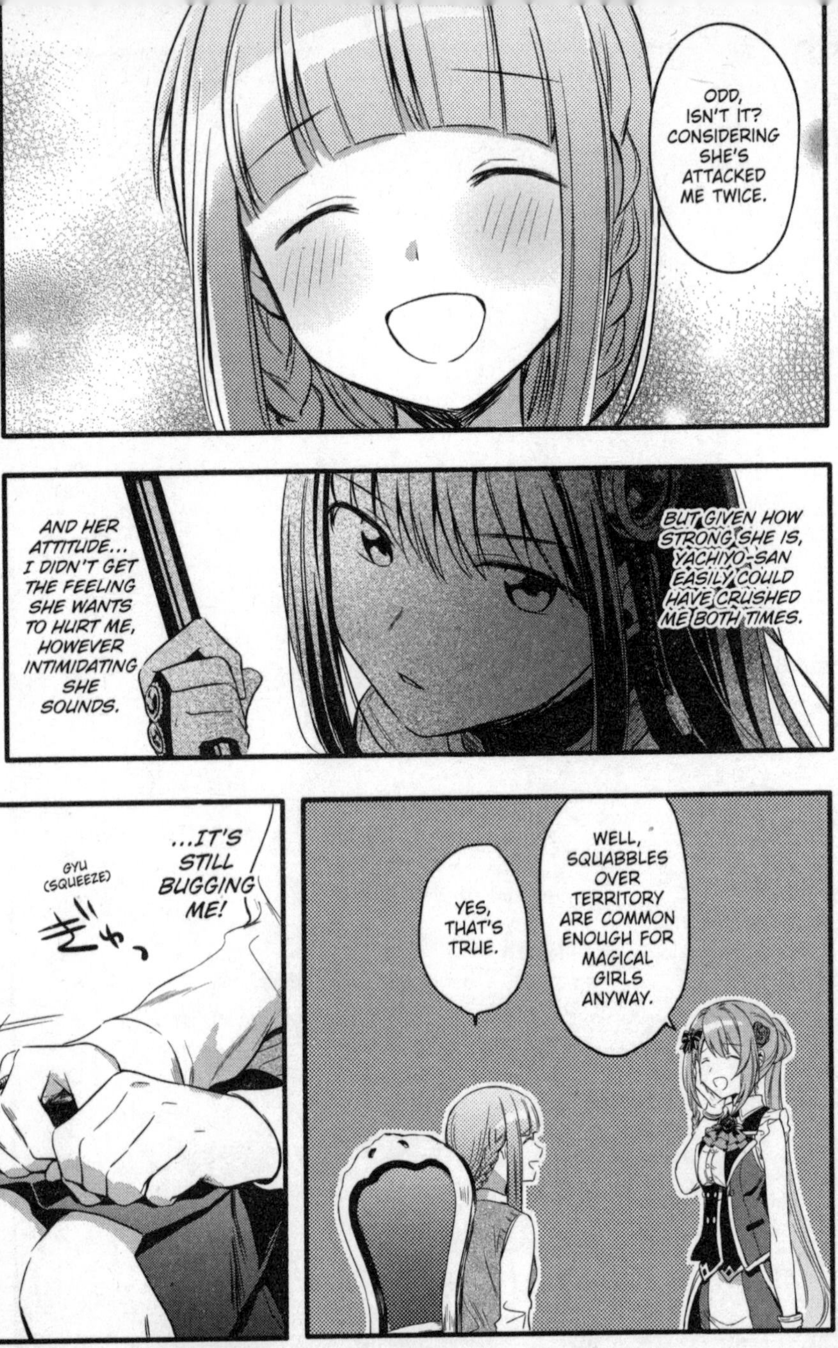
ODD, ISN'T IT? CONSIDERING SHE'S ATTACKED ME TWICE.
BUT GIVEN HOW STRONG SHE IS, YACHIYO-SAN EASILY COULD HAVE CRUSHED ME BOTH TIMES.
AND HER ATTITUDE... I DIDN'T GET THE FEELING SHE WANTS TO HURT ME, HOWEVER INTIMIDATING SHE SOUNDS.
WELL, SQUABBLES OVER TERRITORY ARE COMMON ENOUGH FOR MAGICAL GIRLS ANYWAY.
YES, THAT'S TRUE.
...IT'S STILL BUGGING ME!
GYU (SQUEEZE)
ぎゅっ

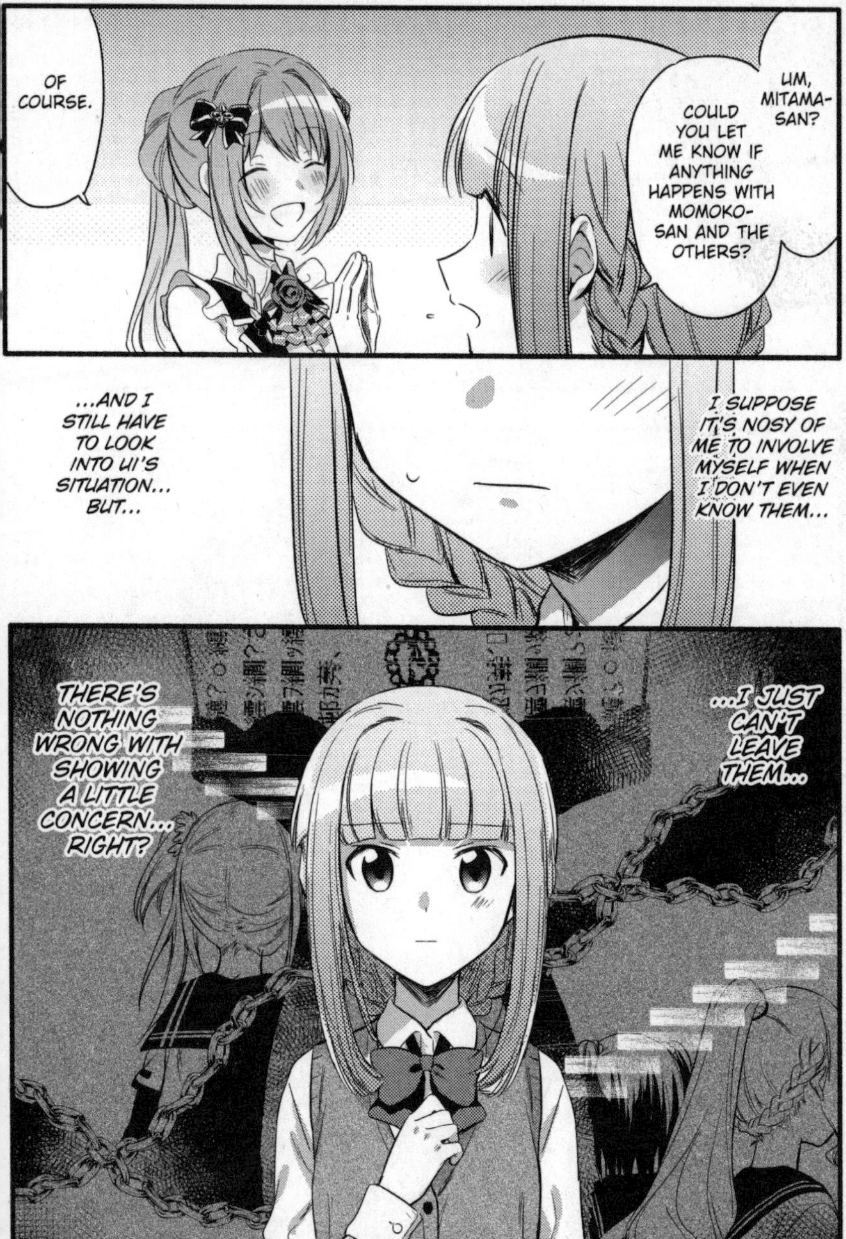
UM, MITAMA-SAN?
COULD YOU LET ME KNOW IF ANYTHING HAPPENS WITH MOMOKO-SAN AND THE OTHERS?
OF COURSE.
I SUPPOSE IT'S NOSY OF ME TO INVOLVE MYSELF WHEN I DON'T EVEN KNOW THEM...
...AND I STILL HAVE TO LOOK INTO UI'S SITUATION... BUT...
...I JUST CAN'T LEAVE THEM...
THERE'S NOTHING WRONG WITH SHOWING A LITTLE CONCERN... RIGHT?

AFTERWORD

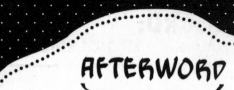

I'D LIKE TO THANK YOU FOR TAKING TIME TO PICK UP THE FIRST VOLUME OF *MAGIA RECORD: PUELLA MAGI☆MADOKA MAGICA SIDE STORY*! IF YOU'D TOLD ME A FEW YEARS AGO THAT ONE DAY I'D HAVE THE OPPORTUNITY TO CONTRIBUTE TO THE *MADOKA* SERIES I WAS WATCHING ON TV, YOUNGER ME WOULD HAVE FAINTED...

I'M REALLY ENJOYING THE CHALLENGES EACH EPISODE PRESENTS IN TERMS OF EXPRESSING THE "FEEL" OF THE WORLD OF THE *MADOKA* SERIES AND DRAWING THE CHARACTERS IN *MAGIRECO* TO BEST PRESENT THEIR CHARM TO THE READER!!

OF COURSE, I INEVITABLY LET MY SOUL GEM GO BLACK PRETTY QUICK, AND THAT OFTEN LEAVES MY EDITOR CLEANING UP AFTER ME. MY EDITOR IS VERY MUCH MY GRIEF SEED!

WHILE THE STORY IN KAMIHAMA IS JUST GETTING STARTED IN THIS VOLUME, THE PACE OF EVENTS PICKS UP QUITE A BIT WITH VOLUME 2 AND NEVER LETS UP, SO I'LL DO MY BEST TO CONTINUE GROWING AS AN ARTIST AS IROHA AND COMPANY GROW AS MAGICAL GIRLS.

I'D BE FLATTERED IF YOU CONTINUE TO WATCH OVER US.

AS AN ASIDE, IS THERE SOME WAY THE GAME DEVS CAN RAISE THE ODDS THAT THE COMIC ADAPTATION ARTIST WILL RECEIVE FOUR-STAR CHARACTERS? (NO.)   EITHER THE APP OR PC VERSION WOULD WORK!!

富士フジノ 拝
FUJINO FUJI

Special Thanks

MY EDITOR: N-SAN
COVER DESIGN: KISUKE-SAN
   (THANK YOU FOR THE AWESOME DESIGN!)

EVERYONE AT F4SAMURAI
UME AOKI-SENSEI
GEKIDAN INU CURRY (MUTT)-SAMA
EVERYONE AT SHAFT

and You!!!

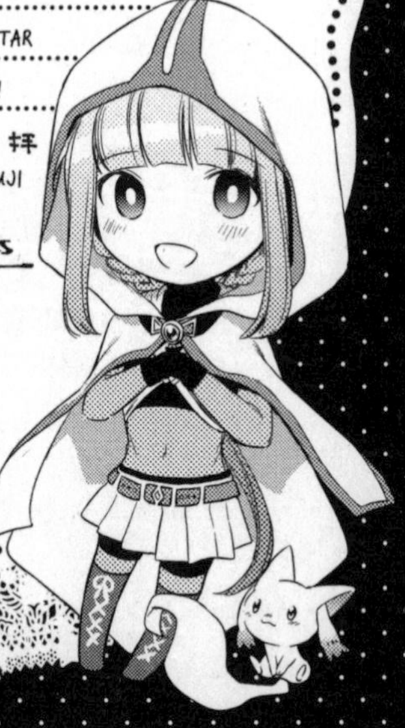

MAGIA RECO[RD]
PUELLA MAGI MADOKA ☆ MAGICA SI[DE STORY]

MAGICA QUARTET
FUJINO FUJI

Translation: Noboru Akimoto　•　**Lettering: Abigail Blackman**

MAGIA RECORD: MAHO SHOJO MADOKA ☆ MAGICA GAIDEN vol. 1
© Magica Quartet / Aniplex, Madoka Partners, MBS. All rights reserved. First published in Japan in 2019 by HOUBUNSHA CO., LTD, Tokyo. English translation rights in United States, Canada, and United Kingdom arranged with HOUBUNSHA CO., LTD. through Tuttle-Mori Agency, Inc., Tokyo.

English translation © 2019 by Yen Press, LLC

Yen Press
150 West 30th Street, 19th Floor
New York, NY 10001

Visit us at yenpress.com
facebook.com/yenpress
twitter.com/yenpress
yenpress.tumblr.com
instagram.com/yenpress

First Yen Press Edition: December 2019

Yen Press is an imprint of Yen Press, LLC.
The Yen Press name and logo are trademarks of Yen Press, LLC.

Library of Congress Control Number: 2019950197

ISBNs: 978-1-9753-8757-0 (paperback)
       978-1-9753-0945-9 (ebook)

10 9 8 7 6 5 4 3 2 1

WOR

Printed in the United States of America